T0281526

Lecture Notes in Computer Science   11501

Commenced Publication in 1973
Founding and Former Series Editors:
Gerhard Goos, Juris Hartmanis, and Jan van Leeuwen

More information about this series at http://www.springer.com/series/7407

Michèle Weiland · Guido Juckeland ·
Carsten Trinitis · Ponnuswamy Sadayappan (Eds.)

High Performance Computing

34th International Conference, ISC High Performance 2019
Frankfurt/Main, Germany, June 16–20, 2019
Proceedings

Editors
Michèle Weiland (iD)
University of Edinburgh
Edinburgh, UK

Carsten Trinitis (iD)
Technical University of Munich
Munich, Germany

Guido Juckeland (iD)
Helmholtz-Zentrum Dresden-Rossendorf
(HZDR)
Dresden, Germany

Ponnuswamy Sadayappan (iD)
Ohio State University
Columbus, USA

ISSN 0302-9743   ISSN 1611-3349 (electronic)
Lecture Notes in Computer Science
ISBN 978-3-030-20655-0   ISBN 978-3-030-20656-7 (eBook)
https://doi.org/10.1007/978-3-030-20656-7

LNCS Sublibrary: SL1 – Theoretical Computer Science and General Issues

This Springer imprint is published by the registered company Springer Nature Switzerland AG
The registered company address is: Gewerbestrasse 11, 6330 Cham, Switzerland

Preface

ISC High Performance, formerly known as the International Supercomputing Conference, was founded in 1986 as the Mannheim Supercomputer Seminar. Originally organized by Hans Meuer, Professor of Computer Science at the University of Mannheim and former director of its computer center, the seminar brought together a group of 81 scientists and industrial partners who shared a common interest in high-performance computing. Since then, the annual conference has become a major international event in the high-performance computing community and, accompanying its growth in size over the years, the conference has moved from Mannheim via Heidelberg, Dresden, Hamburg, and Leipzig to Frankfurt. With a record-breaking 3,505 attendees in 2018, we were looking forward to further growth in the number of attendees. Their expertise made ISC High Performance 2019, again, a powerful and memorable event.

Twelve years ago, in 2007, the scientific part of the conference was strengthened by having selected talks on research results arising within or relevant to the HPC community. These research paper sessions were then held on a separate day preceding the conference, and slides and accompanying papers were made available via the conference website. The research paper sessions have since evolved into an integral part of the conference, and the scientific presentations now take place over a period of three days and culminate in these archival proceedings.

For ISC High Performance 2019, the call for participation was issued in autumn 2018, inviting researchers and developers to submit the latest results of their work to the Program Committee. In all, 75 papers were submitted from authors all over the world. The Research Papers Program Committee consisted of 93 members selected from 20 countries throughout the world. Furthermore, 20 external expert reviewers from the community were invited to help with specific papers. After initial reviews were in place, a rebuttal process gave authors an opportunity to respond to reviewers' questions and help clarify any issues the reviewers might have. To come to a final consensus on the papers for the program and these proceedings, a face-to-face meeting was held in Frankfurt in February 2019, where each paper was discussed. Finally, the committee selected 17 papers for publication and for presentation in the research paper sessions, out of which four papers had to undergo a shepherding process.

Emerging Technologies was introduced as a track in 2019 and attracted papers this year touching on the intersection of quantum computing and HPC.

For the past several years, the ISC High Performance conference has presented an ISC-sponsored award to encourage outstanding research in high-performance computing and to honor the overall best research paper submitted to the conference. Two years ago, this annual award was renamed the Hans Meuer Award in memory of the late Dr. Hans Meuer, general chair of the ISC conference from 1986 through 2014, and a co-founder of the TOP500 benchmark project. From all research papers submitted, the Research Papers Program Committee nominated two papers as finalists for the award, and, based on the final presentations during the conference, elected the best paper.

We would like to express our gratitude to all our colleagues for submitting papers to the ISC scientific sessions, as well as to the members of the Program Committee and the external reviewers for organizing this year's attractive program.

June 2019

Carsten Trinitis
Ponnuswamy Sadayappan
Michèle Weiland
Guido Juckeland

Organization

Research Papers Program Committee

Research Papers Chair and Deputy Chair

Carsten Trinitis	Technical University of Munich, Germany
Saday Sadayappan	Ohio State University, USA

Architectures and Networks

Jonathan Beard	ARM Inc., USA
Anastasiia Butko	Lawrence Berkeley National Lab, USA
David D. Donofrio	Lawrence Berkeley National Lab, USA
Holger Fröning	University of Heidelberg, Germany
Michael Klemm	Intel Deutschland GmbH, Germany
John Leidel	Tactical Computing Laboratories, Texas Tech University, USA
Miquel Moreto	UPC, BSC, Spain
Ivy Peng	Oak Ridge National Laboratory, USA
Alejandro Rico	ARM Ltd., UK
Antonino Tumeo	Pacific Northwest National Laboratory, USA

Artificial Intelligence and Machine Learning

Yufei Ding	University of California Santa Barbara, USA
Yaoqing Gao	Huawei, Canada
David Gregg	Trinity College Dublin, Ireland
Seung-Hwan Lim	Oak Ridge National Lab, USA
Frank Mueller	North Carolina State University
Dimitrios Nikolopoulos	Queen's University Belfast, UK
Paolo Rech	UFRGS, UFRG, Brazil
Xipeng Shen	North Carolina State University (NCSU), NCSU, USA
Yu Wang	Leibniz Supercomputing Centre, Germany
Jin Wang	NVIDIA, USA
Youngmin Yi	University of Seoul, South Korea
Zhijia Zhao	University of California Riverside, USA

Data, Storage, and Visualization

Rita Borgo	King's College London, UK
André Brinkmann	University of Mainz, Germany
Toni Cortes	Barcelona Supercomputing Center, UPC, Spain
Elsa Gonsiorowski	Lawrence Livermore National Laboratory, USA

Hideyuki Kawashima	University of Tsukuba, Center for Computational Sciences, Japan
Jay Lofstead	Sandia National Laboratories, USA
Suzanne McIntosh	New York University, USA
Kathryn Mohror	Lawrence Livermore National Laboratory, USA
Misbah Mubarak	Argonne National Laboratory, USA
Valerio Pascucci	University of Utah, USA
Maria S. Perez	Universidad Politecnica de Madrid, Spain
Osamu Tatebe	University of Tsukuba, Center for Computational Sciences, Japan
Tom Vierjahn	Westphalian University of Applied Sciences, Germany

HPC Algorithms

Mehmet E. Belviranlı	Oak Ridge National Laboratory, USA
Xing Cai	Simula Research Laboratory, Norway
Anshu Dubey	Argonne National Laboratory, University of Chicago, USA
Xiaohu Guo	STFC, UK
H. Howie Huang	The George Washington University, USA
Kamer Kaya	Sabancı University, Turkey
Hatem Ltaief	KAUST, Saudi Arabia
Philipp Neumann	German Climate Computing Center, University of Hamburg, Germany
Tan Nguyen	Lawrence Berkeley National Laboratory, USA
Lena Oden	Forschungszentrum Jülich, Germany
Catherine Olschanowsky	Boise State University, USA
Didem Unat	Koç University, Turkey
Ana Lucia Varbanescu	University of Amsterdam, The Netherlands

HPC Applications

Srinivas Aluru	Georgia Institute of Technology, USA
Tobin Isaac	Georgia Institute of Technology, USA
Ananth Kalyanaraman	Washington State University, USA
Alba Cristina Melo	University of Brazil, Brazil
Kengo Nakajima	University of Tokyo, Japan
Gabriel Noaje	NVIDIA, Singapore
Siva Rajamanickam	Sandia National Laboratories, USA
Christian Schulz	University of Vienna, Austria, Austria
Sudip Seal	ORNL, USA
Edgar Solomonik	University of Illinois at Urbana-Champaign, USA
Bora Ucar	CNRS; LIP, ENS-Lyon, France, France
Sathish Vadhiyar	Indian Institute of Science, India

Performance Modeling and Measurement

Alexandru Calotoiu	Technical University of Darmstadt, Germany
Susan Coghlan	Argonne National Laboratory, USA
Jan Eitzinger	Erlangen Regional Computing Center, FAU Erlangen-Nuremberg, Germany
Marc-André Hermanns	Jülich Supercomputing Centre, Forschungszentrum Jülich, Germany
Daniel Holmes	EPCC, The University of Edinburgh, UK
Arnaud Legrand	LIG - Bâtiment IMAG, France
Allen Malony	University of Oregon, USA
Marek Michalewicz	ICM, University of Warsaw, Poland
Bernd Mohr	Jülich Supercomputing Centre, Germany
Fabrizio Petrini	Intel Corporation, Parallel Computing Labs, USA
Josef Weidendorfer	Leibniz Supercomputing Centre/Technical University of Munich, Germany

Programming Models and Systems Software

Ron Brightwell	Sandia National Laboratories, USA
Bradford L. Chamberlain	Cray Inc., USA
Sunita Chandrasekaran	University of Delaware, USA
Angeles Gonzalez Navarro	Universidad de Malaga, Spain
Bilel Hadri	KAUST Supercomputing Laboratory, Saudi Arabia
Jesús Labarta	Barcelona Supercomputing Center, Spain
Helena Liebelt	Intel, Technical University of Deggendorf, Germany
Simon McIntosh-Smith	University of Bristol, UK
Josh Milthorpe	The Australian National University, Australia
Dhabaleswar Panda	Ohio State University, USA
Swaroop S. Pophale	ORNL, USA
Sven-Bodo Scholz	Heriot-Watt University, UK
Martin Schulz	Technical University of Munich, Germany
Kenjiro Taura	University of Tokyo, Japan
Christian Terboven	RWTH Aachen University, Germany

Emerging Technologies

Ron Brightwell	Sandia National Laboratories, USA
Thomas Häner	Microsoft, Switzerland
Justin Hogaboam	Intel, USA
Martin Roetteler	Microsoft, USA
Mathias Soeken	EPFL Lausanne, Switzerland
Damian Steiger	Microsoft, Switzerland

PHD Forum Program Committee

Florina Ciorba (Chair)	University of Basel, Switzerland
Christian Engelmann	Oak Ridge National Laboratory, USA

Research Posters Program Committee

Sabine Roller	University of Siegen, Germany
Daisuke Takahashi	University of Tsukuba, Japan
Jesmin Jahan Tithi	INTEL CORP, USA
Vadim Voevodin	RCC MSU, Russia
Cheng Wang	Microsoft, USA

Project Posters Program Committee

Alvaro Aguilera	Technische Universität Dresden, Germany
Samar Aseeri	KAUST, Saudi Arabia
Valeria Bartsch	Fraunhofer ITWM, Germany
Peter Dueben	ECMWF, UK
Anja Gerbes	Center for Scientific Computing, Germany
Weicheng Huang	National Center for High-Performance Computing, Taiwan
Nabeeh Jumah	University of Hamburg, Germany
Julian Kunkel	University of Reading
Martin Lanser	Universität zu Köln, Germany
Glenn K. Lockwood	Lawrence Berkeley National Laboratory, USA
George S. Markomanolis	Oak Ridge National Laboratory, USA
Philipp Neumann (Deputy Chair)	German Climate Computing Center, University Hamburg, Germany
Ying Qian	East China Normal University, China
Yuichi Tsujita	RIKEN AICS, Japan
Ekaterina Tyutlyaeva (Chair)	RSC Technologies, Russia
Benjamin Uekermann	TUM, Germany
Tobias Weinzierl	Durham University, UK
Tianqi Xu	Preferred Networks Inc., Japan
Rio Yokota	Tokyo Institute of Technology, Japan

Tutorials Committee

Damian Alvarez	Forschungszentrum Jülich, Germany
Katie Antypas	Lawrence Berkeley National Laboratory, USA
Ritu Arora	Texas Advanced Computing Center, UT Austin, USA
Rosa M. Badia	Barcelona Supercomputing Center, Spain
Pavan Balaji	Argonne National Laboratory, USA
Janine Bennett (Deputy Chair)	Sandia National Laboratories, USA
Alejandro Duran	Intel, USA
Robert Henschel	Indiana University, USA
David Lecomber	ARM Ltd., UK
Simon McIntosh-Smith	University of Bristol, UK
C. J. Newburn	NVIDIA, USA
Dhabaleswar Panda	Ohio State University, USA

Tapasya Patki	Lawrence Livermore National Laboratory, USA
Olga Pearce	Lawrence Livermore National Laboratory, USA
Christian Plessl	Paderborn University, Germany
Mohan Sarovar	Sandia National Laboratories, USA
William Barton Sawyer	CSCS, Switzerland
Paul Springer	NVIDIA, USA
Sandra Wienke (Chair)	RWTH Aachen University, Germany
Michael Wong	Codeplay Software, UK

BoFs Committee

David Bader	Georgia Institute of Technology, USA
Claudia Blaas-Schenner	TU Wien, VSC Research Center, Austria
Sunita Chandrasekaran	University of Delaware, USA
Nahid Emad	University of Versailles, France
Dominik Göddeke	University of Stuttgart, Germany
José Gracia	University of Stuttgart, HLRS, Germany
Harald Köstler	FAU Erlangen-Nuremberg, Germany
Oana Marin	MCS, USA
Simon McIntosh-Smith (Chair)	University of Bristol, UK
Lawrence Mitchell	Imperial College London, UK
Marie-Christine Sawley	Intel, France
Masha Sosonkina (Deputy Chair)	Old Dominion University, USA
Vladimir Voevodin	Moscow State University, Russia
Jan Wender	Atos BDS science+computing AG, Germany
Andreas Wierse	SICOS BW GmbH, Germany
Xingfu Wu	Argonne National Laboratory, University of Chicago, USA
Roman Wyrzykowski	Czestochowa University of Technology, Poland

Workshop Committee

Sadaf Alam (Chair)	Swiss National Supercomputing Centre, Switzerland
Hartwig Anzt	Karlsruhe Institute of Technology, Germany, University of Tennessee, USA
Bruce D'Amora	IBM, USA
Anthony Danalis	University of Tennessee Knoxville, USA
Giuseppe Fiameni	CINECA, Italy
Joachim Hein	Lund University, Sweden
Heike Jagode (Deputy Chair)	University of Tennessee Knoxville, USA
Andreas Knuepfer	Technische Universität Dresden, Germany
John Linford	Arm, USA
Hatem Ltaief	KAUST, Saudi Arabia

Shirley Moore   ORNL, USA
Akihiro Nomura   Tokyo Institute of Technology, Japan
Melissa Smith   Clemson University, USA
Jonathan Sparks   Cray, USA
Ugo Varetto   Pawsey Centre, CSIRO, Australia
Edward Walker   NSF, USA

Contents

Architectures, Networks and Infrastructure

Evaluating Quality of Service Traffic Classes on the Megafly Network

Misbah Mubarak[1]([✉]), Neil McGlohon[3], Malek Musleh[2], Eric Borch[2],
Robert B. Ross[1], Ram Huggahalli[2], Sudheer Chunduri[4], Scott Parker[4],
Christopher D. Carothers[3], and Kalyan Kumaran[4]

[1] Mathematics and Computer Science Division, Argonne National Laboratory,
Lemont, IL, USA
mmubarak@anl.gov
[2] Intel Corporation, Santa Clara, CA, USA
[3] Rensselaer Polytechnic Institute, Troy, NY, USA
[4] Argonne Leadership Computing Facility (ALCF), Argonne National Laboratory,
Lemont, IL, USA

Abstract. An emerging trend in High Performance Computing (HPC)
systems that use hierarchical topologies (such as dragonfly) is that the
applications are increasingly exhibiting high run-to-run performance
variability. This poses a significant challenge for application developers, job schedulers, and system maintainers. One approach to address
the performance variability is to use newly proposed network topologies
such as megafly (or dragonfly+) that offer increased path diversity compared to a traditional fully connected dragonfly. Yet another approach
is to use quality of service (QoS) traffic classes that ensure bandwidth
guarantees. In this work, we select HPC application workloads that have
exhibited performance variability on current 2-D dragonfly systems. We
evaluate the baseline performance expectations of these workloads on
megafly and 1-D dragonfly network models with comparably similar network configurations. Our results show that the megafly network, despite
using fewer virtual channels (VCs) for deadlock avoidance than a dragonfly, performs as well as a fully connected 1-D dragonfly network. We then
exploit the fact that megafly networks require fewer VCs to incorporate
QoS traffic classes. We use bandwidth capping and traffic differentiation
techniques to introduce multiple traffic classes in megafly networks. In
some cases, our results show that QoS can completely mitigate application performance variability while causing minimal slowdown to the
background network traffic.

1 Introduction

With modern high-performance computing (HPC) systems shifting to hierarchical and low-diameter networks, dragonfly networks have become a popular
choice. They have been deployed in multiple high-performance systems including
Cori, Trinity, and Theta systems at NERSC, Los Alamos National Laboratory,

© Springer Nature Switzerland AG 2019
M. Weiland et al. (Eds.): ISC High Performance 2019, LNCS 11501, pp. 3–20, 2019.
https://doi.org/10.1007/978-3-030-20656-7_1

and Argonne National Laboratory, respectively [2,11,16]. Dragonfly is a hierarchical topology that uses short electrical links to form groups of routers using a 1-D or 2-D all-to-all interconnect. These groups are then connected all-to-all via optical links. While this design offers low diameter and cost, it increases contention for the link bandwidth among multiple applications which introduces performance variability [5]. For next-generation systems, HPC designers are considering variations of the dragonfly topology that offer increased path diversity, fairness, and scalability [17]. One such topology that has been recently proposed is the dragonfly+, or megafly, which uses a two-level fat tree to form groups of routers. These groups are then connected all-to-all via optical links. Megafly networks use the path diversity of a two-level fat tree to alleviate the communication bottlenecks that can be introduced with standard dragonfly networks. Megafly networks also have the added advantage of using only two virtual channels (VCs) for deadlock prevention as opposed to up to four virtual channels used in a fully connected 1-D dragonfly network. Prior work [8] has shown that while the design of megafly networks helps mitigate performance variability to some extent, it does not completely eliminate it.

Although quality of service (QoS) has been investigated and implemented on TCP/IP networks and data-centers [3], the mechanism remains largely unexplored in the context of HPC networks. Our work is one of the early studies to investigate the role of QoS traffic classes in reducing performance variability caused by communication interference on the now popular hierarchical networks. In this work, we use HPC application workloads that demonstrate performance variability on current dragonfly systems as shown by Chunduri et al. [5]. We replay the workloads on CODES packet-level interconnect simulations [14,20] to answer questions about dragonfly and megafly network topologies: How does the performance of a megafly network compare with a fully connected dragonfly network? How do traffic classes help with performance variability on a megafly network?

The contributions of this work are as follows. (1) We evaluate the performance variability of HPC application workloads on both a megafly and a 1-D dragonfly network using similar network configurations. We compare the performance of a megafly network with a 1-D dragonfly to determine whether megafly network is better resistant to perturbation. (2) We exploit the fact that megafly requires fewer virtual channels for deadlock prevention (as compared to conventional dragonfly), and we use the unused VCs to introduce QoS traffic classes. We evaluate two mechanisms through which QoS can be introduced in HPC networks. First, using bandwidth capping and traffic prioritization, we quantify the impact of QoS when an entire high-priority traffic class is dedicated to an application or set of applications. Second, we dedicate the high-priority traffic class to latency-sensitive operations such as MPI collectives and observe the performance improvement. (3) We extend the CODES simulation framework to perform packet-level simulation of HPC networks in an online mode driven by the scalable workload models (SWM) [18] for use in the above-mentioned experiments.

2 Exploring Quality of Service on HPC Networks

In the past, HPC systems were often constructed with torus networks, and jobs were allocated onto partitions of the network that reduced resource sharing and communication interference. With hierarchical networks sharing resources such as switches and links, partitioning becomes more difficult and introducing traffic classes becomes an important step to mitigate communication interference. The slowdown caused by communication interference can significantly impact the overall application performance as the typical range of communication time in communication intensive applications is in the range of *50–80%* [6]. Significant performance variability due to communication interference has been reported in [5], where a slowdown of up to 2x is seen on a production system.

Current 2-D dragonfly networks use up to 4 virtual channels to prevent deadlocks, which is typically all the VCs available. Megafly networks use only 2 VCs for deadlock prevention, thus making them a better candidate for enabling multiple traffic classes. Figure 1 shows one way to implement quality of service on HPC networks. In this implementation, a bandwidth monitor component in each switch tracks the bandwidth consumption of each traffic class for every port. The bandwidth monitoring is done over a static time window t_w. Each traffic class is assigned a certain fraction of maximum available link bandwidth, which serves as the upper bandwidth cap for that traffic class while the link is oversubscribed. If the bandwidth consumption of a traffic class reaches the cap and the link is oversubscribed, the traffic class is designated as inactive for the remaining duration of the static window t_w. An inactive traffic class has the lowest priority and it gets scheduled only if there are no packets in the remaining higher priority traffic classes. At the start of the window t_w, the bandwidth statistics for each traffic class are reset to zero, and the traffic class(es) marked as inactive are activated again. If all the traffic classes are violating their bandwidth cap, then a round-robin scheduling policy is used for arbitration.

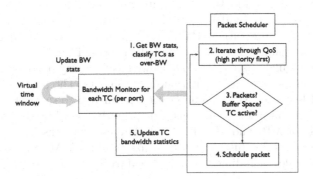

Fig. 1. Enabling quality of service on HPC networks (TC – traffic class, BW – bandwidth, QoS – quality of service)

The implementation of QoS can be beneficial in reducing communication interference on hierarchical networks. For instance, a common problem exhibited on such networks is that communication-intensive (or bandwidth-hungry) applications can "bully" less-communication-intensive applications [20]. With QoS-enabled networks, bandwidth-hungry applications can be prevented from exceeding their permissible bandwidth limits. This approach allows less-communication-intensive applications to have their fair share. Alternatively, one can assign a high-priority traffic class to latency-sensitive operations such as MPI collectives. We report on experiments with both of these QoS mechanisms in Sect. 5.

3   Evaluation Methodology

In this section, we discuss the simulation environment, network configurations, workloads, rank-to-node mapping policies, and routing algorithms used in the study.

3.1   HPC Simulation Environment

The CODES simulation framework provides high-fidelity, massively parallel simulations of prototypical next-generation HPC architectures. The framework has been extensively used for performance analysis of modern interconnect topologies (fat tree, torus, dragonfly, express mesh and slim fly) [14]. The network models have been validated against real architectures [15]. Prior to this work, the CODES simulation framework supported system simulations with post mortem communication traces. Although traces can illustrate realistic system behavior (for a given problem size), their use inhibits flexibility and simulation scalability as compared to other workload representations. Therefore, we extended the CODES simulation suite to replay workloads in an online or in situ mode using the Scalable Workload Models (SWMs) presented in [18].

Scalable workload models are a workload representation approach that focuses on representing the communication patterns, dependencies, computation-communication overlap, and algorithms. The SWM code[1] is decoupled from the original application code as well as from any particular simulator, enabling use across different simulation environments. The SWM runtime supports a set of low-level API communication primitives to support a number of MPI-based communication operations. The primitives used by the SWM closely resemble those of MPI and SHMEM, but they are not constrained to specific syntax or semantics. In this paper, we utilize several SWM representations for multiple HPC codes including Nekbone, LAMMPS and nearest neighbor [18].

---

[1] The Scalable Workload Models code is available at the git repo: https://xgitlab.cels.anl.gov/codes/workloads.git.

3.2 Topology and Routing Description

The dragonfly network topology, proposed by Kim et al. [10], consists of groups of routers that are connected to each other with one or more optical channels. Within each group, the routers are directly connected to each other in an all-to-all manner via electrical links. In this paper, we refer to this configuration as a 1-D dragonfly. A variation of a dragonfly topology, deployed in the Cray XC systems, uses a 2-D all-to-all within each group instead of all-to-all connections. We refer to this configuration as a 2-D dragonfly. A 2-D dragonfly traverses almost double the number of hops as a 1-D dragonfly. The hop count traversed in a 1-D dragonfly is close to that of a megafly network. Therefore, we compare megafly with a 1-D dragonfly to ensure a reasonable comparison. Various forms of adaptive routing have been proposed for a dragonfly, which detect congestion and determine whether the packet should take a minimal or non-minimal route. We use the progressive adaptive routing algorithm (PAR) provided in [19]. The PAR algorithm in the simulation re-evaluates the minimal path until either the packet decides to take a nonminimal route or the packet reaches the destination group on a minimal path. In this work, we use four virtual channels for progressive adaptive routing in a dragonfly network, as suggested in [19].

What separates various dragonfly topologies from each other is largely based on the interconnect within a group. Megafly is a topology that belongs to the Dragonfly class of interconnection networks. At a high level, it is classified as having groups of routers which are, in turn, connected to each other with at least one global connection between any two groups. Megafly is characterized by its connectivity in the form of a two-level Fat Tree network in each group. This locally defined network is also known as a complete bipartite graph: a graph with two sub-groups where all nodes within one subgroup are connected to all nodes in the other subgroup. There are no connections between the routers within the same subgroup. The two levels in each group have routers that will be referred to as *Leaf Routers*, those that have terminal/compute node connections but no global connections, and *Spine Routers*, those that have global connections to other groups but no terminal/compute node connections [8,17]. In this paper, we use the progressive adaptive routing algorithm proposed in prior studies on Megafly networks [8]. Megafly requires only two virtual channels (VCs) to avoid deadlock and none to avoid congestion in the intermediate group.

3.3 Network Configurations

To perform a comparison of the megafly network with a 1-D dragonfly, we maintain similar router radix and similar node counts. We used a router radix of 32 ports for both networks. Across the group, the routers are connected via global channels. The configurations of the 1-D dragonfly and megafly are given in Table 1.

Table 1. Configurations of megafly and 1-D dragonfly used for performance comparison. Link bandwidth for each network is 25 GiB/s (GC - Global Channels)

	Radix	Groups	Nodes/Group	Node count	GC/Group	Nodes per router
Megafly	32	33	256	8448	256	16 (Leaves Only)
1D Dragonfly	32	65	128	8320	128	8

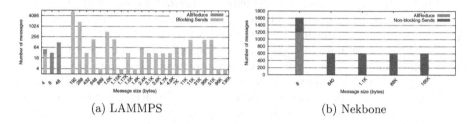

(a) LAMMPS   (b) Nekbone

Fig. 2. Message distributions for Nekbone and LAMMPS application workloads

3.4   Workloads

In order to quantify the slowdown of a particular job due to communication interference, multiple jobs need to be running in parallel to exhibit interference. We conduct two types of interference experiments: (i) replay HPC applications that serve as foreground communication traffic in conjunction with a job that generates synthetic background communication to understand the interference in a controlled manner, and (ii) replay multiple HPC applications in parallel to capture the dynamism of multi-phased communication and quantify the impact of perturbation.

Foreground Traffic. Previous work demonstrates the performance variability shown by LAMMPS, Nekbone, and MILC applications on the Cray XC40 system [5]. Thus, we use LAMMPS and Nekbone workloads as foreground workloads for our experimental analysis. We also use a 3-D nearest-neighbor communication pattern, which is a commonly used pattern in several HPC applications.

LAMMPS is a large-scale atomic and molecular dynamics code that uses MPI for communication. We use the SWM code that derives its communication pattern from the LAMMPS application. Figure 2(a) shows the message distribution of LAMMPS SWM per rank in a problem involving 2,048 ranks. The LAMMPS workload uses MPI_AllReduce with small messages as well as blocking sends and nonblocking receives for point-to-point communication with large messages.

Nekbone is a thermal hydraulics mini-app that captures the structure of the computational fluids dynamics code Nek5000. Nekbone's SWM communication pattern is derived from the Nekbone benchmark. Figure 2(b) shows the message distribution of the Nekbone SWM on a per rank basis in a problem with 2,197 ranks. Nekbone performs a large number of MPI collective operations with small 8-byte messages. It uses nonblocking sends and receives to transmit medium-sized messages.

Cartesian neighborhood communication is a pattern commonly used in multiple scientific applications including Hardware Accelerated Cosmology Code (HACC), fast Fourier transform solvers, and adaptive mesh refinement (AMR) codes. We use a 3-D nearest-neighbor SWM in this work that transmits large messages (64 KiB and 128 KiB) on a per rank basis with multiple iterations of MPI nonblocking sends and receives followed by MPI_Wait_All. A problem size of 4,096 ranks is used with the nearest neighbor SWM.

Background Traffic. The background communication traffic is needed to interfere with the foreground workloads. To ensure an even distribution of traffic that covers a significant fraction of the network, we use a uniform random communication pattern. This is generally considered a benign traffic pattern for dragonfly networks. However, with large messages randomly sent in the network, uniform random causes hotspots at multiple network locations and becomes a source of interference. We varied the amount of data transmitted via uniform random traffic and observed the effect of different data transmission rates on the foreground traffic. The background traffic generation is modeled as a separate job that runs in parallel with the foreground traffic and occupies at least 25% to 50% of the entire network. The background injection rates depend on the available compute node to router link bandwidth in the network. We inject traffic at a percentage of the available link bandwidth and vary the injection rates between 2% to 36.5% of the link bandwidth. At the 36.5% rate, each node is injecting 9 GiB/s of background traffic with an aggregate network background interference of 18 TiB/s. At this rate, we see significant slowdown (up to $4x$ for uniform random and up to $7x$ for random permutation) in application communication times for both networks. Therefore, we keep that as the maximum background injection rate.

We experiment with two different background communication patterns: (i) a uniform random synthetic pattern where a rank randomly chooses a destination rank and transmits large messages and (ii) a random permutation traffic where a pair of ranks communicate and transmit data until a certain threshold is reached.

Multiple Applications. As a specific instance of representative HPC scenarios, we ran the three foreground workloads in parallel (Nekbone, nearest neighbor, and LAMMPS). We also ran each of these workloads in isolation on the network to determine the baseline performance and observed the slowdown introduced when the workloads are running in parallel.

3.5 Rank-to-Node Mappings

Ranks are placed on network nodes in a manner similar to that for production HPC systems, where clusters of available network nodes are assigned to a job. Therefore, we use a geometric job placement policy in which multiple clusters of network nodes are assigned to jobs. In the simulation, the clusters are formed by using the inverse transform sampling method for creating random samples from a given distribution. The experiments in the paper were performed with three different rank to node mappings; however, we did not observe a noticeable difference between the statistics reported by each mapping.

4 Quantifying Interference on 1-D Dragonfly and Megafly Networks

In this section, we analyze the communication interference on both 1-D dragonfly and megafly networks following the methodology described in Sect. 3. Each simulation experiment was conducted three times with different geometric job allocation policies and the performance difference observed between each run was less than 2%. The communication latency of an application is determined by the rank that incurs the maximum latency across all the participating ranks. Given that the distribution of the latencies of ranks potentially contain long tails [13] corresponding to ranks that are effected by congestion, using maximum latency across the ranks is the appropriate metric. Before discussing the QoS experiments, we compare the baseline communication performance of megafly and 1-D dragonfly networks and further quantify the performance degradation with QoS disabled. We then incorporate QoS mechanisms in the megafly networks to evaluate the performance with and without such mechanisms enabled.

Uniform Random Background Traffic. Figure 3(a) shows the communication time of LAMMPS SWM with varying degrees of background traffic, starting from no background traffic, on both megafly and 1-D dragonfly. LAMMPS uses a mix of point-to-point and collective communication as shown in Fig. 2. The performance results in the figure show that megafly performs better than a 1-D dragonfly in most of the background traffic injection rates. For the worst case background injection rate, 1-D dragonfly outperforms megafly.

Figure 3(b) shows the communication time of Nekbone SWM with and without uniform random background traffic on both megafly and 1-D dragonfly networks. Nekbone uses a large number of 8-byte MPI collectives as shown in Fig. 2. Additionally, of the studied workloads, Nekbone is the most communication volume intensive application: it transmits 4x more data than the LAMMPS or nearest-neighbor SWM workloads do. The performance results in the figure show that megafly performs up to 60% better than a 1-D dragonfly in all except one background traffic injection rates. For the worst case background injection rate, 1-D dragonfly outperforms megafly.

Figure 3(c) shows the performance of nearest-neighbor communication on both 1-D dragonfly and megafly networks. Since we are using geometric job mapping that allocates cluster of network nodes, the nearest-neighbor pattern involves extensive communication between two groups. In this case, megafly consistently outperforms the dragonfly network because of multiple reasons: (i) megafly has larger group sizes (more nodes available within a group), which increases locality of communication within a group. The locality of communication is beneficial for nearest neighbor traffic, and (ii) Dragonfly has a single

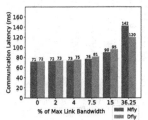 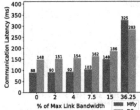 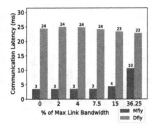

(a) LAMMPS communication times comparison

(b) Nekbone communication times comparison

(c) Nearest-neighbor communication times comparison

Fig. 3. Performance of megafly vs. 1-D dragonfly with (a) geometrically allocated 2048/2048 ranks for LAMMPS/uniform random workloads and (b) geometrically allocated 2197/2197 ranks for Nekbone/uniform random workloads, and (c) geometrically allocated 4096/4096 ranks for nearest-neighbor/uniform random workloads. The intensity of the background traffic was scaled at a percentage of the maximum link capacity.

minimal path between two routers within a group whereas megafly has 16 different minimal path options for this route, which reduces intra-group congestion. Since nearest-neighbor communication exchanges are based exclusively on point-to-point operations between two groups, it is less impacted by the background traffic.

Random Permutation Background Traffic. While uniform random traffic with large message sizes can cause dynamic hotspots in the network, we also considered random permutation traffic to introduce more persistent network interference. Similar to uniform random, the random permutation background traffic pattern sends packets to a randomly selected node in the network. We use a rotating random permutation pattern that will send continually to the same randomly selected destination (on a per node basis) until a certain number of bytes have been transmitted before choosing a new random destination. Figures 4 shows the performance of megafly and dragonfly networks. The foreground workloads see a slowdown in communication time as the number of bytes exchanged in the background traffic is increased. Since nearest neighbor traffic involves point to point operations (mostly to the neighboring group), it is not significantly impacted by the rotating random background traffic. While the performance of LAMMPS workload is comparable on both networks, the Nekbone workload is less perturbed on a megafly network than a 1-D dragonfly. Our conjecture is that the better performance of megafly can be attributed to the additional path diversity of its minimal routes. The results demonstrate that there is nearly a linear slowdown in the performance of the foreground job as the number of bytes exchanged in the background traffic increases.

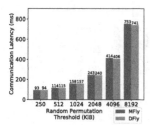 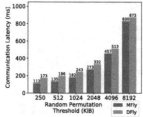 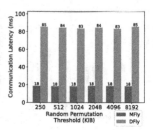

(a) LAMMPS communica-   (b) Nekbone communica-   (c) Nearest-neighbor com-
tion times comparison   tion times comparison   munication times compari-
                                                                son

Fig. 4. Performance of megafly vs. 1-D dragonfly with (a) geometrically allocated 2048/2048 ranks for LAMMPS/random permutation workloads (b) geometrically allocated 2197/2197 ranks for Nekbone/random permutation and (c) geometrically allocated 2197/2197 ranks for nearest-neighbor/Random Permutation workloads. The amount of data exchanged between two nodes in a rotating random permutation was scaled from 250 KiB to 8 MiB.

Multiple Applications in Parallel. In the third case, as a specific instance of representative HPC scenarios, we run the three workloads (LAMMPS, Nekbone, and nearest neighbor) in parallel without any synthetic communication traffic. This scenario clearly mimics a common system state, with multiple jobs completing for shared resources. Figure 5 shows the communication time of the three applications when running in parallel and in isolation on both dragonfly and megafly networks. We can see that with both LAMMPS and Nekbone, the applications are much less perturbed on a megafly network than on a 1-D dragonfly network.

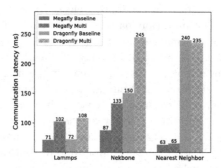

Fig. 5. Communication times of LAMMPS (2,048 ranks), Nekbone (2,197 ranks), and nearest neighbor (2,048 ranks) when running in parallel on 1-D dragonfly and dragonfly+ networks. Baseline indicates the application runs in isolation.

After introducing different forms of background communication traffic with foreground workloads, our analysis shows that in maximum cases, the performance of megafly network is comparable to a 1-D dragonfly network. In majority of the cases, Megafly performs better than a 1-D dragonfly. For LAMMPS and Nekbone workloads with worst case background traffic, a 1-D dragonfly gets relatively less perturbed than a megafly. On both networks, however, HPC applications see a significant slowdown in communication ranging up to 700% in the presence of intense background communication traffic.

5   Evaluating Quality of Service on Megafly Networks

Enabling quality of service on HPC networks requires that each traffic class have its own set of virtual channels. Megafly networks require a fewer number of virtual channels for deadlock prevention. When a fixed, limited number of VCs are available in the switch hardware, megafly needs half as many VCs as a dragonfly and has the opportunity to use the extra VCs for QoS. The mechanism for quality of service was introduced in Sect. 2. In this section, we perform experiments to analyze the impact of QoS on traffic interference and application slowdown that was seen in Sect. 4. Due to space constraints, the results shown are for Megafly networks even though a 1-D dragonfly network performs in a similar manner with QoS turned on. Since there can be a large number of permutations for bandwidth caps, we performed a sensitivity analysis by sweeping different bandwidth values and picked the values that were most effective. The static window over which the bandwidth statistics were monitored was kept to 5 ms throughout these experiments. We explore two configurations through which QoS can be introduced in megafly networks:

5.1   QoS Mechanism I: Prioritizing Entire Applications

With our first QoS mechanism, a higher priority and high bandwidth are assigned to the entire application (or set of applications) so that they face minimal slowdown relative to other traffic. We use uniform random background traffic and both LAMMPS and Nekbone foreground workloads that exhibited slowdown on megafly networks in Sect. 4 (Nearest neighbor was not getting significantly perturbed). To understand the impact on background traffic, we measure the performance of both foreground workload and background traffic. The background traffic performance is measured by the maximum time to complete a message (all messages have the same size in the synthetic workload).

The benefit of using this QoS approach is that if the foreground application is not utilizing the full bandwidth allocated to it, then the background workload can consume the unutilized bandwidth. Figure 6 compares the performance of LAMMPS workload with and without QoS enabled on a megafly network. It also shows the slowdown to background communication traffic. The LAMMPS workload is not as communication intensive because it involves point-to-point messages along with a small number of MPI_AllReduce messages. Therefore, the perturbation to background traffic is not significant. Because of the high priority given to LAMMPS, it does not see any slowdown even though it is running in parallel with intense background traffic. Additionally, while we observe a significant speedup with LAMMPS, the background traffic observes only a small degree of slowdown as compared with the no-QoS case.

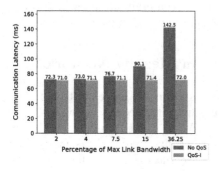

(a) LAMMPS communication times

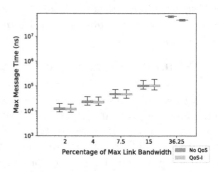

(b) Background traffic performance

Fig. 6. QoS Mechanism I (Application Priority): performance of LAMMPS and background traffic on megafly network with QoS enabled and disabled. The entire LAMMPS application is given a high priority and high bandwidth (70%).

Nekbone SWM is a communication-intensive workload that transmits 4x more data than does LAMMPS SWM, and a majority of the communication involves collectives. Figure 7 shows the performance of the Nekbone SWM when QoS is enabled. Once again we see Nekbone having minimal slowdown when QoS is enabled while causing minimal slowdown to background communication traffic. The primary reason for the improved performance is that both Nekbone and LAMMPS are given high priority and high bandwidth yet they do not consume all the bandwidth assigned to them. Therefore, the background traffic is able to get the required bandwidth that it needs while observing little slowdown.

Both these results demonstrate that traffic differentiation with bandwidth shaping and prioritization can mitigate (or eliminate) communication interference to HPC workloads while causing minimal slowdown to the background traffic. Assigning a high priority to an application can eliminate the perturbation to that application while experiencing a reasonable slowdown in the remaining network traffic.

5.2   QoS Mechanism II: Prioritizing and Guaranteeing Bandwidth to Latency-Sensitive Operations

Several HPC applications rely on the performance of MPI collective operations. In a majority of the cases, collectives comprise small messages, and the application performance suffers when heavy background network traffic interferes with the transmission of these messages. An alternative application of QoS is to assign a high priority and guaranteed bandwidth to collective operations.

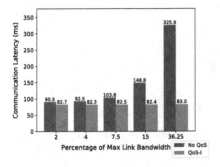
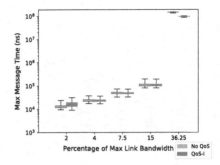

(a) Nekbone communication times   (b) Background traffic performance

Fig. 7. QoS Mechanism I (Application Priority): performance of Nekbone and background traffic on megafly network with QoS enabled and disabled. The entire Nekbone application is given a high priority and high bandwidth (70%).

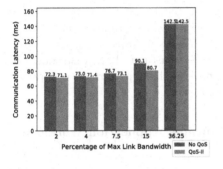
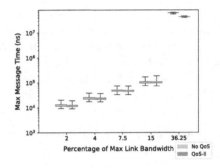

(a) LAMMPS communication times   (b) Background traffic performance

Fig. 8. QoS Mechanism II (Collective Priority): performance of LAMMPS and background traffic on megafly network with application-based QoS enabled and 10% bandwidth guaranteed to collectives.

Figure 8 shows the performance of LAMMPS when high priority is given to collectives and compares it with the case where no QoS is enabled. In this case, we are assigning a high priority but a small fraction of bandwidth to collective operations; the point-to-point operations and background traffic are given a lower priority and higher bandwidth cap (90%). We see that although there is some slowdown in foreground traffic when the background traffic becomes intense, the foreground workload is still 10% faster than the case where no QoS is enabled (specifically in the case of 15% background traffic injection). LAMMPS uses more point-to-point operations and has fewer collective operations, which is why the speedup is not as significant as Nekbone that relies heavily on collective performance.

Figure 9 shows the performance of Nekbone when given high priority and a guaranteed bandwidth to collectives. Nekbone relies heavily on collective

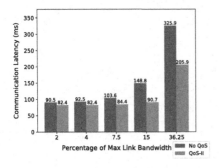

(a) Nekbone communication times

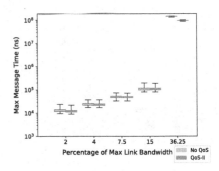

(b) Background traffic performance

Fig. 9. QoS Mechanism II (Collective Priority): performance of Nekbone and background traffic on megafly network with application-based QoS enabled and 10% bandwidth guaranteed to collectives.

operations. *Therefore, we see a significant performance improvement of up to 60% speedup in communication time compared with the case where no QoS is enabled.* The background communication traffic does not show a slowdown in message communication times; instead it shows a slight performance improvement compared to no-QoS options in one case.

5.3 Applying QoS Mechanisms to Multiple Application Workloads in Parallel

In this section, we examine both QoS mechanisms in the case where multiple applications are running in parallel, which is a specific instance of a representative HPC system. We compare the QoS-enabled performance with the case where there are multiple applications running without any QoS. For the first QoS mechanism, since Nekbone is more communication intensive than LAMMPS and nearest neighbor (shown in Fig. 2) we assign it a separate traffic class with a bandwidth cap of 30% and a high priority. The rest of the bandwidth is available to both LAMMPS and nearest neighbor. For the second QoS mechanism, we assign a higher priority to all collective communication in both LAMMPS and Nekbone and then see the impact on application performance.

Figure 10 shows the performance of multiple applications running in parallel with and without QoS enabled. In short, both schemes are beneficial, and lead to reduced communication time. With the QoS Mechanism I, we give a high priority and assign one third of link bandwidth as a cap to Nekbone. Nekbone is communication intensive; and with a high priority and the bandwidth cap, it does not get any slowdown due to background communication traffic. In contrast, LAMMPS and nearest neighbor have a lower priority, and they still see a performance improvement compared with the case where there was no QoS enabled. *Adding bandwidth caps on Nekbone (which is a bandwidth-intensive application) helps improve the performance of LAMMPS and nearest neighbor as well.*

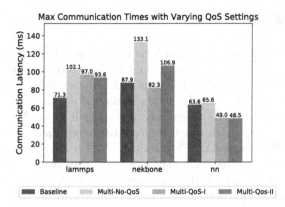

Fig. 10. Communication times of Nekbone, LAMMPS, and nearest-neighbor workloads when running in parallel. Both mechanisms of application-based QoS were enabled. The comparison is done with (i) the worst case when no QoS is enabled (Multi No QoS) and (ii) the best case when the workload is running in isolation with no interference (baseline).

With the QoS Mechanism II, where collective communication is given priority, both LAMMPS and Nekbone benefit by seeing a 10% and 20% speedup, respectively, compared with the case where QoS is not enabled. One interesting observation is the performance of the nearest-neighbor workload, which is much faster with QoS enabled than when the workload is running in isolation. Looking at the adaptive routing statistics, we see that the nearest-neighbor workload when running in isolation takes the maximum number of minimal routes because of the bias toward minimal routes. With QoS enabled, nearest-neighbor traffic has a lower priority with QoS mechanisms enabled, which causes it to take more nonminimal routes, coincidentally helping with the congestion points. Thus the workload sees improved performance. A similar phenomena is observed with Nekbone when it is running with QoS Mechanism I.

These experiments demonstrate the effectiveness of applying QoS to reduce or eliminate communication interference. With both mechanisms, Nekbone, being more bandwidth intensive, sees a 20% to 350% speedup in communication time compared with the case where QoS is not enabled. LAMMPS sees a 10% to 200% improvement in communication time compared with the case where QoS is not enabled. Nearest neighbor is indirectly impacted by bandwidth capping and sees a performance improvement of 25%. Additionally, all applications (both foreground and background traffic) benefit from QoS; the low priority applications are guaranteed to get a share in bandwidth which avoids performance degradation. The takeaway is that adding traffic differentiation in HPC networks can bring performance improvement to all traffic classes.

6   Related Work

There are different approaches to address run-to-run variability on HPC systems. One approach is based on partitioning the networks and providing an isolated partition for a job. While this approach has successfully worked for low-radix networks such as torus [21], it is a challenge to implement partitioning on networks such as dragonfly or megafly, due to their hierarchical nature. The other approach is QoS, which can be enforced through various mechanisms on data centers and HPC networks. Flow control [7,12] is a high-level approach for avoiding interference in large-scale and datacenter-scale networks which takes a coarser-grained look at data within the network. Alizedah et al. [1] studied the impacts of sacrificing a portion of the total bandwidth while lowering the threshold for congestion sensing to provide a buffer zone within links in an attempt to reduce the overall latency of applications in a datacenter environment. On the algorithmic routing side of QoS implementation, many different approaches exist, from centralized global information methods to distributed routing algorithms with limited or incomplete network information and hierarchical algorithms that bridge the gap between globally and locally available information when making routing decisions. Chen and Nahrstedt [3] presented an overview of various routing algorithms solving different QoS problems for both unicast and multicast applications. Most of the literature available on quality of service is intended for data-centric and TCP/IP networks and does not explore HPC workloads, routing, and flow control mechanisms. Cheng et al. [4] provided high-level details about implementing quality of service on data-centric and HPC networks. Jakanovic et al. [9] provided an efficient QoS policy for HPC systems with InifiBand network (fat tree topology).

7   Discussion and Conclusion

With HPC applications showing performance variation on recent hierarchical interconnects, we analyze communication interference for both megafly and dragonfly networks. We extend the CODES parallel simulation framework to replay the communication pattern of HPC applications using the Scalable Workload Models (SWM). We introduce moderate to intense background communication traffic during the execution of these communication workloads and compare the slowdown on megafly network with a 1-D dragonfly network. We demonstrate that performance variability is experienced in both topologies, while observing that in several experiments the performance implication is less severe for megafly.

To further mitigate the variability, we introduce traffic differentiation and quality of service mechanisms and show the results on a megafly network. We explore two different QoS mechanisms for HPC workloads (i) prioritizing and bandwidth capping entire HPC applications (ii) prioritizing and guaranteeing bandwidth to latency sensitive collective operations with small messages. With the first mechanism, performance results show that when a high priority and a bandwidth cap is given to entire HPC applications, it can eliminate performance variability while the rest of the background traffic also sees minimal impact. For the second mechanism, we show that when a small fraction of bandwidth is guaranteed to latency sensitive operations like the MPI collectives, it can mitigate the performance variability by 10% to 60% depending upon the intensity of collective communication in the application. This dramatic performance improvement from QoS on megafly can make up for its shortcomings in high-interference runs with no additional hardware cost. In both cases, we saw that both high and low priority applications have a better performance with QoS than the case with no QoS, which implies that having traffic differentiation is beneficial for all applications on a HPC network as it allows a fair share of bandwidth to each traffic class.

While this work is aimed to provide a proof of concept that QoS is effective in mitigating communication interference for realistic HPC workloads, there are a number of avenues that need to be further explored. First, real HPC systems have tens to hundreds of jobs running. Giving a high priority to more than one HPC application (as shown in QoS mechanism I) can introduce interference within the traffic class, which can slowdown high priority applications. Secondly, one would need to explore how to expose the traffic classes to the MPI interfaces and the job scheduler.

Acknowledgment. This research was supported by the Exascale Computing Project (17-SC-20-SC), a joint project of the U.S. Department of Energy's Office of Science and National Nuclear Security Administration, responsible for delivering a capable exascale ecosystem, including software, applications, and hardware technology, to support the nation's exascale computing imperative. The work has used resources from the Argonne's Leadership Computing Facility (ALCF), Rensselaer's CCI supercomputing center and Argonne's Laboratory Computing Resource Center (LCRC).

References

1. Alizadeh, M., Kabbani, A., Edsall, T., Prabhakar, B., Vahdat, A., Yasuda, M.: Less is more: trading a little bandwidth for ultra-low latency in the data center. In: Proceedings of the 9th USENIX Conference on Networked Systems Design and Implementation, pp. 19–19. USENIX Association (2012)
2. Argonne Leadership Computing Facility (ALCF): Theta, Argonne's Cray XC System. https://www.alcf.anl.gov/theta
3. Chen, S., Nahrstedt, K.: An overview of quality of service routing for next-generation high-speed networks: problems and solutions. IEEE Netw. **12**(6), 64–79 (1998)
4. Cheng, A.S., Lovett, T.D., Parker, M.A.: Traffic class arbitration based on priority and bandwidth allocation. Google Patents, December 2016
5. Chunduri, S., et al.: Run-to-run variability on Xeon Phi based Cray XC systems. In: Proceedings of the International Conference for High Performance Computing, Networking, Storage and Analysis, p. 52. ACM (2017)
6. Chunduri, S., Parker, S., Balaji, P., Harms, K., Kumaran, K.: Characterization of MPI usage on a production supercomputer. In: Characterization of MPI Usage on a Production Supercomputer. IEEE (2018)

7. Curtis, A.R., Mogul, J.C., Tourrilhes, J., Yalagandula, P., Sharma, P., Banerjee, S.: DevoFlow: scaling flow management for high-performance networks. In: ACM SIGCOMM Computer Communication Review, vol. 41, pp. 254–265. ACM (2011)
8. Flajslik, M., Borch, E., Parker, M.A.: Megafly: a topology for exascale systems. In: Yokota, R., Weiland, M., Keyes, D., Trinitis, C. (eds.) ISC High Performance 2018. LNCS, vol. 10876, pp. 289–310. Springer, Cham (2018). https://doi.org/10.1007/978-3-319-92040-5_15
9. Jokanovic, A., Sancho, J.C., Labarta, J., Rodriguez, G., Minkenberg, C.: Effective quality-of-service policy for capacity high-performance computing systems. In: 2012 IEEE 14th International Conference on High Performance Computing and Communication & 2012 IEEE 9th International Conference on Embedded Software and Systems (HPCC-ICESS), pp. 598–607. IEEE (2012)
10. Kim, J., Dally, W.J., Scott, S., Abts, D.: Technology-driven, highly-scalable dragonfly topology. In: 35th International Symposium on Computer Architecture 2008. ISCA 2008, pp. 77–88. IEEE (2008)
11. Los Alamos National Laboratory: Trinity Cray XC40 system. http://www.lanl.gov/projects/trinity/
12. McKeown, N., et al.: OpenFlow: enabling innovation in campus networks. ACM SIGCOMM Comput. Commun. Rev. **38**(2), 69–74 (2008)
13. Mubarak, M., et al.: Quantifying I/O and communication traffic interference on dragonfly networks equipped with burst buffers. In: 2017 IEEE International Conference on Cluster Computing (CLUSTER), pp. 204–215. IEEE (2017)
14. Mubarak, M., Carothers, C.D., Ross, R.B., Carns, P.H.: Enabling parallel simulation of large-scale HPC network systems. IEEE Trans. Parallel Distrib. Syst. **28**(1), 87–100 (2017)
15. Mubarak, M., Ross, R.B.: Validation study of CODES dragonfly network model with Theta Cray XC system (2017). https://doi.org/10.2172/1356812
16. NERSC: Cori. https://www.nersc.gov/users/computational-systems/cori/
17. Shpiner, A., Haramaty, Z., Eliad, S., Zdornov, V., Gafni, B., Zahavi, E.: Dragonfly+: low cost topology for scaling datacenters. In: 2017 IEEE 3rd International Workshop on High-Performance Interconnection Networks in the Exascale and Big-Data Era (HiPINEB), pp. 1–8. IEEE (2017)
18. Thompson, J.: Scalable workload models for system simulations background and motivation. Technical report (2014). http://hpc.pnl.gov/modsim/2014/Presentations/Thompson.pdf
19. Won, J., Kim, G., Kim, J., Jiang, T., Parker, M., Scott, S.: Overcoming far-end congestion in large-scale networks. In: 2015 IEEE 21st International Symposium on High Performance Computer Architecture (HPCA), pp. 415–427. IEEE (2015)
20. Yang, X., Jenkins, J., Mubarak, M., Ross, R.B., Lan, Z.: Watch out for the bully! job interference study on dragonfly network. In: International Conference for High Performance Computing, Networking, Storage and Analysis, SC16, pp. 750–760. IEEE (2016)
21. Zhou, Z., et al.: Improving batch scheduling on Blue Gene/Q by relaxing 5D torus network allocation constraints. In: 2015 IEEE International Parallel and Distributed Processing Symposium (IPDPS), pp. 439–448. IEEE (2015)

Artificial Intelligence and Machine Learning

Densifying Assumed-Sparse Tensors

Improving Memory Efficiency and MPI Collective Performance During Tensor Accumulation for Parallelized Training of Neural Machine Translation Models

Derya Cavdar[3], Valeriu Codreanu[4], Can Karakus[3], John A. Lockman III[1],
Damian Podareanu[4], Vikram Saletore[5], Alexander Sergeev[2], Don D. Smith II[1],
Victor Suthichai[3], Quy Ta[1], Srinivas Varadharajan[1(✉)], Lucas A. Wilson[1(✉)],
Rengan Xu[1], and Pei Yang[1]

[1] Dell EMC, Austin, TX, USA
{s_varadharajan,luke_wilson}@dell.com
[2] Uber, Seattle, WA, USA
[3] Amazon, Seattle, WA, USA
[4] SURFSara, Utrecht, The Netherlands
[5] Intel, Portland, OR, USA

Abstract. Neural machine translation - using neural networks to translate human language - is an area of active research exploring new neuron types and network topologies with the goal of dramatically improving machine translation performance. Current state-of-the-art approaches, such as the multi-head attention-based transformer, require very large translation corpuses and many epochs to produce models of reasonable quality. Recent attempts to parallelize the official TensorFlow "Transformer" model across multiple nodes have hit roadblocks due to excessive memory use and resulting out of memory errors when performing MPI collectives.

This paper describes modifications made to the Horovod MPI-based distributed training framework to reduce memory usage for transformer models by converting assumed-sparse tensors to dense tensors, and subsequently replacing sparse gradient gather with dense gradient reduction. The result is a dramatic increase in scale-out capability, with CPU-only scaling tests achieving 91% weak scaling efficiency up to 1200 MPI processes (300 nodes), and up to 65% strong scaling efficiency up to 400 MPI processes (200 nodes) using the Stampede2 supercomputer.

1 Introduction

Neural Machine Translation (NMT) [1,2,19] offers numerous improvements and advantages in translation quality compared to traditional machine translation systems, such as statistical phrase-based systems [10]. NMT also paved the way to translate multiple languages using a single model [9]. Continued active research interest in the field of NMT has created many interesting architectures which produce models of high translation quality [22]. Recent research also shows

© Springer Nature Switzerland AG 2019
M. Weiland et al. (Eds.): ISC High Performance 2019, LNCS 11501, pp. 23–39, 2019.
https://doi.org/10.1007/978-3-030-20656-7_2

how reduced precision and large batch training could speed-up the training while maintaining translation quality [12].

There are several challenges when scaling out Deep Neural Network (DNN)-based models, such as efficiently exchanging gradients across multiple nodes, scaling up the batch size while maintaining generalized performance, and selecting appropriate hyper-parameters which efficiently train the model while preventing divergence and over-fitting. NMT approaches such as the transformer model [22], which shares the weight matrix between the embedding layer and linear transformation before the *softmax* layer, must ensure that the gradients from these two layers are updated appropriately without causing performance degradation or out-of-memory (OOM) errors.

In this paper, we begin by understanding the basics of a NMT model, and try to explore the reasons that restrict it's scalability. We then show how our current solution of forcibly densifying assumed-sparse tensors achieves high scaling efficiency – both weak and strong – when trained with up to 300 nodes on both the Zenith supercomputer at Dell EMC and the Stampede2 supercomputer at TACC. We also illustrate that even when trained with very large batch sizes (402k, 630k and 1 Million tokens), we are still able to achieve comparable or slightly better translation quality when compared to the official TensorFlow benchmark results.

The software changes which we discuss in this paper have been incorporated into Horovod 0.15.2 and later, providing other researchers the opportunity to apply this approach on any models that may benefit.

2 Background

NMT models work much like source-to-source compilers, taking input from a source language (e.g., Fortran) and converting it to a target language (e.g., binary machine code). An NMT model first reads a sentence in a source language and passes it to an encoder, which builds an intermediate representation. This intermediate representation is then passed to the decoder, which processes the intermediate representation to produce the translated sentence in the target language.

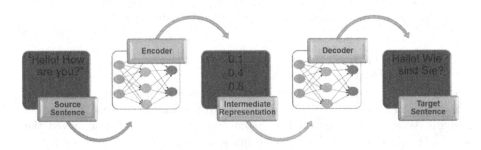

Fig. 1. Encoder-decoder architecture

Figure 1 shows an encoder-decoder architecture. The English source sentence, "Hello! How are you?" is read and processed by the architecture to produce a translated German sentence "Hallo! Wie sind Sie?". Traditionally, Recurrent Neural Networks (RNN) were used in encoders and decoders [2], but other neural network architectures such as Convolutional Neural Networks (CNN) [4] and attention mechanism-based models [16] are also used.

The transformer model [22] is one of the interesting architectures in the field of NMT, which is built with variants of attention mechanism in the encoder-decoder part, eliminating the need for traditional RNNs in the architecture [3]. This model was able to achieve state of the art results in English-German and English-French translation tasks.

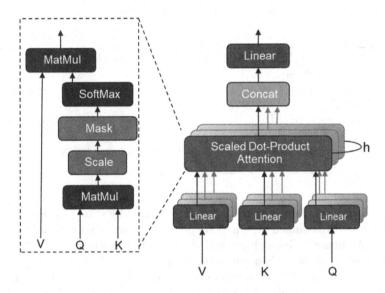

Fig. 2. Multi-head attention block [22]

Figure 2 illustrates the multi-head attention block used in the transformer model. At a high-level, the scaled dot-product attention can be imagined as finding the relevant information, values (V) based on Query (Q) and Keys (K) and multi-head attention could be thought as several attention layers in parallel to get distinct aspects of the input.

3   Issues with Scaling the Transformer Model

Encoder-decoder models for NMT make use of an attention mechanism to help the decoders obtain the vital information from the source tokens while discarding irrelevant information. The main structure of the transformer model is the multi-head attention, which provides a way to get different linear transformations of all the inputs. These components allow an NMT model to learn more robustly. But a particular design consideration that needs to be looked at for improving the scaling capabilities is the weight matrix that is shared between the embedding layer and the projection matrix. This type of similar design is also seen in other NMT models such as [4]. Hence, understanding the cause and effect of these specific design considerations is vital for the NMT research community.

This particular design would cause performance degradation or OOM errors if the gradients from these layers are not accumulated correctly. Specifically, gradients from the embedding layer are sparse whereas the gradients from the projection matrix are dense. In TensorFlow both gradients are updated together as a sparse `IndexedSlices` objects. This has a dramatic effect on TensorFlow's determination of a gradient accumulation strategy, and subsequently on the total size of the accumulated gradient tensor.

Algorithm 1. Tensor Accumulation Strategy in TensorFlow [20]

1: **if** $|GRAD_{in}| < 2$ **then**
2:     $GRAD_{out} \leftarrow GRAD_{in}$ ▷ Pass-through
3: **else if** $type(g) = Tensor \; \forall g \in GRAD_{in}$ **then**
4:     $GRAD_{out} \leftarrow \sum GRAD_{in}$ ▷ Output is a dense Tensor (reduce)
5: **else**
6:     $GRAD_{out} \leftarrow \widehat{GRAD}_{in}$ ▷ Output is a sparse IndexedSlice (gather)
7: **end if**

Algorithm 1 describes the algorithm used in TensorFlow to accumulate gradients, based on the assumed type and shape of the gradients being accumulated (see [20]). At present, TensorFlow will either: (1) do nothing if there are less than 2 output gradients, (2) accumulate gradients by reduction if all gradients are expressed as dense tensors with defined shapes, or (3) convert everything to indexed slices and accumulate by concatenation (performing a gather operation).

In this particular use case, the embedding lookup is performed using `tf.gather`, which returns an `IndexedSlice` object. This forces TensorFlow (based on the accumulation algorithm - Algorithm 1) to convert the remaining dense tensors to indexed slices, even though all the gradients being accumulated are dense.

The result of this decision to convert and assume that the gradient tensors are sparse is to accumulate by gathering, rather than reduction. This applies not only to single-node tensor accumulation, but to multi-node accumulation through Horovod due to the use of the main TensorFlow graph in determining which collective operations Horovod will perform using MPI. The result is extremely large message buffers (exceeding 11 GB - see Fig. 3a), which cause segmentation faults or out-of-memory (OOM) errors.

Because of the message buffer sizes, we were unable to scale beyond 32 MPI processes, and saw quickly diminishing scaling efficiency, or fraction of ideal scaled speedup. Figure 4 shows the scaled speedup of the training process up

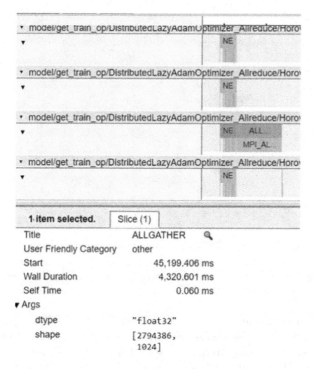

(a) Before: tf.gather/MPI_Gather

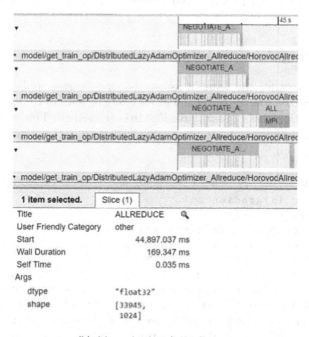

(b) After: tf.reduce/MPI_Reduce

Fig. 3. Horovod timelines for 64 MPI process tests before and after modification

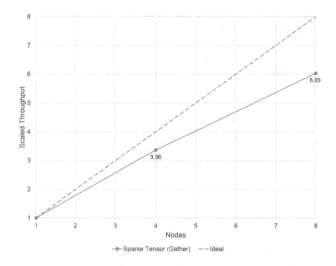

Fig. 4. Scaled speedup with sparse tensor accumulation strategy (gather)

to the maximum achievable 32 MPI processes (8 nodes with 4 processes per node). Scaling efficiency – which is visually expressed as distance from the ideal line – declines rapidly, going from 84% with 4 nodes to 75% for 8 nodes. Eventually scaled speedup would (if the training could be parallelized further) reach an asymptotic limit where additional resources do not further accelerate the algorithm.

4   Densifying Assumed-Sparse Tensors

In order to correct for the issue of assumed-sparse tensors in TensorFlow, we have implemented a forced-conversion of all gradient tensors to dense representation inside of Horovod's `DistributedOptimizer` method. This will then force TensorFlow to accumulate those tensors via reduction, rather than aggregation (see Listing 1).

Listing 1. Horovod code for converting IndexedSlices to Tensors [5]

```
for grad, var in gradients:
    if grad is not None:
        if self._sparse_as_dense and
            isinstance(grad, tf.IndexedSlices):
            grad = tf.convert_to_tensor(grad)
```

The result is an 82x reduction in the amount of memory required (from 11.4 GB to 139 MB - see Fig. 3a and b, respectively) when using 64 nodes (1 MPI process per node, batch size 5000 tokens). Additionally, the time needed to perform the accumulate operation drops from 4320 ms to 169 ms, which is a 25x reduction (see Fig. 5 for a comparison of accumulate size and time).

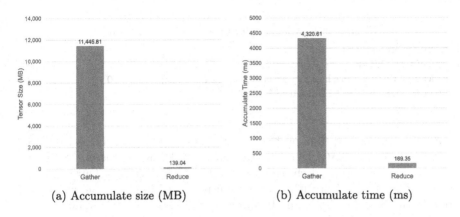

(a) Accumulate size (MB)   (b) Accumulate time (ms)

Fig. 5. Space/time for tensor accumulate (sparse gather vs. dense reduce)

These small changes reduce the memory footprint per process to a degree that we can both scale up the batch size per MPI process and increase the number of MPI processes per run. They also reduce the tensor exchange time significantly enough to maintain near-linear scaling when running in a multi-node environment.

This algorithmic change can be made in Horovod 0.15.2 or later by setting the `sparse_as_dense` option when initializing `DistributedOptimizer`:

```
opt = hvd.DistributedOptimizer(opt, sparse_as_dense=True)
```

5   Experimental Results

The models were trained using the WMT-17 English-German parallel corpus with 4.5M sentence pairs. The newstest2014 dataset was used as unseen test data to capture the translation quality. All the pre-processing and BLEU [13] calculations were in accordance with TensorFlow's official benchmarks in order to compare performance and translation quality. We also used hyper parameter settings based on best practices in [12,15]. Model training experiments were run on the Zenith cluster in the Dell EMC HPC & AI Innovation Lab, as well as the Stampede2 cluster at the Texas Advanced Computing Center (TACC) in Austin, Texas.

Each Zenith node contains dual Intel®Xeon®Scalable Gold 6148/F processors, 192 GB of memory, and an M.2 boot drive to house the operating system that does not provide user-accessible local storage. Nodes are interconnected by a 100 Gbps Intel®Omni-path fabric, and shared storage is provided by a combination of NFS (for HOME directories) and Lustre [17] filesystems.

For our Zenith tests, we used Python 2.7, with Intel's MKL-optimized version of TensorFlow (1.12). The version of Horovod used for these experiments was a private branch for testing purposes, but all of these optimizations have now been made a part of Horovod 0.15.2. Table 1 gives a complete breakdown of the software environment used for the Zenith experiments, while Listing 2 provides the runtime settings for the experiments.

Listing 2. Runtime settings for Zenith Experiments

```
OMP_NUM_THREADS=10
KMP_BLOCKTIME=0
KMP_AFFINITY=granularity=fine,verbose,compact,1,0
HOROVOD_FUSION_THRESHOLD=134217728
```

We also ran scaling tests on the Stampede2 cluster at the Texas Advanced Computing Center (TACC) at The University of Texas at Austin [18]. Stampede2 has two partitions, each with a different set of processors. Our tests were performed on the SKX partition, which consists of 1,736 nodes, each with dual Intel®Xeon®Scalable Platinum 8160 processors, 192 GB of memory, and 200 GB internal SSD drive for the operating system and local /tmp. The second KNL partition consists of 4,200 nodes, each with a single Intel®Xeon Phi™ 7250 processor with 16 GB of on-package MCDRAM, 94 GB of main memory, and a 200 GB SSD for the operating system and local /tmp. All nodes are interconnected with 100 Gbps Intel®Omni-path fabric and connected to Lustre-based shared filesystems.

For our Stampede2 tests, we used Python 2.7, with Intel's MKL-optimized version of TensorFlow (1.12). The version of Horovod used for these experiments was a private branch for testing purposes, but all of these optimizations have now been made a part of Horovod 0.15.2. Table 2 gives a complete breakdown of the software environment used for the Zenith experiments.

Table 1. Software environment for Zenith experiments

Package	Version
Python	2.7.13
TensorFlow	Anaconda TensorFlow 1.12.0 with Intel®MKL
Horovod	0.15.2
MPI	MVAPICH2 2.1

5.1 Weak Scaling Performance

The difference in reducing the output gradient size can be seen when comparing the scaling efficiency – the ratio between observed scaled speedup and ideal – between the default sparse tensor accumulation strategy (gather) and the dense tensor accumulation strategy (reduce). Dense tensor accumulations show significantly better scaling efficiency out to 32 MPI processes (95%) than the default sparse tensor accumulation (75%) (see Fig. 6).

The reduced output gradient size and improved scaling efficiency mean that we can scale to larger process counts than was previously possible. Additional weak scaling experiments on Zenith using 4 processes per node (PPN) on up to 300 compute nodes (1200 MPI processes) show near-linear scaling, with efficiency

Table 2. Software environment for Stampede2 experiments

Package	Version
Python	2.7.13
TensorFlow	Anaconda TensorFlow 1.12.0 with Intel®MKL
Horovod	0.15.2
MPI	MVAPICH2 2.3

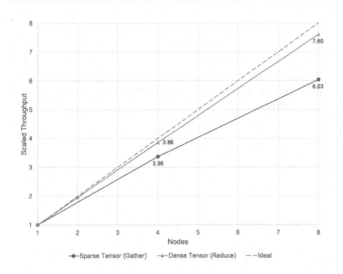

Fig. 6. Comparison of weak scaling on Zenith up to 8 nodes (4PPN) between sparse and dense tensor accumulation strategies

dropping from 95% for 8 nodes to 91.5% for 300 (see Figs. 7 and 8). For these particular experiments on Zenith, batch size per process was held constant at 5000 tokens, or 20000 tokens per node. This means in the largest case (1200 MPI processes) we are training with a global batch size of 6M tokens.

The ability to maintain very high weak scaling efficiency above 90% suggests that continued scale-out is worthwhile. We will seek to perform additional experiments on systems larger than Zenith.

5.2 Strong Scaling

Besides good weak scaling efficiency, the reduced output gradient size also gives us the possibility to perform strong scaling experiments. For this purpose, we have selected a global batch size of 819,200 that allows us to produce a near-state-of-the-art model in terms of translation quality (as measured by BLEU score [13]), and as discussed in the following section. Obtaining good strong scaling efficiency is significantly more challenging compared to the weak scaling case, as the effective batch size per worker decreases when increasing the node count.

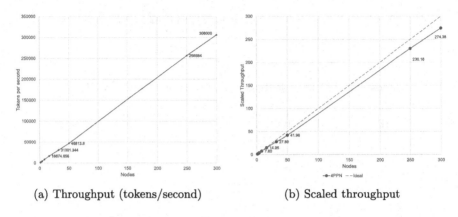

(a) Throughput (tokens/second)   (b) Scaled throughput

Fig. 7. Weak scaling on Zenith cluster from 1 to 300 nodes (4 PPN) using dense tensor accumulation strategy (reduce)

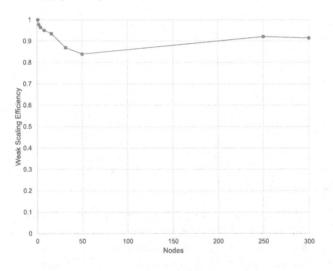

Fig. 8. Weak scaling efficiency on Zenith up to 300 nodes (1200 processes)

We have performed strong scaling experiments on both on the Zenith cluster and on the Stampede2 supercomputer from TACC. We have used up to 200 nodes on Zenith, and up to 512 nodes on Stampede2, both systems showing significant reductions in terms of time to solution.

Figures 9 and 10 illustrate the strong scaling behavior that can be expected on the Zenith system. When going from 16 nodes up to 200 nodes, we can improve the throughput by a factor exceeding 8 (out of a maximum of around 12). In all these strong scaling cases, we only use 2 processes per node, each being scheduled to run on one socket and exploiting the NUMA affinity. This setting is more appropriate in this scenario, as the batch size that can be used per worker is double compared to the case when using 4 processes per node.

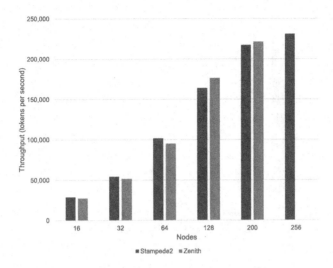

Fig. 9. Strong scaling throughput on up to 200 nodes of Zenith (Dell EMC) and 256 nodes of Stampede2 (TACC) with global batch size of 819,200 tokens

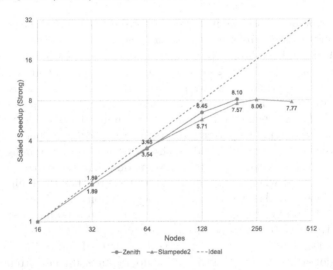

Fig. 10. Scaled speedup (strong scaling) up to 200 nodes on Zenith (Dell EMC) and 256 nodes on Stampede2 (TACC) with a global batch size of 819,200 tokens

The impact of having good strong scaling efficiency is that training times can be dramatically reduced. This can be best visualized in Fig. 11, where the time to solution drops from around one month when using a single node, down to slightly over 6 h when using 200 nodes (121 times faster), therefore significantly increasing the productivity for NMT researchers when using CPU-based HPC infrastructures. The results observed were based on the models achieving a baseline BLEU score (case-sensitive) of 27.5.

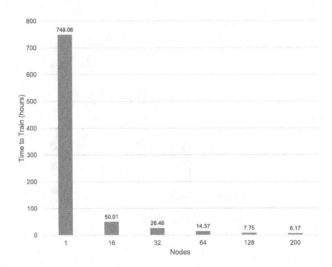

Fig. 11. Time to solution (strong scaling) on up to 200 Zenith nodes

For the single node case, we have used the largest batch size that could fit in a node's memory, 25,600 tokens per worker. For all other cases we use a global batch size of 819,200, leading to per-worker batch sizes of 25,600 in the 16-node case, down to only 2,048 in the 200-node case. The number of training iterations is similar for all experiments in the 16–200 node range, and is increased by a factor of 16 for the single-node case (to compensate for the larger batch).

On Stampede2, the behavior is similar to zenith up to 200 nodes. Since Stampede2 is a larger system, we performed larger strong scaling experiments. However, we noticed that using a 819,200 batch size would limit the scaling efficiency when using over 256 nodes. The 200 to 256 node range show improvements in time-to-solution, but when using 400 nodes we have reached the limits of strong scaling, and begin to observe performance degradation. This is due to the fact that a small (1,024) per-worker batch size is used in the 400 nodes experiment. To test that this is the case, we performed a larger experiment using a per-worker batch size of 1,536, and a total of 1,024 workers divided across 512 nodes. This leads to a global batch size of 1,572,864, and requires further attention to in order to reach the translation accuracy performance targets. However, from a throughput perspective, this run is 56% faster compared to a similar 256-node run. This shows that there will be performance improvements as we increase the per-worker batch size to a reasonably large size (>1536).

5.3 Model Accuracy

Scaling out transformer model training using MPI and Horovod improves throughput performance, while producing models of similar translation quality (see Fig. 12). Models of comparable quality can be trained in a reduced amount of time by scaling computation over many more nodes, and with larger global batch sizes (GBZ). Our experiments on Zenith demonstrate ability to train models of comparable or higher translation quality (as measured by BLEU score [13]) than the reported best for TensorFlow's official model [21], even when training with batches of a million or more tokens.

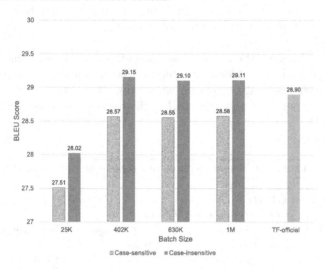

Fig. 12. Translation quality (BLEU) when trained with varying batch size on Zenith (Color figure online)

6   Discussion

Our experiments have demonstrated that converting assumed-sparse tensors to dense tensors improves memory utilization as well as time to accumulate, thanks to a switch from gathering to reduction (see Fig. 5). Unlike similar solutions implemented directly within optimized NMT models, such as NVIDIA's OpenSeq2Seq package [11], our approach *does not limit usability strictly to one specific package repository or model implementation*. Instead, our approach provides greater generalized use and potential applicability to other models.

Applicability to Other Models. We believe the solution that is now implemented in Horovod will prove useful to most neural network model classes, including various language translation models, image segmentation models, voice/text translation models across multiple voice datasets, time-series models, etc. Future work will quantify the impact of the current solution to these use cases. We also foresee this as a potential workaround for issues in custom architectures, such as multi-branch neural networks [7,23–25]. These architectures are typically recollecting gradient data from multiple "separated" neural network branches, which would be likely to encounter similar sparse tensor encoding issues.

Specificity to TensorFlow. While we have identified a specific edge case within the TensorFlow code base, we do not believe that this particular edge case is common to other deep learning frameworks, such as Caffé2 [8] and PyTorch [14]. However, TensorFlow's current and continuing popularity and the abundance of pre-built models in TensorFlow mean that any performance benefits we can communicate back to that community are important.

Incorporating Changes into TensorFlow. Long-term, we believe that the ideal solution is to add additional logic into TensorFlow's gradient accumulation algorithm to convert and reduce tensors when **any** of the tensors is dense (see Algorithm 2), rather than only when **all** of the tensors are dense (as is the case in Algorithm 1).

Algorithm 2. Proposed Tensor Accumulation Strategy for TensorFlow

---

1: **if** $|GRAD_{in}| < 2$ **then**
2:    $GRAD_{out} \leftarrow GRAD_{in}$ ▷ Pass-through
3: **else if** $type(g) = Tensor \ \forall g \in GRAD_{in}$ **then**
4:    $GRAD_{out} \leftarrow \sum GRAD_{in}$ ▷ Output is a dense Tensor (reduce)
5: **else if** $\exists g \in GRAD_{in} \ type(g) = Tensor$ **then**
6:    $GRAD_{conv} \leftarrow \{conv\_to\_tensor(g), \ \forall g \in GRAD_{in}\}$ ▷ Convert all to Tensor
7:    $GRAD_{out} \leftarrow \sum GRAD_{conv}$ ▷ Output is a dense Tensor (reduce)
8: **else**
9:    $GRAD_{out} \leftarrow \widehat{GRAD}_{in}$ ▷ Output is a sparse IndexedSlice (gather)
10: **end if**

In the case of Algorithm 2, we propose the addition of an extra conditional block (lines 5–7), which would handle the case that there exists at least 1 tensor which is dense, in which case all of the tensors to be accumulated would be converted to dense and accumulated by reduction. More research has to be done in order to ensure that incorporating this conditional block into the TensorFlow accumulation strategy would not adversely effect other well-behaved tensor accumulations, and we will be testing this inclusion and proposing back to TensorFlow in the future.

7 Future Work and Conclusion

Scaling Neural Machine Translation (NMT) models to multiple nodes can be difficult due to the large corpuses needed for reasonable translation, and the all-to-all mapping nature of the intermediate representation encodings. If tensor accumulation is not performed in a memory and compute-optimized fashion, excessively large tensors can cause buffer overruns which prevent scaling beyond a few MPI processes. These models can take weeks or months to train at low node counts, making it all the more critical that they can be efficiently scaled to hundreds or thousands of MPI processes.

We have identified an edge case in TensorFlow's tensor accumulation strategy which leads to sub-optimal memory and compute utilization, which prevents scaling of multi-head attention-based transformer models beyond a relatively small number of processes without very large memory buffers. We have proposed and implemented a fix via the Horovod MPI-based framework for distributed memory scaling of TensorFlow models by forcibly converting – through the use of an option to `DistributedOptimizer` – all tensors to be accumulated to dense and subsequently reducing tensors rather than aggregating them. The result is a more than 82x reduction in memory needed and 25x reduction in time to complete the accumulation step at 64 MPI processes, and the enabled ability to scale the translation model to a thousand MPI processes or more with batches of millions of word part tokens.

These modifications have been incorporated into Horovod, and are available as of version 0.15.2 [6], so that other teams can scale neural machine translation tasks or any other tasks which use similar topologies. We have proposed a potential fix within TensorFlow as a more long-term solution to this issue, and we will be pursuing this going forward once we have determined that there are no additional side-effects from the addition of the new tensor accumulation strategy.

Going forward, we intend to investigate whether other neural network architectures besides multi-head attention can benefit from being able to expressly densify sparse tensor encodings, as well as whether custom architectures could potentially benefit from this solution.

Acknowledgement. The authors acknowledge the Texas Advanced Computing Center (TACC) at The University of Texas at Austin for providing HPC resources that have contributed to the research results reported within this paper http://www.tacc.utexas.edu.

References

1. Bahdanau, D., Cho, K., Bengio, Y.: Neural machine translation by jointly learning to align and translate. Computing Research Repository (CoRR), abs/11409.0473v7, September 2014
2. Cho, K., van Merrienboer, B., Gulcehre, C., Bougares, F., Schwenk, H., Bengio, Y.: Learning phrase representations using RNN encoder-decoder for statistical machine translation. Computing Research Repository (CoRR), abs/1406.1078v3, September 2014
3. Collobert, R., Puhrsch, C., Synnaeve, G.: Wav2Letter: an End-to-End ConvNet-based speech recognition system. Computing Research Repository (CoRR), abs/1609.03193v2, September 2016
4. Gehring, J., et al.: Convolutional sequence to sequence learning. Computing Research Repository (CoRR), abs/1705.03122v3, July 2017
5. Horovod. compute_gradients() in horovod/tensorflow/__init__.py. https://github.com/uber/horovod/blob/085cb1b5f3b30734a34d047841b098c15a6e1bae/horovod/tensorflow/__init__.py#L195

6. Horovod. Release 0.15.2. https://github.com/uber/horovod/releases/tag/v0.15.2
7. Hu, J., Shen, L., Sun, G.: Squeeze-and-excitation networks. In: Proceedings of the IEEE Conference on Computer Vision and Pattern Recognition, pp. 7132–7141 (2018)
8. Jia, Y., et al.: Caffe: convolutional architecture for fast feature embedding. In Proceedings of the 22nd ACM International Conference on Multimedia, pp. 675–678, November 2014
9. Johnson, M., et al.: Google's multilingual neural machine translation system: enabling zero-shot translation. Computing Research Repository (CoRR), abs/1611.04558v2, August 2017
10. Koehn, P., Och, F.J., Marcu, D.: Statistical phrase-based translation. In: Proceedings of 2003 Human Language Technology Conference (HLT-NAACL), pp. 48–54, June 2003
11. Kuchaiev, O., Ginsburg, B., Gitman, I., Lavrukhin, V., Case, C., Micikevicius, P.: Mixed-precision training for NLP and speech recognition with OpenSeq2Seq. Computing Research Repository (CoRR), abs/1805.10387v2, November 2018
12. Ott, M., Edunov, S., Grangier, D., Auli, M.: Scaling neural machine translation. Computing Research Repository (CoRR), abs/1806.00187v3, September 2018
13. Papineni, K., Roukos, S., Ward, T., Zhu, W.-J.: BLEU: a method for automatic evaluation of machine translation. In: Proceedings of the 40th Annual Meeting on Association for Computational Linguistics, pp. 311–318. Association for Computational Linguistics (2002)
14. Paszke, A.: Automatic differentiation in PyTorch, December 2017
15. Popel, M., Bojar, O.: Training tips for the transformer model. Computing Research Repository (CoRR), abs/1804.00247v2, May 2018
16. Rush, A.M., Chopra, S., Weston, J.: A neural attention model for abstractive sentence summarization. Computing Research Repository (CoRR), abs/1509.00685v2, September 2015
17. Schwan, P., et al.: Lustre: building a file system for 1000-node clusters. In: Proceedings of the 2003 Linux Symposium, vol. 2003, pp. 380–386 (2003)
18. Stanzione, D., et al.: Stampede 2: the evolution of an XSEDE supercomputer. In: Proceedings of the Practice and Experience in Advanced Research Computing 2017 on Sustainability, Success and Impact, PEARC 2017, pp. 15:1–15:8. ACM, New York (2017)
19. Sutskever, I., Vinyals, O., Le, Q.V.: Sequence to sequence learning with neural networks. In: NIPS Proceedings Advances in Neural Information Processing Systems 27, pp. 3104–3112, December 2014
20. TensorFlow. _AggregatedGrads() in tensorflow/python/ops/gradients_impl.py. https://github.com/tensorflow/tensorflow/blob/c95ca05536144451ef78ca6e2c15f0 f65ebaaf95/tensorflow/python/ops/gradients_impl.py#L1183
21. TensorFlow. Official Transformer Model. https://github.com/tensorflow/models/ blob/cdcd3ec276bdccd77a9a35c38f5aaec39c15cc0b/official/transformer/ README.md
22. Vaswani, A., et al.: Attention is all you need. Computing Research Repository (CoRR), abs/1706.03762v5, December 2017
23. Xie, S., Girshick, R., Dollár, P., Tu, Z., He, K.: Aggregated residual transformations for deep neural networks. In: Proceedings of the IEEE Conference on Computer Vision and Pattern Recognition, pp. 1492–1500 (2017)

24. Yamashita, T., Hirasawa, K., Hu, J.: Application of multi-branch neural networks to stock market prediction. In: Proceedings. 2005 IEEE International Joint Conference on Neural Networks 2005, vol. 4, pp. 2544–2548. IEEE (2005)
25. Yamashita, T., Hirasawa, K., Hu, J., Murata, J.: Multi-branch structure of layered neural networks. In: Proceedings of the 9th International Conference on Neural Information Processing 2002, ICONIP 2002, vol. 1, pp. 243–247. IEEE (2002)

Learning Neural Representations
for Predicting GPU Performance

Shweta Salaria[1,2(✉)], Aleksandr Drozd[1,2], Artur Podobas[3],
and Satoshi Matsuoka[1,3]

[1] Tokyo Institute of Technology, Tokyo, Japan
salaria.s.aa@m.titech.ac.jp, alex@smg.is.titech.ac.jp, matsu@acm.org
[2] AIST-Tokyo Tech RWBC-OIL, Tokyo, Japan
[3] RIKEN Center for Computational Science, Kobe, Japan
artur.podobas@gmail.com

Abstract. The graphic processing units (GPUs) have become a primary source of heterogeneity in today's computing systems. With the rapid increase in number and types of GPUs available, finding the best hardware accelerator for each application is a challenge. For that matter, it is time consuming and tedious to execute every application on every GPU system to learn the correlation between application properties and hardware characteristics. To address this problem, we extend our previously proposed collaborating filtering based modeling technique, to build an analytical model which can predict performance of applications across different GPU systems. Our model learns representations, or embeddings (dense vectors of latent features) for applications and systems and uses them to characterize the performance of various GPU-accelerated applications. We improve state-of-the-art collaborative filtering approach based on matrix factorization by building a multi-layer perceptron. In addition to increased accuracy in predicting application performance, we can use this model to simultaneously predict multiple metrics such as rates of memory access operations. We evaluate our approach on a set of 30 well-known micro-applications and seven Nvidia GPUs. As a result, we can predict expected instructions per second value with 90.6% accuracy in average.

Keywords: Performance prediction · GPU · Collaborative filtering ·
Matrix factorization · Multi-layer perceptron

1 Introduction

Graphics Processing Units (GPUs) are today the de-facto source of performance in High-Performance Computing (HPC), and the vast majority of current top supercomputers [24] include them in their system setup. These powerful devices are explicit vector machines, whose programming model allows the programmer to leverage the large amount of parallelism they offer. Unlike general-purpose processors, which focus on exploiting instruction-level parallelism (and

M. Weiland et al. (Eds.): ISC High Performance 2019, LNCS 11501, pp. 40–58, 2019.
https://doi.org/10.1007/978-3-030-20656-7_3

focus on latency), GPUs focus on thread-level parallelism, masking/hiding long-latency operations (e.g. external memory accesses) by time-sharing computational resources. Despite their similar programming model, GPUs are constantly undergoing architectural changes across generation (e.g. mixed-precision Arithmetic Logic Units, per thread program counters, diverse amount of floating-point units), which makes their performance non-trivial to reason around and *predict*.

Performance prediction is (and will continue to be) a core pillar in computer science, and is used to assess the performance (or other metrics such as power-consumption) of a (non-) fictional system prior to acquisition. The usage of predicting system performance ranges from users' reasoning around which cloud solution fits their performance and budget requirements the best, to HPC system administrators understanding what components to expand their system with, all the way to researchers attempting to map and reason around performance trends and directions. And with the end of Moore's law near [8], prediction and understanding performance is more crucial than ever before.

Predicting GPU performance is a challenging and hard task. Despite sharing a programming model (CUDA [7] and OpenCL [21]), their architectural differences between generations can be substantial. Furthermore, with the advent and popularity of Deep-Learning, the type and target audience of GPUs is diversifying. As a result, GPUs specialized in inference, training, gaming, and scientific computing are emerging [19]. Given this vast array of current and emerging GPU types, *how do users choose which to invest in?* Today, most users blindly buy the fastest next-generation accelerator for their workload, which is more than likely not the most optimal choice. The Nvidia's Maxwell vs. Kepler architecture is one such example where the older generation has an order of magnitude higher double-precision performance. Thus, there is a need for a *simple* and effective performance model that assists users in choosing accelerators suitable for their workloads.

Existing methods to predict GPU performance are either constrained by the programming environment (and the necessity of mapping algorithms to existing GPU features) [10,15], or based on compiler-based approaches [2] to extract GPU-specific micro-architectural features. Such methods often work well on the targeted GPU, but are inapplicable across GPU types and architectures as these methods are *system-specific*. We focus on building a prediction model that does not burden users to needlessly execute an application on all target systems. We recently proposed a collaborative filtering (CF) based prediction model and showed that it worked well on general-purpose processors (CPUs) that were diverse in both instruction set architecture (ISA) and architecture, even when the sampling data was sparse [22]. In this paper, we extend our CF-based prediction method to GPU-based systems and propose a new model which further improves the prediction accuracy.

The main contributions of this work are as follows:

1. We show that CF can be used to capture and predict performance for GPUs.
2. We introduce a neural network architecture to learn representations of applications and systems and test whether using auxiliary training objectives can further improve its predictive power.

3. We evaluate and analyze our performance model empirically on a large and diverse set of well-known benchmarks and multiple generations of Nvidia GPUs, quantifying the prediction accuracy.

2 Background and Motivation

2.1 Related Work

Many modeling methods have been proposed to estimate the performance of codes on GPUs. Low-level simulators, such as GPGPU-Sim [3] are relatively accurate but they are many orders of magnitude slower than other methods. Abstract analytical models like the roofline model [25] provide fast estimation but are difficult to use without in-depth knowledge of the algorithm (or, in worse case, the micro-architecture) at hand.

Baghsorkhi et al. proposed a compiler-based approach to develop a work flow graph based prediction model that heavily relies on extracting micro-architectural features of a target GPU [2]. Luo and Suda proposed a GPU power and performance model based on analyzing PTX codes to calculate memory accesses and execution time [16]. They showed good accuracy on two older GPUs presented in their study but it would not deal well with advances like multi-level caches.

Kerr et al. presented a framework for automating the generation of GPU performance models using PCA-based statistical method [14]. They profiled 12 benchmarks using a simulator and used PCA to find groups of similar workloads in order to build their models. They evaluated their framework using 3 Nvidia GPUs corresponding to Fermi micro-architecture. It is however not known how this approach will work with different micro-architectures.

Wu et al. predicted power and performance across hardware configurations corresponding to AMD Graphics Core Next micro-architecture [26], while we predicted performance across different generations of GPU micro-architectures. They used only one real GPU in their work and 448 hardware configurations were obtained by varying its compute units, memory and core frequencies. We used seven Nvidia GPUs from four different generations ranging from Kepler to Volta. They used 22 performance counters to capture AMD Graphics Core Next micro-architecture features and it is likely that this number will change considerably as we consider another micro-architecture; e.g. we can record 81 hardware events using Nvidia Pascal but 139 using Kepler. In such case, finding an optimal set of features becomes a new challenge which is the main motivation behind using latent features in our work.

The number of different GPU micro-architectures and accelerators per architecture available in today's market brings new challenges towards projecting an application's performance across different systems. Our prediction model can help in pruning this search space resulting to a few systems, which can then be studied for architectural insights using any other complementary modeling approach. In this way, we are complementing (not replacing) existing techniques.

2.2   Explicit Features

The performance of a program on a given system is guided by the complex inter-actions between the program's properties and system's characteristics. The most common approach taken towards building analytical models is to first perform a detailed characterization of applications on systems and collect various performance metrics such as execution time, hardware counters [12,27]. Second, it needs to explicitly list all the features that can capture the inter-dependencies between the application and system at hand such as clock rate, cache size, floating point operations per second (FLOPS) etc. Most previous works use an intuitive approach when selecting the number of features in order to determine a set of good explanatory features. However, missing just one crucial feature from these carefully handpicked features can greatly (and negatively) affect the prediction accuracy. Third, we need to test each possible subset of those features finding the one which minimizes the error. This is an exhaustive search of the feature space, and is computationally expensive and unfeasible for all but the smallest of feature sets. Feature selection algorithms come handy when it comes to finding the most impactful feature subsets but it comes with an extra effort of selecting the appropriate algorithm and its parameters.

While considering tens or more of applications and systems, manually defining features for each set of application and system is practically impossible. For building a cross-architecture predictive model, such as the one we are targeting, we focus on two things: (1) We do not want to manually define feature for each application and system (2) we want our model to learn the features automatically from the known performance of a subset of applications executed on a subset of systems and leverage this information to predict performance.

2.3   Representation Learning

The concept of representation learning is grounded in the idea that often the information needed to characterize or classify high dimensional data can be found in a low-dimensional manifold, or mapped into a dense vector. For instance, natural language processing systems use word embeddings to represent (embed) words in a continuous vector space where semantically similar words have similar vector representations (embeddings) [17]. Recommender systems employ similar representations to describe its entities (e.g. users and items) and call them as *latent features*.

We assume that there is a number of important features, called latent features, which characterize systems and applications. We use a machine learning model to learn these features as a by-product of predicting known runtime metrics. In our model, we have application and system feature vectors. Two or more applications can be similar in one latent feature (they both benefit from high memory bandwidth) but different in others (only one benefits from high core clock frequency).

2.4   Collaborative Filtering

Collaborative filtering [1] is considered to be the most popular and widely implemented technique in recommender systems. It automatically generates predictions (filtering) about the interests of a user by collecting preferences or information from many users (collaborating) present in the system. One of its most publicized applications is the Netflix challenge for improving Netflix's movie recommender system, Cinematch, by providing valid movie recommendations to its users. The prize was won by using a combination of different collaborative filtering techniques.

Model-based CF methods transform both users and items to the same latent feature space. The latent space is then used to explain ratings by characterizing both products and users in terms of factors automatically inferred from user feedback.

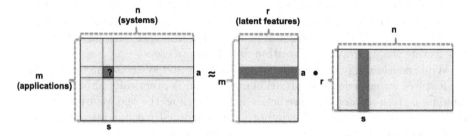

Fig. 1. Mapping of applications and systems into a shared latent space using matrix factorization.

We recently investigated different CF-based methods to predict performance across different processor architectures [22]. We used a model-based CF method called matrix factorization (MF) to model the interactions between applications and systems. While training, MF associates each of m applications and n systems with real-valued vectors of latent features of size r as shown in Fig. 1. It infers these latent features automatically by uncovering hidden patterns in performance observed on systems. In order to predict performance of a benchmark a on system s, MF calculates the predicted score by taking the dot product of their latent features.

3   Prediction Model

We first discuss the limitations of matrix factorization and then present a neural network architecture that can learn complex application-system representations using additional training objectives.

3.1   Multi-layer Perceptron Model

MF models the two-way interactions of applications and systems as a dot product of their latent features in a latent space. However, the linear combination of latent features with the same weight can limit its capability to model all application-system interactions in the low-dimensional latent space. Also, using a large number of latent features in order to capture both linear and non-linear interactions may affect the generalization of the model by overfitting the data. We address this limitation of MF by learning latent features using a feedforward neural network.

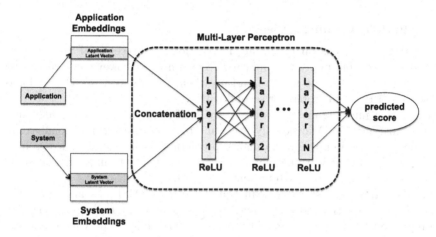

Fig. 2. Multi-layer perceptron model using latent features

We propose a multi-layer perceptron (MLP) to learn the correlation between application and system latent features as shown in Fig. 2. Each application and system in dataset is identified by a sparse vector with one-hot encoding. For example, representing two applications or systems using one-hot encoding would result in two vectors i.e. [1, 0] and [0, 1]. These sparse representations are used to create dense vectors called embeddings. The size of each application (system) embedding vector is determined by the number of features to be used by the model. In the beginning, each embedding vector is initialized with a scaled uniform distribution. These embeddings are fed into a multi-layer neural network to learn the interaction between the corresponding application and system from a training dataset. For that purpose, an optimizer is used to iteratively optimize these embeddings vectors based on training losses. The obtained application (system) embedding can be seen as the latent feature vector for application (system) in the context of matrix factorization model.

Let x_a and y_s denote the embeddings for application a and system s, respectively. Then, the MLP model is defined as:

$$l_1 = (x_a, y_s) = [x_a \ y_s]$$
$$\phi(l_1) = a_1(W_1 l_1 + b_1),$$
$$\ldots\ldots$$
$$\phi(l_n) = a_n(W_n l_n + b_n),$$

(1)

where W_x, b_x, a_x and (x_a, y_s) denote the weight matrix, bias vector, activation function for the xth's layer perceptron and concatenation of x_a and y_s embeddings respectively.

3.2 Multiple Training Objectives

In our study, we focus on predicting instructions per second (IPS) metric as the most reasonable proxy to application performance; however we can easily collect additional runtime metrics and use them for training. We choose loads per second (LPS) and stores per second (SPS).

Predicting multiple metrics is useful by itself for gaining better insight into application behavior. Additionally, we want to investigate if additional training objectives can improve performance prediction itself. Auxiliary losses have been used in machine learning models in various domains to improve statistical efficiency and to build better representations [13,18,28].

As with IPS, we use root mean squared error (RMSE) as an actual loss function for each of the additional metrics. We sum all losses for backpropagation and report only IPS component of total loss for fair comparison with the model which is trained with single metric.

3.3 Automated Architecture Search

We assume that a neural network that works better in the case of training with a single metric would not necessarily be the same as for training with multiple objectives. Although our model is elegantly simple and it is not uncommon to develop such models manually, we would like to avoid possible pitfall of subconsciously dedicating more attention to fine-tuning a model. As if it performs better, it would support our hypothesis of handpicking features. Additionally, because the problem is relatively small, we can afford to train and evaluate multiple architectures in a short time. For these reasons we perform a grid search for the best model architectures for cases of training with single and auxiliary objectives. We constrain the model to be a multi-layer feed forward network with an arbitrary number of layers and neurons in each layer.

4 Experiment Setup

4.1 Machine Specification

To demonstrate robustness of our approach, we selected GPUs as shown in Table 1. These hardware accelerators are commonly used in both HPC and cloud systems. The heterogeneity of these accelerators are with respect to micro-architecture[1] (Kepler, Maxwell, Pascal and Volta) and the number of streaming multiprocessors (SM), L2 cache size, core frequency and memory bandwidth within accelerators having similar micro-architectures. We also show the type of Intel Xeon processor used along with each GPU in our experiments.

Table 1. Specifications of the GPUs used in our experiments.

GPU	arch	SMs	cores/SM	L2[a]	mem[b]	corefreq.[c]	bandwidth[d]	cpu used
K20m	Kepler	13	192	1.5	5	706	208	E5-2670v3
K20X	Kepler	14	192	1.5	6	732	250	E5-2650
K40c	Kepler	15	192	1.5	12	745	288	E5-2699v3
GTX-980Ti	Maxwell	22	128	3	6	1225	337	E5-2650v3
P100-PCIE	Pascal	56	64	4	16	1329	721	E5-2650v3
P100-SXM2	Pascal	56	64	6	16	1480	721	E5-2630v4
V100-SXM2	Volta	80	64	6	16	1530	897	Gold 6140

[a]L2 size in MiB.
[b]Memory size in GiB.
[c]Core frequency in MHz.
[d]Peak memory bandwidth in GB/s.

4.2 Benchmarks

We selected a diverse set of benchmarks from a variety of domains, as shown in Table 2. These workloads are from two well-known benchmark suites: Rodinia benchmark suite [6] version 3.3.1 and Polybench GPU version 1.0 [11].

The benchmarks were compiled using CUDA version 9.2.88 on P100-PCIE, V100-SXM2 and CUDA version 9.1.85 on all the other systems. We used nvprof [20] to collect three performance metrics which are inst_executed (instructions executed), gld_transactions (global load transactions) and gst_transactions (global store transactions). We executed each benchmark in isolation and recorded the total execution time for each benchmark.

---

[1] We tried adding Nvidia RTX 2070 and RTX 2080Ti GPUs from Turing micro-architecture in our study however we faced two issues: (1) nvprof profiling is not supported on these devices and a new profiling tool, Nsight Compute is recently introduced. However, some nvprof metrics (such as global load and store transactions) can't be recorded using Nsight Compute when SM < 7.0. (2) Also, Nsight Compute records global load transactions in *sector* while nvprof records the same performance metric in *bytes*.

Table 2. Workloads used in our experiments along with their domains.

Domain	Benchmark
Linear algebra	gaussian, 2 mm, 3 mm, atax, bicg, gemm, gesummv, gramschmidt, mvt, syrk, syr2k
Data mining & pattern recognition	correlation, covariance, nearest neighbor (nn), back-propogation (backprop)
Stencils	2dconvolution, 3dconvolution, fdtd-2d
Signal processing	discrete wavelet transform 2D (dwt2d)
Image processing	heartwall, srad, particlefilter
Simulation	hotspot2D, hotspot3D, myocyte
Graph traversal	breadth-first search (bfs), b+tree, pathfinder
Fluid and molecular dynamics	lavamd
Bioinformatics	needleman-wunsh (nw)

4.3   Methodology

Problem Formulation. Let M and N denote the number of applications and systems, respectively. We construct an application-system interaction matrix, $Y \in \mathbb{R}^{M \times N}$. Each cell in the matrix Y has value as:

$$y_{as} = \begin{cases} p_{as}, & \text{if application } a \text{ was executed on system } s \\ 0, & \text{otherwise} \end{cases} \quad (2)$$

Here p_{as} indicates the observed performance score when application a was executed on system s. Our goal is to predict all the zero entries of Y.

Datasets. We constructed three datasets with IPS, LPS and SPS values respectively for our experiments. In order to map these scores to a continuous scale, we performed z-score normalization of scores in each of the datasets. For each application a, we obtained mean score, $\bar{p}_a$ and standard deviation, σ_a in performance exhibited by the application on all the systems. The normalization of a performance score, p_{as} can be obtained as:

$$zscore(p_{as}) = \frac{p_{as} - \bar{p}_a}{\sigma_a} \quad (3)$$

Evaluation. We used Chainer [23] to construct the MLP with Rectifier Linear Units (ReLU) [9] as the activation function. The network was trained to minimize RMSE and the optimizations were done by performing stochastic gradient descent (SGD) [4].

Let $\hat{p}_{as}$ be the predicted performance score of application a corresponding to system s. We divide the performance scores into a training set y_{train}, which is used to learn, and a test set y_{test}, which is used to calculate the prediction accuracy. 80% of the dataset was used for training and 20% was used for testing in out study. RMSE [5] is a de-facto method to measure accuracy of CF algorithms. We used RMSE to evaluate the accuracy of our models as:

$$RMSE = \sqrt{\frac{1}{|y_{test}|} \sum_{p_{as} \in y_{test}} (\hat{p}_{as} - p_{as})^2} \qquad (4)$$

5 Results and Discussions

In this section, we conduct experiments with the aim of answering the following research questions:

R1 Does collaborative filtering based matrix factorization approach work with GPUs?
R2 Can we improve the prediction quality by using deep neural networks?
R3 Does training with other performance metrics alongside IPS improve the prediction accuracy?

5.1 Performance of Matrix Factorization (R1)

Figure 3a shows the performance of MF with respect to the number of latent features on the IPS dataset. When we use one latent feature to represent each benchmark as well as system, the RMSE is 0.57. As we increase the features, MF projects each benchmark and system as data points in a higher dimensional space that describes the correlations between benchmarks and systems. As a result, the prediction improves by analyzing the linear associations between benchmarks and systems. The best RMSE is 0.40 when each benchmark and system is defined by five features. As we further increase the number of latent features to six, MF starts over-fitting the training data that performs poorly on the test dataset thereby increasing the error.

We show the training and test losses when using five latent features in Fig. 3b. We can see that with more epochs, the training and test RMSE gradually decrease. The most effective updates are observed in the first 100 iterations for the training dataset. Although for the test dataset, the loss keeps decreasing and it starts saturating after 175 iterations at a RMSE of 0.4.

Figure 3c shows the scatter plot of actual vs predicted normalized IPS scores. Ideally, all the points in the plot should lie on or close to the regressed diagonal line. First, this plot tells us that the normalized actual scores lie within the range of -1.6 to 2.3. Second, MF make predictions close to the diagonal line when the actual value is greater than -1.5 and less than 1.5. While some of the values lie on the diagonal line showing accurate predictions, many fall close to the line. There are two cases when the actual score is near 1.0, that are estimated rather incorrectly. Third, when the actual value is greater than 2.0, MF underestimates the actual scores. On further inspection, we found that the three of these underestimated predictions are related to benchmarks mvt, pathfinder and backprop on K20m.

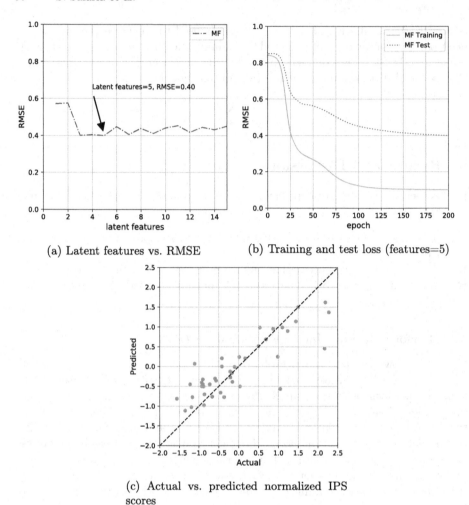

(a) Latent features vs. RMSE

(b) Training and test loss (features=5)

(c) Actual vs. predicted normalized IPS
scores

Fig. 3. Prediction performance of matrix factorization using latent features with IPS dataset.

Table 3 shows the accuracy of MF on 42 pairs of benchmarks and GPUs selected from the test set. We can see that our model is able to predict a wide range of IPS values (with a minimum of 95.33 and a maximum of 6.9×10^8). The minimum IPS value corresponds to gaussian elimination application (gaussian) from the Rodinia benchmark using data file as matrix4.txt. We also measured the prediction accuracy for each benchmark and GPU pair and reported the average accuracy across all those pairs. We used the absolute value of the relative error $\left(\frac{Actual - Predicted}{Actual} * 100 \right)$ to evaluate the accuracy. MF achieves an average (relative) error of 15.8% and geometric mean (Gmean) of 7.4%, with minimum error of **0.02%** and maximum error of 52.31%.

Answer to R1: We extended collaborative filtering based matrix factorization approach to seven GPUs using 30 benchmarks. Overall, MF achieves predictions with an average error of 15.8% (**84.2%** accuracy) and geometric mean of 7.4%.

5.2   Performance of Multi-layer Perceptron (R2)

We constructed MLPs with one hidden layer (MLP-1) as well as two hidden layers (MLP-2) to predict IPS as described in Sect. 3.1. We tested each network with number of neurons in each layer as [2, 4, 8, 16, 32, 64], the embedding size of 1 to 15.

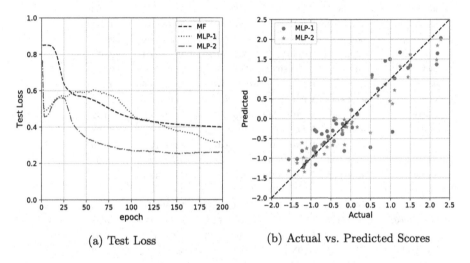

(a) Test Loss   (b) Actual vs. Predicted Scores

Fig. 4. Test loss and the scattered plot of actual vs predicted normalized IPS scores using MLP.

We present the findings of our experiments in Table 4. MF serves as the baseline performance with an RMSE of 0.40 with 5 latent features. MLP-1 with one hidden layer of 4 neurons and embedding size of 11 results in 20% decrease in RMSE thereby increasing prediction accuracy. While, MLP-2 with 32 and 8 neurons in the first and second hidden layer respectively (32→8) achieves the best RMSE of 0.25 which accounts for 37.5% improvement over the baseline.

Figure 4 shows the test loss and actual vs. predicted normalized IPS scores for both MLP-based models. We can see that MLP-1 test loss decreases with more epochs and it starts predicting better than MF after 130 epochs in Fig. 4a. Whereas, for MLP-2 the prediction performance on test dataset starts improving after 25 epochs. The above findings w.r.t prediction performance i.e. MLP-2 > MLP-1 > MF provide empirical evidence for the effectiveness of using deeper layers to improve prediction accuracy.

We show the advantage of using a deep network to predict IPS in Fig. 4b. MLP-2 plots data points closer to the diagonal line than MLP-1. It is to be noted

Table 3. Accuracy of the matrix factorization model.

Benchmark	Suite	GPU	Actual IPS	Predicted IPS	Relative error%
mycoyte	rodinia	V100-SXM2	12362329.33	12440673.99	0.63
hotspot2d	rodinia	V100-SXM2	628213.33	707013.49	12.54
mvt	polybench	K20m	2446784.0	1465271.07	40.11
gaussian	rodinia	K20m	95.33	92.74	2.72
srad1	rodinia	K40c	169454.77	184485.42	8.87
mvt	polybench	K40c	699081.14	914765.62	30.85
2 mm	polybench	K20m	685834240.0	699268041.2	1.96
atax	polybench	P100-PCIE	1204320.0	1254020.08	4.13
pathfinder	rodinia	K20m	651904.0	574757.98	11.83
gemm	polybench	K20X	6277120.0	5636040.41	10.21
backprop	rodinia	K40c	805745.29	1123610.02	39.45
gesummv	polybench	P100-PCIE	1557440.0	1572621.1	0.97
backprop	rodinia	GTX980Ti	1395922.2	1397639.04	0.12
atax	polybench	K20m	1631189.33	1630874.66	0.02
bicg	polybench	V100-SXM2	941926.4	1142419.5	21.29
heartwall	rodinia	P100-SXM2	97238507.25	87104974.98	10.42
nn	rodinia	K20X	9102.8	9657.58	6.09
mvt	polybench	P100-PCIE	963456.0	1322472.2	37.26
covariance	polybench	V100-SXM2	70272888.89	57696629.18	17.9
gesummv	polybench	P100-SXM2	2076629.33	2076142.74	0.02
gramschmidt	polybench	P100-PCIE	2316.76	3166.81	36.69
fdtd2d	polybench	K20X	110436.15	135592.53	22.78
covariance	polybench	K20X	47624371.2	59948517.91	25.88
backprop	rodinia	K20m	1880072.33	1569359.24	16.53
3dconvolution	polybench	K20X	4145.14	5518.12	33.12
syrk	polybench	K20X	39819673.6	35606924.25	10.58
3dconvolution	polybench	P100-PCIE	4204.9	4497.67	6.96
mycoyte	rodinia	K20m	12547497.2	14798852.29	17.94
gramschmidt	polybench	K20m	7524.22	6787.84	9.79
b+tree	rodinia	V100-SXM2	2646457.0	2541856.97	3.95
3dconvolution	polybench	GTX980Ti	5667.48	4943.69	12.77
heartwall	rodinia	GTX980Ti	54529707.29	56063846.0	2.81
syr2k	polybench	V100-SXM2	526275925.33	333587189.11	36.61
syrk	polybench	V100-SXM2	37499699.2	41851043.74	11.6
gesummv	polybench	K20m	2054570.67	1936674.13	5.74
syrk	polybench	P100-PCIE	44900352.0	43516292.35	3.08
mvt	polybench	GTX980Ti	963481.6	1203747.72	24.94
2dconvolution	polybench	K40c	3294354.29	3665771.31	11.27
syrk	polybench	GTX980Ti	30632618.67	39903543.09	30.26
backprop	rodinia	V100-SXM2	1186206.2	1144560.7	3.51
covariance	polybench	P100-PCIE	48332996.27	61818140.88	27.9
syr2k	polybench	K20X	268763136.0	409358367.43	52.31
Average					15.8
Gmean					7.4

Table 4. Results of grid search for MLP-1 and MLP-2 parameters.

Model	Network	Features	Epoch	RMSE	↓ in RMSE
MF	-	5	199	0.40	-
MLP-1	4	11	194	0.32	20%
MLP-2	32→ 8	3	154	**0.25**	**37.5%**

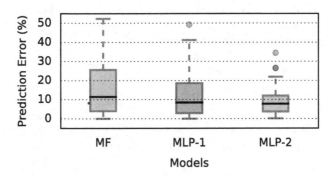

Fig. 5. Accuracy of MF, MLP-1 and MLP-2 using IPS dataset

that for all the actual values underestimated by MLP-1 such as when the actual values are between 0.5 and 1.0 and also greater than 2.0, MLP-2 with just one more layer learns better and make predictions near to their actual values.

Table 5 shows the relative errors using MLP-1 and MLP-2 models. For fair comparison, we selected the same pairs of benchmarks and GPUs as evaluated for MF and presented the accuracy of all the three models. First, the average error as well as geometric mean show the same trend that MLP-2 > MLP-1 > MF. Second, overall, MLP-1 predicts better than MF specially when the relative error when using MF is greater than 20%. However, there are a few corner cases where MLP-1 underestimates the actual value when MF has an error of less than 1%. This can be attributed to those cases when a simple model is enough to describe the linear correlation between benchmark and system properties. In that case, using linear layers with ReLU as an activation unit may cause some irregularities in prediction performance. Since the main point of focus of this work is not to reason on how many and what features are important to model performance across benchmarks and systems, a model like MLP-1 which caters to the many of the cases is a better choice.

MLP-2 further decreases the large errors seen in MF and achieves the lowest average error across all the predictions. It is to note that the maximum error seen in MF is 51%, while in MLP-1 and MLP-2 are 49.26% and 34.45%. We summarize our results for MF, MLP-1 and MLP-2 in Fig. 5. An outlier which is common to MLP-1 and MLP-2 in the box plot corresponded to a simulation application, myocyte from the Rodinia benchmark suite on V100-SXM2.

Table 5. Relative error using MF, MLP-1 and MLP-2 on the test set.

Benchmark	Suite	GPU	Error MF%	Error MLP-1%	Error MLP-2%
srad1	rodinia	K40c	8.87	8.09	5.51
b+tree	rodinia	V100-SXM2	3.95	0.86	1.79
backprop	rodinia	GTX980Ti	0.12	19.44	4.52
gaussian	rodinia	K20m	2.72	1.96	9.25
backprop	rodinia	V100-SXM2	3.51	2.03	8.09
mycoyte	rodinia	K20m	17.94	22.69	19.99
mvt	polybench	P100-PCIE	37.26	23.04	26.55
mycoyte	rodinia	V100-SXM2	0.63	49.26	34.45
heartwall	rodinia	P100-SXM2	10.42	9.97	6.36
mvt	polybench	GTX980Ti	24.94	8.5	8.86
gesummv	polybench	K20m	5.74	3.08	7.42
gramschmidt	polybench	P100-PCIE	36.69	0.02	16.58
syr2k	polybench	K20X	52.31	1.19	15.98
syrk	polybench	P100-PCIE	3.08	3.46	6.95
gesummv	polybench	P100-SXM2	0.02	2.95	2.18
nn	rodinia	K20X	6.09	20.82	6.43
backprop	rodinia	K40c	39.45	28.29	13.3
pathfinder	rodinia	K20m	11.83	3.27	3.71
atax	polybench	P100-PCIE	4.13	0.41	4.63
covariance	polybench	V100-SXM2	17.9	8.42	3.82
3dconvolution	polybench	GTX980Ti	12.77	7.56	11.29
syrk	polybench	V100-SXM2	11.6	6.51	2.33
gramschmidt	polybench	K20m	9.79	12.51	2.31
mvt	polybench	K20m	40.11	18.82	16.11
2dconvolution	polybench	K40c	11.27	15.5	10.61
atax	polybench	K20m	0.02	2.39	3.65
3dconvolution	polybench	P100-PCIE	6.96	1.55	8.69
heartwall	rodinia	GTX980Ti	2.81	5.62	2.51
mvt	polybench	K40c	30.85	22.86	3.29
gesummv	polybench	P100-PCIE	0.97	1.35	9.38
syrk	polybench	K20X	10.58	8.0	10.93
syrk	polybench	GTX980Ti	30.26	41.17	10.62
bicg	polybench	V100-SXM2	21.29	20.23	8.97
covariance	polybench	P100-PCIE	27.9	9.15	6.33
fdtd2d	polybench	K20X	22.78	9.66	0.83
hotspot2d	rodinia	V100-SXM2	12.54	15.31	3.35
3dconvolution	polybench	K20X	33.12	17.73	26.46
covariance	polybench	K20X	25.88	7.34	0.15
syr2k	polybench	V100-SXM2	36.61	31.29	15.3
2 mm	polybench	K20m	1.96	13.4	0.09
gemm	polybench	K20X	10.21	1.26	21.93
backprop	rodinia	K20m	16.53	11.58	12.17
Average			15.8	11.9	9.4
Gmean			7.4	6.3	6.0

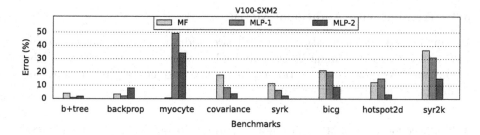

Fig. 6. Evaluation of MF, MLP-1 and MLP-2 on V100-SXM2 GPU

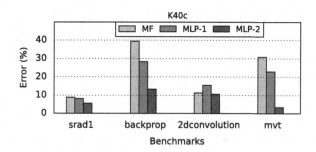

Fig. 7. Performance of MF, MLP-1 and MLP-2 on K40c GPU

We show the prediction performance of MF, MLP-1 and MLP-2 on V100-SXM2 GPU and K40c in Figs. 6 and 7 respectively. MLP-2 predicted the best in all the cases except for benchmarks myocyte and backprop on V100-SXM2. We executed myocyte with the default parallelization mode 0, which, based on the benchmark author's description, has issues with performance scaling on GPUs to the point that the overhead of host to device memory transfer and kernel launch become non-negligible. Hence, other components of the system like CPU, motherboard and memory also become involved in the final performance which are not considered in our model. Thus, myocyte's performance can be highly variable across different GPUs which affects the construction of its latent features, thereby affecting the prediction accuracy.

Answer to R2: We investigated MLP with a curiosity to see whether using a deep network structure is beneficial to the prediction. The MLP-1 (MLP with one hidden layer) predicted with an average error of 11.9% (88.1% accuracy) and geometric mean of 6.3%. While the MLP-2 (MLP with two hidden layers) predicted with an average error of 9.4% (**90.6%** accuracy), geometric mean of 6% as compared to 84.2% accuracy, geometric mean of 7.4% achieved with MF.

5.3   Training with Additional Metrics (R3)

We augmented training data (IPS) with two additional performance metrics, LPS and SPS to determine if using multiple training objectives improve the predictions. We performed a grid search for the best neural architectures for training with additional objectives.

Table 6. Performance of MLP when using additional training metrics, LPS and SPS.

Metric	MLP-1				MLP-2			
	Network	Features	RMSE	Error%	Network	Features	RMSE	Error%
IPS	4	11	0.32	11.9%	32→8	3	0.25	**9.4%**
IPS+LPS	32	9	0.32	12%	16→32	5	0.28	11.5%
IPS+LPS+SPS	32	12	0.33	12.2%	32→32	8	0.28	10.7%

Table 6 show the results of the grid search in order to find the best model corresponding to different training metrics. Training MLP-1 with IPS and LPS, we find that a network with 32 neurons and embedding size of 9 shows the similar predictive performance as with training MLP-1 with IPS. When we look at three metrics case using MLP-1, there is a slight increase in RMSE and the average error across all predictions. Overall, we can say that augmenting additional performance metrics with IPS using MLP-1 results in a similar performance.

We repeated the grid search to find the best parameters using MLP-2 as well. First, when training the model with IPS+LPS, the number of neurons increases from 16 to 32. So, it seems to be trading off the number of training metrics for depth as it goes through the layers. By using an embedding size greater than while training with only IPS, the model manages to achieve an average error of 11.5%. Similarly, for 3 metrics case, by increasing the number of neurons in the first layer and the embedding size, the average error becomes marginally lower though the RMSE remains the same.

Answer to R3: This shows that IPS is only metric that we need to predict performance across different benchmarks and GPUs. Using more additional optimization objectives in the predictive model does not improve accuracy of predicted IPS values in this study.

6   Conclusions

In this work, we demonstrated that it is possible to collect performance metrics and use collaborative filtering for GPU-based applications. We evaluated a set of 30 micro-applications on seven different GPUs. Using the vanilla matrix factorization method of collaborative filtering resulted in 84.2% accuracy when the actual IPS has a wide range of values, with a minimum of 95.3 and a maximum of $6.9 * 10^8$. We then introduced a neural network architecture to further improve the prediction accuracy. While for predicting performance, IPS is only metric that we need, we showed that using additional optimization objectives in the predictive model (other metrics such as LPS and SPS) results in the similar accuracy of predicted IPS values. In total, we achieved 90.6% accuracy in average, with a geometric error mean of 6% with our multi-layer perceptron model. We showed that the confidence of predictions made varies between different kinds of applications. We leave it to future work to develop a model which can predict this uncertainty explicitly.

Acknowledgment. This work was partially supported by JST CREST Grant Numbers JPMJCR1303, JPMJCR1687 and JSPS KAKENHI Grant Number JP16F16764.

References

1. Almazro, D., Shahatah, G., Albdulkarim, L., Kherees, M., Martinez, R., Nzoukou, W.: A survey paper on recommender systems. CoRR abs/1006.5278 (2010)
2. Baghsorkhi, S.S., Delahaye, M., Patel, S.J., Gropp, W.D., Huw, W.M.: An adaptive performance modeling tool for GPU architectures. In: Proceedings of the 15th ACM SIGPLAN Symposium on Principles and Practice of Parallel Programming, PPoPP 2010, pp. 105–114 (2010)
3. Bakhoda, A., Yuan, G.L., Fung, W.W.L., Wong, H., Aamodt, T.M.: Analyzing CUDA workloads using a detailed GPU simulator. In: 2009 IEEE International Symposium on Performance Analysis of Systems and Software, pp. 163–174, April 2009. https://doi.org/10.1109/ISPASS.2009.4919648
4. Bottou, L.: Large-scale machine learning with stochastic gradient descent. In: Proceedings of COMPSTAT 2010, pp. 177–186 (2010)
5. Chai, T., Draxler, R.R.: Root mean square error (RMSE) or mean absolute error (MAE) - arguments against avoiding RMSE in the literature. Geosco. Model Dev. **7**, 1247–1250 (2014)
6. Che, S., et al.: Rodinia: a benchmark suite for hetrogenous computing. In: International Symposium on Workload Characterization (IISWC) (2009)
7. NVIDIA Corporation. https://docs.nvidia.com/cuda/cuda-c-programming-guide/index.html
8. Dean, J., Patterson, D., Young, C.: A new golden age in computer architecture: empowering the machine-learning revolution. IEEE Micro **38**(2), 21–29 (2018)
9. Glorot, X., Bordes, A., Bengio, Y.: Deep sparse rectifier neural network. In: Proceedings of the Fourteenth International Conference on Artifical Intelligence and Statistics. PMLR 15, pp. 315–323 (2011)
10. Govindaraju, N.K., Larsen, S., Gray, J., Manocha, D.: A memory model for scientific algorithms on graphics processors. In: Proceedings of the 2006 ACM/IEEE Conference on Supercomputing, November 2006 (2006)
11. Grauer-Gray, S., Xu, L., Searles, R., Ayalasomayajula, S., Cavazos, J.: Auto-tuning a high-level language targeted to GPU codes. In: Innovative Parallel Computing (InPar) (2012)
12. Hong, S., Kim, H.: An integrated GPU power and performance model. In: Proceedings of the 37th Annual International Symposium on Computer Architecture, ISCA 2010, pp. 280–289 (2010)
13. Jaderberg, M., et al.: Reinforcement learning with unsupervised auxiliary tasks. CoRR abs/1611.05397 (2016)

14. Kerr, A., Anger, E., Hendry, G., Yalamanchili, S.: Eiger: a framework for the automated synthesis of statistical performance models. In: 2012 19th International Conference on High Performance Computing, pp. 1–6 (2012)
15. Liu, W., Schmidt, B.: Performance predictions for general-purpose computation on GPUs. In: Proceedings of 2007 International Conference on Parallel Processing, ICPP (2017)
16. Luo, C., Suda, R.: A performance and energy consumption analytical model for GPU. In: 2011 IEEE Ninth International Conference on Dependable, Autonomic and Secure Computing, pp. 658–665 (2011)
17. Mikolov, T., Sutskever, I., Chen, K., Corrado, G.S., Dean, J.: Distributed representations of words and phrases and their compositionality. In: Advances in Neural Information Processing Systems 26. Curran Associates, Inc. (2013)
18. Mirowski, P.W., et al.: Learning to navigate in complex environments. CoRR abs/1611.03673 (2016)
19. Nvidia Turing GPU Architecture. https://www.nvidia.com/content/dam/en-zz/Solutions/design-visualization/technologies/turing-architecture/NVIDIA-Turing-Architecture-Whitepaper.pdf
20. NVProf. https://docs.nvidia.com/cuda/profiler-users-guide/index.html
21. The OpenCL Specification. https://www.khronos.org/opencl/
22. Salaria, S., Drozd, A., Podobas, A., Matsuoka, S.: Predicting performance using collaborative filtering. In: Proceedings of the 2018 IEEE International Conference on Cluster Computing, pp. 504–514. CLUSTER (2018)
23. Tokui, S., Oono, K., Hido, S., Clayton, J.: Chainer: a next generation open source framework for deep learning. In: Proceedings of Workshop on Machine Learning Systems in NIPS (2010)
24. Top500. https://www.top500.org
25. Williams, S., Waterman, A., Patterson, D.: Roofline: an insightful visual performance model for multicore architectures. Commun. ACM **52**(4), 65–76 (2009)
26. Wu, G., Greathouse, J.L., Lyashevsky, A., Jayasena, N., Chiou, D.: GPGPU performance and power estimation using machine learning. In: 2015 IEEE 21st International Symposium on High Performance Computer Architecture (HPCA), pp. 564–576, February 2015
27. Xhang, Y., Owens, J.D.: A quantitative performance analysis model for GPU architectures. In: Proceedings of the 17th IEEE International Symposium on High Performance Computer Architecture, HPCA 2011 (2011)
28. Yuting, Z., Kibok, L., Honglak, L.: Augmenting supervised neural networks with unsupervised objectives for large-scale image classification. In: Proceedings of the 33rd International Conference on International Conference on Machine Learning, ICML 2016, vol. 48, pp. 612–621. JMLR.org (2016)

Data, Storage and Visualization

SLOPE: Structural Locality-Aware Programming Model for Composing Array Data Analysis

Bin Dong$^{(\boxtimes)}$, Kesheng Wu, Suren Byna, and Houjun Tang

Lawrence Berkeley National Laboratory, 1 Cyclotron Rd, Berkeley, CA 94720, USA
{dbin,kwu,sbyna,htang4}@lbl.gov

Abstract. MapReduce brought on the Big Data revolution. However, its impact on scientific data analyses has been limited because of fundamental limitations in its data and programming models. Scientific data is typically stored as multidimensional arrays, while MapReduce is based on key-value (KV) pairs. Applying MapReduce to analyze array-based scientific data requires a conversion of arrays to KV pairs. This conversion incurs a large storage overhead and loses structural information embedded in the array. For example, analysis operations, such as convolution, are defined on the neighbors of an array element. Accessing these neighbors is straightforward using array indexes, but requires complex and expensive operations like self-join in the KV data model. In this work, we introduce a novel 'structural locality'-aware programming model (SLOPE) to compose data analysis directly on multidimensional arrays. We also develop a parallel execution engine for SLOPE to transparently partition the data, to cache intermediate results, to support in-place modification, and to recover from failures. Our evaluations with real applications show that SLOPE is over ninety thousand times faster than Apache Spark and is 38% faster than TensorFlow.

Keywords: Multidimensional array · Programming model ·
Structural locality · Composable data analysis · User-defined function ·
ArrayUDF · Apache Spark · TensorFlow · MapReduce · Array cache

1 Introduction

The MapReduce (MR) programming model [11] transformed the way of developing data analysis algorithms and led to advanced data analysis systems, such as Spark [42]. These systems enable users to compose complex data analysis algorithms without implementing the details of parallel execution, data management, error recovery, among other challenging tasks. Unfortunately, the MR programming model could not be effectively used for scientific data analysis due to its lack of support for multidimensional array data model and their limited support for accessing neighbors in arrays [13,24]. As arrays are prevalent in scientific data, such as 2D sky survey images [4], we propose a programming model that

© Springer Nature Switzerland AG 2019
M. Weiland et al. (Eds.): ISC High Performance 2019, LNCS 11501, pp. 61–80, 2019.
https://doi.org/10.1007/978-3-030-20656-7_4

operates directly on arrays and an execution engine to run composite analysis on massively parallel computing systems efficiently.

A programming model for data analysis conceptually includes an abstract data type and a set of generic operators. The abstract data type defines input and output data structures for generic operators. This abstract data model for the MR programming model is the key-value (KV) pairs and the corresponding generic operators are *Map* and *Reduce*. The *Map* and *Reduce* execute user customized procedures on a list of KV instances. To apply MapReduce to a multi-dimensional array, array elements need to be converted into KV pairs. Common analysis operations, such as convolution [7,24], access a group of neighboring array elements to compute a new value. In array representation, these neighbors are near each other – we refer to this feature as structural locality [13,24]. This structural locality is lost when the values are represented as KV pairs. Although there are many ways to improve MapReduce systems [7,42], these intrinsic limitations still exist within its programming model.

Array databases (e.g., SciDB [33] and RasDaMan [2]) use multidimensional array as the native model. Their built-in operators, such as *window*, can capture structural locality, but they only allow performing uniform aggregation on all window cells, i.e., running non-discriminative operations (e.g., *sum*) on all window cells. Moreover, the definition of a *window* as *(starting indices, ending indices)* limits its shape to be rectangular bounding boxes. However, data analysis tasks on scientific data, such as computing gradients or slope [13,22], need different operations on distinct window cells, which together may form non-rectangular shapes. Blanas et al. [3] also show that loading scientific array data from their native file formats (e.g., HDF5 [38]) into array databases is a time-consuming and error-prone process.

Recent efforts, such as ArrayUDF [13], support user customized data analysis on array file formats and represent structural locality for the aforementioned data analysis operations. However, ArrayUDF lacks a formally defined programming model, which is essential for composing analysis tasks as discussed previously. ArrayUDF only allows operation on a single array with only one attribute, and its input and output arrays must have the same dimensions and the data have to be stored on disk. The lack of caching intermediate data in memory limits its performance with significant I/O overhead. TensorFlow [1] uses tensor abstraction to represent an array in machine learning applications. However, it only provides customized operations (e.g., *conv2d*) for specific tasks. Tuning existing operations and adding new ones still need non-trivial amount of code development for data management, parallelization and other tasks.

To address the gaps in composing various data analysis operations for multi-dimensional arrays, we propose a new "structural locality"-aware programming model (SLOPE), describe the design and implementation for its parallel execution engine, and present a thorough evaluation comparing with state-of-the-art Big Data systems. SLOPE offers a formally defined abstraction for users to customize various data analyses directly on multidimensional arrays. Each array, as an input of SLOPE, can have multiple attributes. The output array may have different dimensions from the input array. SLOPE has a distributed DRAM-based cache layer to stage the intermediate array of the analysis pipeline. In summary, contributions of this effort include:

- A formally defined structural locality-aware programming model (Sect. 3) and its parallel execution engine (Sect. 4.1). SLOPE has a novel new data structure – namely *Stencil* – and a generic operator (*SLApply*) to capture and express structural locality existing in multidimensional array data access and analysis. SLOPE allows customizable analysis operations directly on multidimensional array stored in native scientific data formats. A vectorization interface of SLOPE allows it to compose data analysis involving multiple attributes of one or more arrays.
- A distributed DRAM-based cache layer (Sect. 4.1) to store intermediate output arrays. SLOPE supports asynchronous checkpoint method for cached array. SLOPE also has a asynchronous halo exchange algorithm that synchronizes array cached in distributed DRAMs.
- Describe optimization features of SLOPE, such as mirror values and in-place data modification, to improve performance and semantics of data analysis on multidimensional array (Sect. 4.1).

We demonstrate the performance of SLOPE by using it to compose real scientific data analysis tasks on a supercomputer with 2, 388 Intel Xeon processors. These data analysis tasks come from applications: CAM5 [28,40], VPIC [8,22], and BISICLES [10,44]. We also compare SLOPE with state-of-the-art data analysis systems, such as Apache Spark [42] and TensorFlow [1]. SLOPE achieves up to $\approx$90,000× performance speedup over Apache Spark and $\approx$38% speedup over TensorFlow. We show that SLOPE can scale linearly as the data size and the number of CPU cores increase, achieving 512 GB/sec ($\approx$128 GFLOPs) processing bandwidth using 16K CPU cores.

2   Preliminaries

2.1   Multidimensional Array

A d-dimensional array has dimensions $D = D_1, D_2, \ldots, D_d$ and a set of m attributes $A = A_1, A_2, \ldots, A_m$ [5]. Each dimension is a continuous range of integer values in $[0, N-1]$. Each indices $[i_1, i_2, \ldots, i_d]$ defines an array cell. All cells have the same data type for an attribute. An array can be expressed as a function mapping defined over dimensions and taking value attributes tuples: $Array : [D_0, D_1, \ldots, D_{d-1}] \mapsto < A_0, A_1, \ldots, A_{m-1} >$. In array, cells are stored in well-defined layouts, such as row-major and column-major orders. The row-major order is popular in scientific data formats, such as HDF5 [38] and NetCDF [21], and its last dimension is stored contiguously in storage devices. Offsets from the beginning to a cell at $(i_1, i_2, \ldots, i_d)$ is given by $\sum_{k=0}^{d-1} \prod_{l=k+1}^{d-1} D_l i_k$.

2.2 User-Defined Function and Programming Model

User-defined function (UDF) is a classic mechanism in database systems [26] to extend their query language. With the prevalence of MapReduce (MR), UDF evolves into a stand-alone *programming model* [11,32]. The MR has an abstract KV data model and two generic operators: *Map* and *Reduce*. *Map* and *Reduce* accept UDF defined on KV data model from users for different purposes. MR has achieved a lot of successes since its emergence. MR, however, has several intrinsic issues in supporting array data analysis:

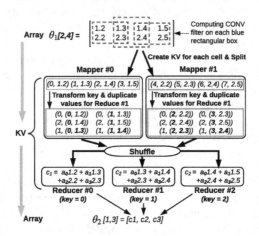

Fig. 1. An example of using MapReduce to compose convolution computing (*CONV*) from array θ_1 to θ_2. θ_1 is first linearized to a 1D KV list. *Mappers* then unify the key of KV pairs belonging to the same CONV filters (i.e., blue dashed rectangular boxes). Based on the index of a cell in original rectangular box, a secondary key (light green) is added to find corresponding filter weight in later *Reducers*. Also, KV pairs for *Reducer* #1 (denoted as red) are added via duplicating existing values. After shuffle, *Reducers* perform a weighted summary to compute *CONV* ({$a_0, \ldots, a_3$} are weight). Obviously, MapReduce is an inefficient programming model for array because of the conversion between array and KV and the duplication of values for *Reducers*. We propose a new programming model that enable users to directly customize and execute operations from θ_1 to θ_2 without data model conversion and with negligible duplications. (Color figure online)

- **KV data model makes MapReduce perform poorly on multidimensional arrays.** Multidimensional arrays have to be linearized into KV list before using them as the input of MapReduce. First, this linearization may need to explicitly handle array index. Second, the linearization breaks the array structural locality, which exists in many data analysis operations such as convolution [19] and gradient computing [13]. In Fig. 1, we give an example of using MapReduce to compute convolution on a 2D array and discuss its problems. The discrete convolution [6] is expressed as $*$ operator: $(f * g)(n) = \sum_{m=-\infty}^{\infty} f(m)g(n-m)$, where f, g are two complex-valued functions on the set Z of integers. For a single convolution on array, it needs a few neighborhood cells. Linearization breaks the structural locality by scattering these neighborhood cells in different Mappers. The penalty is the extra cost to rebuild this structural locality though *Shuffle* and *Reduce*. Although using linearization methods (e.g., SFC [35]) may preserve structural locality, developing these methods and converting operations originally defined on multidimensional array to ones on KV are still cumbersome tasks for users.

- **A set of KV pairs processed by a *Reducer* is independent from the set of KV pairs processed by another *Reducer*.** Assuming $S1$ and $S2$ are two sets of KV pairs belonging to two *Reducers*, it is common to have intersection $S1 \cap S2$ in use cases, such as convolution [19]. Because MapReduce schedules and executes these two *Reducers* separately, duplicating KV pairs in $S1 \cap S2$ for two *Reducers* are required to make parallel processing on $S1$ and $S2$ work properly. As shown in Fig. 1, the input KV pairs for Reducers #1 are added by MapReduce through duplication. These duplicated KV pairs consume memory for storing and network bandwidth for shuffling and therefore degrade overall data analysis performance.

3   SLOPE Programming Model

As discussed above, multidimensional arrays and KV pairs are different data models. Using the MapReduce to handle multidimensional arrays requires converting them into a KV list. Therefore, it is critical to explore a programming model with multidimensional arrays as the first-class citizens. Toward that goal, we focus on addressing the following question: what are the abstract data types and generic operators for a comprehensive programming model supporting data analytics on multidimensional arrays? We answer these questions with the proposal of SLOPE that contains a new abstract data type, called *Stencil* and a generic operator *SLApply*. Details are reported in following subsections.

3.1   Abstract Data Type—*Stencil*

An abstract data type represents both the input and output data structures of generic data analytic operators in a programming model. In other words, the abstract data type describes the data structure for the smallest subsets of array data in composite data analysis. In this work, we present a new abstract data type, called *Stencil*, which is inspired by the stencil-based numerical computing [14]. Being different from these existing work, we focuses on generalizing these ideas for modern data analysis (e.g., convolution neural network). Conceptually, a *Stencil* can represent a geometric neighborhood of an array, which further contains a *center* cell and a few neighborhood cells at different *relative offsets* from the center. We use the **absolute index** (c) of an array cell to refer the *center* cell and use the **relative offsets** ($\vec{o}$) to represent the neighborhood cells, which can be expressed as $(c, \vec{o})$. For example, in a 2D array, a geometric neighborhood expression using *Stencil* can be $\Big((1,1), \big((0,0),\ (0,-1),\ (0,1),\ (-1,0),\ (1,0) \big) \Big)$, where $c = (1,1)$ is the absolute index of the center cell and $\vec{o} = \Big((0,0),\ (0,-1),\ (0,1),\ (-1,0),\ (1,0) \Big)$ contains relative offsets for the center cell itself, the cell on the left, the cell on the right, the cell on the top, and the cell below. This geometric neighborhood is visually shown in Fig. 2(b).

In the following description, we use the symbol S to refer an instance of *Stencil* and use $S_{o_1,o_2,\ldots,o_d}$ to refer a single cell at the relative offset $[o_1, o_2, \ldots, o_d]$. In the above example, $S_{0,0}$ is the center cell and $S_{0,-1}$ is the cell at the left. The value of the cell in a *Stencil* is represented by dot "." operator on the symbol S. For example, during an array with multiple attributes A_j $(j \in [1, m])$, the value of the attribute A_j is represented as $S_{o_1,o_2,\ldots,o_d}.A_j$. The value of all attributes is represented as a vector $\overrightarrow{S_{o_1,o_2,\ldots,o_d}.A}$ or $\vec{S.A}$. In the array with a single attribute, we use $S_{o_1,o_2,\ldots,o_d}$ to represent its value by omitting the dot operator and attribute name. We conclude the properties of *Stencil* as follows:

- **A *Stencil* abstraction provides a new way to logically partition a large array into subsets.** Compared with chunking in array databases [31], *Stencil* splits array into even smaller subsets for processing. *Stencil* obeys the structure locality of array data access by allowing relative offset from a center cell, which is important in many data analytic operations [13].
- **A *Stencil* has flexible size.** By taking a *2 by 2* array as an example, $S_1 = \Big((0,0),\ \big((0,0) \big) \Big)$ contains the first cell. $S_2 = \Big((0,0),\ \big((0,0),\ (0,1),\ (1,0),\ (1,1) \big) \Big)$ represents the whole array. Such flexibility enables users to group any number of desired cells for analysis.
- **Cells within a *Stencil* can form any geometric shape.** One can specify any cell as the center of a *Stencil* and add any other cell into the *Stencil*. So, the cells within a *Stencil* can form any shape. A few examples of typical *Stencils* are visually presented in Fig. 2, which will be further discussed in

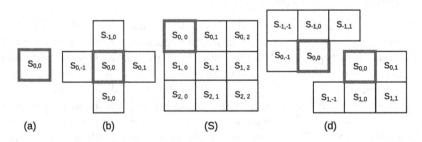

Fig. 2. Example of geometric neighborhoods expressed by *Stencil* on a 2D array: (a) a single cell neighborhood; (b) a neighborhood containing a center cell and four surrounding cells; (c) a neighborhood contains a center cell and its neighbors at right-bottom; (d) a forward-scan neighborhood (at top) and a backward-scan neighborhood (at bottom). These examples are presented from the point-view of users. The center of each is ignored and will be automatically handled by the execution engine in following Sect. 4. Usages of these examples in real applications are presented in Sect. 3.3.

the following Sect. 3.3. By comparison, *window* in SciDB is defined as *(start indices, end indices)* and it can only represent rectangular shape. Compared with *sliding* idea of the Spark [42] on a 1D KV list and the *window* idea of SQL database systems [26, 41] on relational tables, our *Stencil* can express more diverse geometric shapes on top of a multidimensional array.

3.2   SLOPE Programming Model

The *Stencil* abstract data type provides a flexible way to represent a small set of array cells with structural locality. We use it as the input and the output data type of a generic operation in our programming model. Hence, we refer our programming model as Structural Locality-aware Programming Model (SLOPE). Inspired by the *Apply* primitive in R [15] and in several other languages, our SLOPE has a generic operator, named $\underline{S}$tructural $\underline{L}$ocality $\underline{Apply}$, or *SLApply* for short. Hence, the SLOPE model can be represented as the following two-element tuple: $(Stencil, SLApply)$, where *Stencil* is the generic data type and *SLApply* is the generic operator. Given two arrays θ_1 and θ_2, the generic operator *SLApply* is expressed as,

$$SLApply : \vec{S} \xmapsto{f} \vec{S'}, \quad S \subset \theta_1, S' \subset \theta_2, \tag{1}$$

Semantically, *SLApply* maps the *Stencil* instance $\vec{S}$ to the result *Stencil* instance $\vec{S'}$. The $\vec{S}$ and $\vec{S'}$ represents geometric neighborhoods from input array θ_1 and output array θ_2, respectively. The UDF f defines the desired operation for the map. Within function f, users can use the *Stencil* abstraction and its member cells to describe any desired operation. The $\rightarrow$ (hat) symbol on *Stencil* means both input and output can be a vector *Stencil* across all attributes of input and output arrays. In following parts, we uses $\theta_2 = SLApply(\theta_1, f)$ to represent the execution of function f from θ_1 to θ_2. Users also control the return value of function f which is used to initialize output *Stencil*.

In SLOPE implementation, the *SLApply* internally executes the function f on all instances of *Stencil* abstraction. There are two ways for *SLApply* to create *Stencil* instances and execute function f:

- By default, *SLApply* creates *Stencil* instance for each array cell in θ_1. Then, it executes f on each *Stencil* instance. This default method works for most data analysis tasks (such as *filter*) which run an operation on the whole array. The value of output *Stencil* is the return value of function f. The output *Stencils* inherit the coordinate of the center cell of the input *Stencil*.
- Additionally, *SLApply* can create *Stencil* instances for certain cells and execute f only on them. For example, users can specify a skipping parameter on θ_1 to avoid creating *Stencil* instances, i.e., calling function f for certain cells. One example operation is convolution computing which may run filter on every two cells on each dimension.

In most cases, output S' only has a single cell, but it can also include a set of neighborhood cells. By default, the semantic of *SLApply* only allows "read only" on original array θ_1. But SLOPE provide users an option namely *"In-place Modifications"* (in Sect. 4.5) to change the semantic to update θ_1 as the propagation of f onto the whole array.

```
//User customized functions
Gradient(S):
    return 4S_{0,0} − (S_{−1,0} + S_{0,−1} + S_{0,1} + S_{1,0})

θ_2 = SLApply(θ_1, Gradient)

Interpolation:(S)
    return BilinearInter(S_0.X, S_0.Y, θ_2)

SLApply(θ_3, Interpolation)
```

Fig. 3. Gradient computing and interpolation with SLOPE on a 2D field data θ_1 and on a 1D particle data θ_3. The θ_3 has two attributes X and Y. It first invokes *SLApply* to execute *Gradient* on θ_1. Then, the *Interpolation* is applied onto θ_3, which uses θ_2 from first *SLApply* too. For simplicity, we use *BilinearInter* (omitted) to denote the interpolation formula. In parallel execution, θ_2 can be cached in memory and broadcast to all processes for performance.

```
//Three user customized functions
CONV(S):
    return [S_{0,0}, S_{0,1}, ..., S_{2,2}]  [a_{0,0} ... a_{0,k}; ...; a_{8,0} ... a_{8,k}]
POOL(S):
    return max([S_{0,0,0}, S_{0,0,1}, ...S_{0,0,2}])
ReLU(S):
    return max(0, S_{0,0,0})
//Execution by chaining three SLApplys on array θ_1
SLApply(SLApply(SLApply(θ_1,CONV),ReLU), POOL)
```

Fig. 4. Expression of CNN on a 2D array θ_1 with SLOPE. The convolution has k kernels whose parameters are $a_{ij}, i \in [0,8]$ and $j \in [0,k]$. The output of each *CONV* is a vector, turning θ_1 into a 3D array. *CONV* is applied onto array θ_1 at first. Then, *ReLU* and *POOL* are applied onto the result of *CONV*. Users can define and add more layers to have a deep architecture.

3.3 Example Data Analysis Using SLOPE

SLOPE can express various single data analysis operations, such as *filter, moving average*, etc. Here we use SLOPE to compose a few advanced data analytic algorithms with multiple steps:

- **Gradient and interpolation computations.** Magnetic reconnection is an important phenomenon in plasma particle acceleration research [22]. Data analysis pipeline used to study the reconnection phenomenon involves computing gradients on the magnetic field mesh data and then interpolate the gradient value for all particles scattered in space. An example of using SLOPE to express this data analysis pipeline on a 2D filed data is shown in Fig. 3. The gradient procedure uses the *Stencil* shown in Fig. 2(b). The interpolation uses the *Stencil* from Fig. 2(a).
- **Convolutional neural network (CNN).** CNN [19] is a deep feed-forward artificial neural network, typically used in recognizing images. A CNN has been applied to identify extreme weather events [27]. CNN usually includes three main layers: convolution, ReLU, and pooling. Figure 4 shows expressions of these three layers with SLOPE. The *Stencil* for convolution and pooling is shown in Fig. 2(c). The ReLU uses a single cell *Stencil*, as shown in Fig. 2(a).
- **Connected Component Labeling (CCL).** CCL [34] is one fundamental algorithm in pattern recognition. CCL assigns each connected component member with a unique label. The standard CCL repeatedly applies an 8-way connection detection for each point to replace its label with the minimum label of its neighbors. CCL converges until no such replacement happens. To accelerate the converge process, advanced CCL algorithms break the connection detection into forward and backward passes, as shown in Fig. 5. The *Stencil* in Fig. 2(d) are used during forward and backward passes in advanced CCL.

4 Parallel Execution Engine

This section introduces a parallel execution engine for SLOPE. We especially focus on following problems: (1) how to enable the user-defined operation defined on *Stencil* to run parallel. (2) how to cache intermediate data of analytic pipeline in DRAM to avoid expensive I/O operations.

4.1 Overview of Parallel Execution Engine

SLOPE execution engine follows single program and multiple data (SPMD) pattern [16, 29, 30], where multiple SLOPE processes are launched with the same analysis program and each process handles different data. Within a process, an *SLApply* executes an user-defined operation. An example of SLOPE on three nodes processing a 2D array in parallel is shown in Fig. 6. The input array is partitioned by SLOPE into chunks. SLOPE augments each chunk with halo layers

```
//Two user customized functions
ForwardScan(S):
   return min(S_{0,0}, S_{-1,-1}, S_{-1,0}, S_{-1,1}, S_{0,-1})
BackwardScan(S):
   return min(S_{0,0}, S_{0,1}, S_{1,0}, S_{1,1}, S_{1,-1})

//Repeatedly executing two SLApplys on array θ_1
do
   θ_1 = SLApply(SLApply(θ_1, ForwardScan), BackwardScan)
while (NOT converged)
```

Fig. 5. CCL algorithm on a 2D array θ_1 expressed with SLOPE. It includes a backward scan and a forward scan. The converged status is reached when no new label is found for all cells. For simplification, we omit the functions to detect converged status and to switch execution direction.

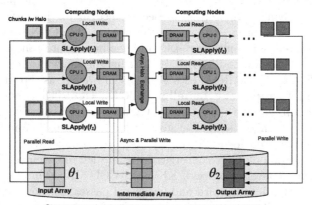

Fig. 6. Example of SLOPE execution for two user customized analysis functions (f_1 and f_2) on a 2D array θ_1. The θ_1 is split into 6 (3 × 2) chunks and read into 3 computing nodes for parallel processing. The intermediate array from f_1 is cached locally in memory for f_2 to read. Before actual read, a halo exchange algorithm is executed to augment cached chunks with halo layer. The intermediate array can be written onto disk for fault tolerance. The final output array is θ_2. Both θ_1 and θ_2 are stored as scientific data formats, e.g., HDF5, in storage systems.

(or called ghost zones) to avoid possible accessing cells from different nodes during execution. The output array of *SLApply* can be cached in memory. Caching the output from the previous *SLApply* allows the following *SLApply* to quickly access input data. SLOPE execution engine uses a halo exchange algorithm to synchronize each cached chunk for cache array. While storing the intermediate array in memory is prone to software and hardware failures, SLOPE supports asynchronously checkpointing intermediate arrays to persistent storage system.

4.2 Data Partitioning and Halo Layer

An array is split into chunks for parallel processing in SLOPE. The chunk in SLOPE is defined as *(starting indices, ending indices)*, where *indices* is a vector. SLOPE augments each chunk with a halo layer. The halo layer eliminates the need to retrieve cells from other chunks. Users can specify the size of the halo layer as the maximum offset used by *Stencil* in the user-defined function f. Note that the halo layer in SLOPE introduces a small amount of duplicated cells at boundary. However, these duplications has a negligible performance impact since halo layer is usually smaller than a chunk. In contrast, MapReduce (as shown in Fig. 1) duplicates KV instances for each operation across the whole chunk, which significantly increases data size to be processed.

4.3 Data and Computing Scheduling

The scheduling method in SLOPE assigns chunks among processes with the structural locality at chunk level to reduce the ghost zone exchanges when the array is needed by following *SLApplys*. By default, array chunks are linearized by the row-major order and the linearized index is used as the 'ID' of the chunk (denoted as id_{chunk}). Given p processes, the chunk id_{chunk} is assigned to the process at rank $\lfloor id_{chunk}/\lfloor \frac{id_{chunk}}{p} \rfloor \rfloor$. SLOPE also allows users to choose the assignment in the reverse direction, i.e., from the end to the beginning along linearized order. Within a single chunk, cells are also scheduled by their row-major order.

4.4 Output Array Dimension

Mostly, the output array from a *SLApply* has the same number of dimensions and size as the input array. However, the output array may have different number of dimensions and size. SLOPE detects these attributes for output array based on information extracted from input array and the user customized function on it. For example, the convolution operation (in Fig. 4) converts a 4×4 2D data to an $4 \times 4 \times 8$ 3D array. In the *CONV* function, the return value for a single array cell is a vector with 8 cells. *SLApply* detects the size of this return vector and uses it as the size of the third dimension in output array.

4.5 Advanced Features

In SLOPE, we also provide various advanced and optional features that may apply only to selected data analytic tasks.

Intermediate Array Cache. To support efficient data movement between multiple *SLApply* operations, we support caching [43] intermediate data on distributed memory instead of storing on file systems. The in-memory cache layer has a metadata table containing array dimensions, cell type, and other array related attributes [36]. This metadata table is created when the intermediate array is produced through the output array dimension reasoning method discussed before. Based on the SPMD pattern of SLOPE, each SLApply can have its own copy of metadata table to avoid communication when it writes or reads data. Intermediate arrays are stored as chunks and each is produced by its corresponding input chunk on the same process. Each chunk does not contain the halo layer when it is produced. SLOPE builds halo layers for the following *SLApply* when needed using an **asynchronous halo exchange** method. SLOPE uses classic halo exchange algorithm [18] but we improve it with MPI asynchronous primitives *MPI_Isend* and *MPI_Ireceive* to improve its performance.

Asynchronous Check Point Method. Caching intermediate arrays in memory is prone to data loss because of potential hardware or software faults [20]. SLOPE allows to asynchronously checkpoint intermediate arrays [37]. SLOPE provides interface for users to control the checkpoint frequency, which can be calculated via: $\frac{V}{T \times E}$, where V is the data size, T the bandwidth of storage system, and E the time of executing a *SLApply*.

Mirror Value. Invoking a user customized function incurs overhead. In reality, there are some operations that have defined mapping from the input value to the output values, e.g., values greater than or equal to zero in *ReLU* used by CNN. The SLOPE introduces a mirror value feature to allow *SLApply* to skip invoking customized function for these points.

In-Place Modification. During real-world data analysis, computing on a cell may need the result from previous cells. For example, in CCL, the label of the previous point can be used to find the label for the current one. To optimize for these operators, SLOPE allows users to replace input of *SLApply* with its output. By contrast, Spark does not allow analysis operation to modify the original data, which may create lots of RDDs in long pipeline.

Multiple Arrays. SLOPE allows users to compose data analysis on multiple arrays. For example, the user-defined Interpolation function in Fig. 3 describes the operations on array θ_3 and on array θ_2. This operation is similar to the map-side join in MapReduce.

4.6   Implementation of SLOPE

Based on ArrayUDF [13], we provide an implementation[1] of SLOPE in plan C++ with its template feature to support different data types. Specially, it provides two C++ classes, e.g., *Stencil* and *Array*, which are included in header file *"ArrayUDF.h"*. The *Stencil* class implements abstract type *Stencil* in Sect. 3.1. The *Array* contains all functions related to execution engine in Sect. 4. The *Array* has a method namely *Apply* (i.e., *SLApply*) to run UDF on its data. The UDF is standard C++ function and is passed to *SLApply* as function pointer. An example for using SLOPE to implement CCL code (with a single step and 8-way check) is presented in Fig. 7. User can use standard C++ compiler to compile it. MPI is required to run it in parallel for both intra-node and inter-node.

---

[1] https://bitbucket.org/arrayudf/.

```
#include <ArrayUDF.h>
//Define function to find minimum label for a Cellhood
float  ccl_check(Stencil<float> c){
         return Min(c(-1,-1), c(-1, 0), c(-1, 1), c(0,-1),\
                    c( 0 ,0), c( 0, 1), c( 1,-1), c( 0, 1), c(1, 1));
}
//Initialize chunk_size & ghost_size for parallel processing
//Initialize Array instance A with a 2D array "data" from
//      a HDF5 file "file.h5"
//Apply ccl_check on array A, output is ignored
void main(){
         vector<int>   chunk_size{10,10}, ghost_size{1,1};
         Array<float>  A("file.h5", "/data",chunk_size,ghost_size);
         A->Apply(ccl_check);
}
```

Fig. 7. SLOPE C++ example code for CCL (with a single step and 8-way check).

5 Evaluation

We demonstrate the effectiveness of SLOPE on the Cori supercomputer at The National Energy Research Scientific Computing Center, or NERSC[2] with over 2,400 computing nodes. We compare SLOPE with following systems:

- **Apache Spark** [42] represents state-of-the-art MapReduce. We use new technologies including H5Spark [23] and file pooling [9] to realize a fair comparison between Spark and SLOPE on supercomputer. We also have a test in non-supercomputer environment to compare Spark and SLOPE.
- **ArrayUDF** [13] provides a native user-defined function on array. However, it lacks a clearly defined programming model and supports for multiple attributes, multiple arrays and in memory cache. We use a few customized operations to compare ArrayUDF to match its capability.
- **TensorFlow** [1] includes hand-tuned and public available procedures for data analytics. The goal to use TensorFlow in tests is to show how fast/slow the analytic tasks that are expressed through Spark and SLOPE.
- **C++ Imp**, developed by authors, represents the way users implement data analytic function without programming model. C++ Imp only implements the data analytic logics (e.g., convolution) with hand-tuned codes (e.g., directly calculating convolution on array in memory). The C++ Imp has the same data management (e.g., cache) as we have done in SLOPE.

5.1 Evaluation Using Synthetic Data Analysis

Our evaluation in this section uses a two-layer convolutional neural network (CNN) on a 2D synthetic float typed array with the dimension of *64,000 by 64,000*. Specifically, we focus on a single forward pass computing of the CNN. Unless otherwise noted, all experiments use 256 CPU cores and *4096 by 4096* chunk size. The size of halo layer is set to 1. The two-layer CNN has a *convolution (CONV)* layer and a *ReLU* layer. *CONV* is configured with a *8 2 by 2* kernels. *ReLU* is: $f(x) = max(0, x)$, where x is the input to a neuron.

---

[2] https://www.nersc.gov/.

Comparing SLOPE with ArrayUDF. We use customized workloads from CNN described above to match the capability of ArrayUDF. Specifically, we use a single convolution kernel to keep both input and output arrays have the same size, which is supported by ArrayUDF. As discussed before, SLOPE allows input and output arrays to have different sizes. We find out that cache feature of SLOPE enable it to be at most 10× faster in accessing data. In following parts, we will focus on comparing SLOPE with Spark and hand-tuned code.

Comparing SLOPE, Spark, TensorFlow, and C++ Imp. This test uses a 2 layered CNN workload. TensorFlow uses *tf.nn.conv2d* and *tf.nn.relu* for *CONV* and *ReLU*, respectively. Spark uses a chain of *Map* and *Reduce* to express *CONV* and *ReLU* (as shown in Fig. 1). The expression of *CONV* and *ReLU* in SLOPE is presented in Fig. 4. To isolate impact of supercomputer software, such as MPI and Lustre, we have two separate tests on non-supercomputer environment and supercomputer environment, as discussed below:

- **Non-supercomputer environment.** This test uses a single Linux box. For Spark, in order to clearly measure performance for each step, we test it without its Lazy Evaluation (LE) optimization [42]. We report test results in Fig. 8. Spark without LE spends 11% of time to read data and 38% of time to shuffle data. As explained in Fig. 1, the read function accesses data from the disk and converts the array into KV pairs. The shuffle function aggregates the inputs for *Reduce*. Both read and shuffle are expensive. Spark's LE optimization improves its performance by 3X. Based on this observation, we test Spark only with the LE optimization in following sections. The "C++ Imp" has the best performance. TensorFlow is ≈15% slower than SLOPE. TensorFlow may implement *CONV* as expensive matrix multiplication [1]. Overall, SLOPE has comparable performance as hand-tuned code and is much faster than Spark.
- **Supercomputer environment.** On a parallel environment with Lustre and MPI, we scaled above tests from 1 CPU core to 16 CPU cores. Note that, to be fair, we only consider the computation time of these systems because we believe TensorFlow and Spark are not originally designed and optimized for Lustre. For Spark, we force the read operation to complete before *Map* and *Reduce* starts. The results are presented in Fig. 9. The trend in these results are consistent with the one from non-supercomputer environment. On average, SLOPE is 13× faster than Spark. SLOPE maintains structural locality in the assignment of array cells and partitions, eliminating the need for communication. Spark has to shuffle data between *Map* and *Reduce*. SLOPE is 38% faster than TensorFlow. As explained in previous paragraph, TensorFlow may convert *CONV* into large and expensive matrix multiplications.

Scalability Tests of SLOPE. We evaluated both weak scaling and strong scaling of SLOPE using the number of CPU cores from 256 to 16K. In weak scaling tests, the data size for each process is fixed at 64 MB, totaling 1 TB at 16K CPU cores. In strong scaling tests, the file size is fixed at 1 TB. We use the parallel efficiency to measure the result. The parallel efficiency for strong scaling is defined as

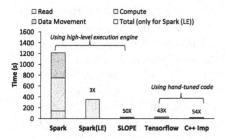

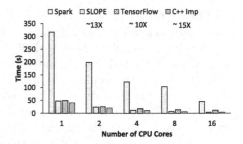

Fig. 8. Comparing SLOPE with Spark and hand-tuned codes to perform *CONV* for a 2D array on a Linux server. The Spark was tested with and without Lazy Evaluation (LE).

Fig. 9. The computing time (only) for executing CNN with SLOPE, Spark and hand-tuned codes (i.e., TensorFlow and C++ Imp) on a supercomputer.

$t_1/(N*t_N)*100\%$, where t_1 is the time to finish a work unit with 1 process and t_N is the time to finish the same work unit with N process. For weak scaling, its parallel efficiency is $t_1/t_N*100\%$. Results are presented in Fig. 10. Both cases show that SLOPE has high parallel efficiency. Actually, processing a 1 TB data takes around 2 s, giving around 512 GB/sec throughput at 16K CPU cores. The primary reason SLOPE can achieve such scalability is that it can maintain structural locality on processing multiple dimensional array and all computing can happen on a local node without communication across nodes.

5.2   Evaluation for SLOPE and Spark Using Real Applications

In this section, we compare SLOPE with Spark in executing data analysis operations for three applications: CAM5 [28,40], VPIC [8,22], and BISICLES [10,44]. All datasets are stored in the HDF5 files. Spark uses H5Spark [23] to read HDF5 data into RDDs. Since H5Spark does not support writing RDDs back to HDF5, we compare read performance and execution performance.

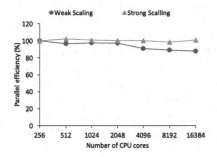

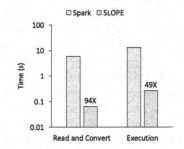

Fig. 10. Strong and weak scaling test results for SLOPE with upto 16K CPU cores.

Fig. 11. Test results of executing CAM5's CNN with SLOPE.

CAM5's Convolution Encoder. The CAM5 is widely used by the climate community to study the global climate change and prediction [40]. The dataset in test is from a simulation run with 25 km spatial resolution for the years spanning from 1979 to 2005. Each frame of the global atmospheric state is a 768×1152 image. CNN [28] has been used to predict extreme weather events, such as atmospheric rivers, from this data. We have used SLOPE and Spark to compose three key steps of CNN: *CONV*, *ReLU*, and *Pooling*. Following the work [28], we consider the layer close to the Earth's surface and the variables, namely *TMQ*, for atmospheric rivers detection. We use the output data for the year *1979*, which is a 768×1152 2D array. Spark uses two sets of *Map* and *Reduce* to express *CONV* and *Pooling* layers, respectively. The *ReLU* is expressed with a *Map*. The implementation with SLOPE is shown in Fig. 4. Test results are reported in Fig. 11. The read time required by Spark is around 94× slower than that of SLOPE. This performance benefit is because SLOPE directly handles multidimensional array without flattening it into KV pairs. Spark needs to convert the array into KV pairs during read. When comparing the execution time, SLOPE is 49× faster than Spark. Also, as discussed in the previous section, linearization to a 1D KV causes significant communication overhead for *Reduce* to gather inputs. SLOPE reduces communication to synchronize only a small number of halo layers with the preserved structure locality.

VPIC's Gradient and Interpolation Operations. VPIC simulates the magnetic reconnection phenomenon [22]. Magnetic reconnection study involves two key steps: calculating gradient on 3D field mesh and finding gradient field value for each particle via interpolation. These operations involve four arrays, M, X, Y, and Z, where M is a 3D magnetic field mesh data and X, Y and Z contains particle locations. The gradient computing for M uses a Laplace operation, i.e., 3D version of the one in Fig. 3. Using Spark, the gradient on M is expressed with a *Map* and a *Reduce*, where the *Map* duplicates each cell for its neighbors and the *Reduce* operation performs the Laplace calculation. Then, a tri-linear operation is finished with a map-side join, where the gradient value of M is broadcasted to each executor and then a *Map* is used to find the gradient field value of each particle. Implementation with SLOPE is a 3D version of the algorithm in Fig. 3. Since Spark has a limit on the size of broadcast data, we have set the test to use a small 256 MB ($512 \times 256 \times 256$) field data. The particle data has 263 GB with ~23 billion particles. The tests used *128* CPU cores on 16 nodes. A performance comparison is shown in Fig. 12, where SLOPE performs 106× faster than Spark to execute the analysis. In reading the input data, SLOPE is 45× times faster. Since Spark has to duplicate a lot (~6×) cells to help *reduce* to calculate the Laplace operator, its performance is poor. In contrast, SLOPE uses logical partitioning without duplications to finish the Laplace operator. Explicitly processing and communicating array index for particle data in Spark consumes CPU time and network bandwidth and therefore degrades its performance.

BISICLES's CCL Algorithm. Connected component labeling (CCL) has been used to detect ice calving events on Antarctica, simulated by BISICLES [44]. We have used both Spark and SLOPE to compose CCL. The data size

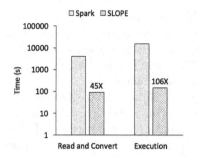

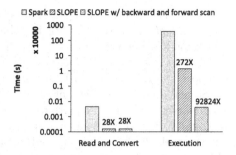

Fig. 12. Test results of executing VPIC's gradient & interpolation analysis with SLOPE.

Fig. 13. Test results of executing BISICLES's connected component labeling (CCL) with SLOPE.

is 12288×12288 and we test it with 16 CPU cores on 4 nodes. We implemented a standard multi-pass algorithm for CCL with an 8-way connection detection [34] for both Spark and for SLOPE. We report the execution time in Fig. 13. The 8-way connection detection based CCL algorithm needs 10868 iterations to converge and SLOPE is 272× faster than Spark. The main reason for Spark's slower performance is that it needs to duplicate a large number of array cells for neighborhood-based connection detection, while SLOPE needs to duplicate only a small halo layer. SLOPE also can use advanced features, such as in-place data modification and back-forward execution, which can accelerate the convergence of the CLL algorithm [34] (in Fig. 5). The CCL algorithm with these advanced features can not be implemented with Spark as its immutable RDD concept, where in-place data modification is not allowed. By enabling the feature in SLOPE, it converges after 8 steps. Comparing the performance of Spark, SLOPE is 92824× faster.

6 Related Work

Relational [26,41] and array [2,5,24] DBMS provide built-in operators and a UDF mechanism for customization operations. Our SLOPE shares certain similarity with these systems in expressing UDF operation. SLOPE differs from them in its new abstract data type *Stencil* and programming model. The *Stencil* of SLOPE supports a flexible way to logically subset array into any shapes for analytic operations. In DBMS, their *window* operator only subsets array into rectangular boxes and each member in *window* operator is treated equally. In contrast, each member of *Stencil* can be customized with different operations in SLOPE.

MapReduce has a KV data type and two generic operations, *Map* and *Reduce*. Spark [42] introduces a memory cache layer for iterative analysis. SciHadoop [7] provides a scheduling optimization for adopting MapReduce to analyze data in arrays. Our SLOPE has a structural locality-aware programming model on multidimensional array and generalizes both *Map* and *Reduce* into a single operator, *SLApply*, on array. SLOPE has the similar cache mechanism as the one in Spark for KV but the cache in SLOPE works for multidimensional array. The SciHadoop has similar goal as SLOPE. But SciHadoop still uses MapReduce to compose analysis and SLOPE is a new programming model.

Stencil domain-specific languages (DSL) [12,17,25] are mostly developed to solve partial differential equation(PDE) problem. Our SLOPE is a data analysis framework that generalizes MapReduce for multidimensional arrays. SLOPE uses Stencil idea to extend the Map functions (on a single element) to a set of neighborhood array cells towards composing data analysis tasks, e.g., connected component labeling (CCL). Technologically, SLOPE is implemented by plain C++ without compiler extension/new language definition. Stencil DSL may need compiler extension or even new language definition.

SAGA [39] supports aggregator operation on array file formats. R [15] uses *Apply* operators and its parallel version *dmapply* to customize operations over a list or a vector. But, none of these *Apply* operators can express the structure locality on array. ArrayUDF [13] provides a simple API to accept UDF but it can only run a single UDF on a single array stored on disk. TensorFlow [1] provides hand-optimized code for machine learning but has not programming model defined. SLOPE defines programming model and in-memory cache to compose complex analytic operations with multiple stages and multiple arrays.

7   Conclusions and Future Work

Data analysis operations on multidimensional arrays are typically defined on a set of neighborhood cells in diverse geometric shapes. This structural locality is lost in the programming models, such as MapReduce, making them perform poorly in composing deep data analytic pipeline for multidimensional arrays. In this work, based on multidimensional array data model, we proposed a new structure locality-aware programming model (SLOPE) and its implementation. We also present multiple data analysis examples with SLOPE, such as convolutional neural network, gradient computing, and connected component labeling. In tests with real scientific data analysis, SLOPE is $49\times \sim 92824\times$ faster than Spark, which represents state-of-the-art MapReduce programming model. In our future work, we plan to expand SLOPE to compose diverse operations without strong locality of reference.

Acknowledgment. This effort was supported by the U.S. Department of Energy (DOE), Office of Science, Office of Advanced Scientific Computing Research under contract number DE-AC02-05CH11231 (program manager Dr. Laura Biven). This research used resources of the National Energy Research Scientific Computing Center (NERSC), a DOE Office of Science User Facility.

References

1. Abadi, M., et al.: Tensorflow: a system for large-scale machine learning. In: OSDI 2016 (2016)
2. Baumann, P., Dehmel, A., Furtado, P., Ritsch, R., Widmann, N.: The multidimensional database system RasDaMan. SIGMOD Rec. **27**(2), 575–577 (1998)
3. Blanas, S., Wu, K., Byna, S., Dong, B., Shoshani, A.: Parallel data analysis directly on scientific file formats. In: SIGMOD 2014 (2014)
4. Bloom, J.S., Richards, J.W., et al.: Automating discovery and classification of transients and variable stars in the synoptic survey era. PASP **124**(921) (2012)
5. Brown, P.G.: Overview of SciDB: large scale array storage, processing and analysis. In: SIGMOD (2010)
6. Brown, P.G.: Convolution is a database problem (2017)
7. Buck, J.B., Watkins, N., et al.: SciHadoop: array-based query processing in Hadoop. In: Supercomputing Conference (SC) (2011)
8. Byna, S., Chou, J., Rübel, O., Prabhat, Karimabadi, H., et al.: Parallel I/O, analysis, and visualization of a trillion particle simulation. In: SC (2012)
9. Chaimov, N., Malony, A., Canon, S., Iancu, C., et al.: Scaling spark on HPC systems. In: HPDC 2016 (2016)
10. Cornford, S.L., et al.: Adaptive mesh, finite volume modeling of marine ice sheets. J. Comput. Phys. (2013)
11. Dean, J., Ghemawat, S.: MapReduce: simplified data processing on large clusters. Commun. ACM **51**(1), 107–113 (2008)
12. Denniston, T., Kamil, S., Amarasinghe, S.: Distributed halide. SIGPLAN Not. **51**(8), 5:1–5:12 (2016)
13. Dong, B., Wu, K., Byna, S., Liu, J., Zhao, W., Rusu, F.: ArrayUDF: user-defined scientific data analysis on arrays. In: HPDC (2017)
14. Durlofsky, L.J., Engquist, B., Osher, S.: Triangle based adaptive stencils for the solution of hyperbolic conservation laws. J. Comput. Phys. **98**(1), 64–73 (1992)
15. The R Foundation: The R Project for Statistical Computing. https://www.r-project.org/
16. Gropp, W., Lusk, E., Doss, N., Skjellum, A.: A high-performance, portable implementation of the MPI message passing interface standard. Parallel Comput. **22**(6), 789–828 (1996)
17. Gysi, T., Osuna, C., Fuhrer, O., Bianco, M., Schulthess, T.C.: STELLA: a domain-specific tool for structured grid methods in weather and climate models. In: SC 2015 (2015)
18. Laoide-Kemp, C.: Investigating MPI streams as an alternative to halo exchange. Technical report, The University of Edinburgh (2014)
19. Lecun, Y., Bengio, Y., Hinton, G.: Deep learning. Nature **521**(7553), 436–444 (2015)
20. Li, D., Vetter, J.S., Yu, W.: Classifying soft error vulnerabilities in extreme-scale scientific applications using a binary instrumentation tool. In: SC (2012)
21. Li, J., Liao, W.-K., Choudhary, A., et al.: Parallel netCDF: a high-performance scientific I/O interface. In: SC 2003, p. 39. ACM, New York (2003)
22. Li, X., Guo, F., Li, H., Birn, J.: The roles of fluid compression and shear in electron energization during magnetic reconnection (2018)
23. Liu, J., Racah, E., Koziol, Q., et al.: H5Spark: bridging the I/O gap between spark and scientific data formats on HPC systems. In: Cray User Group (2016)
24. Marathe, A.P., Salem, K.: A language for manipulating arrays. In: VLDB (1997)

25. Maruyama, N., et al.: Physis: an implicitly parallel programming model for stencil computations on large-scale GPU-accelerated supercomputers. In: SC 2011 (2011)
26. Momjian, B.: PostgreSQL: Introduction and Concepts. Addison-Wesley Longman Publishing Co., Inc., Boston (2001)
27. Racah, E., Beckham, C., Maharaj, T., Kahou, S.E., Prabhat, M., Pal, C.: Extremeweather: a large-scale climate dataset for semi-supervised detection, localization, and understanding of extreme weather events. In: NIPS (2017)
28. Racah, E., et al.: Extremeweather: a large-scale climate dataset for semi-supervised detection, localization, and understanding of extreme weather events. In: NIPS (2017)
29. Shi, R., et al.: Designing efficient small message transfer mechanism for inter-node MPI communication on infiniband GPU clusters. In: HiPC (2014)
30. Shi, R., et al.: HAND: a hybrid approach to accelerate non-contiguous data movement using MPI datatypes on GPU clusters. In: ICPP (2014)
31. Soroush, E., Balazinska, M., Wang, D.: ArrayStore: a storage manager for complex parallel array processing. In: SIGMOD 202011. ACM (2011)
32. Sousa, M., Dillig, I., Vytiniotis, D., Dillig, T., Gkantsidis, C.: Consolidation of queries with user-defined functions. SIGPLAN Not. 49(6), 554–564 (2014)
33. Stonebraker, M., et al.: Requirements for science data bases and SciDB. CIDR 7, 173–184 (2009)
34. Suzuki, K., Horiba, I., Sugie, N.: Linear-time connected-component labeling based on sequential local operations. Comput. Vis. Image Underst. 89(1), 1–23 (2003)
35. Tang, H., Byna, S., et al.: In situ storage layout optimization for AMR spatio-temporal read accesses. In: ICPP (2016)
36. Tang, H., et al.: SoMeta: scalable object-centric metadata management for high performance computing. In: CLUSTER 2017, pp. 359–369. IEEE (2017)
37. Tang, H., et al.: Toward scalable and asynchronous object-centric data management for HPC. In: CCGRID 2018, pp. 113–122. IEEE (2018)
38. The HDF Group. HDF5 User Guide (2010)
39. Wang, Y., Nandi, A., Agrawal, G.: SAGA: array storage as a DB with support for structural aggregations. In: SSDBM 2014. ACM, New York (2014)
40. Wehner, M., Prabhat, et al.: Resolution dependence of future tropical cyclone projections of CAM5.1 in the U.S. CLIVAR hurricane working group idealized configurations. JCLI (2015)
41. Widenius, M., Axmark, D.: MySQL Reference Manual. O'Reilly & Associates Inc., Sebastopol (2002)
42. Zaharia, M., et al.: Resilient distributed datasets: a fault-tolerant abstraction for in-memory cluster computing. In: NSDI 2012 (2012)
43. Zhang, W., et al.: Exploring memory hierarchy to improve scientific data read performance. In: CLUSTER 2015, pp. 66–69. IEEE (2015)
44. Zou, X., et al.: Parallel in situ detection of connected components in adaptive mesh refinement data. In: CCGrid 2015 (2015)

A Near-Data Processing Server Architecture and Its Impact on Data Center Applications

Xiaojia Song[1(✉)], Tao Xie[1(✉)], and Stephen Fischer[2(✉)]

[1] San Diego State University, 5500 Campanile Dr, San Diego, CA 92182, USA
{xsong2,txie}@sdsu.edu
[2] Samsung Semiconductor, 3655 N 1st St, San Jose, CA 95134, USA
sg.fischer@samsung.com

Abstract. Existing near-data processing (NDP) techniques have demonstrated their strength for some specific data-intensive applications. However, they might be inadequate for a data center server, which normally needs to perform a diverse range of applications from data-intensive to compute-intensive. How to develop a versatile NDP-powered server to support various data center applications remains an open question. Further, a good understanding of the impact of NDP on data center applications is still missing. For example, can a compute-intensive application also benefit from NDP? Which type of NDP engine is a better choice, an FPGA-based engine or an ARM-based engine? To address these issues, we first propose a new NDP server architecture that tightly couples each SSD with a dedicated NDP engine to fully exploit the data transfer bandwidth of an SSD array. Based on the architecture, two NDP servers ANS (ARM-based NDP Server) and FNS (FPGA-based NDP Server) are introduced. Next, we implement a single-engine prototype for each of them. Finally, we measure performance, energy efficiency, and cost/performance ratio of six typical data center applications running on the two prototypes. Some new findings have been observed.

Keywords: Near data processing · Data center server · FPGA · ARM embedded processor · Data-intensive · Compute-intensive

1 Introduction

A spectrum of near-data processing (NDP) work [1,3,6,10,16–18,24,27,29,30] have been proposed recently. Although they target data at different levels of the memory hierarchy, they share a common idea: deploying some hardware data processing accelerators (hereafter, NDP engines) such as FPGAs and embedded processors in or near memory devices to process data locally. NDP is a one-stone-two-birds approach. It largely reduces the pressure of data transfer as the size of processed data is normally smaller than that of raw data. Also, it alleviates the burden of host CPUs by offloading part or all computations to NDP engines.

© Springer Nature Switzerland AG 2019
M. Weiland et al. (Eds.): ISC High Performance 2019, LNCS 11501, pp. 81–98, 2019.
https://doi.org/10.1007/978-3-030-20656-7_5

However, existing NDP techniques might not be able to provide a satisfying solution to a data center server, which usually needs to perform a diverse range of applications from data-intensive to compute-intensive. This is mainly because they only aim at improving performance and energy-efficiency for some specific data-intensive applications such as databases [11,15,17,27], word count [3], linear regression [3], and scan [3]. It is understandable that they concentrate on data-intensive applications. After all, the major incentive of NDP is to reduce the increasingly heavy data transfer pressure of data-intensive applications. Recently, the processing power of NDP engines has been substantially increased [20]. For example, ARM Cortex-A53, a state-of-the-art embedded processor, is a quad-core 64-bit processor operating at 1.1 GHz [9]. The Xilinx VCU1525 FPGA board released in 2017 is equipped with 16 GB DDR4 memory and a Kintex UltraScale FPGA chip, which has 5k DSP slices, 1M logic cells, and 75.9 Mb block RAM [28]. We argue that NDP now also has a potential to benefit compute-intensive applications by considerably alleviating the computational burden of host CPUs as well as reducing their data movement. Thus, building a versatile NDP server that can benefit a wide range of data center applications becomes feasible. Unfortunately, such NDP server is not available yet. Besides, a good understanding of the impact of NDP on data center applications is still missing. For example, whether a compute-intensive application can also benefit from NDP remains an open question. In addition, FPGAs [6,27,29] and embedded processors (e.g., ARM processors) [3,24] are two main types of NDP engines. Which type of NDP engine is a better choice for an NDP server? In order to answer this question, a quantitative comparison between the two types of NDP engines in terms of performance, energy efficiency, and cost/performance ratio is required. Still, it cannot be found in the literature.

To address these issues, in this research we first propose a new versatile NDP server architecture (see Fig. 1a), which employs an array of NDP engines between host CPUs and an SSD array. Based on the architecture, two NDP servers called FNS (**FPGA-based NDP Server**) and ANS (**ARM-based NDP Server**) are then introduced. In both ANS and FNS, there are multiple SSDs with each having its corresponding NDP engine. Next, we implement a single-engine prototype for each of them based on a conventional data center server (hereafter, conventional server). While SANS (**Single-engine ANS**) utilizes an ARM Cortex-A53 processor [9] as its NDP engine, SFNS (**Single-engine FNS**) employs FPGA logic as its NDP engine (see Sect. 4). Further, we measure performance, energy efficiency, and cost/performance ratio for six typical data center applications (see Sect. 4.3) on the two prototypes. Finally, we obtain some new findings after analyzing our experimental results. To the best of our knowledge, this is the first study that provides a quantitative comparison between the two major types of NDP engines. Also, this research is the first investigation on the impact of NDP on compute-intensive applications.

2   Related Work

According to the location of NDP engines in the memory hierarchy, existing NDP techniques can be generally divided into three groups: in-storage

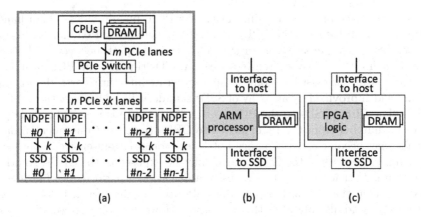

Fig. 1. (a) NDP server; (b) ARM-based NDP engine; (c) FPGA-based NDP engine.

computing (ISC), in-memory computing (IMC), and near-storage computing (NSC). Although various ISC and IMC techniques have shown their strength in the laboratory, so far none of them is publicly available. NSC, however, is more practical as one can develop an NSC-based computer using some commodity products (e.g., a server and FPGA). Thus, in this research we employ NSC to study the impact of NDP on data center applications.

NSC techniques usually insert computing devices on the path between storage devices (e.g., SSDs) and host CPUs to accelerate data processing. Ibex [27] is developed as an FPGA-based SQL engine that accelerates relational database management systems, whereas Netezza [5] builds a server equipped with one FPGA between main memory and storage to extract useful data. Firebox [2] consists of many fine-grained components of SoCs and memory modules connected with high-radix switches. Hewlett-Packard utilizes configurable fine-grained processing cores and memory pools to build a "machine" by connecting them with a photonic network [26]. Interconnected-FPGAs [29] proposes to build a computer system with one FPGA-based NDP engine to accelerate join operations in a database. While all existing NSC techniques only utilize one NDP engine in a server, ANS/FNS adds an NDP engine for each SSD of an SSD array to fully exploit the parallelism among the SSDs.

3   NDP Server Architecture

In this section, we first introduce the architecture of a conventional server. Next, we propose a versatile NDP server architecture, which inspires ANS and FNS.

3.1   The Architecture of a Conventional Server

The architecture of a conventional server with all flash storage can be envisioned from Fig. 1a by removing the NDP engine (i.e., NDPE) array. Its main components include one or multiple multi-core CPUs, DRAM, PCIe bus, PCIe switch, an array of SSDs, and network interface. The PCIe bus provides a high bandwidth data path between the CPUs and SSDs. There are k PCIe lanes ($k \geqslant 1$) for each SSD. A PCIe switch is in charge of the data path between CPUs and SSDs. The host CPUs concurrently access all SSDs through the PCIe switch.

Two limitations exist in a conventional server architecture. First, data transfer bandwidth provided by an array of SSDs is underutilized because the number of PCIe lanes from SSDs to the PCIe switch (i.e., $n \times k$) is usually much larger than that number from the PCIe switch to CPUs (i.e., m). Consequently, data transfer may become a performance bottleneck for a data-intensive application as the full bandwidth of the SSD array cannot be exposed to the CPUs. Another limitation is that for a compute-intensive application a performance bottleneck could occur on the CPUs. It seems that allocating engines (e.g., FPGAs) near host CPUs could also alleviate this limitation. However, doing so would require all raw data to be transferred from SSDs to the DRAM of host CPUs through the PCIe bus and PCIe switch (see Fig. 1a), which decreases the performance and energy-efficiency. Besides, deploying engines close to host CPUs is useless for a data-intensive application as its data transfer bottleneck cannot be solved.

To address the two limitations, we propose a new NDP server architecture that employs an NDP engine array between the PCIe switch and the SSD array so that each SSD is coupled with an NDP engine (see Fig. 1a). The rationale behind the new architecture is that deploying data processing engines near SSDs could benefit both data-intensive and compute-intensive applications. In addition, tightly coupling one SSD with one NDP engine enables an NDP server to fully exploit the storage bandwidth. Also, it makes the server scale well. Based on this new architecture, two NDP servers (i.e., ANS and FNS) are introduced.

3.2   The New NDP Server Architecture

Figure 1a shows the architecture of our proposed NDP server. The only difference between a conventional server and an NDP server based on the new architecture is that the latter has an extra layer of NDP engines. Each NDP engine consists of four key components: a processing element (PE), DRAM, an interface to host, and an interface to SSD. For an ANS, a PE is simply an embedded processor like an ARM Cortex-A53 (see Fig. 1b). For an FNS, the FPGA logic used by an application kernel (i.e., a partition of an FPGA chip) serves as a PE (see Fig. 1c). This is because an FPGA chip is relatively expensive. Multiple SSDs sharing one FPGA chip is more practical than each SSD owning an FPGA chip. Note that application kernels generated from one FPGA chip can concurrently process data from distinctive SSDs. The DRAM stores metadata. Also, it works as a buffer for data movement among an SSD, an NDP engine, and host CPUs.

A data processing procedure is always launched by host CPUs, which are in charge of the following tasks: (1) managing the operating system of the server; (2) monitoring the statuses of all NDP engines; (3) executing the host-side application; (4) offloading the application kernel to all NDP engines; (5) writing the arguments to an application kernel in an NDP engine and then enabling it to read and process the data from its corresponding SSD.

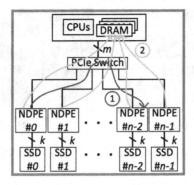

Fig. 2. Data transfer in an NDP server.

In the NDP architecture proposed by [29], each server (called computing node in [29]) only has one NDP engine and NDP engines belong to different servers are interconnected in order to reduce the communication cost caused by data exchange between different NDP engines. In our proposed NDP server architecture, however, NDP engines are not directly connected to each other because doing so will make hardware connection routing very complicated considering that each NDP server proposed in this research can have dozens of NDP engines.

Instead, when an NDP engine has a need to transfer data to one of its peers, it leverages a PCIe peer-to-peer (P2P) communication strategy [19], which is a part of the PCIe specification. The PCIe P2P communication enables regular PCIe devices (i.e., NDP engines in our case) to establish direct data transfer without the need to use host memory as a temporary storage or use the host-CPU for data movement. Thus, data transfer from a source NDP engine to a destination NDP engine can be accomplished through the PCIe switch in a DMA (Direct Memory Access) manner. PCIe P2P communication significantly reduces the communication latency and does not increase hardware design complexity. The data path 1 shown in Fig. 2 illustrates this process. After all NDP engines finish their data processing, the results from each NDP engine will be aggregated at the host-DRAM for a further processing in CPU. The data path 2 shown in Fig. 2 clarifies this case. Compared to the NDP architecture proposed in [29], our proposed NDP server architecture lays a burden on the host when an application needs to frequently exchange data or messages between different NDP engines. However, our architecture has two advantages: (1) the design complexity is greatly reduced; (2) it is more compatible with a conventional server. In addition, the fine-grained coupling of NDP engines with SSDs (i.e., each SSD has an exclusive NDP engine) in a shared-nothing architecture leads to a very high degree of parallelism in data transfer and data processing. It also delivers a very good scalability to the proposed server architecture.

Fig. 3. (a) The SANS prototype; (b) The SFAN prototype.

4 Implementations

In this section, we first explain our implementation methodology. Next, we describe how we implement the two single-engine NDP server prototypes SANS and SFNS, which are all extended from a state-of-the-art server with two 18-core Intel Xeon CPUs and 36 PCIe SSDs [22]. Finally, we provide implementation details of six data center applications.

4.1 Implementation Methodology

To develop two NDP servers (i.e., ANS and FNS) based on our proposed architecture shown in Fig. 1a, 36 Fidus Sidewinder-100 boards [9] and 36 Xilinx VCU1525 FPGA boards [28] are needed. In addition, each board needs two separate PCIe interfaces to connect an SSD and the PCIe switch, respectively. The high hardware cost and massive hardware revision are beyond our capacity. Fortunately, the major goal of this research is to understand the impact of NDP on data center applications instead of building two fully-fledged NDP servers. Therefore, we only build one NDP engine for each of the two proposed NDP servers shown in Fig. 3. Six applications are executed on the two single-engine NDP server prototypes, and then, the results are extrapolated to the case of the two full-size NDP servers (i.e., ANS and FNS), respectively.

The procedure of data processing in an NDP server can be divided into four steps: (1) SSD: data transfer from SSDs to NDP engines; (2) NDP: data processing in NDP engines; (3) NDP2CPU: data transfer from NDP engines to host-DRAM; (4) CPU: data processing in host-CPU. These four steps are organized in a pipelined fashion. If the data throughput bandwidth of each step is denoted as *BW (* is SSD, NDP, NDP2CPU, or CPU), then the system performance of the NDP server is determined by:

$$\text{Min}\{\text{SSDBW}, \text{NDPBW}, \text{NDP2CPUBW}^*\alpha, \text{CPUBW}\}, \tag{1}$$

where α is equal to the size of NDP engine input data divided by the size of NDP engine output data. An example of using this equation can be found in Sect. 5.1. Based on our tests, the read bandwidth of an SSD is approximately 3 GB/s and NDP2CPUBW is about 36 GB/s (see Table 1). When all 36 SSDs work concurrently the SSDBW is equal to 108 GB/s (i.e., 36×3 GB/s). The NDPBW is

Table 1. Platform setup

	Specifications
Server	Two CPU sockets; 36 SSDs m = 48; n = 36; k = 4 (see Fig. 1a)
CPU [14]	Xeon 6154: 64 bit, 3.0 GHz, 18 cores, 36 threads
PCIe	48 lanes attached to host CPUs (36 GB/s) 144 lanes attached to SSDs (108 GB/s)
SSD	PCIe×4; 3 GB/s
ARM platform	Quad-core Cortex-A53: 64-bit, 1.1 GHz [9]
FPGA platform	Xilinx VCU1525 platform [28]

equal to NDPEBW×n, where NDPEBW denotes the data processing bandwidth of one NDP engine and n is the total number of NDP engines. Obviously, the values of NDPEBW and CPUBW depend on the characteristics of applications. These values of applications will be measured in Sect. 5. We will use Eq. 1 to calculate the performance of the six applications running on ANS/FNS.

4.2 Implementation of SANS and SFNS

The PE of each NDPE of an ANS is a quad-core Cortex-A53 ARM processor embedded in a Fidus Sidewinder-100 SoC board [9]. Table 1 summarizes the specifications of the conventional server we used and the Fidus board. The board's PCIe Gen3 NVMe interfaces enable the ARM cores to directly read data from an attached SSD. Its PCIe × 8 host interface and 1 Gigabit Ethernet interface provides a channel for data movement and communication from/to the host CPUs. In our experiments, an application is first compiled by a cross-platform compiler aarch64-linux-gnu-g++. Next, the executable file is offloaded from host CPUs to the ARM cores in an NDPE. Finally, a data processing procedure is launched by the ARM cores. For each application, we measure its performance, energy efficiency and cost/performance ratio.

In an SFNS, the PE of an NDPE is built by FPGA logic (see Fig. 1c). We use a Xilinx VCU1525 FPGA board [28] to implement that NDPE. The specifications of the FPGA board are presented in Table 1. The FPGA board is plugged into a PCIe slot of the server (see Fig. 3b). The six applications are implemented in C++ and then compiled into binary files using Vivado High-Level Synthesis (HLS) [28] tool chain. The OpenCL framework is employed for a general management of the kernel running on NDP engines, which includes programing the device, setting arguments for the kernel, and launching the kernel. The pseudo code of the management is shown as below.

An SDAccel [28] development environment is used to evaluate the applications on FNS. It includes a system compiler, RTL level synthesis, placement, routing, and bitstream generation [28]. The system compiler employs underlying tools for HLS. The VCU1525 FPGA board is plugged into a PCIe Gen3 × 8 slot of the conventional server (see Fig. 3b).

```
for kernel ← 0 to N − 1 do
    cl::Program::Program(context, devices, binaryfile)
    //create a program project
    cl::Program::Kernel(program, kernel_name)
    //create a kernel object
    cl_int cl::Kernel::setArg()
    //set argument and workload for kernel
    cl::CommandQueue::enqueueTask(kernel)
    //program the FPGA and launch the kernel
end
```

In the SDAccel development environment, the OpenCL (Open Computing Language) [13] standard is used for parallel programming. It provides a programming language and runtime APIs to support the development of applications on the OpenCL platform model, which includes the host CPUs and FPGAs. Details of SDAccel and OpenCL can be found in [28]. Note that the data flow of SFNS is different from that of the OpenCL framework, which is shown in Fig. 4. The primary benefit of NDP comes from reducing data movement by directly reading/processing data from where they are stored (i.e., SSDs in the case of FNS). Thus, an FNS engine is expected to be able to fetch data from an SSD to the DRAM of an NDP engine (step 1 in Fig. 4a). And then, the data are transferred to the FPGA to be processed, after which the results are sent back to the DRAM in the NDP engine (step 2 in Fig. 4a). Finally, the results will be transferred to the host-CPU (step 3 in Fig. 4a). Unfortunately, the proposed NDP engine in an SFNS is built in the OpenCL framework, which always starts data processing from host-CPU. When there is a need to execute an application kernel on the FPGA board, the host-CPU first reads data from an SSD to the host-DRAM (step 1 in Fig. 4b). Next, the host-CPU writes the data to the DRAM in an NDP engine (step 2 in Fig. 4b). After the data have been processed in the NDP engine (step 3 in Fig. 4b), they are eventually transferred to the host-DRAM (step 4 in Fig. 4b).

Since it is difficult, if not impossible, to change the data flow of the OpenCL framework to the way that an SFNS desires, we find a workaround to bypass this issue. In particular, we use the steps 2–4 in Fig. 4b to emulate the steps 1–3 in Fig. 4a in our experiments in order to estimate an application's wall

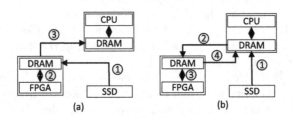

Fig. 4. (a) Data flow in SFNS; (b) Data flow in OpenCL framework.

time when it is running on an SFNS. The only difference between these two sets of steps lies in where to fetch the raw data. While SFNS is expected to achieve this by reading data from an SSD to the DRAM of an NDP engine (step 1 in Fig. 4a), the OpenCL framework actually accomplishes this task by transferring raw data from host-DRAM to the DRAM of an NDP engine (step 2 in Fig. 4b). However, the VCU1525 FPGA board can deliver a 10 GB/s data transfer bandwidth [28] in step 2 shown in Fig. 4b, which is much higher than the 3 GB/s data transfer bandwidth provided by an SSD (see Table 1) in step 1 shown in Fig. 4a. Therefore, a delay is injected to deliberately lower the data transfer bandwidth from 10 GB/s to 3 GB/s, by which we achieve our goal. To balance the workload among all NDP engines, the data set is equally split across the SSD array. In fact, the amount of workload for each kernel is set on the host program during its argument stetting phase for a kernel.

4.3   Implementation of the Applications

Six applications with distinct characteristics are chosen to study the impact of NDP on data center applications. They are run on CNS, SANS, and SFNS, respectively.

Linear Classifier (LC). In the field of machine learning, a linear classifier achieves statistical classification by making a classification decision based on the value of a linear combination of the features [23]. If the input feature vector to the classifier is a real vector $\boldsymbol{x}$, then the output score is $y = f(\boldsymbol{w} \cdot \boldsymbol{x}) = f\left(\sum_j w_j x_j\right)$. In our experiments, j is set to 8, which makes LC a data-intensive application. A parallel implementation of this algorithm can be found at [23]. The size of the dataset used for this application is 37 GB. Since the classification for each data point is independent from the other points, the classifying of each point can be parallelized among the 36 NDP engines.

Histogram Equalization (HE). Histogram equalization is a computer image processing technique used to improve contrast in images. Histogram equalization transforms pixel intensities so that the histogram of the resulting image is approximately uniform. This allows for areas of lower local contrast to gain a higher contrast [23]. A parallel implementation of this algorithm can be found at [23]. The dataset size used for this application is 3.4 GB. The execution of histogram equalization on different pictures can be done concurrently across the 36 NDP engines.

k-NN_2, k-NN_6, and k-NN_8. Given a set S of n reference data points in a dimensional space and a query point q, the k-NN algorithm [21] returns the k points in S that are closest to point q. Main steps of k-NN include: (1) computing n squared Euclidean distances between the query point q (x1, x2, ..., xi) and the n reference points of the set S (s1, s2, s3, ..., si);

$$distance = (x1 - s1)^2 + (x2 - s2)^2 + ... + (xi - si)^2 \qquad (2)$$

(2) sorting the n distances while preserving their original indices specified in S. The k nearest neighbors would be the k points from the set S corresponding to

the k lowest distances of the sorted distance array. The dimension of the data in our experiments is set to 9. Since the distance calculation for each point in the database is independent, step 1 can be executed concurrently among all 36 NDP engines. In step 2, the calculated distances are aggregated and then sorted in order to discover the k nearest points of the query point. This step is carried out in the host CPUs after all results from step 1 are aggregated to the host-DRAM. The computational complexity of k-NN depends on the number of features of each data point. The number behind the word k-NN represents the number of features of each data point. For example, k-NN_8 stands for a k-NN algorithm with each data point having 8 features. A larger number of features for each data point implies a more complex k-NN problem. The CPU and ARM codes start from a parallel implementation of the k-NN algorithm from the Rodinia library [21]. The dataset used for this application is totally 130 GB [21].

FFT. FFT is an algorithm that samples a signal over a period of time (or space) and then divides it into its frequency components. It is probably the most ubiquitous algorithm employed to analyze and manipulate digital or discrete data. It is also a well-recognized compute-intensive application [12]. The algorithm consists of two 1D FFTs, i.e., a row-wise FFT and a column-wise FFT. Note that for each picture its three color (i.e., R, G, B) values can be processed in parallel as shown in Fig. 5. To obtain the best performance on CNS, we employ MKL (Math Kernel Library) [25] for the implementation of 2D FFT on the Xeon CPUs. A 2D FFT implementation on FPGA adopts 1D FFT IP core from Xilinx and it mainly consists of a 256×256 size row-wise 1D FFT module, buffer, and column-wise 1D FFT module (see Fig. 5). This design is implemented at the RTL level. We run 2D FFT on 800 colorful pictures with total size of 238.54 MB [7].

Among the six applications, LC is the most data-intensive, whereas FFT is the most compute-intensive. Their data processing complexity increases in the following order: LC, HE, k-NN_2, k-NN_6, k-NN_8, FFT. In the same order, they become less data-intensive, which can be seen from the "System BW" columns shown in Tables 3 and 7. While LC, HE, and FFT only rely on NDP engines to process their input data, the three KNN applications require both NDP engines and host CPUs to accomplish the data processing task. In Sect. 5, we will run these six applications with distinct data processing complexities on CS, SANS, and SFNS separately. After that, the impact of proposed NDP server on them will be talked.

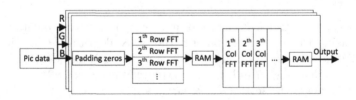

Fig. 5. 2D FFT on FPGA.

5   Evaluation

In this section, we measure the performance, energy efficiency, and cost/performance ratio of the six applications running on the conventional server (hereafter, CS), SANS, and SFNS, respectively. The results of ANS and FNS are extrapolated from real measurements of SANS and SFNS, respectively. In ANS and FNS, 36 NDPEs and 36 SSDs are assumed to be employed. Performance is defined as data processing bandwidth of an application when it is running on a server. Energy efficiency is represented by the amount of data that can be processed per joule (i.e., MB/joule). Cost/performance ratio is defined as a server's cost divided by its data processing bandwidth (i.e., dollar/(MB/second)). Obviously, an NDP server is more expensive than a CS because it is equipped with an array of NDP engines, which do not exist in a CS. However, it can deliver a higher performance. Therefore, measuring their cost/performance ratios is a fair method to compare their cost-effectiveness.

5.1   Evaluation of FFT & LC & HE

Performance Evaluation: Tables 2 and 3 show the performance of FFT, LC, and HE on the five servers in terms of wall time and data processing bandwidth, respectively. While "App" shown in Table 2 is a shorthand for "application", "BW" shown in Table 3 is an abbreviation of "data processing bandwidth" (see Eq. 1). "All" stands for "all three applications". Since there is no NDP engine in CS, "NA" (i.e., not applicable) is used for the three applications' "Wall time of NDP" and "BW of NDP" columns. Besides, since the three applications are entirely implemented and executed in the NDP engines, there is no computing task for host CPUs. Thus, their values of "Wall time of CPU" and "BW of CPU" are "0" and "$+\infty$", respectively.

The BW of either an NDP engine or host CPUs is equal to the size of dataset divided by wall time. The wall time of ANS/FNS is derived by the wall time of SANS/SFNS divided by 36 as 36 NDP engines can work in parallel assuming that the dataset has been evenly distributed among the 36 SSDs. "System BW" of an application is derived by Eq. 1. It represents the application's performance.

Table 2. Performance of six applications

| App | Wall time (s) | | | | | |
| | NDP/CPU | | | | | |
	LC	HE	FFT	k-NN_2	k-NN_6	k-NN_8
CS	NA/0.98	NA/0.13	NA/2.05	NA/17.22	NA/31.33	NA/47.45
SANS	16.67/0	1.98/0	132.60/0	825.50/0.62	1843/0.62	2354/0.62
SFNS	13.45/0	1.14/0	3.02/0	36.31/0.62	34.39/0.62	32.83/0.62
ANS	0.46/0	0.06/0	3.68/0	22.93/0.62	51.21/0.62	65.40/0.62
FNS	0.37/0	0.03/0	0.08/0	1.01/0.62	0.96/0.62	0.91/0.62

Table 3. Performance of LC & HE & FFT

	BW (GB/s)					System BW (GB/s)		
	NDP/CPU			SSD(s)	NDP2CPU			
App	LC	HE	FFT	All	All	LC	HE	FFT
CS	NA/37.76	NA/26.15	NA/0.11	108	36	36	26.15	0.11
SANS	2.22/+∞	1.72/+∞	$1.80e^{-3}$/+∞	3	36	2.22	1.72	$1.80e^{-3}$
SFNS	2.75/+∞	2.98/+∞	0.08/+∞	3	36	2.75	2.98	0.08
ANS	80.43/+∞	56.67/+∞	0.06/+∞	108	36	80.43	36	0.06
FNS	100.00/+∞	113.33/+∞	2.91/+∞	108	36	100.00	36	2.91

Table 4. Energy efficiency of LC & HE & FFT

	NDP (Watt)			Server only (Watt)		Energy consumption (Joule)			Energy efficiency (MB/Joule)		
				Active	Idle						
App	LC	HE	FFT	All	All	LC	HE	FFT	LC	HE	FFT
CS	0	0	0	613.70	30.33	601.43	79.78	1258.10	63.00	43.64	0.19
ANS	207.50	207.50	207.50	613.70	30.33	109.40	14.27	875.21	346.33	243.98	0.27
FNS	421.20	743.40	259.56	613.70	30.33	167.07	23.21	23.19	226.78	150.00	10.29

Take LC for example, its execution wall time on the NDP engine of SFNS is 13.45 s (see Table 2). Since the size of its dataset is 37 GB, its NDPBW is 2.75 (GB/s) (i.e., 37/13.45, see Table 3). Meanwhile, its SSDBW, NDP2CPUBW, CPUBW are 3 GB/s (only one SSD is used in SFNS), 36 GB/s (see Table 1), and "+∞", respectively. Based on Eq. 1, the performance of LC on SFNS is 2.75 GB/s. Unlike FFT and HE whose size of dataset is unchanged after NDP engine processing, the size of dataset of LC is reduced by 8 times (i.e., $\alpha = 8$) after NDP engine processing [23]. To saturate NDP2CPUBW (i.e., 36 GB/s), its NDPBW should be at least $36 \times 8 = 288$ GB/s, which is much higher than 80.43 GB/s and 100 GB/s (i.e., NDPBW of LC using ANS and FNS). That is why the performance of LC on ANS and FNS is decided by NDPBW rather than NDP2CPUBW.

Energy Efficiency: Table 4 summarizes energy consumption and energy efficiency of the three servers. All values of power (Watt) in this table are measured by the power meter shown in Fig. 3a. The "Server Only" column provides the power of the CS server. In the CS, since there is no NDPE, a "0" shows up in the "NDP (Watt)" column for the three applications. The total energy consumption of a server is the sum of energy consumption of NDPEs, energy consumption of CPU in active status, and energy consumption of CPU in idle status. For example, the energy consumption of ANS running LC is $(207.5 + 30.33) \times 0.46 = 109.40$ J. Thus, its energy efficiency is $(37 \times 1024)/109.4 = 346.33$ MB/J.

Cost/Performance Ratio: Cost/performance ratios of the three servers are provided in Table 5. Although in ANS and FNS the host CPUs are not involved in data processing, their costs are still taken into account as we are calculating

Table 5. Cost/performance ratios of FFT & LC & HE

System	Cost ($)			Cost/Performance ($/(MB/s))		
APP	FFT	LC	HE	FFT	LC	HE
CS	3,543	7,086	7,086	31.45	0.19	0.26
ANS	3,723	7,266	7,266	60.60	0.09	0.20
FNS	5,863	7,504	13517	1.97	0.07	0.37

Table 6. FPGA utilization of 36 NDPEs in FNS

App/Board	LUT	REG	BRAM	DSP slices
FPGA [28]	1,182,240	2,364,480	2,160	6,840
LC	108,108 (9.14%)	125,568 (5.31%)	72 (3.33%)	180 (2.63%)
HE	1,673,352 (140.54%)[b]	1,961,604 (82.96%)	6300[a] 0	0 0
k-NN_2	129,816 (10.98%)	172,512 (7.30%)	72 (3.33%)	432 (6.32%)
k-NN_6	227,016 (19.20%)	364,140 (15.40%)	288 (13.33%)	1,440 (21.10%)
k-NN_8	272,916 (23.08%)	444,960 (18.81%)	288 (13.33%)	1,944 (28.42%)
FFT	481,932 (40.81%)	643,608 (27.21%)	180 (8.28%)	3,456 (50.50%)

[a]Off-chip DRAM used for the overfilled BRAM;
[b]Larger than 100% means more than one FPGA chip needed.

the cost of an entire system. The prices of CPUs, ARM, and FPGA can be found at [14], [4], and [28], respectively. We will take FFT as an example to show how to obtain its cost/performance ratio on CS, ANS, and FNS, respectively. Since MKL [25] recommends using just one thread per host CPU core for FFT to achieve the best performance, we divide the total CPUs' price by two, which is $3,543. So, the cost/performance ratio of FFT on CS is $3,543/0.11 GB/s (see Table 3) = 31.45 $/(MB/s). In an ANS, the total price of the server is the sum of the price of CS and 36 ARM processors [4]. In an FNS, most resources that the 36 NDPEs consume are DSP slices, which account for 50.5% of the FPGA resources (see Table 6). Thus, the cost of FFT on an FNS is the price of host CPUs (i.e., $3,543) plus a 50.5% of FPGA price (i.e., $4,593.75 [8]), which is equal to $5,863. Since the performance of FFT on FNS is 2.91 GB/s (see Table 3), its cost/performance ratio is $5,863/2.91 GB/s = 1.97 $/(MB/s).

5.2   Evaluation of the Three k-NN Applications

Performance Evaluation: Tables 2 and 7 show the performance of k-NN_2, k-NN_6, and k-NN_8 on the five servers in terms of wall time and data processing bandwidth separately. Unlike FFT, LC and HE, an execution of a k-NN

Table 7. Performance of k-NN_2 & k-NN_6 & k-NN_8

	BW (GB/s)					System BW (GB/s)		
	NDP/CPU			SSD(s)	NDP2CPU			
k-NN_	2	6	8	All	All	2	6	8
CS	NA/7.55	NA/4.15	NA/2.74	108	36	7.55	4.15	2.74
SANS	0.16/209.68	0.07/209.68	0.06/209.68	3	36	0.16	0.07	0.06
SFNS	3.58/209.68	3.78/209.68	3.96/209.68	3	36	3	3	3
ANS	5.67/209.68	2.54/209.68	1.99/209.68	108	36	5.67	2.54	1.99
FNS	128.71/209.68	136.42/209.68	142.86/209.68	108	36	108	108	108

Table 8. Energy efficiency of k-NN_2 & k-NN_6 & k-NN_8

	NDP (Watt)			Server only (Watt)		Energy consumption (Joule)			Energy efficiency (MB/Joule)		
				Active	Idle						
KNN_	2	6	8	All	All	2	6	8	2	6	8
CS	0	0	0	613.70	30.33	10568	19227	29120	12.60	6.92	4.57
ANS	207.50	207.50	207.50	613.70	30.33	5815.10	12541	15916	22.89	10.61	8.36
FNS	420.53	429.85	431.87	613.70	30.33	817.06	803.46	782.29	162.93	165.68	170.17

application on an NDP server (i.e., ANS or FNS) involves both host CPUs and NDPEs. There are two steps in an execution of a k-NN application. While the first step (i.e., computing n squared Euclidean distances between the query point q and the n reference points of the set S) is performed in NDPEs, the second step (i.e., sorting the n distances while preserving their original indices specified in S) is carried out in host CPUs. Note that in the first step distance calculations can be performed in parallel as there is no data dependency among the distances. While the values in the "NDP" column show the performance of step 1 in NDP engines, the values in the "CPU" column demonstrate the performance of step 2 in host CPUs (see Table 7). The only difference among the three k-NN applications is the number of features used for the distance calculation in step1.

Energy efficiency and **Cost/performance ratio** of the three k-NN applications are summarized in Tables 8 and 9.

5.3 Impact of NDP on Data Center Applications

Figure 6 summarizes experimental results from Tables 3, 4, 5, 6, 7, 8 and 9. A quantitative comparison between CS and the two NDP servers (i.e., ANS and FNS) is also given in Table 10. Based on Fig. 6 and Table 10, several new findings on the impact of NDP on data center applications can be obtained.

Table 10 shows that in terms of performance ANS outperforms CS by 2.23× and 1.38× for LC and HE, respectively. **Finding 1:** *For data-intensive but compute-light applications, ANS can provide performance benefits by offloading*

Table 9. Cost/performance ratios of three k-NNs

System	Cost ($)			Cost/Performance ($/(MB/s))		
k-NN_	2	6	8	2	6	8
CS	7,086	7,086	7,086	0.92	1.67	2.53
ANS	7,266	7,266	7,266	1.25	2.79	3.57
FNS	7,591	7,968	8,390	0.07	0.07	0.08

Table 10. Comparisons among the three servers in three metrics.

Comparison with CS		LC	HE	k-NN_2	k-NN_6	k-NN_8	FFT
ANS	Performance	2.23x	1.38x	0.75x	0.61x	0.73x	0.55x
	Energy efficiency	5.49x	5.59x	1.81x	1.53x	1.83x	1.42x
	Cost/performance ratio	2.11x	1.30x	0.74x	0.60x	0.71x	0.50x
FNS	Performance	2.78x	1.38x	14.30x	26.02x	39.42x	26.45x
	Energy efficiency	3.6x	3.44x	12.93x	23.94x	37.23x	54.16x
	Cost/performance ratio	2.71x	0.70x	13.14x	23.86x	31.63x	15.46x

computation from host CPUs to NDP engines that are close to data. The performance benefits stem from ANS' capability of exploiting the full bandwidth of the SSD array, and thus, avoiding the data transfer bottleneck on the path from the PCIe switch to host CPU DRAM (see Fig. 1a). Table 10 also shows that ANS is inferior to CS in terms of performance for k-NN_2 (0.75x), k-NN_6 (0.61x), k-NN_8 (0.73x), and FFT (0.55x), which all have a data processing complexity higher than that of LC and HE. **Finding 2:** *ANS cannot benefit compute-intensive applications in terms of performance.* Although offloading computation to near-data processing engines enables ANS to enjoy the high data throughput bandwidth of the SSD array, for compute-intensive applications these benefits cannot offset the significant discrepancy in computational capacity between a 1.1 GHz embedded processor and a 3.0 GHz Xeon CPU. The trend shown in Finding 1 and Finding 2 can also be observed in Fig. 6.

Can a compute-intensive application also enjoy the benefits of NDP? The answer is yes, which is confirmed by the Performance row of FNS in Table 10. **Finding 3:** *FNS can offer performance benefits not only for data-intensive applications but also for compute-intensive applications.* The FPGA's hardware-level acceleration capability in FNS remedies the weakness of an embedded processor in ANS. This advantage of FNS and the benefits brought by NDP (i.e., fully exploiting the high data throughput of the SSD array, and thus, reducing data movement) together explain this finding. The performance benefits cannot be gained by simply putting data processing engines at the host CPU side because data transfer from the PCIe switch to host CPU could become a system performance bottleneck if doing so (see NDP BW 142.86 GB/s and NDP2CPU BW 36 GB/s of k-NN_8 in Table 7).

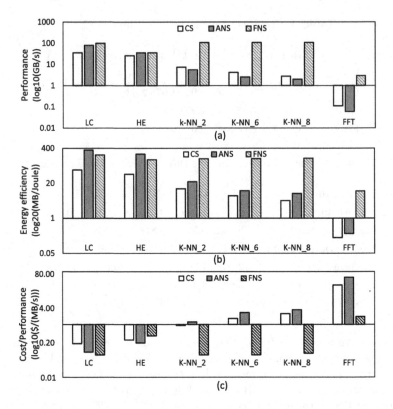

Fig. 6. Comparisons among the three servers in three metrics.

From Table 10, we obtain the following findings. **Finding 4:** *FNS offers more benefits in terms of performance and energy efficiency for applications with a higher data-processing complexity, which is contrary to ANS.* **Finding 5:** *Compared with CS both ANS and FNS can deliver a higher energy efficiency for all six applications.* The reason is that host CPUs are not energy efficient in nature. Offloading more computational load to an NDP engine not only relieves the computational burden of host CPU but also reduces the data movement, which can better improve energy efficiency of the entire system. Table 10 shows that ANS can provide a better cost/performance ratio for LC and HE only compared with CS. For the rest four applications, it offers a worse cost/performance ratio. However, FNS can improve cost/performance ratio for all applications except HE. This is because HE consumes too many LUTs (see Table 6). **Finding 6:** *FNS can improve cost/performance ratio for a diverse range of data center applications, whereas ANS can do so only for some compute-light applications.* The conclusion is that FNS is better than ANS in terms of cost-effectiveness.

6   Conclusions

In this paper, we first propose a new NDP server architecture for data center applications. The goal of the new architecture is to benefit a wide range of data center applications from data-intensive to compute-intensive. Next, we implement two single-engine NDP server prototypes. Finally, we evaluate six typical data center applications on a conventional data center server and the two prototypes. Based on our experimental results, several new findings have been obtained. These findings answer some open questions about how NDP impacts data center applications. Now we understand that a compute-intensive application can also benefit from NDP in the three metrics when FPGA-based NDP engines are employed. In addition, we find that compared with an ARM-based NDP engine an FPGA-based NDP engine is more capable of benefiting a wide range of data center applications. Currently, the main merit of an ARM-based NDP engine is to improve energy efficiency and reduce cost/performance ratio for some data-intensive but compute-light applications. For most applications, an FPGA-based NDP engine is superior to an ARM-based NDP engine, and thus, it should be considered first when NDP is applied to a data center server.

Acknowledgment. This research was supported by Samsung Memory Solution Laboratory (MSL). We thank our colleagues from MSL who provided insight and expertise that greatly assisted the research. This work is also partially supported by the US National Science Foundation under grant CNS-1813485.

References

1. Ahn, J., Hong, S., Yoo, S., Mutlu, O., Choi, K.: A scalable processing-in-memory accelerator for parallel graph processing. ACM SIGARCH Comput. Architect. News **43**(3), 105–117 (2016)
2. Asanovic, K., Patterson, D.: Firebox: a hardware building block for 2020 warehouse-scale computers. In: USENIX FAST, vol. 13 (2014)
3. Cho, S., Park, C., Oh, H., Kim, S., Yi, Y., Ganger, G.R.: Active disk meets flash: a case for intelligent SSDs. In: Proceedings of the 27th International ACM Conference on International Conference on Supercomputing, pp. 91–102. ACM (2013)
4. CNXSoft: Allwinner A64 a quad core 64-bit ARM cortex A53 SoC for tablets (2015)
5. Davidson, G.S., Cowie, J.R., Helmreich, S.C., Zacharski, R.A., Boyack, K.W.: Data-centric computing with the netezza architecture. Technical report, Sandia National Laboratories (2006)
6. De, A., Gokhale, M., Gupta, R., Swanson, S.: Minerva: accelerating data analysis in next-generation SSDs. In: FCCM, pp. 9–16. IEEE (2013)
7. Deng, J., Dong, W., Socher, R., Li, L.J., Li, K., Fei-Fei, L.: Imagenet: a large-scale hierarchical image database. In: CVPR. IEEE (2009)
8. Digikey: Price of VCU1525 board (2018). https://www.digikey.com/products/en?keywords=VCU1525
9. Fidus Systems, Inc.: Fidus sidewinder-100 (2017). https://www.xilinx.com/products/boards-and-kits/1-o1x8yv.html

10. Gao, M., Ayers, G., Kozyrakis, C.: Practical near-data processing for in-memory analytics frameworks. In: 2015 International Conference on PACT, pp. 113–124 (2015)
11. Gu, B., et al.: Biscuit: a framework for near-data processing of big data workloads. In: ISCA, pp. 153–165. IEEE (2016)
12. He, H., Guo, H.: The realization of FFT algorithm based on FPGA co-processor. In: Second International Symposium on Intelligent Information Technology Application, IITA 2008, vol. 3, pp. 239–243. IEEE (2008)
13. The Khronos Group, Inc.: The open standard for parallel programming of heterogeneous systems (2018). https://www.khronos.org/opencl/
14. Intel: Intel® Xeon® Gold 6154 Processor. https://ark.intel.com/products/120495/Intel-Xeon-Gold-6154-Processor-24.75M-Cache-3.00-GHz
15. István, Z., Sidler, D., Alonso, G.: Caribou: intelligent distributed storage. Proc. VLDB Endowment 10(11), 1202–1213 (2017)
16. Jo, I., et al.: YourSQL: a high-performance database system leveraging in-storage computing. Proc. VLDB Endowment 9(12), 924–935 (2016)
17. Jun, S.W., Liu, M., Lee, S., Hicks, et al.: BlueDBM: an appliance for big data analytics. In: Computer Architecture (ISCA), pp. 1–13 (2015)
18. Koo, G., et al.: Summarizer: trading communication with computing near storage. In: Proceedings of the 50th Annual IEEE/ACM International Symposium on Microarchitecture, pp. 219–231. ACM (2017)
19. Mayhew, D., Krishnan, V.: PCI express and advanced switching: evolutionary path to building next generation interconnects. In: Proceedings of the High Performance Interconnects, pp. 21–29 (2003)
20. Nurvitadhi, E., Sheffield, D., Sim, J., Mishra, A., Venkatesh, G., Marr, D.: Accelerating binarized neural networks: comparison of FPGA, CPU, GPU, and ASIC. In: FPT, pp. 77–84. IEEE (2016)
21. Rodinia: accelerating compute-intensive applications with accelerators (2009)
22. Samsung: Mission peak NGSFF all flash NVMe reference design (2017). http://www.samsung.com/semiconductor/insights/tech-leadership/mission-peak-ngsff-all-flash-nvme-reference-design/
23. Talbot, J., Yoo, R.M., Kozyrakis, C.: Phoenix++: modular mapreduce for shared-memory systems. In: Proceedings of the Second International Workshop on MapReduce and its Applications, pp. 9–16. ACM (2011)
24. Tiwari, D., et al.: Active flash: towards energy-efficient, in-situ data analytics on extreme-scale machines. In: FAST, pp. 119–132 (2013)
25. Wang, E., et al.: Intel math kernel library. In: High-Performance Computing on the Intel® Xeon Phi^{TM}, pp. 167–188. Springer, Cham (2014). https://doi.org/10.1007/978-3-319-06486-4_7
26. Whitman, M., Fink, M.: HP labs: the future technology. HP discover Las Vegas (2014). https://news.hpe.com/content-hub/memory-driven-computing/
27. Woods, L., István, Z., Alonso, G.: Ibex: an intelligent storage engine with support for advanced SQL offloading. Proc. VLDB Endowment 7(11), 963–974 (2014)
28. Xilinx virtex ultrascale+ FPGA VCU1525 (2017). https://www.xilinx.com/products/boards-and-kits/vcu1525-a.html
29. Yoshimi, M., Oge, Y., Yoshinaga, T.: Pipelined parallel join and its FPGA-based acceleration. TRETS 10(4), 28 (2017)
30. Zhang, D., Jayasena, N., Lyashevsky, A., Greathouse, J.L., Xu, L., Ignatowski, M.: TOP-PIM: throughput-oriented programmable processing in memory. In: HPDC, pp. 85–98. ACM (2014)

Comparing the Efficiency of In Situ Visualization Paradigms at Scale

James Kress[1,2(✉)], Matthew Larsen[3], Jong Choi[1], Mark Kim[1], Matthew Wolf[1], Norbert Podhorszki[1], Scott Klasky[1], Hank Childs[2], and David Pugmire[1]

[1] Oak Ridge National Laboratory, Oak Ridge, TN 37830, USA
{kressjm,choij,kimmb,wolfmd,pnorbert,klasky,pugmire}@ornl.gov
[2] University of Oregon, Eugene, OR 97403, USA
hank@uoregon.edu
[3] Lawrence Livermore National Laboratory, Livermore, CA 94550, USA
larsen30@llnl.gov

Abstract. This work compares the two major paradigms for doing in situ visualization: in-line, where the simulation and visualization share the same resources, and in-transit, where simulation and visualization are given dedicated resources. Our runs vary many parameters, including simulation cycle time, visualization frequency, and dedicated resources, to study how tradeoffs change over configuration. In particular, we consider simulations as large as 1,024 nodes (16,384 cores) and dedicated visualization resources with as many as 512 nodes (8,192 cores). We draw conclusions about when each paradigm is superior, such as in-line being superior when the simulation cycle time is very fast. Surprisingly, we also find that in-transit can minimize the total resources consumed for some configurations, since it can cause the visualization routines to require fewer overall resources when they run at lower concurrency. For example, one of our scenarios finds that allocating 25% more resources for visualization allows the simulation to run 61% faster than its in-line comparator. Finally, we explore various models for quantifying the cost for each paradigm, and consider transition points when one paradigm is superior to the other. Our contributions inform design decisions for simulation scientists when performing in situ visualization.

1 Introduction

The processing paradigm for visualizing simulation data has traditionally been post hoc processing. In this mode, the simulation writes data to disk, and, at a later time, a visualization program will read this data and perform desired analyses and visualizations. However, this mode is severely handicapped on today's HPC systems, as computational capabilities are increasingly outpacing I/O capabilities [3, 11].

© Springer Nature Switzerland AG 2019
M. Weiland et al. (Eds.): ISC High Performance 2019, LNCS 11501, pp. 99–117, 2019.
https://doi.org/10.1007/978-3-030-20656-7_6

To alleviate this pressure on the I/O systems, in situ processing methods [8] are now being used for analysis and visualization of simulation data while it is still in memory, i.e., before reaching disk. In situ methods are varied, but in broad terms can be placed in two categories: in-line in situ and in-transit in situ.

In the in-line in situ paradigm (sometimes also referred to as tightly coupled in situ), the simulation and the visualization will directly share the same set of resources. In this paradigm, generally speaking, the simulation will compute a specified number of cycle iterations and then pause while the visualizations are performed. Once the visualizations have been computed, the simulation will continue on to the next time step. In the in-transit in situ paradigm (sometimes also referred to as loosely coupled in situ), the simulation and visualization use separate resources. In this paradigm, the simulation will compute a specified number of cycle iterations and then transfer the simulation data over the network to the dedicated visualization resources. Once this transfer is completed, the simulation runs concurrently to the visualization tasks being performed.

Both paradigms have been applied successfully for real HPC applications. In a typical application, any publication evaluating in situ processing will generally include only anecdotal information that shows the simulation benefited from in situ processing, perhaps including comparisons with the post hoc paradigm. However, there has been substantially less research dedicated to how these two paradigms directly compare. As a result, it is difficult to understand which paradigm to use for a particular situation. A thorough comparison requires consideration of many different axes [17], e.g., execution time, cost, ease of integration, fault tolerance, etc. In this work, we focus our scope to execution time and cost. The goal of this work is to understand the performance of these two paradigms for a number of simulation configurations.

Our hypothesis entering this work was that both paradigms (in-transit and in-line) are useful, i.e., some workloads favor one paradigm with respect to execution time and cost, and other workloads favor the other, and a major contribution of this work is confirmation for that hypothesis. In particular, we have found that visualization workloads are different than the more general analysis workloads that have been studied previously, and so the best approaches for visualization differ. Specifically, we find that the rendering operation inherent to visualization has parallel coordination costs, which makes in-transit more competitive in comparison to analysis-centric workloads, since in-transit will often run with fewer nodes and so the coordination costs are reduced. Further contributions of this work include additional analysis of when to choose which processing paradigm and why, with respect both to time to solution and to resources used.

2   Related Work

While the constraints of the I/O systems in current HPC systems have made in situ visualization an important topic, many of the central ideas go back to the early years of computing. Bauer et al. [8] provide a detailed survey of the history of in situ visualization.

Over the years, a number of infrastructures for doing in situ visualization have been widely used. SCIRun [23] is a problem solving environment that allowed for in situ visualization and steering of computations. Cactus [16] provides a framework to assist in building simulation codes with plug-ins that can perform tasks such as in situ visualization. LibSim [26] is a library that allows simulations to use the full set of features of the VisIt [10] visualization tool for in situ exploration, extraction, analysis and visualization. ParaView Catalyst [6] offers a similar in situ functionality for the ParaView [4] visualization tool. ADIOS [19] is an I/O middleware library that exposes both in-line and in-transit paradigms to a simulation through a POSIX-like API. Its in-transit capabilities are provided by a number of different data transport methods, including DataSpaces [13], DIMES [27], and FlexPath [12]. Damaris/Viz [14] provides both in-line and in-transit visualization using the Damaris I/O middleware. Ascent [18] is a fly-weight in situ infrastructure that supports both distributed-memory and shared-memory parallelism. SENSEI [5] is a generic data interface that allows transparent use of the LibSim, Catalyst, and ADIOS in situ frameworks.

Several large studies have been done on using in situ methods in HPC simulations. Bennett et al. [9] use both in-line and in-transit techniques for analysis and visualization of a turbulent combustion code. Ayachit et al. [7] performed a study of the overheads associate with using the generic SENSEI data interface to perform in situ visualization using both in-line and in-transit methods. These and other studies are focused on the particular methods chosen for in situ visualization. They do not do a comparison between in-line and in-transit methods, nor discuss the tradeoffs associated with each.

Adhinarayanan et al. [2] on the other hand look at characterizing in-line in situ vs. post-hoc processing from the energy usage point of view. Their goal was to see if in-line in situ was more energy efficient for a simulation vs. post-hoc processing. Similarly, Gamell et al. [15] look at energy usage vs. performance for an in-line in situ analytics pipeline, and explore ways of reducing the energy usage with in situ processing. Rodero et al. [25] use the same concept and expand it to look at different configurations of simulation and visualization nodes to reduce energy usage.

Our work takes a different view than any of these works. First, we focus specifically on in situ visualization pipelines, which tend to have different communication and computation scaling curves than a full scale simulation. Second, we focus specifically on in-line in situ vs. in-transit in situ, and look specifically at visualization frequency, resource requirements, and how different combinations of all of these factors impact the bottom line of simulation scientists in terms of compute time used for visualization pipelines.

The closest comparator to our own work comes from Oldfield et al. [22]. Their work also considered in-line and in-transit in situ. However, their work was primarily focused on analysis use cases, where our work is focused on scientific visualization use cases. This difference is essential, because scientific visualization use cases involve rendering which requires parallel image compositing. This image compositing can become a bottleneck at large scale. This bottleneck is particularly relevant to this problem because the in-line approach operates with higher concurrency and thus suffers a bigger delay, while the in-transit approach performs image compositing at lower concurrence and thus less delay. As a result, our findings differ than those of Oldfield et al., specifically that in transit is superior for a much higher percentage of workloads than Olfield's analysis-based study. We also consider a wider array of factors, including varying the number in-transit resources, the simulation cycle time, and perform additional evaluation by including a total cost model.

3   Experimental Overview

In evaluating the characteristics of the in-transit and in-line in situ paradigms, we hypothesize that there are particular configurations for the simulation and analysis such that one paradigm outperforms the other. This includes both performance metrics under consideration in this work: execution time and resource cost. One intuition is that in-transit in situ has a chance to execute the analysis algorithms using fewer overall cycles, since it will use lower node counts and suffer less busywaiting from bottlenecks. This potential benefit, however, must offset the cost of allocating extra nodes, as well as transferring data from the simulation. To test our hypothesis, we designed a set of experiments to study the behaviors of both paradigms.

For this study, we use CloverLeaf3D [1,20], a hydrodynamics proxy-application that solves the compressible Euler equations. Cloverleaf3D spatially decomposes the data uniformly across distributed memory processes, where each process computes a spatial subset of the problem domain; it does not overlap communication with computation. To couple CloverLeaf3D with both in-transit and in-line in situ, we leveraged the existing integration with Ascent [18]. For in-transit visualization, Ascent's link to the Adaptable I/O System (ADIOS) [19] was used to transport data, and then the distributed memory component of VTK-m [21] was used to perform the visualization tasks. For in-line visualization, Ascent applied the distributed memory component of VTK-m directly. As a result, the same visualization code was being called on the same data sets in both settings, with the only differences being (1) whether Ascent used ADIOS to transport the data and (2) the number of nodes dedicated to visualization.

Visualization Tasks: The visualization tasks performed were isocontouring and parallel rendering. These tasks were chosen because they are widely used in scientific visualization, and parallel rendering is a communication-heavy algorithm that allowed testing of the performance bottleneck hypothesis. After each simulation time step, isocontours of the energy variable were computed at values of 33% and 67% between the minimum and maximum value for each time step. Since energy is a cell-centered quantity in CloverLeaf3D, the variable had to be re-centered, i.e., cell values surrounding each point were averaged. After the isocontours are computed, the geometry is rendered to an image using a parallel rendering algorithm. As we are operating in a distributed memory environment, each MPI process locally rendered the data it contained, then all of the locally rendered images were composited using radix-k.

In-line Visualization Setup: In-line visualization is accomplished via Ascent. Ascent's main visualization capability is effectively as a distributed memory version of VTK-m. The visualization is described through a set of actions. Ascent combines these actions into a data flow graph, then executes the graph. The in-line setup is illustrated in Fig. 1a. Again, for this case, the simulation and visualization share the same resources.

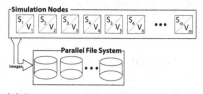
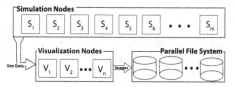

(a) Representation of the in-line visualization used as part of this study. With this mode, the simulation and visualization alternate in execution, sharing the same resources.

(b) Representation of the in-transit visualization used as part of this study. With this mode, the simulation and visualization operate asynchronously, and each have their own dedicated resources.

Fig. 1. Comparison of the two workflow types used in this study.

In-transit Visualization Setup: In-transit visualization is accomplished via Ascent's link with ADIOS. ADIOS is only used in the in-transit case because the data needs to be moved off node before visualization can take place, whereas visualization is done in place in the in-line case. ADIOS supports memory-to-memory data transports between processes or applications. I.e., it supports transporting data in a memory space of one application to the memory space of another. For this study, we used the DIMES data transport method. In the DIMES data transport method, the writing process transports the data asynchronously over the remote direct memory access network (RDMA) to the reading process. Additionally, DIMES requires the use of metadata servers to hold indexing information for the reading processes. The in-transit setup is shown in Fig. 1b. Here, a dedicated set of resources are used for the visualization. After the simulation has computed a time step, the data are transferred over the network to the visualization resources where visualization is performed asynchronously. Comparisons between these two methods are presented in Sect. 4. Because the two paradigms use different numbers of resources, we use two evaluation metrics to make a fair comparison. The first, time to solution, is discussed in Sect. 4.1, and the second, total cost, is discussed in Sect. 4.2.

Experiments: There are several different variations of each in situ paradigm. Examples include whether the same memory space is used for in-line in situ, or how proximate the visualization resources are for in-transit in situ. In this study we focus on the most common variation for each. We also consider configurations that directly affect in situ performance, such as simulation cycle time, visualization frequency, and resources dedicated to in-transit in situ. We evaluate the implications of these configurations both in terms of total time to run the simulation, and in terms of total resources used. We also explore the scalability of in situ visualization in both paradigms, and the implications of visualization performed at various levels of concurrency.

The experiments were designed to build a better understanding of the performance of the in-line and in-transit in situ paradigms. To aid in the analysis of this experiment, we ran a number of different in situ configurations:

- **Sim only:** Baseline simulation time with no visualization
- **In-line:** Simulation time with in-line visualization
- **Alloc(12%):** In-transit visualization allocated an additional 12% of simulation resources
- **Alloc(25%):** In-transit visualization allocated an additional 25% of simulation resources
- **Alloc(50%):** In-transit visualization allocated an additional 50% of simulation resources

For the in-transit paradigm, predetermined percentages of simulation resources for visualization were selected. These percentages, listed above, were selected based off of a rule of thumb in the visualization community where 10% of resources are traditionally devoted to visualization. We used that rule as a starting point and used two additional higher allocations to explore a range of options for simulation scientists. This also allows enough range to study the right ratio of simulation and visualization resource allocations. We also initially considered in-transit allocations that were below 10%, but due to the memory limitations on Titan (32 GB per node), the visualization nodes ran out of memory. Because of this, we omitted these experiments from our study. In the in-line case, visualization had access to all of the simulations resources. Finally, for all tests, we ran each one of these configurations in a weak scaling study with concurrency ranging between 128 and 16,384 processes, with 128^3 cells per process (268M cells to 34.4B cells).

Because CloverLeaf3d is a mini-app using a simplified physics model, the simulation has a relatively fast cycle time. This fast cycle time is representative for some types of simulations, but we also wanted to study the implications with simulations that have longer cycle times. To simulate these longer cycle times, we configured CloverLeaf3D to pause after each cycle completes, using a sleep command. This command was placed after the simulation computation, and before any visualization calls were made. To ensure no simulation communication was done asynchronously during the sleep call or visualization routines, the simulation tasks were synchronized before entering sleep. The three cases used were:

- **Delay(0):** simulation ran with no sleep command.
- **Delay(10):** a 10 s sleep was called after each simulation step.
- **Delay(20):** a 20 s sleep was called after each simulation step.

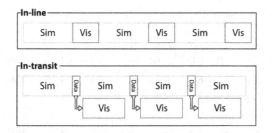

Fig. 2. Gantt chart showing how the simulation and visualization progress over time (from left to right) with both in-line and in-transit in situ. In this notional example, the data transfer for in-transit is faster than the visualization step for in-line, meaning the in-transit simulation can advance more quickly (four cycles versus three).

Conceptually, longer cycle times benefit in-transit visualization. Figure 2 demonstrates how visualization latency is hidden in in-transit vs. in-line visualization. After the data have been transferred to the visualization resources, the simulation and visualization proceed in parallel allowing in-transit to hide the latency of the visualization. In-line visualization cannot take advantage of latency hiding.

Lastly, in the bulk of the experiments we fixed the visualization frequency to once every time step. This is a common setup in codes that evolve quickly, where skipping timesteps could cause events to be missed. By having very frequent visualization, we can see an upper bound for how visualization will impact the simulation. To contrast these results we did a small study with a visualization frequency of once every three simulation cycles to see how the simulation is impacted. This scenario, where visualizations are performed every n cycles, is also common, and we wanted to understand how the frequency of visualization compared in terms of time and cost.

Hardware: The experiments in this study were performed on the Titan supercomputer deployed at the Oak Ridge Leadership Compute Facility (OLCF) at Oak Ridge National Laboratory. Titan is a Cray XK7, and is the current production supercomputer in use at the OLCF. It contains 18,688 compute nodes and has a peak performance of 27 petaflops. Because the mini-app we used for our study runs on CPUs only, we restricted this study to simulations and visualizations run entirely on the CPU. This also simplifies the analysis as we are not concerned with data movement within the node (from GPU to network).

Launch Configuration: The configuration for each experiment performed is shown in Table 1. Because CloverLeaf3D is not an OpenMP code, the in-line in situ and the simulation only configurations were launched with 16 ranks per node. The in-transit configurations used 4 ranks per visualization node and 4 OpenMP threads to process data blocks in parallel. Therefore, in-transit and in-line both used 16 cores per node. In the in-transit configuration, each rank will be assigned multiple blocks. Additionally, the in-transit configuration required

Table 1. Resource configuration for each of the tests performed in our scaling study.

Test	Sim processes	128	256	512	1024	2048	4096	8192	16384
configuration	Tot. data cells	648^3	816^3	1024^3	1296^3	1632^3	2048^3	2592^3	3264^3
In-line	**Total nodes**	**8**	**16**	**32**	**64**	**128**	**256**	**512**	**1024**
In-transit	Vis nodes	1	2	4	8	16	32	54	128
Alloc(12%)	Staging nodes	1	2	2	4	4	8	8	16
	Total nodes	**10**	**20**	**38**	**76**	**148**	**296**	**584**	**1168**
In-transit	Vis nodes	2	4	8	16	32	64	128	256
Alloc(25%)	Staging nodes	1	2	2	4	4	8	8	16
	Total nodes	**11**	**22**	**42**	**84**	**164**	**328**	**648**	**1296**
In-transit	Vis nodes	4	8	16	32	64	128	256	512
Alloc(50%)	Staging nodes	1	2	2	4	4	8	8	16
	Total nodes	**13**	**26**	**50**	**100**	**196**	**392**	**776**	**1552**

the use of dedicated staging nodes to gather the metadata from the simulation in order to perform RDMA memory transfers from the simulation resource to the visualization resource. These additional resources are accounted for in Table 1.

4   Results

The objective of our experiments was to understand the performance of in situ visualization using both in-line and in-transit paradigms and explore the hypotheses presented in Sect. 3. Our results focus on time to solution (Sect. 4.1), total cost (Sect. 4.2), and performance and load balancing of visualization algorithms (Sect. 4.3).

4.1   Time to Solution

Figure 3 shows the total runtime for each study configuration. There are several insights that can be drawn from Fig. 3. First, the in-line visualization operations in our study are subject to poor performance as concurrency increases (see Sect. 4.3 for a discussion on scalability). Second, the simulation cycle has a large impact on how many resources are required for in-transit visualization to outperform in-line visualization. In *Delay*(0), where simulation cycle times are very quick, the *Alloc*(50%) configuration is required for the in-transit resources to keep up with the simulation. As the simulation cycle time increases in *Delay*(10) and *Delay*(20), fewer visualization resources are required to out perform. In the case of *Delay*(20), the performance of all the in-transit configurations are nearly identical.

The times for each configuration are a result of the work required to perform in situ visualization, and are different for each paradigm. In Fig. 3, the added time for in situ visualization is indicated by the gap between the "Sim Only"

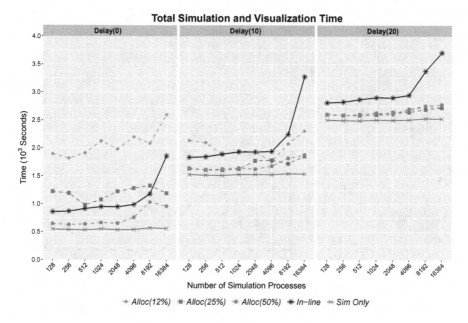

Fig. 3. Total execution time for the three simulation configurations ($Delay(0)$, $Delay(10)$, $Delay(20)$) using in-line visualization, and three configurations of in-transit visualization ($Alloc(12\%)$, $Alloc(25\%)$, $Alloc(50\%)$).

line, and the in situ configuration lines. For example, in the $Delay(0)$ case with 16,384 processes, the sim-only time was 561 s, while the in-line time was $1,858$ s, and increase of $1,297$ s to do visualization. This gap is a result of the simulation stalling for the visualization. For in-line visualization, the simulation will stall until the visualization operations are complete, at which point the simulation will continue with the next time step. For in-transit visualization, the simulation is stalled while the data are transferred to the visualization resources. Once the transfer is complete, the simulation will continue with the next time step, and the visualization will be performed concurrently on the dedicated resources (see Fig. 2). In-transit visualization is also subject to second type of stall, which can occur when the time to complete the visualization tasks exceeds the cycle time of the simulation. We permit such stalls to occur in our experiments. An alternative would have been to only begin visualization tasks if resources are available (i.e., drop time slices of data). We felt permitting stalls showed more interesting behavior, as the result from dropping time slices is approximately the same as increasing the simulation cycle time—which we cover in other experiments.

For in-line visualization, the simulation stall is the direct cost of the visualization operations. The amount of simulation stall increases with the level of concurrency, and is a result of a drop in the scalability of the visualization operations. This effect can be seen at higher level of concurrency, and will be discussed later in Sect. 4.3.

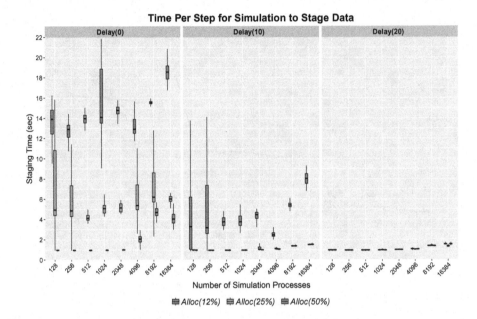

Fig. 4. Boxplot of the time it took to write data from the simulation to the staging resource at each step during the simulation. Results are shown for the three simulation configurations of in-transit visualization. This chart demonstrates the extent to which in-transit visualization slowed down the simulation. The lower the staging time, the less time it took the simulation to write data and continue on to the next cycle. Note that the majority of the time to stage data is due to the simulation being stalled while waiting for the visualization resources to free up (Delay(0) case), and in general staging the data is a quick operation (Delay(20) case).

For in-transit visualization, the simulation stalling in Fig. 3 is more complicated. In these cases, the simulation is stalled by the data transfer time, and in some cases, while waiting for the visualization processes to catch up. For example, in the in-transit *Delay*(0) *Alloc*(25%) case in Fig. 3, there is a rise in time between 1024 and 8192 processes. Figure 4 shows the range of data transfer times over all time steps in the simulation. Larger boxes in Fig. 4 indicates longer data transfer times which corresponds to the stalling described above. There is a correspondence between the stall times in Fig. 4, and the total times in Fig. 3. For example, looking at concurrency of 1024, 2048, 4096 and 8192 for *Delay*(0) *Alloc*(25%) cases in Figs. 3 and 4 shows the increase in time is due to stalling. As the simulation cycle time increases in *Delay*(10) and *Delay*(20), and the visualization has more time to keep up with the simulation, the stalling decreases.

Figure 5 is a metric that quantifies the impact to the simulation by the visualization. Given a fixed time allocation of 500 s, the graphs show how many simulation time steps can be completed with each configuration. The case where no visualization is performed is the high water mark for each graph.

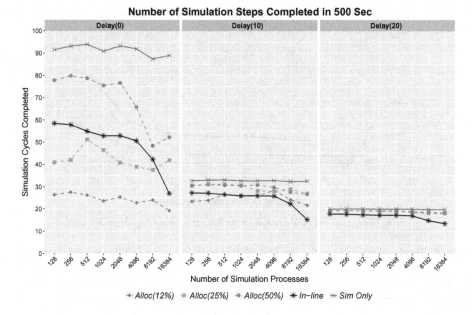

Fig. 5. Illustrating the cost of doing visualization. This figure plots the number of simulation cycles that could be completed in 500 s. The number of completed cycles are shown for the three simulation configurations using in-line visualization, and three configurations of in-transit visualization. This chart demonstrates that based on simulation time and resources, the simulation can proceed further with in-transit visualization vs. in-line visualization.

For example, a $Delay(0)$ configuration with 16384 simulation processors can complete 26 cycles using in-line visualization and 42 cycles using in-transit ($Alloc(25\%)$). This means that a 25% increase in compute power led to a 61% increase in productivity ($42/26 \times 100\% - 100\%$). Similarly, $Delay(0)$ and $Alloc(50\%)$ yields a 100% increase in productivity (26 cycles to 52 cycles) for 50% more resources, $Delay(10)$ and $Alloc(12\%)$ yields a 46% increase (15 cycles to 22 cycles) for 12% more resources, and $Delay(10)$ and $Alloc(25\%)$ yields an 80% increase (15 cycles to 27 cycles) for 25% more resources.

Figure 6 shows the total times for the $Delay(0)$ configuration where visualization was performed on every cycle, and every third cycle. For in-line visualization, the reduction in total time and reduction of frequency are nearly identical at 1/3. For the in-transit $Alloc(12\%)$ case, the reduction in total time is much more dramatic. When the visualization frequency is every simulation cycle, the simulation is stalled because there are not enough resources to keep up with the simulation. However, with a reduction in visualization frequency, the reduced allocation can keep up with the simulation, and the total time drops dramatically.

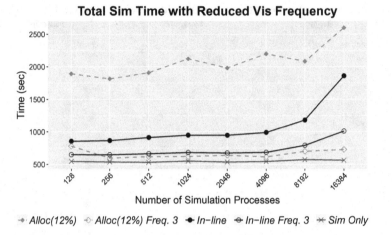

Fig. 6. Total execution time for the $Delay(0)$ simulation using in-line visualization and the $Alloc(12\%)$ in-transit visualization at two different frequencies, an image every step, and an image every third step. This chart demonstrates the large time savings that can be gained for in-transit visualization by reducing visualization frequency.

4.2   Total Cost

Figure 7 shows the cost of the node allocation for the selected configurations. We define this cost simply as $TotalTime \times TotalNodes$. This formulation takes into account that the in-transit method uses additional resources, allowing for the comparison to consider all resources used. In the in-transit case, because the simulation allocation is much larger than the visualization allocation, the costs are much higher where more simulation stalling occurs. This can be seen in the $Delay(0)$ configuration, particularly for $Alloc(12\%)$ in-transit visualization. In $Delay(10)$ and $Delay(20)$, we see nearly identical costs for the in-line and in-transit $Alloc(25\%)$ and $Alloc(50\%)$ configurations up to 8192 processes. For these cases, the extra resources pay for themselves.

The $Alloc(12\%)$ and $Delay(20)$ configuration is notable as the cost for in-transit becomes less than the cost for the in-line configuration at higher concurrency. This is a case where adding additional resources results in both a reduced time to solution, and a reduced allocation cost.

4.3   Scalability of Visualization Algorithms

The visualization pipeline used in this study consists of two operations: isocontouring and parallel rendering.

The isocontouring operation for both in-line and in-transit visualization cases selects values based on the minimum and maximum data values at each time step, which requires global communication of extents, i.e., two doubles per process. The cost of computing isocontours is a function of how much output geometry

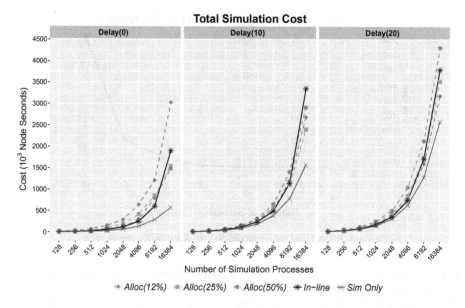

Fig. 7. Total cost in node-seconds to run the three simulation configurations using in-line visualization and three configurations of in-transit visualization.

is produced, which is dependent on the input data. Data blocks that do not contain the isovalues can be ignored. Workload imbalance is possible because the amount of work to perform is not the same for each data block.

The parallel rendering algorithm consists of two stages. First, each process renders the geometry produced by the isocontour operation, and second, these rendered images are combined using a parallel compositing algorithm to produce the final image. The parallel compositing algorithm requires significant communication.

Figure 8 shows the total time for rendering for simulation $Delay(0)$ using both in-line and in-transit paradigms. A sharp rise in rendering time occurs for in-line visualization at levels of concurrency above 2048. As described previously, the parallel rendering algorithm consists of two stages: rendering of data blocks, and parallel image compositing. The performance of in-line visualization is impacted by both stages of the parallel rendering algorithm. The input to the rendering are the isocontours generated in the previous step of the pipeline. The data blocks that contain more geometry will take more time to render. Likewise, the data blocks with less geometry will take less time to render.

For in-line visualization, each process has a single data block, and all of the processes will wait until the longest process is finished. Second, and more impactful, the performance of the parallel compositing algorithm is a function of the concurrency. Higher levels of concurrency require more communication, reducing the performance [24].

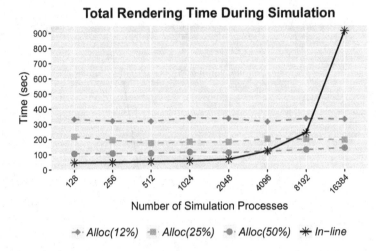

Fig. 8. Total time spent during rendering for the $Delay(0)$ configuration of the simulation for in-line and in-transit visualization. A communication bottleneck can be observed at high concurrency with in-line in situ as the time to perform rendering increases dramatically.

For in-transit visualization, a different situation exists. First, each visualization process is assigned multiple data blocks. When multiple blocks are assigned to each process, better load balancing is more likely to naturally occur. Second, and more impactful, the parallel compositing algorithm is run at lower concurrency, and so the performance is better.

Figure 9 shows a histogram of the idle times for the in-line and the $Alloc(50\%)$ in-transit case running on the $Delay(20)$ simulation at 16384 processors. The idle timings provide a higher-level look at the overall performance of the visualization operations. The idle time captures the amount of time each process spends waiting for other processes to complete. For in-line visualization, the histogram shape indicates significant idle time for a large number of processes. Note that there are a couple of in-line processes with little to no idle time, they are just not visible on this plot. On the other hand, the idle times for in-transit visualization lie much closer to zero, indicating much better load balancing across the entire visualization pipeline. These effects are the result of the load imbalance in isocountouring and rendering, and the decreased scalability in parallel compositing that were described above.

5   Discussion

In this section we revisit the results presented in Sect. 4, and consider them in the broader context of the tradeoffs associated with in-line and in-transit in situ. Simulations, along with their requirements and resources, are unique. The same simulations could have different requirements based on the type of run

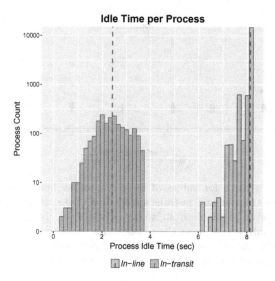

Fig. 9. Log scale histogram showing the idle time for each process during a single visualization step. The data shown are from the $Delay(20)$ simulation configuration run on 16384 processes, using in-line, and in-transit $Alloc(50\%)$ configurations for visualization. The dotted vertical lines give the mean value for both cases. This chart shows that in-line in situ causes higher per process idle times, driving up the total simulation time. Note that there are a couple of processes for each paradigm with no idle time, but they are not visible on this plot.

being performed, when the results are required, and the available resources. The major tradeoffs to consider are related to the time to solution (see Sect. 4.1) and the cost (see Sect. 4.2). When resources are available, time to solution might be the primary driver. Conversely, if resources are restricted, the cost might become the primary driver.

In Sect. 5.1 we discuss a cost model for both in situ visualization paradigms and provide some analysis that can help inform decisions. In Sect. 5.2 we discuss factors for consideration when time to solution is a primary driver.

5.1   In-line and In-transit Cost Models

The model for the cost of in-line visualization (C_V) can be described as:

$$C_V = (S + V)N_S \tag{1}$$

where S is the time to compute the simulation, V is the time to compute visualization, and N_S is the number of nodes used.

The model for the cost of in-transit visualization (C_T) can be described as:

$$C_T = (S + T_{IN})(N_S + N_D) \tag{2}$$

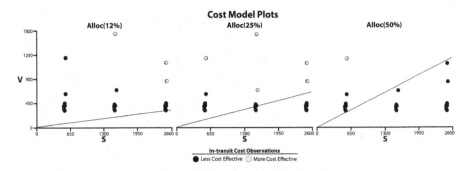

Fig. 10. Solutions of Eq. 3 for values of T_{IN}. A contour line of $T_{IN} = 0$ is shown representing a data transfer and in-transit stall time of 0 s. Below this line in-transit visualization will never be viable from a cost perspective, given that any amount of transfer time will make it cost more than in-line. The data points for each experiment in the study are also shown, and indicate if the experiment cost more (black) or less (white) than the comparable in-line test.

where S and N_S are as defined above. T_{IN} is the simulation stall time caused by transferring data to visualization resources, as well as any stall from the simulation when waiting for the visualization to complete. N_D is the number of nodes used for visualization.

The costs of in-line and in-transit visualization are equal when Eqs. 1 and 2 are equal. Setting them equal, and solving for T_{IN} gives:

$$T_{IN} = \frac{V N_S - S N_D}{(N_S + N_D)} \tag{3}$$

Given a simulation time (S), in-line visualization time (V), and a particular resource allocation $(N_S$ and $N_D)$, Eq. 3 gives the in-transit visualization data transfer time required for the costs of both paradigms to be equal. Smaller time values of T_{IN} will lower the cost of in-transit visualization with respect to in-line visualization. Conversely, larger time values of T_{IN} will raise the cost of in-transit visualization with respect to in-line visualization.

Figure 10 shows the solution to Eq. 3 as a function of S and V for the fixed configurations $(N_S$ and $N_D)$ used in our study. The black line in each chart denotes where $T_{IN} = 0$ for each (S, V) pair for Eq. 3. That is, in order for in-transit visualization to cost less than in-line visualization, the value of T_{IN}, must be zero. This is not physically possible, so (S, V) pairs below that line will always cost more using in-transit visualization. For (S, V) locations above the line, the in-transit visualization time must be less or equal to the value of T_{IN} in Eq. 3 in order for the cost to be less than in-line visualization.

Data points from our study are also shown in Fig. 10. For each configuration (N_S, N_D) in our study, the experiment generates values for S, V, and T_{IN}. Each point indicates an (S, V) data value, and the color of the point indicates if T_{IN} was less than (white) or greater than (black) the value in Eq. 3. The slope of the

$T_{IN} = 0$ contour provides an indicator of the performance requirements for in-transit visualization. As the slope increases (and resources used rises), increased performance is required.

5.2   In-Line and In-Transit Time to Solution

When time to solution is the primary driver, understanding the performance characteristics of the visualization and analysis algorithms used is important. If the algorithms scale well with respect to the number of simulation resources, in-transit visualization is likely to be slower, since it will be bottlenecked by both the network transfer time and the time to complete the analysis routine on the separate smaller set of resources. That is, if the visualization and analysis algorithms scale well, the time to perform them in-line will likely be faster than the time it would take to transfer the data across the network. Conversely, if the algorithm does not scale well, i.e. requires a lot of global or inter rank communication, then in-transit may be faster overall. This phenomenon of algorithms performing poorly at scale was demonstrated in our study as the parallel rendering was scaled up, as in Fig. 8. In such situations, the reduced concurrency provided by the in-transit paradigm translates into significant time savings.

6   Conclusion and Future Directions

In this paper, we have presented a study that compares the performance of the two major in situ paradigms: in-line and in-transit visualization. We believe understanding tradeoffs in execution time and cost between these two paradigms are critical for the efficient use of in situ methods to handle the growing data problem. Without this understanding, it is difficult to make informed decisions when designing analysis and visualization workflows. If one technique significantly outperforms the other (in either time or cost), the community is likely to favor that technique. Further, if the techniques have similar performance, then other axes of consideration can be used in the decision making process.

This work provides two major contributions towards that end. First, we present a study and analysis for both paradigms on a simulation running on an HPC system at scale. We varied control parameters that define how each paradigm is configured, and analyze the performance tradeoffs for each. Second, we have explored various models for quantifying the costs of performing visualization using each in situ paradigm.

Further, our experiments gave insight into our hypothesis presented at the beginning of Sect. 3. First, we demonstrated that there are particular configurations for the simulation and analysis such that one in situ paradigm outperforms the other. This is a somewhat surprising result for the in-transit paradigm, as it means that allocating additional resources for analysis can lead to not just faster execution time for the simulation, but faster to the extent that there are fewer cycles used even when considering the additional resources. Second, we demonstrated that a communication heavy algorithm (parallel rendering) can cause bottlenecks when using an in-line paradigm at high concurrency, but by using a lower concurrency in-transit paradigm those bottlenecks would decrease. We further demonstrated that an in-transit paradigm can provide better load balancing for visualization algorithms. Lastly, we provided models that quantify the cost of in situ visualization, and identified important relationships between the factors in each model and how they affect overall in situ cost.

In the future, we will perform follow up studies to better understand the behavior of both paradigms under different situations. These studies will include more visualization pipelines, different simulation codes, consider optimal numbers of visualization tasks to place per node in-transit, GPU's, and variations of both in-line and in-transit visualization that go beyond the common model. With this work we focused on a comparison based purely on time to solution and resource cost. There are additional factors of consideration [17] we would like to investigate in future work as well, as they provide insight into broader aspects when evaluating in situ visualization paradigms.

Acknowledgments. This material is based upon work supported by the U.S. Department of Energy, Office of Science, Office of Advanced Scientific Computing Research, Scientific Discovery through Advanced Computing (SciDAC) program. This research used resources of the Oak Ridge Leadership Computing Facility, which is a DOE Office of Science User Facility supported under Contract DE-AC05-00OR22725. This work was partially performed by UT-Battelle, LLC, with the US Department of Energy. This work was partially performed under the auspices of the U.S. Department of Energy by Lawrence Livermore National Laboratory under contract DE-AC52-07NA27344. Lawrence Livermore National Security, LLC (LLNL-CONF-769101).

References

1. Cloverleaf3d. http://uk-mac.github.io/CloverLeaf3D/. Accessed 19 Dec 2018
2. Adhinarayanan, V., Feng, W.C., Rogers, D., Ahrens, J., Pakin, S.: Characterizing and modeling power and energy for extreme-scale in-situ visualization. In: IEEE Parallel and Distributed Processing Symposium (IPDPS), pp. 978–987 (2017)
3. Ahern, S., et al.: Scientific Discovery at the Exascale: Report for the DOE ASCR Workshop on Exascale Data Management, Analysis, and Visualization, July 2011
4. Ahrens, J., Geveci, B., Law, C.: ParaView: an end-user tool for large-data visualization. In: The Visualization Handbook, pp. 717–731 (2005)
5. Ayachit, U., et al.: The SENSEI generic in situ interface. In: Workshop on In Situ Infrastructures for Enabling Extreme-Scale Analysis and Visualization (ISAV), pp. 40–44, November 2016
6. Ayachit, U., et al.: ParaView catalyst: enabling in situ data analysis and visualization. In: Workshop on In Situ Infrastructures for Enabling Extreme-Scale Analysis and Visualization (ISAV), pp. 25–29 (2015)
7. Ayachit, U., et al.: Performance analysis, design considerations, and applications of extreme-scale *In Situ* infrastructures. In: ACM/IEEE Conference for High Performance Computing, Networking, Storage and Analysis (SC16), November 2016
8. Bauer, A.C., et al.: *In Situ* methods, infrastructures, and applications on high performance computing platforms, a state-of-the-art (STAR) report. Comput. Graph. Forum **35**(3), 577 (2016). Proceedings of Eurovis 2016

9. Bennett, J.C., et al.: Combining in-situ and in-transit processing to enable extreme-scale scientific analysis. In: Proceedings of the International Conference on High Performance Computing, Networking, Storage and Analysis, pp. 49:1–49:9 (2012)
10. Childs, H., et al.: A contract-based system for large data visualization. In: Proceedings of IEEE Visualization 2005, pp. 190–198 (2005)
11. Childs, H., et al.: Extreme scaling of production visualization software on diverse architectures. IEEE Comput. Graph. Appl. (CG&A) 30(3), 22–31 (2010)
12. Dayal, J., et al.: Flexpath: type-based publish/subscribe system for large-scale science analytics. In: IEEE/ACM International Symposium on Cluster, Cloud and Grid Computing (CCGRID) (2014)
13. Docan, C., et al.: Dataspaces: an interaction and coordination framework for coupled simulation workflows. Cluster Comput. 15(2), 163–181 (2012)
14. Dorier, M., et al.: Damaris/viz: a nonintrusive, adaptable and user-friendly in situ visualization framework. In: IEEE Symposium on Large-Scale Data Analysis and Visualization (LDAV), pp. 67–75, October 2013
15. Gamell, M., et al.: Exploring power behaviors and trade-offs of in-situ data analytics. In: International Conference on High Performance Computing, Networking, Storage and Analysis (SC), pp. 1–12 (2013)
16. Goodale, T., et al.: The cactus framework and toolkit: design and applications. In: Palma, J.M.L.M., Sousa, A.A., Dongarra, J., Hernández, V. (eds.) VECPAR 2002. LNCS, vol. 2565, pp. 197–227. Springer, Heidelberg (2003). https://doi.org/10.1007/3-540-36569-9_13
17. Kress, J., et al.: Loosely coupled in situ visualization: a perspective on why it's here to stay. In: Workshop on In Situ Infrastructures for Enabling Extreme-Scale Analysis and Visualization (ISAV), pp. 1–6, November 2015
18. Larsen, M., et al.: The ALPINE in situ infrastructure: ascending from the ashes of strawman. In: Workshop on In Situ Infrastructures on Enabling Extreme-Scale Analysis and Visualization (ISAV), pp. 42–46 (2017)
19. Liu, Q., et al.: Hello ADIOS: the challenges and lessons of developing leadership class I/O frameworks. Concurrency Comput. Pract. Experience 26(7), 1453–1473 (2014)
20. Mallinson, A., et al.: Cloverleaf: preparing hydrodynamics codes for exascale. The Cray User Group (2013)
21. Moreland, K., et al.: VTK-m: accelerating the visualization toolkit for massively threaded architectures. Comput. Graph. Appl. 36(3), 48–58 (2016)
22. Oldfield, R.A., Moreland, K., Fabian, N., Rogers, D.: Evaluation of methods to integrate analysis into a large-scale shock shock physics code. In: Proceedings of the 28th ACM International Conference on Supercomputing, pp. 83–92. ACM (2014)
23. Parker, S., Johnson, C.: SCIRun: a scientific programming environment for computational steering. In: ACM/IEEE Conference on Supercomputing, p. 52 (1995)
24. Peterka, T., Ma, K.L.: Parallel image compositing methods. In: High Performance Visualization: Enabling Extreme-Scale Scientific Insight (2012)
25. Rodero, I., et al.: Evaluation of in-situ analysis strategies at scale for power efficiency and scalability. In: IEEE/ACM Symposium on Cluster, Cloud and Grid Computing (CCGrid), pp. 156–164 (2016)
26. Whitlock, B., Favre, J., Meredith, J.: Parallel in situ coupling of simulation with a fully featured visualization system. In: Proceedings of the 11th Eurographics Conference on Parallel Graphics and Visualization, pp. 101–109 (2011)
27. Zhang, F., et al.: In-memory staging and data-centric task placement for coupled scientific simulation workflows. Concurrency Comput. Pract. Experience 29(12), e4147 (2017)

Emerging Technologies

Layout-Aware Embedding for Quantum Annealing Processors

Jose P. Pinilla$^{(\boxtimes)}$ and Steven J. E. Wilton

University of British Columbia, Vancouver, BC, Canada
{jpinilla,stevew}@ece.ubc.ca

Abstract. Due to the physical limit in connectivity between qubits in Quantum Annealing Processors (QAPs), when sampling from a problem formulated as an Ising graph model, it is necessary to *embed* the problem onto the physical lattice of qubits. A valid mapping of the problem nodes into qubits often requires qubit chains to ensure connectivity.

We introduce the concept of layout-awareness for *embedding*; wherein information about the layout of the input and target graphs is used to guide the allocation of qubits to each problem node. We then evaluate the consequent impact on the sampling distribution obtained from D-Wave's QAP, and provide a set of tools to assist developers in targeting QAP architectures using layout-awareness. We quantify the results from a layout-agnostic and a layout-aware embedding algorithm on (a) the success rate and time at finding valid embeddings, (b) the metrics of the resulting chains and interactions, and (c) the energy profile of the annealing samples. The latter results are obtained by running experiments on a D-Wave Quantum Annealer, and are directly related to the ability of the device to solve complex problems.

Our technique effectively reduces the search space, which improves the time and success rate of the embedding algorithm and/or finds mappings that result in lower energy samples from the QAP. Together, these contributions are an important step towards an understanding of how near-future Computer-Aided Design (CAD) tools can work in concert with quantum computing technologies to solve previously intractable problems.

Keywords: Quantum annealing · Minor-embedding · QUBO

1 Introduction

As quantum computing technologies evolve, Quantum Annealing Processors (QAPs) have emerged as a promising path for the use of quantum effects to solve the minimization of Quadratic Unconstrained Binary Optimization (QUBO) problems. Commercial implementations of QAPs, such as those from D-Wave, have been made available for almost a decade [19]. With recent open access for the general public [14], this technology is now in reach of the masses, allowing its impact to be felt broadly. Central to the use of QAPs is the formulation of

© Springer Nature Switzerland AG 2019
M. Weiland et al. (Eds.): ISC High Performance 2019, LNCS 11501, pp. 121–139, 2019.
https://doi.org/10.1007/978-3-030-20656-7_7

QUBO or Ising Spin Glass (ISG) graphical models for NP problems [20,27,32]. These problems must then be mapped to qubits available on the QAP lattice, and repeatedly put through quantum annealing to collect *samples* that minimize the total energy of the ISG formulation; or Ising model. This mapping step, or *minor-embedding*, typically requires the use of extra qubits solely to provide connections between qubits which are otherwise not coupled in the architecture, leading to "qubit chains". Besides wasting qubits which could otherwise be used for computation, long chains can lead to annealing solutions that poorly approximate the optimum solution to the original problem being solved.

The limited connectivity between qubits in the QAP, as well as the presence of defective qubits which must be avoided, makes this mapping problem difficult, and has been shown to be NP-Hard [11]. Yet, finding a good solution to the problem is vital for at least two reasons: (a) the capabilities of the mapping algorithm can determine the size (or complexity) of the problems that can be solved, especially in the presence of defective qubits, and (b) the quality (energy levels) of the annealing samples depends on the structure of the mapping. We anticipate that future QAP architectures will achieve several improvements over the current generation [23], e.g. number of qubits, higher connectivity, lower parameter noise, and more control on the annealing schedule (required for fair sampling [24,28]); but will continue to require the step of *minor-embedding* due to the graph's connectivity not being complete [10,13].

Degradation effects from qubit *chains* on the overall performance of quantum annealing has been the focus of previous studies [17,30,39,44]. In this paper, we extend the study beyond the effects seen for artificial qubit chains, and consider real problems to better understand the impact of long chains, and more generally, to understand the capabilities of the algorithm used for *minor-embedding*. We then use these findings to develop a new algorithm that takes advantage of layout information available in many optimization problems, but also attainable for any Ising model. To ensure our results are meaningful, energy results are gathered on a D-Wave 2000Q with 2038 operating qubits. The topology of the qubits in this machine is a 16×16 Chimera graph [10] with 8 nodes per tile as in Fig. 1.

The potential impact of this work is two-fold. First, the data presented here will motivate future development into *minor-embedding* algorithms, and will provide important resources and tools to guide future investigation in this area. For quantum annealing technologies to continue to advance as a feasible approach for quantum computing, work in this area is critical. Second, and more generally, this work is a step towards goals set forth for near-future Computer-Aided Design (CAD) tools for Noisy Intermediate-Scale Quantum (NISQ) technologies [36]. We expect that, in the long term, *minor-embedding* algorithms will be as critical to computing as placement algorithms are to VLSI design today.

This paper is organized as follows. Section 2 first presents background related to QAPs and *minor-embedding*. Section 3 then motivates and introduces the concept of layout-awareness for *minor-embedding*, with layout-aware embedding methods detailed in Sect. 4. Finally, in Sect. 5 we evaluate our work with real-world problems in terms of the ability of the algorithm to find valid embeddings and the energies of the samples from those embeddings.

2   Background

2.1   Quantum Annealing

Programming D-Wave's QAP requires the description of a problem as the minimization of the dimensionless energy of an Ising graph model, as in (1); with N variables (nodes), $s_i \in \{-1, +1\}$, describing the ith site's spin; and parameters h_i and J_{ij} for the local longitudinal magnetic fields (bias) and the coupling between sites (edge weights), respectively. D-Wave's device samples from low energy spin configurations $s = \{s_1, s_2, ..., s_N\}$ of the Ising model through Quantum Annealing (QA) [19].

$$E(s) = \sum_{i=1}^{N} h_i s_i + \sum_{i<j} J_{ij} s_i s_j \tag{1}$$

In QA, the initial and problem Hamiltonians, $\hat{H}_I$ and $\hat{H}_P$, describe the system according to the time-dependent $\hat{H}(t)$ in (2); with annealing time T, $t \in [0, T]$, and Pauli[1] operators $\hat{\sigma}_\alpha^{(i)}$ acting on qubit i. At any point in time the system is relaxing towards the lowest-energy states or eigenvectors $|s_1 s_2 ... s_N\rangle$ with the smallest eigenvalues of $\hat{H}(t)$. Solving for the lowest-energy state, or ground state, of $\hat{H}_P$ is the same as finding the $\arg \min_s$ of the energy function (1).

$$\hat{H}(t) = \overbrace{-\frac{1}{2} \sum_{i=1}^{N} \Delta_i(t) \hat{\sigma}_x^{(i)}}^{\hat{H}_I} + \frac{1}{2} \mathcal{E}(t) \hat{H}_P$$

$$\hat{H}_P = \sum_{i=1}^{N} h_i \hat{\sigma}_z^{(i)} + \sum_{i<j} J_{ij} \hat{\sigma}_z^{(i)} \hat{\sigma}_z^{(j)} \tag{2}$$

QA is achieved through the gradual introduction of $\hat{H}_P$, and the reliance on the adiabatic theorem which implies that the system will remain in its ground state, or the lowest energy configuration, throughout the anneal. Initially, $\hat{H}_I$ is programmed to dominate the system by setting a high transverse energy for all qubits using $\Delta_i(t)$, while scaling down the longitudinal energies h_i using $\mathcal{E}(t)$; $\Delta_i(0) \gg \mathcal{E}(0) \approx 0$. The process runs until $\mathcal{E}(T) \gg \Delta_i(T) \approx 0$, at which point, the state of the system is governed by $\hat{H}_P$. With this, the new ground state of the system encodes a solution to the optimization problem. Our experiments use D-Wave's default annealing schedule with time $T = 20\,\mu s$ per sample. The correct setting of the anneal schedule, given by the energy scales $\mathcal{E}(t)$ and $\Delta_i(t)$, affects the likelihood of obtaining the lowest energy. Having a very fast schedule

---

[1] With $\hat{\sigma}_x = \begin{pmatrix} 0 & 1 \\ 1 & 0 \end{pmatrix}$; $\hat{\sigma}_y = \begin{pmatrix} 0 & -i \\ i & 0 \end{pmatrix}$; $\hat{\sigma}_z = \begin{pmatrix} 1 & 0 \\ 0 & -1 \end{pmatrix}$; $\hat{\sigma}_\alpha^{(i)} = \overbrace{I \otimes ... \otimes I}^{i-1} \otimes \hat{\sigma}_\alpha \otimes \overbrace{I \otimes ... \otimes I}^{N-i}$.

might cause the system to leave the ground state set with $\hat{H}_I$ and "jump" to an excited state during the anneal. This jumps are made easier if the *minimum energy gap* between the ground and first excited states is smaller [30]. The finite temperature operation of QAPs allows those "jumps", and therefore contribute to the indeterminism and non-optimality of the distribution of results.

2.2 Minor-Embedding

The limited connectivity of the QAP means a straightforward one-to-one mapping, from variables to qubits, is not likely to lead to a successful implementation, and may require the use of qubit *chains*. A *chain* is an extension of a problem vertex over multiple connected qubits. Mapping of the problem graph $\mathcal{G} = \{\mathbf{P}, \mathbf{E}\}$, with nodes $\mathbf{P}$ and edges $\mathbf{E}$, to the Chimera graph $\mathcal{H} = \{\mathbf{Q}, \mathbf{C}\}$, with qubits $\mathbf{Q}$ and couplers $\mathbf{C}$, can be formulated as a *minor-embedding* problem [11].

Definition. *A graph $\mathcal{G}$ is a minor of $\mathcal{H}$ if $\mathcal{G}$ is isomorphic to a graph obtained from a subgraph of $\mathcal{H}$ by successively contracting edges.*

Therefore, a QAP samples from the energy function in (3), which differs from the source formulation (1) in that qubit *chains* and split qubit *interactions* are put in place to have the formulation match the QAP's topology. A qubit chain of length λ_i is given by $Q_i = \{s_i^{(k)} | k \in [1, \lambda_i]\}$, with $s_i^{(k)}$ being the kth physical qubit mapped to the ith variable s_i. The number of *interactions* is the connectivity κ_{ij} between chains Q_i and Q_j; also interpretable as the size of the *cut-set* $\{(k, l) \in \mathbf{C} | k \in Q_i, l \in Q_j\}$. Chains are connected using a *ferromagnetic coupling* $J_{FM} = 1.0$; also called *chain strength*.

Long chains are detrimental to the QA algorithm. Samples from a QAP may return results with "broken chains", which are mismatched physical qubits for the same variable. The *chain break method* of choice, to determine the sample value of i from a broken chain, is the majority vote with random tiebreaker [1,4,37]; $s_i = sign(\sum_k^{\lambda_i} s_i^{(k)})$. Having larger λ_i and κ_{ij} may also increase the resolution required for the parameters to represent the problem, which is undesirable [12].

$$E_{emb}(\boldsymbol{s}) = \sum_i^N \sum_k^{\lambda_i} \frac{h_i}{\lambda_i} s_i^{(k)} + \sum_{i<j}^{\lambda_i} \sum_k^{\lambda_j} \sum_l \frac{J_{ij}}{\kappa_{ij}} s_i^{(k)} s_j^{(l)} - J_{FM} \sum_i^N \sum_{k<l} s_i^{(k)} s_i^{(l)} \quad (3)$$

The dimension, topology, and connectivity of the target graph grows with new generations of physical annealing machines and, due to manufacturing limitations, some qubits in the QAP graph may not be functional. Therefore, the problem should consider both $\mathcal{G}$ and $\mathcal{H}$ as inputs.

There are two common approaches for minor-embedding described in previous QAP applications. Some approaches use systematic methods that are specific to their Ising model formulation [1,20,47]. Others, more often, rely on running the heuristic provided by D-Wave [11] for multiple iterations and selecting the "best" embedding in that batch [16, 18, 22, 34, 45, 48]. The "best" embedding is the one with the lowest qubit count, and/or lowest maximum chain length. This ambiguity in the preferred metrics is witnessed specially when choosing embeddings for fully-connected graphs [2, 4, 26, 31].

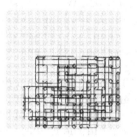 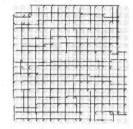 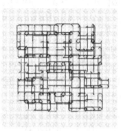

(a) Layout-Agnostic [11]   (b) Layout-Aware Disperse   (c) Layout-Aware Combined
Total: 648. Max Chain: 7.   Total: 553. Max Chain: 4.   Total: 529. Max Chain: 4.
Avg Chain±Stdev: Avg Chain±Stdev: Avg Chain±Stdev:
2.53±1.34.   2.16±0.76.   2.07±0.86.

Fig. 1. Qualitative and quantitative comparison between embedding methods. (Color figure online)

3 Layout-Awareness

The adjacency of graph $\mathcal{G}$, which is the user's input to the embedding algorithm, represents the problem to be solved. For many problems, nodes in the problem graph may have natural "location information" that can be deduced by understanding how the graph is created from the problem instance; or artificially generated using graph drawing heuristics. Existing embedding heuristics are based only on the immediate adjacency when mapping each problem node to qubits. In our approach, we use the location information to help guide the mapping heuristics.

In this section, we motivate our work by showing that the inclusion of this location information in embedding algorithms, which we refer to as *layout-awareness*, can have a significant effect on the characteristics of the resulting mapping and, as a result, on the energy profile produced by a QAP sampling from that mapping.

To show this, in this section we focus on a single test case: a 16×16 two-dimensional grid with all biases h_i set to 0, and all $J_{i,j}$ set to a random value from a uniform distribution inside the range $(-1, 1)$. Presenting results for a test case such as this provides insight into the relationship between layout, embedding metrics, and energy. In Sect. 5 we consider more complex test cases to understand how well our approach solves real-world problems; i.e. irregular non-planar graphs with higher density and connectivity.

We use three embedding algorithms to characterize layout-awareness. The first we refer to as *Layout-Agnostic*; this is the default algorithm used in the commercial D-Wave programming flow [11,15]. The second and third, which we refer to as *Disperse* and *Combined* respectively, use layout information to guide the embedding heuristic. These algorithms are described in detail in the next section, but results are presented here to motivate our approach. We make use of spatial layout information to either initiate the search of qubit assignments from candidate regions of the target graph, in the *Disperse* method; or to produce an initial placement that is further optimized using the heuristic in [11] to generate a valid embedding, in the *Combined* method.

To represent each method, we ran each algorithm 10 times, each with a different seed, producing 10 embeddings of our 16×16 grid for each algorithm. The mappings in Fig. 1 are the ones found with the lowest qubit count from the sets of 10. Qualitatively, layout-awareness can be observed in the chains plotted in Fig. 1, where each colour represents a node in the input problem. The *Agnostic* method results in a congested, irregular mapping of the otherwise regular structure of the grid. The *Disperse* method, using each tile (8 qubits) in the 16×16 Chimera graph as candidate set for each problem node, preserves layout information while also avoiding disabled qubits, and yields an embedding that is more "spread out" in favour of consistent spacing and reduced congestion during routing. The *Combined* method preserves some of the regularity of the grid, while also generating a more concentrated use of qubits in the target graph. Quantitatively, the layout-agnostic approach results in higher values for all observed metrics, i.e. total number of qubits, maximum chain length, and standard deviation; while both layout-aware methods deliver results that take advantage of the regular planar layout of the 2D grid, both having a lower maximum chain length. Moreover, the *Combined* approach is able to minimize the total number of qubits, compared to the *Disperse* result, which, in turn, minimizes deviation in the results. These results suggest that the choice of algorithm can significantly impact the chain length metrics in the resulting embeddings and that the guidance given by layout-awareness is a useful addition to minor-embedding heuristics. Our experiments can be reproduced using our open source tools [35].

We now relate the embedding metrics to the energies of the samples obtained from the D-Wave machine. To gather these results, we collected 10000 samples for each of the 30 different embeddings described in this section. All experiments were run on the same D-Wave 2000Q machine available through D-Wave's online service [14]. The energy values correspond to the "unembedded" Ising model [12], after resolving broken chains. We use the median for energy, not the mean, because the results from each run (10000 samples) are skewed and not normally distributed [41]; which makes quantiles a more meaningful choice of metric. Each plot in Fig. 2 shows results for all 30 embeddings. For each embedding, we measured maximum and average chain length λ_i, and maximum interactions κ_{ij}, against the minimum and median of the energies sampled from the QAP, and plotted one point in each graph. The plots for minimum energy also include a

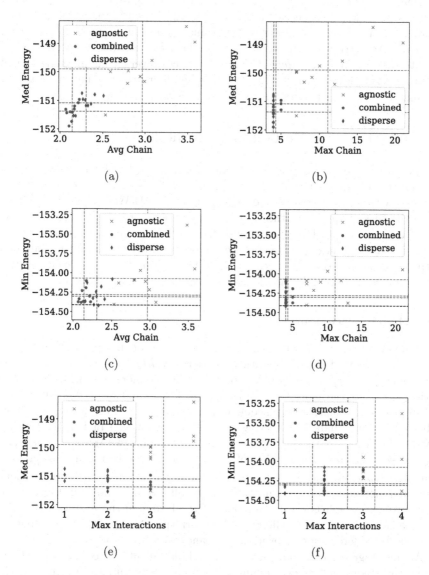

Fig. 2. D-Wave energy statistics from 10000 Samples for 10 16 × 16 2D grid embeddings using three different methods. The x position for each dot is an embedding metric, while the y position is either median or minimum energy of the results for each of the 10000 samples. The dotted lines represent the averages across the 10 embeddings. The dotted black line is the solution found classically using tabu search. Note that presenting results in terms of minimum and median energy is different from previous work where the results are fit to an expected Boltzmann distribution [25]; we do not have enough data to be confident that any particular distribution is appropriate.

solution, of the original problem, found classically using tabu search and allowed an indiscriminately long processing time. As can be seen in the graphs, the best results, that is, those with lower energy values, were found by the layout-aware methods. We attribute this observation to the fact that, for this example, the layout-aware methods minimize the maximum and average chain length, which in turn, leads to lower energy solutions. This highlights the role layout-awareness can play in obtaining results optimized towards those goals.

4 Layout-Aware Embedding Methods

We propose a 2-stage minor-embedding algorithm using layout-aware global placement and detailed routing. During the first stage, each node $p \in \mathbf{P}$ is matched with a set of *candidate* qubits $Q_p \subset \mathbf{Q}$. For D-Wave's 2000Q QAP, we chose the tiles (8 qubits in tile j, k) of the Chimera[2] graph as candidate bins. Then, a routing algorithm for each node finds a qubit, or *chain* of qubits, guided by the initial candidate assignment. We explore two alternative routing methods, both based on negotiated congestion. The first method is the *Disperse* router, detailed in Sect. 4.3, while the second method in Sect. 4.4 is based on [11].

4.1 Global Placement

The global placement stage uses each node's location in the problem layout (x_p, y_p) and the grid size of the target Chimera (N, M), to superpose a *stretched out* geometry (x_p', y_p') of the problem on top of the Chimera tiles grid. The qubits in tile (j_p, k_p) are the candidates for node p; $j_p = \lfloor x_p' \rfloor$ and $k_p = \lfloor y_p' \rfloor$. Although a routing guided by this initial placement may result in a valid solution, stretching will lead to long chains connecting distant nodes, as seen in Fig. 1b. Usually, downscaling the superposed layout is enough to meet a target *concentration* $(d_{j,k} = \frac{P_{j,k}}{S_{j,k}})$, given as the number of problem nodes mapped to a tile $P_{j,k}$, over that tile's *supply* of functional qubits $S_{j,k}$; the latter is to account for qubit yield. A down-scaled candidate assignment for a graph layout is shown in Fig. 3a. The input problem graph is the Ising model of the layout in the inset; see Sect. 5.1 for details. In that Figure, different colors correspond to qubits in the same tile occupied by different nodes; overlapping candidates are allowed.

At this stage, we can transform the initial placement to meet two objectives: (1) spread nodes out of overpopulated regions (*diffusion*) to ensure that the demand for each tile $P_{j,k}$ does not exceed the supply $S_{j,k}$; and (2) migrate nodes from sparsely populated regions into denser regions (*compaction*) in order to improve resource utilization. We propose a diffusion-based migration algorithm targeting those objectives. A diffusion-based method is appealing because it is $O(|\mathbf{P}|)$; $|\mathbf{P}|$ being the size of the input problem. Layout-aware algorithms, however, are not constrained to the use of this method for layout transformations.

---

[2] We also developed a flow for future QAP architectures, such as Pegasus [8], but Pegasus machines have not been made available for public usage.

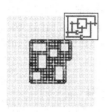

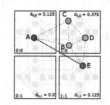

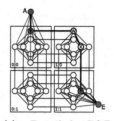

(a) Global Placement with highlighted candidates for a QCA layout.

(b) Global Placement with final tile concentrations $d_{j,k}$.

(c) Detailed P&R with highlighted shortest path A to E.

Fig. 3. Layout-aware embedding flow. (Color figure online)

4.2 Diffusion-Based Migration

The concept of diffusion has been applied to CAD tools in the context of VLSI and FPGA placement [3,38]. Migration (movement of nodes over time $\frac{\partial d_{x,y}}{\partial t}$) is proportional to the local curvature of the *concentration* gradient, and the diffusivity of the medium D. We define D in (4) as the overall density of the embedding, times an expected occupancy α, or the number of qubits expected to be used per problem node; we chose $\alpha = 3$. The choice of D causes higher migration for low global densities, and lower migration for limited qubit availability.

$$\frac{\partial d_{x,y}}{\partial t} = D\nabla^2 d_{x,y}; \qquad D = 1 - \frac{\alpha|\boldsymbol{P}|}{|\boldsymbol{Q}|}; \qquad \alpha = 3 \qquad (4)$$

(1) Diffusion can be achieved by applying a velocity field which, in the space discretized by the Chimera tiles, translates to the equations in (5), dependent on the concentration in each tile and its neighbours, at discretized time step n; where $t = n\Delta t$ and a choice of $\Delta t = 0.2$.

$$v_{j,k}^X(n) = -\frac{d_{j+,k}(n) - d_{j-,k}(n)}{2d_{j,k}(n)}; \qquad v_{j,k}^Y(n) = -\frac{d_{j,k+}(n) - d_{j,k-}(n)}{2d_{j,k}(n)} \qquad (5)$$

(2) Compaction is achieved by forcing the migration of nodes to the centre of the tile grid using a modified velocity field $v'_{j,k}(n)$. To do this, in (6), we replace one of the concentration terms with a high concentration using a node limit $P_{LIM} = 6$ over the Maximum supply $S_{MAX} = 8$, while the other term is replaced with the concentration at the "attractor" tiles; or the concentrations at the neighbouring tiles of (j, k) that are horizontally (d_h), vertically (d_v), and oblique (d_o) towards the centre of the grid.

$$v'^X_{j,k}(n) = -\frac{\frac{P_{LIM}}{S_{MAX}} - \left(d_h(n) + \frac{d_o}{2}(n)\right)}{2d_{j,k}(n)} \qquad v'^Y_{j,k}(n) = -\frac{\frac{P_{LIM}}{S_{MAX}} - \left(d_v(n) + \frac{d_o}{2}(n)\right)}{2d_{j,k}(n)}$$

$$(6)$$

This gradient will have the direction relative to the "attractor" tiles. In (7), in order to translate the gradient into an absolute value and to assign it to a specific node, so that all nodes in a tile do not move equally, we use the x and y components of the distance from the centre of the grid $l_p^{X,Y}$.

$$v_p^X(n) = l_p^X(n)v_{j,k}'^X(n); \qquad v_p^Y(n) = l_p^Y(n)v_{j,k}'^Y(n)$$
$$l_p^X(n) = \frac{2x_p(n)}{N} - 1; \qquad l_p^Y(n) = \frac{2y_p(n)}{M} - 1 \tag{7}$$

Lastly, we use (8), which incorporates the velocity and diffusivity to calculate each node's placement at the next time step. The algorithm iterates until the dispersion, or average distance of the cells from the centre of the tile array, increases or has a cumulative variance lower than a predefined threshold.

$$x_p(n+1) = x_p(n) + Dv_p^X(n)\Delta t \qquad y_p(n+1) = y_p(n) + Dv_p^Y(n)\Delta t \tag{8}$$

As a result, the set of candidates Q_p is given by the qubits in tile ($j_p = \lfloor x_p \rfloor, k_p = \lfloor y_p \rfloor$) at the final iteration. Q_p can be expanded to neighbouring tiles or reduced to specific qubits in each tile. As an example, Fig. 3b shows a global placement for a graph with nodes $\mathbf{P} = \{A, B, C, D, E\}$. In it, the candidate qubits for node A are all the functional qubits in tile $(0,0)$, while the candidate qubits for E are all the functional qubits in tile $(1,1)$.

4.3   Disperse Router

To create the *Disperse* embeddings such as that in Fig. 1b we used the following approach. We create a *Routing graph* $\mathcal{F}$ in which we join the nodes $\mathbf{P}$ from the problem graph ($\mathcal{G} = \{\mathbf{P}, \mathbf{I}\}$) with the connected Chimera graph ($\mathcal{H} = \{\mathbf{Q}, \mathbf{C}\}$), and add edges from each node $p \in \mathbf{P}$ to the candidate qubits Q_p. Figure 3c shows a subgraph of a Routing Graph $\mathcal{F}$ with problem nodes A and E connected to their corresponding candidates. We use the adjacency of $\mathcal{G}$ to formulate a series of minimal Steiner tree problems. We iteratively solve for the minimal Steiner tree between p and the unrouted neighbouring nodes $\mathcal{N}(p)$ in $\mathcal{G}$, through the qubit nodes in $\mathcal{F}$. We use the negotiated congestion routing algorithm described below. Figure 3c shows a shortest path from nodes A to E through graph $\mathcal{F}$ which passes through four qubits (V, W, X, and Y).

We use a negotiated-congestion scheme, which is widely-used for FPGA routing [29], in which overlap of resources is initially allowed but the costs of using each qubit is recalculated until a *legal* solution is found. A solution is *legal* when the occupancy of the qubits do not have conflicts. We define the cost of using one qubit $c_q = b_q s_q h_q$ to depend on a base cost b_q, a present-sharing cost s_q, and a historical-sharing cost h_q. The base cost b_q, given in (9), is calculated using the degree Δ_q of a node in relation to the maximum degree Δ_{MAX}, and the scope cost ς_q, which favours qubits inside the same tile over those in neighbouring tiles.

$$b_q = 1 + \left(1 - \frac{\Delta_q}{\Delta_{MAX}}\right) + \varsigma_q; \quad \varsigma_q = \begin{cases} 0 & \text{if intra} \\ 0.2 & \text{if inter} \end{cases} \tag{9}$$

$$s_q(n) = 1 + \delta_s n k_q(n); \qquad h_q(n) = h_q(n-1) + \delta_h k_q(n); \qquad h_q(0) = 1 \qquad (10)$$

The congestion costs s_q and h_q, defined in (10), depend on the router iteration n, the respective cost steps δ_p and δ_h, and the present qubit occupancy $k_q(n)$. We also ensure that no paths between source and sink pass through only one qubit. We can view our global placement algorithm as an informed reduction of the search space. For each path, the qubit closest to the root is assigned to the root node, and the qubit closest to the sink is occupied by the sink node. In Fig. 3c, qubit V is assigned to node A, and qubit Y is assigned to node E. Qubits in between the source and sink (W, X, and Y in Fig. 3c) can be assigned to either the source or sink. We initially label these nodes as *unassigned*. During routing, if a path to a different sink node is found through an *unassigned* node, that node is assigned to the root node of that path. Once all connections have been routed, we make assignments for all remaining *unassigned* nodes by solving a linear programming problem to minimize the maximum chain length.

4.4 Combined Approach

The *Combined* approach creates a global placement as in Sect. 4.1, followed by the algorithm in [11] with each model initialized with the candidate qubits. In comparison with the *Disperse* router, the heuristic in [11] rips up conflicting or large sized models and performs a tree search starting from the mapped neighbours of the node to be placed. Negotiated Congestion is also used to calculate the cost of each unused vertex. Opposite to the disperse router, this approach allows models to move away from their candidate tiles and move toward more congested areas. As seen in Sect. 3, the *Combined* approach yielded better results in terms of average chain length, and comparable results for maximum chain length, when compared both to the layout-agnostic algorithm [11], and the *Disperse* router. The *Disperse* method tends to be too restrictive, and is outperformed by the *Combined* method for benchmarks with more complexity than the grid shown in Sect. 3. For the following sections we will focus on comparing D-Wave's layout-agnostic [11] heuristic with the layout-aware *Combined* flow.

4.5 Related Work

Our approach differs from problem-type specific, and systematic embedding methods. Problem-type specific methods [5–7,40,42,43] make use of "local" strategies, by embedding subsets of the problem graph, e.g. Constraints in Constraint Satisfaction Problems (CSP), followed by a routing stage connecting those subgraphs. Our approach can be categorized as "global", because problem nodes are allowed to take any location in the target graph. On the other hand, some applications can easily take advantage of systematic approaches for embedding. Three dimensional lattices [20] and complete bipartite graphs [1] can be embedded homogeneously, utilizing the complete fabric of the device. However, the nature of both of these approaches, as well as systematic clique methods [9,47], make them dependent on the regularity of the QAP graph. Imperfections in the qubit yield limit the viability of these methods and/or the feasible problem size to the size of the initial clique, even if the problem graph is not complete.

The programming flow of circuit model quantum computers also requires the mapping of logical qubits into physical qubits. This work does not target circuit model quantum computing fabrics; but due to their limited connectivity, and additional requirement to minimize qubit SWAPs within a decoherence time, we anticipate that layout-awareness could be beneficial in the mapping process.

5   Evaluation

In this section, we consider a larger set of benchmark problems, as shown in Table 1. Among these benchmark problems, we include different size 2D grids and Rook's graphs; models of Quantum-dot Cellular Automata (QCA) Networks, using the Ising formulation explained below; and $LANL1$ which is a problem known to be hard to embed using D-Wave's default algorithm [33] (and witnessed in the valid embedding count in Table 1). Unlike the other benchmarks, $LANL1$ does not have an intrinsic layout. To address this, we generate a spring layout every time we create an embedding. This problem was included in our benchmark set to allow us to demonstrate the applicability of layout-awareness to any type of Ising model. Reproduction of the following results, and open source implementations of our flow are available online [35].

Table 1. Benchmark characteristics and summary of embedding results. These benchmark problems are characterized by graph size $|P|$, number of edges $|E|$, graph density $D = \frac{2|E|}{|P|(|P|-1)}$, and beta index (or connectivity) $\beta = \frac{|E|}{|P|}$. Results are obtained from averaging 100 runs of a layout-agnostic and layout-aware algorithm for embedding time in seconds T(s); maximum, average, and standard deviation (σ) of chain lengths λ_i; maximum connectivity κ_i; and valid embeddings ($\checkmark$).

Benchmark					Agnostic [11]						Combined					
					T	λ_i			κ_i	$\checkmark$	T	λ_i			κ_i	$\checkmark$
Name	$\|P\|$	$\|E\|$	D	β	(s)	Max	Avg	σ	Max		(s)	Max	Avg	σ	Max	
QCA_MAJ5B	13	41	0.53	3.15	0.2	4.7	2.9	1	2.4	100	0.3	4.6	2.9	1	2.4	100
QCA_NOTFT	13	49	0.54	3.5	0.3	5	3.2	1	2.5	100	0.3	4.9	3.1	0.9	2.5	100
GRID2D_4X4	16	24	0.2	1.5	0.1	3	1.6	0.7	1.5	100	0.2	3.1	1.7	0.7	1.4	100
ROOKS_4X4	16	48	0.4	3	0.3	6.1	3.9	1.1	3.5	100	0.4	5.8	3.8	1	3.1	100
QCA_MAJ5A	19	88	0.51	4.63	0.6	7.1	4.5	1.5	3.4	100	0.5	7	4.4	1.6	3.4	100
QCA_SRFF	24	80	0.29	3.33	0.5	5.8	3.3	1.2	3	100	0.5	5.9	3.4	1.3	3	100
GRID2D_5X5	25	40	0.13	1.6	0.3	4	1.9	0.9	1.8	100	0.4	3.5	1.8	0.8	1.8	100
QCA_COPLANX	25	58	0.19	2.32	0.5	4.7	2.4	1.1	2.3	99	0.6	4.8	2.5	1.1	2.4	100
QCA_MUX	25	87	0.29	3.48	0.5	6.1	3.4	1.5	3.1	100	0.6	6.1	3.4	1.5	3.2	100
ROOKS_5X5	25	100	0.33	4	0.9	9.4	5.9	1.7	4.4	100	1	9.3	5.8	1.6	4.3	100
QCA_SOSC	33	112	0.21	3.39	1	6.5	3.5	1.3	3.4	100	0.9	6.3	3.5	1.3	3.4	100
QCA_XOR	77	256	0.09	3.32	2	11.4	4.1	2.2	4.4	100	1.6	6.9	3.6	1.4	4.1	100
QCA_FULLADD	101	305	0.06	3.02	2.9	12.5	3.6	2.1	4	90	1.6	6.8	3.3	1.4	3.9	100
QCA_SERADD	128	391	0.05	3.05	3.7	14.4	3.8	2.3	4.2	91	1.9	7	3.4	1.4	4.2	100
QCA_LOOPMEM	129	412	0.05	3.19	4.3	14.5	4	2.4	4.2	86	1.9	7.7	3.6	1.5	4.3	100
QCA_4BMUX	210	719	0.03	3.42	11.8	20.1	4.1	2.6	5.1	48	4.5	22.3	4.2	2.9	5.2	93
GRID2D_16X16	256	480	0.01	1.88	3.9	14	3	2.1	3.1	95	2.3	4.3	2.3	0.9	2.4	100
LANL1	269	490	0.01	1.82	5.4	27.7	3.4	3.8	3.6	33	3.4	17.9	3.1	2.9	3.7	100
QCA_4BACCUM	290	883	0.02	3.04	12.5	17.6	3.5	2.2	4.8	23	6.3	16.8	3.8	2.4	5.3	99

5.1   Benchmark Problems: Quantum-Dot Cellular Automata

Here we provide more details regarding the QCA simulation benchmarks. QCA [21] is a field-based computing technology based on the polarization of QCA cells, where the geometry of the design determines the polarity of each cell. Each QCA cell, disregarding the physical implementation, can be represented by four quantum dots and two moving charges interacting due to Coulombic repulsion. Therefore, a QCA cell can have state $|0\rangle$ with polarization -1 when charges are in the anti-diagonal $\left[\begin{smallmatrix} \bullet & \circ \\ \circ & \bullet \end{smallmatrix}\right]$, or state $|1\rangle$ with polarization 1 when charges are in the diagonal $\left[\begin{smallmatrix} \circ & \bullet \\ \bullet & \circ \end{smallmatrix}\right]$ dots. Interaction between cells causes each local configuration to propagate to neighbouring cells. QCA circuits, built from the basic components in Fig. 4, and as seen in the inset in Fig. 3a, are typically designed using layout-level tools (e.g. [46]), which makes them especially interesting for our layout-aware algorithm.

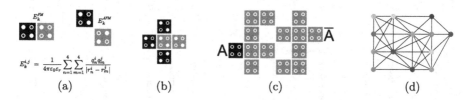

Fig. 4. (a) QCA wire and inverter showing ferromagnetic and anti-ferromagnetic coupling; "kink" energy $E_k^{i,j}$ depends on the locations r_n^i and charges q_n^i at dot n of cell i, and the free space and relative permitivities, ε_0 and ε_r (b) QCA majority voter (c) QCA fault tolerant NOT gate; QCA_NOTFT in Table 1 (d) Ising model graph of the QCA_NOTFT; the adjacency threshold is $r_{a,b} < 2.5$ and the driver cell is replaced by the $E_k^{i,d}$ biases.

In QCA simulation, the problem being solved for each model is to find the solution of the complete quantum mechanical formulation required to simulate cell-to-cell interactions, as given by the two-state approximation in (11).

$$\hat{H} = -\sum_{i=1}^{N} \gamma_i \hat{\sigma}_x(i) - \frac{1}{2}\sum_{i<j} E_k^{i,j}\hat{\sigma}_z(i)\hat{\sigma}_z(j) + \frac{1}{2}\sum_{d}\sum_{i=1}^{N} E_k^{i,d} P_d \hat{\sigma}_z(i) \qquad (11)$$

The three terms in (11) account for: the kinetic energy of moving charges in the cells, the energy due to the geometry of neighbouring cells, and the energy due to driver cells. Here, γ_i is the effective tunnelling energy used to control the "activation" of cells, P_d is the polarization of driver cell d, and $E_k^{a,b}$ is the "kink" energy; or the energy required to change the cell's polarization as a function of its proximity to other cells. When parsing the QCA layout, $E_k^{a,b}$ becomes negligible for distances greater than the span of a few cells due to $E_k^{a,b} \propto r_{a,b}^{-5}$; where $r_{a,b}$ is the distance between a and b. Our models of the adjacency between cells use a threshold for $r_{a,b} < 2.5$ to produce *non-planar* graphs.

Favourably, there is a direct mapping from QCA cells to nodes in an Ising model, and from the QCA tunnelling energy γ_i in (11) to the traverse energy $\Delta_i(t)$ in (2) [39]. After embedding once, the QCA model can be simulated for different test vectors by changing the biases associated to the driver cells. We see this direct mapping, along with recent developments in QCA technology [21], as an opportunity for the use of a layout-aware embedding approach. It is important to remark that layout-awareness for minor-embedding is *not* QCA simulation specific, nor limited to Ising models with intrinsic layouts.

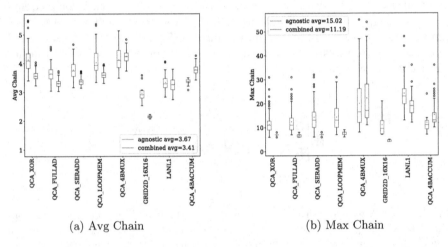

(a) Avg Chain   (b) Max Chain

Fig. 5. Detailed chain metrics for 100 embeddings, using the *Combined* embedding method against the *Agnostic* method [11], for each benchmark with $|P| > 50$. Each box shows the quartiles, with a horizontal line at the median, a dot at the mean, and the whiskers extending until the lowest and highest datum within 1.5 of the interquartile range; outliers are plotted as individual points.

5.2 Embedding Results

From the results in Table 1 we see that in problems with sizes $|P| < 50$ there is no clear advantage for either method, including similar embedding times. However, with increasing problem complexity, we see that the likelihood of finding a valid embedding increases for the *Combined* method, compared to the *Agnostic* method. In particular, for the benchmark *QCA_4BACCUM*, we see that for the *Combined* method, 99 of the 100 trials resulted in a valid embedding, while for the *Agnostic* method, only 23 trials resulted in a valid embedding. The table also shows that for higher complexity problems, the difference between the embedding time for the two methods increases. We have observed that these results are caused by the reduction of congestion provided by layout-awareness.

On the other hand, in our set of results, embeddings for two out of the 19 problems (*QCA_4BACCUM* and *QCA_4BMUX*) tend to have longer chain lengths when using layout-awareness. Figures 5a and b contain more detailed

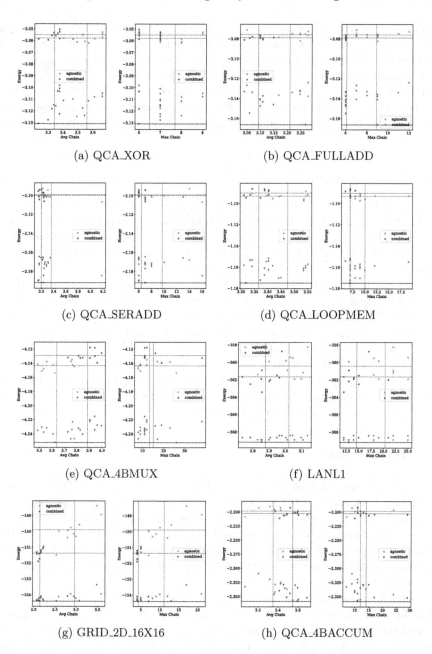

Fig. 6. D-Wave energy statistics from 10000 samples using the 10 best embeddings given by each method. The x position for each dot is a chain metric, while y marks both the median (labelled marker) and minimum energies (▼). A black dotted line marks the lowest energy sampled for that benchmark. The averages over all 10 embeddings, in both axes, are marked by dotted lines in the corresponding colours for each method. (Color figure online)

results for average and maximum chain length of these and other benchmarks with sizes $|P| > 50$. We have observed that these negative results (longer chains) are also associated to the reduction of congestion in the initial stages of the embedding heuristic, which allow the algorithm to yield more valid embeddings faster, but in doing so, will also yield unoptimized embeddings "prematurely". In our results, a higher number of interactions κ suggests higher congestion, or density, in the resulting embedding; more connected nodes are mapped closer to each other.

5.3 Sampling Results

We then performed D-Wave sampling experiments for the problems in our benchmark set with size $|P| > 50$. Each embedding was run on a D-Wave processor. For each embedding, we collected 10000 samples. The results are summarized in Fig. 6 in a similar fashion to those in Sect. 3. Axes relate chain metrics to energy values.

With the inclusion of these results for real-world problems, our observations from Sect. 3 remain. The generation of better embeddings has a direct positive impact on the sampling of lower energy results, and the use of layout-awareness can lead to a minimization of the maximum and average chain lengths. However, in agreement with the results in Table 1, embeddings for both $QCA\_4BACCUM$ and QCA_4BMUX do not seem to benefit from layout-awareness. We recognize in this an opportunity for the exploration of post-embedding optimization methods as an interesting area for future work, given that the embeddings found faster using layout-awareness are less congested.

6 Conclusions

If Quantum Computing is to reach the hands of more users, CAD tools and algorithms that enhance the programmability of these devices need to evolve in tandem with the technologies. In this paper, we introduced the concept of layout-aware minor-embedding for quantum annealing processors. Some of the concepts used in our algorithms, e.g. global placement and migration techniques to reduce routing congestion, come from the mature work on CAD tools for FPGA and VLSI design.

Using layout-awareness we described a method that is fast and highly successful at finding embeddings compared to existing methods, while also being able to yield shorter or equal qubit chain embeddings for most cases. Our approach is fundamentally different from existing methods in that it leverages layout information that is part of the problem instance, and it does so without fixing problem nodes to specific qubits. We are not aware of any other minor-embedding algorithm that leverages layout information in this way. Moreover, our technique can also be applied to problems which do not have intrinsic layout information. In these cases, a layout is generated using graph drawing heuristics. This approach could be broadly applicable to circuit model quantum computing platforms, for which there is an additional constraint on the movement of logical qubits (e.g. using SWAP operations) within the decoherence time.

We anticipate there is much more research to do related to minor embedding and CAD for quantum computers in general. It is likely that there is other information, other than layout information, that can be used to better optimize embeddings. To help accelerate research in this area, we are releasing our tools, experimental data, and methods and utilities for a complete Ising-model to QAP-samples interface with D-Wave's online services. Together, these contributions will help researchers explore this vast area, eventually increasing the use of QAPs to solve many of today's otherwise intractable problems.

References

1. Adachi, S.H., Henderson, M.P.: Application of quantum annealing to training of deep neural networks, p. 18, October 2015. arXiv preprint: arXiv:1510.06356
2. Amin, M.H., Andriyash, E., Rolfe, J., et al.: Quantum Boltzmann machine. Phys. Rev. X 8(2) (2018). https://doi.org/10.1103/PhysRevX.8.021050
3. Asghar, A., Parvez, H.: An improved diffusion based placement algorithm for reducing interconnect demand in congested regions of FPGAs. Int. J. Reconfigurable Comput. 2015, 1–10 (2015). http://www.hindawi.com/journals/ijrc/2015/756014/
4. Benedetti, M., Realpe-Gómez, J., Perdomo-Ortiz, A.: Quantum-assisted Helmholtz machines: a quantum-classical deep learning framework for industrial datasets in near-term devices. Quantum Sci. Technol. 3(3), 34007 (2018). https://doi.org/10.1088/2058-9565/aabd98
5. Bian, Z., Chudak, F., Israel, R., et al.: Discrete optimization using quantum annealing on sparse Ising models. Front. Phys. 2, 56 (2014). http://journal.frontiersin.org/article/10.3389/fphy.2014.00056
6. Bian, Z., Chudak, F., Israel, R., et al.: Mapping constrained optimization problems to quantum annealing with application to fault diagnosis. Front. ICT 3, 14 (2016). http://journal.frontiersin.org/article/10.3389/fict.2016.00014
7. Bian, Z., Chudak, F., Macready, W.G., et al.: Experimental determination of Ramsey numbers. Phys. Rev. Lett. 111(13) (2013). https://doi.org/10.1103/PhysRevLett.111.130505
8. Boothby, K., Bunyk, P., Raymond, J., Roy, A.: Next-generation topology of D-wave quantum processors. Technical report (2019). https://www.dwavesys.com/sites/default/files/14-1026A-C_Next-Generation-Topology-of-DW-Quantum-Processors.pdf
9. Boothby, T., King, A.D., Roy, A.: Fast clique minor generation in Chimera qubit connectivity graphs. Quantum Inf. Process. 15(1), 495–508 (2016). https://doi.org/10.1007/s11128-015-1150-6
10. Bunyk, P.I., Hoskinson, E.M., Johnson, M.W., et al.: Architectural considerations in the design of a superconducting quantum annealing processor. IEEE Trans. Appl. Supercond. 24(4), 1–10 (2014). https://arxiv.org/abs/1401.5504
11. Cai, J., Macready, W.G., Roy, A.: A practical heuristic for finding graph minors. Quantum (2014). http://arxiv.org/abs/1406.2741
12. Choi, V.: Minor-embedding in adiabatic quantum computation: I. The parameter setting problem. Quantum Inf. Process. 7(5), 193–209 (2008). https://doi.org/10.1007/s11128-008-0082-9

13. Choi, V.: Minor-embedding in adiabatic quantum computation: II. Minor-universal graph design. Quantum Inf. Process. **10**(3), 343–353 (2011). https://doi.org/10. 1007/s11128-010-0200-3
14. D-Wave Systems Inc.: D-Wave Leap (2018). https://cloud.dwavesys.com/leap/
15. D-Wave Systems Inc.: Source Repository for MinorMiner. Version 0.1.7 (2019). https://github.com/dwavesystems/minorminer
16. Djidjev, H.N., Chapuis, G., Hahn, G., Rizk, G.: Efficient combinatorial optimization using quantum annealing, January 2018. https://arxiv.org/abs/1801.08653
17. Dorband, J.E.: Stochastic characteristics of Qubits and Qubit chains on the D-Wave 2X, June 2016. http://arxiv.org/abs/1606.05550
18. Douglass, A., King, A.D., Raymond, J.: Constructing SAT filters with a quantum annealer. In: Heule, M., Weaver, S. (eds.) SAT 2015. LNCS, vol. 9340, pp. 104–120. Springer, Cham (2015). https://doi.org/10.1007/978-3-319-24318-4_9
19. Harris, R., Johnson, M.W., Lanting, T., et al.: Experimental investigation of an eight-qubit unit cell in a superconducting optimization processor. Phys. Rev. B Condens. Matter Mater. Phys. **82**(2), 24511 (2010). https://doi.org/10.1103/ PhysRevB.82.024511
20. Harris, R., Sato, Y., Berkley, A.J., et al.: Phase transitions in a programmable quantum spin glass simulator. Science (New York) **361**(6398), 162–165 (2018). http://www.ncbi.nlm.nih.gov/pubmed/30002250
21. Huff, T., Labidi, H., Rashidi, M., et al.: Binary atomic silicon logic. Nat. Electron. **1**(12), 636–643 (2018). http://arxiv.org/abs/1706.07427, http://www.nature.com/articles/s41928-018-0180-3
22. Jiang, S., Britt, K.A., McCaskey, A.J., et al.: Quantum annealing for prime factorization, April 2018. http://arxiv.org/abs/1804.02733
23. Johnson, M.J.: Future hardware directions of quantum annealing (2018). https:// www.dwavesys.com/sites/default/files/mwj_dwave_qubits2018.pdf
24. Könz, M.S., Mazzola, G., Ochoa, A.J., et al.: Uncertain fate of fair sampling in quantum annealing, June 2018. http://arxiv.org/abs/1806.06081
25. Korenkevych, D., Xue, Y., Bian, Z., et al.: Benchmarking quantum hardware for training of fully visible Boltzmann machines, November 2016. http://arxiv.org/ abs/1611.04528
26. Li, R.Y., Di Felice, R., Rohs, R., Lidar, D.A.: Quantum annealing versus classical machine learning applied to a simplified computational biology problem. NPJ Quantum Inf. **4**(1), 14 (2018). http://www.nature.com/articles/s41534-018-0060-8
27. Lucas, A.: Ising formulations of many NP problems. Front. Phys. **2**, 5 (2014). https://www.frontiersin.org/article/10.3389/fphy.2014.00005
28. Mandrà, S., Zhu, Z., Katzgraber, H.G.: Exponentially biased ground-state sampling of quantum annealing machines with transverse-field driving Hamiltonians. Phys. Rev. Lett. **118**(7), 070502 (2017). https://doi.org/10.1103/PhysRevLett. 118.070502
29. McMurchie, L., Ebeling, C.: PathFinder: a negotiation-based performance-driven router for FPGAs. In: Proceedings of the 1995 ACM Third International Symposium on Field-programmable Gate Arrays, FPGA 1995, pp. 111–117. ACM, New York (1995). http://doi.acm.org/10.1145/201310.201328
30. Mishra, A., Albash, T., Lidar, D.A.: Finite temperature quantum annealing solving exponentially small gap problem with non-monotonic success probability. Nat. Commun. **9**(1), 2917 (2018). http://www.nature.com/articles/s41467-018-05239-9
31. Mott, A., Job, J., Vlimant, J.R., et al.: Solving a Higgs optimization problem with quantum annealing for machine learning. Nature **550**(7676), 375–379 (2017). https://doi.org/10.1038/nature24047

32. Pakin, S.: Performing fully parallel constraint logic programming on a quantum annealer, March 2018. https://doi.org/10.1017/S1471068418000066
33. Pakin, S.: Personal communication via email (2018)
34. Perdomo Ortiz, A., Fluegemann, J., Narasimhan, S., et al.: A quantum annealing approach for fault detection and diagnosis of graph-based systems, February 2015. https://doi.org/10.1140/epjst/e2015-02347-y
35. Pinilla, J.P.: Source repository for embedding methods (2019). https://github.com/joseppinilla/embedding-methods
36. Preskill, J.: Quantum computing in the NISQ era and beyond. Quantum **2**, 79 (2018). https://arxiv.org/abs/1801.00862, https://doi.org/10.22331/q-2018-08-06-79, https://quantum-journal.org/papers/q-2018-08-06-79/
37. Pudenz, K.L., Albash, T., Lidar, D.A.: Quantum annealing correction for random Ising problems. Phys. Rev. A Atomic Mol. Opt. Phys. **91**(4) (2015). https://doi.org/10.1103/PhysRevA.91.042302
38. Ren, H., Pan, D.Z., Alpert, C.J., Villarrubia, P.: Diffusion-based placement migration. In: Proceedings of the 42nd Annual Conference on Design Automation, DAC 2005, p. 515 (2005). http://doi.acm.org/10.1145/1065579.1065712
39. Retallick, J., Babcock, M., Aroca-Ouellette, M., et al.: Embedding of quantum-dot cellular automata circuits onto a quantum annealing processor. In: 2014 Conference on Optoelectronic and Microelectronic Materials and Devices, COMMAD 2014, pp. 200–203, December 2014. https://doi.org/10.1109/COMMAD.2014.7038689
40. Rieffel, E.G., Venturelli, D., O'Gorman, B., et al.: A case study in programming a quantum annealer for hard operational planning problems. Quantum Inf. Process. **14**(1), 1–36 (2014). https://doi.org/10.1007/s11128-014-0892-x
41. Steiger, D.S., Rønnow, T.F., Troyer, M.: Heavy tails in the distribution of time to solution for classical and quantum annealing. Phys. Rev. Lett. **115**(23) (2015). http://arxiv.org/abs/1504.07991, https://doi.org/10.1103/PhysRevLett.115.230501
42. Su, J., He, L.: Fast embedding of constrained satisfaction problem to quantum annealer with minimizing chain length. In: 2017 54th ACM/EDAC/IEEE Design Automation Conference (DAC), pp. 1–6. ACM Press, New York, June 2017. http://dl.acm.org/citation.cfm?doid=3061639.3062246
43. Su, J., Tu, T., He, L.: A quantum annealing approach for Boolean satisfiability problem. In: Proceedings of the 53rd Annual Design Automation Conference, DAC 2016, pp. 1–6. ACM Press, New York (2016). http://dl.acm.org/citation.cfm?doid=2897937.2897973
44. Venturelli, D., Mandrà, S., Knysh, S., et al.: Quantum optimization of fully connected spin glasses. Phys. Rev. X **5**(3) (2015). https://arxiv.org/abs/1406.7553
45. Venturelli, D., Marchand, D.J.J., Rojo, G.: Quantum annealing implementation of job-shop scheduling, June 2015. http://arxiv.org/abs/1506.08479
46. Walus, K., Dysart, T.J., Jullien, G.A., Budiman, R.A.: QCADesigner: a rapid design and simulation tool for quantum-dot cellular automata. IEEE Trans. Nanotechnol. **3**, 26–31 (2004). http://ieeexplore.ieee.org/document/1278264/
47. Zaribafiyan, A., Marchand, D.J., Changiz Rezaei, S.S.: Systematic and deterministic graph minor embedding for Cartesian products of graphs. Quantum Inf. Process. **16**(5), 136 (2017). https://doi.org/10.1007/s11128-017-1569-z
48. Zick, K.M., Shehab, O., French, M.: Experimental quantum annealing: case study involving the graph isomorphism problem. Sci. Rep. **5**(1), 11168 (2015). http://www.nature.com/articles/srep11168

HPC Algorithms

Toward Efficient Architecture-Independent Algorithms for Dynamic Programs

Mohammad Mahdi Javanmard[1], Pramod Ganapathi[2], Rathish Das[1], Zafar Ahmad[1], Stephen Tschudi[3], and Rezaul Chowdhury[1(✉)]

[1] Computer Science, Stony Brook University, Stony Brook, NY, USA
`rezaul@cs.stonybrook.edu`
[2] Computer Science and Engineering, Indian Institute of Technology, Indore, India
[3] Google Inc., Mountain View, CA, USA

Abstract. We argue that the recursive divide-and-conquer paradigm is highly suited for designing algorithms to run efficiently under both shared-memory (multi- and manycores) and distributed-memory settings. The depth-first recursive decomposition of tasks and data is known to allow computations with potentially high temporal locality, and automatic adaptivity when resource availability (e.g., available space in shared caches) changes during runtime. Higher data locality leads to better intra-node I/O and cache performance and lower inter-node communication complexity, which in turn can reduce running times and energy consumption. Indeed, we show that a class of grid-based parallel recursive divide-and-conquer algorithms (for dynamic programs) can be run with provably optimal or near-optimal performance bounds on fat cores (cache complexity), thin cores (data movements), and purely distributed-memory machines (communication complexity) without changing the algorithm's basic structure.

Two-way recursive divide-and-conquer algorithms are known for solving dynamic programming (DP) problems on shared-memory multicore machines. In this paper, we show how to extend them to run efficiently also on manycore GPUs and distributed-memory machines.

Our GPU algorithms work efficiently even when the data is too large to fit into the host RAM. These are external-memory algorithms based on recursive r-way divide and conquer, where r (≥ 2) varies based on the current depth of the recursion. Our distributed-memory algorithms are also based on multi-way recursive divide and conquer that extends naturally inside each shared-memory multicore/manycore compute node. We show that these algorithms are work-optimal and have low latency and bandwidth bounds.

We also report empirical results for our GPU and distribute memory algorithms.

Keywords: GPU · Recursive divide & conquer ·
Dynamic programming · Exascale · Distributed memory ·
Shared memory · I/O efficiency · Communication efficiency

© Springer Nature Switzerland AG 2019
M. Weiland et al. (Eds.): ISC High Performance 2019, LNCS 11501, pp. 143–164, 2019.
https://doi.org/10.1007/978-3-030-20656-7_8

1   Introduction

Many of the world's current fastest supercomputers are networks of distributed-memory hybrid compute nodes where each node houses both latency optimized multicores (a.k.a. fat cores) and throughput optimized manycores (a.k.a. thin cores, e.g., GPU cores) connected through a multilevel memory hierarchy [4][1] which is also what an exascale supercomputer is expected to look like in the near future [41,54]. In addition to allowing various types of parallelism, e.g, distributed-memory, shared-memory, task (on multicores) and data (on manycores), a program running on these supercomputers must exploit data locality at various levels of computation for efficiency. Indeed, higher data locality leads to better intra-node I/O and cache performance and lower inter-node communication complexity, which in turn can reduce running times and lower energy consumption.

We argue in this paper that the recursive divide-and-conquer paradigm is highly suited for designing efficient algorithms for both shared-memory and distributed-memory architectures. The depth-first recursive decomposition of tasks and data is known to allow computations with potentially high temporal locality, and automatic adaptivity when resource availability (e.g., available space in shared caches [13,19]) changes during runtime. Indeed, we show that a class of grid-based parallel recursive divide-and-conquer algorithms for solving dynamic programming problems can be run with provably optimal or near-optimal performance bounds on fat cores (cache complexity), thin cores (data movements), and purely distributed-memory machines (communication complexity) without any change in the algorithm's basic structure.

Dynamic programming (DP) [12,22] is a widely used algorithm design technique for solving optimization problems that can be decomposed into overlapping subproblems whose optimal solutions can be combined to obtain an optimal solution to the original problem. DP is extensively used in computational biology [32,73], and in many other application areas including operations research, compilers, sports, economics, finance, and agriculture (see DP refs in [19]).

Dynamic programs are typically implemented using nested loops that fill out the cells of a DP table using already computed values for other cells. However, such a looping code is usually not suitable for high performance on a modern computer with a memory hierarchy as without any *temporal locality*[2] in its data access pattern it often spends significantly more time in data transfers than in actual computations.

Tiled looping codes reduce the number of data transfers between two specific (adjacent) levels of the memory hierarchy by tiling the DP table so that a

---

[1] As of November 2018, the supercomputers ranked 1 (Summit), 2 (Sierra), 6 (ABCI), 7 (Piz Daint), and 8 (Titan) in order of *Rpeak* (TFlop/s) are networks of hybrid CPU+GPU nodes [4].

[2] Temporal locality — whenever a block of data is brought into a faster level of cache/memory from a slower level, as much useful work as possible is performed on this data before removing the block from the faster level.

constant number of such tiles completely fit in the smaller[3] of the two levels. Whenever a tile is brought into the smaller memory level, as much computation as possible is done with it before replacing it with another tile. In this approach, the code must know the size of the smaller memory level. The tiled code often differs significantly from the standard looping code both in structure and in complexity. Multilevel iterative tiling is possible, but at the expense of significantly increasing the complexity of the code with each additional level. Fixed tile sizes can be problematic when the program shares the smaller memory level with multiple other concurrently running programs because it can adapt neither automatically nor efficiently as the memory space available to it keeps changing during running time [13,19].

Recursive parallel 2-way divide-and-conquer DP algorithms perform an asymptotically optimal number of data transfers between every two adjacent levels of [19,69]. They do not need to know the sizes of the memories in the hierarchy, can passively self-adapt to cache sharing [13,19], and the complexity of the code is independent of the depth of the memory hierarchy. For any given pair of adjacent memory/cache levels the bounds hold under the *ideal cache* model [29] with a fully automatic optimal offline cache replacement policy. LRU replacement policy also works. It has been shown very recently that for a large class of DP problems these recursive parallel algorithms can be generated automatically [19,37].

Recursive 2-way divide-and-conquer algorithms are not suitable for GPUs as those devices have very limited support for recursion and require the programmer to explicitly transfer data between memory levels (e.g., between global and shared memories). Explicit communications among compute nodes are also required during distributed-memory computations. Moreover, these algorithms may lose parallelism because of artificial dependencies among subtasks [18].

Our Contributions. In this paper, we show how to extend 2-way recursive divide-and-conquer algorithms designed to solve DP problems efficiently on shared-memory multicore machines to run efficiently also on manycore GPUs and distributed-memory machines. The same algorithm without any changes in its basic structure runs with provable efficiency on all three platforms. Our approach works for the wide *fractal DP* class [19] that includes Floyd-Warshall's APSP, the parenthesis problem, pairwise sequence alignment, and the gap problem among many others.

(*i*) **[GPU Algorithms].** We design I/O-optimal algorithms for the *fractal DP* class [19].

---

[3] I.e., faster and closer to the processing core(s).

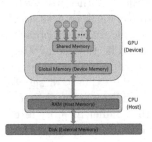

Fig. 1. Memory hierarchy assumed by our GPU algorithms.

Our approach works for arbitrarily deep memory hierarchies. But in this paper, we target the one shown in Fig. 1. We assume that the input DP table is stored either in the RAM or in the disk. Our algorithms are based on r-way recursive divide-and-conquer, where r varies based on the level of recursion (i.e., different levels can have different r values). We use $r = 2$ at every level of recursion until the input size drops below the size of the GPU global memory. At that level we choose r large enough so that the input is decomposed into chunks that are small enough to fit in the GPU shared memory. We do not use the knowledge of the CPU RAM size as the RAM can be maintained as a fully associative memory with an automatic LRU page replacement policy (through STXXL [1]). Through the choice of r we basically resort to iterative tiling once we reach inside the GPU as the device provides only limited support for recursion.

We prove theoretical bounds showing that we perform an asymptotically optimal number of data transfers between every two adjacent levels of the memory hierarchy.

We have implemented our GPU algorithms for four DP/DP-like problems: Floyd-Warshall's APSP, parenthesis problem, gap problem, and Gaussian elimination without pivoting. Our programs run significantly faster than all internal-memory multicore CPU implementations and almost all existing tiled GPU implementations.

(*ii*) **[Distributed-memory Algorithms].** Our distributed-memory algorithms are also based on r-way recursive divide and conquer that extends naturally inside each shared-memory multicore/manycore compute node. Thus these algorithms are, indeed, hybrid distributed-shared-memory algorithms. We show that they are work-optimal and have latency and bandwidth bounds that are within $\log p$ factor of optimal, where p is the number of compute nodes.

We include empirical performance results for Floyd-Warshall's APSP, the parenthesis problem and the gap problem.

Organization. Section 2 presents our approach for designing r-way algorithms. We describe our GPU results in Sect. 3 with the computing model, related work, algorithm design, I/O complexities, and experimental results in Sects. 3.1, 3.2, 3.3, 3.4 and 3.5, respectively. Our distributed-memory results are presented in Sect. 4 with the algorithm design, communication lower bounds, related work, and experimental results in Sects. 4.1, 4.2, 4.3, and 4.4, respectively. Finally, we conclude in Sect. 5.

2   Multi-way Recursive Divide and Conquer

In this section, we describe our methodology for designing multi-way (i.e., r-way) recursive divide-and-conquer algorithms for DP problems in the fractal-DP class [19]. The 2-way and r-way algorithms will be called 2-way and r-way $\mathcal{R}\text{-}\mathcal{DP}$s, respectively.

We will explain our methodology using the parenthesis DP [17,31] which fills out a 2D table $C[0:n, 0:n]$ based on the following recurrence:

$$C[i,j] = \min_{i \leq k \leq j} \{C[i,k] + C[k,j] + w(i,j,k)\} \quad \text{for } 0 \leq i < j - 1 < n;$$

assuming $C[i,j] = \infty$ for $0 \leq i = j \leq n$ and $C[i,j] = x_j$ for $0 \leq i = j - 1 < n$, where, x_j's are given constants and $w(i,j,k)$ does not incur any I/Os.

The class of problems defined by the recurrence above includes optimal chain matrix multiplication, RNA secondary structure prediction, optimal polygon triangulation, string parsing for context-free grammar, and optimal database joins among others. A 2-way $\mathcal{R}\text{-}\mathcal{DP}$ for the problem can be found in [19].

2.1 r-way $\mathcal{R}\text{-}\mathcal{DP}$ Design

We first use either AUTOGEN [19] or Bellmania [37] to automatically derive the standard 2-way $\mathcal{R}\text{-}\mathcal{DP}$ for the given DP problem. We then derive an r-way $\mathcal{R}\text{-}\mathcal{DP}$ from the 2-way $\mathcal{R}\text{-}\mathcal{DP}$. Indeed, assuming $r = 2^t$ for some positive integer t, each level of recursion of an r-way $\mathcal{R}\text{-}\mathcal{DP}$ can be obtained by unrolling t levels of recursion of the corresponding 2-way $\mathcal{R}\text{-}\mathcal{DP}$. The resulting r-way $\mathcal{R}\text{-}\mathcal{DP}$s typically have more parallelism than their 2-way counterparts (see Figure 3 in [64] for an example).

To obtain a multi-way $\mathcal{R}\text{-}\mathcal{DP}$ from a 2-way $\mathcal{R}\text{-}\mathcal{DP}$, we start with $t = 1$ and keep applying the following two refinement steps until we can identify the pattern in which the recursive functions are called in the resulting unrolled $\mathcal{R}\text{-}\mathcal{DP}$.

STEP 1. Take the 2^t-way $\mathcal{R}\text{-}\mathcal{DP}$, and unroll each recursive function call by one level (of recursion) based on the 2-way $\mathcal{R}\text{-}\mathcal{DP}$ version of that function.

STEP 2. To execute the recursive function calls in the unrolled version from step 1 in as few stages as possible, we move each such function call to the lowest possible stage without violating dependency constraints. We follow the following rules where by $\mathbf{W}(\mathcal{F})$ we denote the DP subtable function $\mathcal{F}$ writes to and by $\mathbf{R}(\mathcal{F})$ we denote the set of DP subtables $\mathcal{F}$ reads from. We say that $\mathcal{F}$ is *flexible* provided $\mathbf{W}(\mathcal{F}) \notin \mathbf{R}(\mathcal{F})$, and *inflexible* otherwise. By $\mathcal{F}_1 \to \mathcal{F}_2$ we mean that $\mathcal{F}_1$ is executed before $\mathcal{F}_2$, $\mathcal{F}_1 \leftrightarrow \mathcal{F}_2$ means that order does not matter, and $\mathcal{F}_1 \| \mathcal{F}_2$ indicates parallel execution.

#1: If $\mathbf{W}(\mathcal{F}_1) \neq \mathbf{W}(\mathcal{F}_2)$ and $\mathbf{W}(\mathcal{F}_1) \in \mathbf{R}(\mathcal{F}_2)$, then $\mathcal{F}_1 \to \mathcal{F}_2$.
#2: If $\mathbf{W}(\mathcal{F}_1) = \mathbf{W}(\mathcal{F}_2)$ and only $\mathcal{F}_1$ flexible, then $\mathcal{F}_1 \to \mathcal{F}_2$.
#3: If $\mathbf{W}(\mathcal{F}_1) = \mathbf{W}(\mathcal{F}_2)$ and both $\mathcal{F}_1$ and $\mathcal{F}_2$ are flexible, then $\mathcal{F}_1 \leftrightarrow \mathcal{F}_2$.
#4: If $\mathcal{F}_1$ and $\mathcal{F}_2$ satisfy none of the rules above, then $\mathcal{F}_1 \| \mathcal{F}_2$.

The new 2^{t+1}-way $\mathcal{R}\text{-}\mathcal{DP}$ has potentially more parallelism than its 2^t-way version.

$\mathcal{A}_{par}(X, U, V, d)$

1. $r \leftarrow tilesize[d]$
2. **if** $r \geq m$ **then** $\mathcal{A}_{loop\text{-}par}(X, U, V)$
   else
3. $\quad \delta \leftarrow (j - i), d' \leftarrow d + 1$
4. $\quad$ **parallel:** $\mathcal{A}_{par}(X_{i,j}, U_{i,j}, V_{i,j}, d') \, \forall i, j \in [1, r], \delta = 0$
5. $\quad$ **for** $k \leftarrow 1$ **to** $r - 1$ **do**
6. $\quad\quad$ **parallel:** $\mathcal{C}_{par}(X_{i,j}, U_{i,i+k-1}, V_{i+k-1,j}, d')$
   $\quad\quad\quad \forall i, j \in [1, r], \, \delta \in [k, \min\{2k - 2, r - 1\}]$
7. $\quad\quad$ **parallel:** $\mathcal{C}_{par}(X_{i,j}, U_{i,j-k+1}, V_{j-k+1,j}, d')$
   $\quad\quad\quad \forall i, j \in [1, r], \, \delta \in [k, \min\{2k - 3, r - 1\}]$
8. $\quad\quad$ **parallel:** $\mathcal{B}_{par}(X_{i,j}, U_{i,i}, V_{j,j}, d') \, \forall i, j \in [1, r], \, \delta = k$

$\mathcal{B}_{par}(X, U, V, d)$

1. $r \leftarrow tilesize[d]$
2. **if** $r \geq m$ **then** $\mathcal{B}_{loop\text{-}par}(X, U, V)$
   else
3. $\quad$ Let $\langle U'_{\ell,\ell}, V'_{\ell,j} \rangle = \begin{cases} \langle X_{i,\ell}, V_{\ell,j} \rangle & \text{if } \ell > 0, \\ \langle U_{i,\ell+r}, X_{\ell+r,j} \rangle & \text{if } \ell \leq 0. \end{cases}$
4. $\quad \delta \leftarrow (j - i), d' \leftarrow d + 1, r' \leftarrow 2r - 1$
5. $\quad$ **for** $k \leftarrow 1$ **to** r' **do**
6. $\quad\quad$ **parallel:** $\mathcal{C}_{par}(X_{i,j}, U'_{i,k-r+i-1}, V'_{k-r+i-1,j}, d')$
   $\quad\quad\quad \forall i, j \in [1, r], \delta + r \in [k, \min\{2k - 2, r'\}]$
7. $\quad\quad$ **parallel:** $\mathcal{C}_{par}(X_{i,j}, U'_{i,1+i-r}, V'_{1+i-r,j}, d')$
   $\quad\quad\quad \forall i, j \in [1, r], \delta + r \in [k, \min\{2k - 3, r'\}]$
8. $\quad\quad$ **parallel:** $\mathcal{B}_{par}(X_{i,j}, U_{i,i}, V_{j,j}, d')$
   $\quad\quad\quad \forall i, j \in [1, r], \delta + r = k$

$\mathcal{C}_{par}(X, U, V, d)$

1. $r \leftarrow tilesize[d]$
2. **if** $r \geq m$ **then** $\mathcal{C}_{loop\text{-}par}(X, U, V)$
   else
3. $\quad$ **for** $k \leftarrow 1$ **to** r **do**
4. $\quad\quad$ **parallel:** $\mathcal{C}_{par}(X_{i,j}, U_{i,k}, V_{k,j}, d + 1) \, \forall i, j \in [1, r]$

Fig. 2. An r-way $\mathcal{R}\text{-}\mathcal{DP}$ for parenthesis problem [20]. Here, X, U and V are $m \times m$ tables.

Based on the dimension m of the DP (sub-)table(s) at any given level of recursion of an r-way $\mathcal{R}\text{-}\mathcal{DP}$, r can be set to a constant or a function of either m or both m and a particular cache or memory size such that the resulting tile exactly fits into that memory. When a subproblem fits into a memory of the smallest size, we execute an iterative kernel. Given the original DP table dimension n we precompute the value of r at each recursion level d and store that in $tilesize[d]$.

In Fig. 2 we show an r-way $\mathcal{R}\text{-}\mathcal{DP}$ for the parenthesis problem with functions $\mathcal{A}_{par}$, $\mathcal{B}_{par}$, and $\mathcal{C}_{par}$. The initial function call is $\mathcal{A}_{par}(C, C, C, 1)$, where C is the input DP table. The term m in all the functions represents the dimension length at a particular recursion level. The keyword **parallel** means that the functions can be invoked in parallel (Fig. 3).

2.2 Additional r-way $\mathcal{R}\text{-}\mathcal{DP}$ Algorithms

In this work, we have designed and implemented r-way $\mathcal{R}\text{-}\mathcal{DP}$ algorithms for the following three additional problems.

Gaussian Elimination w/o Pivoting. This DP-like algorithm is used for solving systems of linear equations and LU decomposition of symmetric positive-definite or diagonally dominant real matrices [22].

Floyd-Warshall's APSP. This all-pairs shortest path algorithm [22] uses the recurrence below. Let $D[i, j, k]$ be the length of the shortest path from vertex v_i to vertex v_j with no intermediate vertex higher than v_k. Let $\ell(i, j)$ be the distance between v_i and v_j. Then $D[i, j, k] = 1$ if $k = 0$ and $i = j$; $D[i, j, k] = \ell(v_i, v_j)$ if $k = 0$ and $i \neq j$; and $D[i, j, k] = \min(D[i, j, k - 1], D[i, k, k - 1] + D[k, j, k - 1])$ if

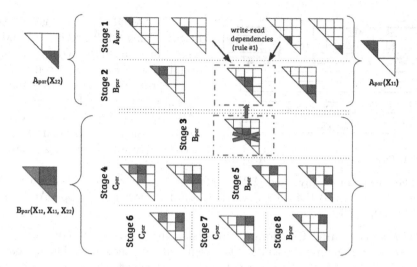

Fig. 3. Reducing the number of parallel stages in $\mathcal{A}_{par}$ after unrolling the recursive function calls by one level.

$k > 0$. The third dimension of D can be dropped to solve the problem in space quadratic in the number of vertices in the graph.

Sequence Alignment with Gap Penalty (Gap Problem). In this problem [30,31,73], a sequence of consecutive deletes or inserts corresponds to a gap and they are handled with generic cost functions w and w'. The optimal alignment cost for strings $X = x_1 x_2 \ldots x_m$ and $Y = y_1 y_2 \ldots y_n$ is defined by the following recurrence: $G[i,j] = 0$ if $i = j = 0$, $G[i,j] = w(0,j)$ if $i = 0 \ \wedge \ j \in [1,n]$, $G[i,j] = w'(i,0)$ if $j = 0 \wedge i \in [1,m]$, and $G[i,j] = \min\{G[i-1,j-1]+S(x_i,y_j),$ $\min_{0 \leq q < j} \{G[i,q] + w(q,j)\}, \ \min_{0 \leq p < i} \{G[p,j] + w'(p,i)\}\}$ otherwise; where, w and w' do not incur any I/Os.

3 External-Memory GPU Algorithms

3.1 GPU Computing Model

We give a brief overview of the GPU architecture, its programming model, and GPU programming challenges.

General Purpose Computing on GPUs. GPUs are attached to CPUs through PCI bus as hardware accelerators. They have a manycore architecture with hundreds to thousands of cores, and are designed to have thousands of light-weight threads, perform highly data-parallel and compute-intensive tasks, and maximize the throughput of the parallel programs. GPUs support multi-threading, SIMD, and instruction-level parallelism.

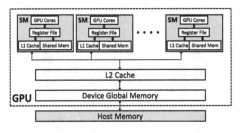

Fig. 4. Organization of an NVIDIA GPU.

An NVIDIA GPU is a set of Streaming Multiprocessors (SMs) employing an SIMT computational architecture. Each SM consists of many processing cores connected to a shared memory/L1 cache. The SMs are connected to the device (global) memory through an L2 cache. Figure 4 shows this memory organization.

The most commonly used APIs for general purpose computing on GPUs include OpenCL, NVIDIA CUDA, Microsoft DirectCompute, OpenACC, and AMD's APP SDK.

GPU Programming Challenges. Recursion and divide-and-conquer are powerful tools for designing efficient (I/O-efficient, energy-efficient, and highly parallel), portable (cache- and processor-oblivious) and robust (cache- and processor-adaptive) algorithms. However, these design techniques involve complicated control logic and hence they are either unsupported or have very limited support in GPUs.

Optimizing a GPU program is hard as many factors have big influence on its performance: thread organization (in blocks of different dimensions with different dimension lengths), warp size (the granularity at which the SMs can execute computations), memory coalescing (consecutive numbered threads access consecutive memory locations), and streams and events (overlapping compute kernel execution and data transfers).

3.2   Related Work (GPU)

Several GPU algorithms exist that solve DP problems: Floyd-Warshall's APSP [14,26,27,34,40,47,49,58,71], parenthesis problem family [51–53,56,61,74], and sequence alignment [45,46,48,62,75]. Most of them are loops tiled for GPU global and shared memories to exploit temporal locality. Some are based on tiling derived from recursive divide-and-conquer algorithms that use only matrix-matrix multiplications on a semiring, e.g., R-Kleene's algorithm [14,23,55] for Floyd-Warshall's APSP. Major limitations of existing results are as follows. First, almost all existing GPU algorithms assume that the entire DP table fits into the GPU global memory, and none of them work when the table is too large for the host RAM. Thus, the size of the problem they can handle is limited by the size of one of those two levels of memory. Second, no general methodology is known that work for a large class of DP problems. Third, theoretical performance guarantees for data transfers and parallelism are often missing.

3.3   GPU Algorithm Design

We will explain how to port the r-way $\mathcal{R}\text{-}\mathcal{DP}$ given in Fig. 2 to a GPU system. The approach works for all fractal-DP problems. For simplicity, we assume the

4-level memory hierarchy shown in Fig. 1. Handling deeper hierarchies, multiple GPUs, and multiple shared memories connected to a global memory are not difficult.

Let us first assume that we know the sizes of the CPU RAM and both GPU memories, and let the input DP table be present in the external memory. Hence, the data from the DP table will pass through CPU RAM, GPU global memory, and GPU shared memory. We define functions host_disk_$\mathcal{A}_{par}$, host_RAM_$\mathcal{F}_{par}$, device_global_$\mathcal{F}_{par}$, and device_shared_$\mathcal{F}_{par}$, where $\mathcal{F} \in \{\mathcal{A}, \mathcal{B}, \mathcal{C}\}$. The suffixes $\mathcal{A}_{par}$, $\mathcal{B}_{par}$, and $\mathcal{C}_{par}$ correspond to the three recursive functions. Functions with keywords host and device run on the CPU and GPU, respectively. Input and the output matrices accessed by functions with keywords disk, RAM, global, and shared reside on CPU disk, CPU RAM, GPU global memory, and GPU shared memory, respectively.

Initially, host_disk_$\mathcal{A}_{par}$ is invoked with the entire DP table as input. The function splits the $n \times n$ DP table into $r_d \times r_d$ subtables each of size $(n/r_d) \times (n/r_d)$, assuming r_d divides n for simplicity. The value of r_d is chosen such that the input subtables for the function exactly fit in the RAM. The function invokes host_RAM_$\mathcal{F}_{par}$, where $\mathcal{F} \in \{\mathcal{A}, \mathcal{B}, \mathcal{C}\}$, as per the r-way $\mathcal{R}$-$\mathcal{DP}$ algorithm, after copying the subtables required by that child function to RAM. We do not define host_disk_$\mathcal{B}_{par}$ and host_disk_$\mathcal{C}_{par}$ as they will never be invoked.

Function host_RAM_$\mathcal{F}_{par}$ splits each of its $(n/r_d) \times (n/r_d)$ sized input/output tables into $r_m \times r_m$ subtables each of size $(n/(r_d r_m)) \times (n/(r_d r_m))$, assuming r_m divides (n/r_d) for simplicity. It invokes appropriate functions device_global_$\mathcal{F}_{par}$ after copying the relevant subtables to the GPU global memory. This process continues till the functions device_shared_$\mathcal{F}_{par}$ are reached. Inside these functions we execute the looping kernels using GPU cores.

Now let's assume that we do not know the size of the CPU RAM, but it is maintained as a fully associative memory with an automatic LRU page replacement policy. Then instead of host_disk_$\mathcal{A}_{par}$ and host_RAM_$\mathcal{A}_{par}$ we will only have host_$\mathcal{A}_{par}$, and similarly host_$\mathcal{B}_{par}$ and host_$\mathcal{C}_{par}$. Initially, the function host_$\mathcal{A}_{par}$ is invoked with the entire DP table as input. The function splits the entire $n \times n$ DP table into 2×2 subtables each of size $(n/2) \times (n/2)$, assuming n is divisible by 2 for simplicity. Now if a $(n/2) \times (n/2)$ subtable fits into the GPU global memory we invoke device_global_$\mathcal{F}_{par}$, otherwise we recursively invoke host_$\mathcal{F}_{par}$.

3.4   I/O Complexities

We present theoretical bounds on the I/O's performed by our GPU algorithms.

Let M_m, M_g, and M_s be the sizes of the CPU main memory, GPU global memory, and GPU shared memory, respectively, and suppose these sizes are known to the algorithm. So there will be exactly three levels of recursion, and in each level the algorithm will choose the largest tile size (i.e., the smallest possible value of r) such that the required number (a constant) of tiles fit in the next smaller level of memory. Let B, B_m, B_g, and B_s denote the block sizes between disk and RAM, RAM and global memory, global memory and shared memory, and shared memory and processor, respectively. All M's, n's, and B's are natural numbers.

Theorem 1 (I/O complexity of GPU algorithms). *When run on the GPU memory hierarchy of Fig. 1, the number of data blocks transferred by the external-memory GPU algorithm (i.e., I/O complexity) between:* **(a)** *disk & RAM:* $\Theta\left(\frac{n^w}{BM_m^{w/d-1}} + \frac{n^w}{M_m^{(w+1)/d-1}}\right)$, **(b)** *RAM & global memory:* $\Theta\left(\frac{n^w}{B_m M_g^{w/d-1}} + \frac{n^w}{M_g^{(w+1)/d-1}}\right)$, *and* **(c)** *global & shared memories:* $\Theta\left(\frac{n^w}{B_g M_s^{w/d-1}} + \frac{n^w}{M_s^{(w+1)/d-1}}\right)$; *where,* $\Theta(n^w)$ *is the total work (i.e., time spent in computation only) performed by the GPU algorithm, and* n^d *is the size of the original input DP table.*

Proof. We assume that the number of submatrices accessed by each recursive function is upper bounded by a constant. Let n_q be the largest tile dimension a function can use while still making sure that the required number of tiles fit into a memory of size M_q. Then $n_m^d = \Theta(M_m)$, $n_g^d = \Theta(M_g)$ and $n_s^d = \Theta(M_s)$.

Let M_L and M_S be the sizes of two adjacent levels of memory and $M_L \geq M_S$. Let B_L be the block transfer size between the two levels. Then the I/O-complexity of filling the smaller memory once is $\mathcal{O}\left(n_S^{d-1}(n_S/B_L + 1)\right)$. The smaller memory will be filled $\Theta\left((n_L/n_S)^w\right)$ times. Hence, the I/O-complexity between the two memories is $\mathcal{O}\left((n_L/n_S)^w n_S^{d-1}(n_S/B_L + 1)\right)$.

We now apply the result above to prove the theorem. The I/O-complexity between disk and RAM is $\mathcal{O}((n/n_m)^w n_m^{d-1}(n_m/B + 1))$. The I/O-complexity between RAM and global memory to work on all data present in RAM is $\mathcal{O}((n_m/n_g)^w n_g^{d-1}(n_g/B_m + 1))$. However, the RAM will be filled $\Theta\left((n/n_m)^w\right)$ times. Hence, the total I/O-complexity between RAM and global is $\mathcal{O}((n/n_g)^w n_g^{d-1}(n_g/B_m + 1))$. We use a similar reasoning to compute the total I/O-complexity between global and shared memories. Putting $n_m^d = \Theta(M_m)$, $n_g^d = \Theta(M_g)$ and $n_s^d = \Theta(M_s)$ we obtain the claimed bounds.

I/O Optimality. The optimality of the I/O bounds presented in Theorem 1 for any given r-way $\mathcal{R}\text{-}\mathcal{DP}$ follows from the known optimality of the corresponding 2-way $\mathcal{R}\text{-}\mathcal{DP}$ proved under the ideal cache model [29]. We compute the I/O complexity of an r-way $\mathcal{R}\text{-}\mathcal{DP}$ as the product of the number of subproblems that exactly fit into the memory and the number of block transfers required to scan the input and output matrices for a subproblem. Say $r = 2^t$ for some $t \in \mathbb{N}$. Then, to compare the I/O complexities of the two algorithms, the r-way $\mathcal{R}\text{-}\mathcal{DP}$ can be viewed as the 2-way $\mathcal{R}\text{-}\mathcal{DP}$ unrolled t times. The number of subproblems that exactly fit in the memory will be asymptotically same for both 2-way and r-way $\mathcal{R}\text{-}\mathcal{DP}$s. Also, the I/Os required to scan the matrices that exactly fit in the memory will also be asymptotically the same for both $\mathcal{R}\text{-}\mathcal{DP}$s. Hence, the I/O complexities of the two $\mathcal{R}\text{-}\mathcal{DP}$s will match.

3.5 GPU Experimental Results

We present empirical results showing the performance benefits of our GPU algorithms.

Setup. All our experiments were performed on a heterogeneous node of the Stampede supercomputer [2,70]. The multicore machine had a dual-socket 8-core 2.7 GHz Intel Sandy Bridge processors ($2 \times 8 = 16$ cores in total) and 32 GB RAM. Each core was connected to a 32 KB private L1 cache and a 256 KB private L2 cache. All cores in a processor shared a 20 MB L3 cache. The node was attached to a single NVIDIA K20 GPU. The GPU had an on-board GDDR5 memory of 5 GB, and 2496 CUDA cores.

All our algorithms were implemented in C++. We used Intel Cilk Plus extension to parallelize and Intel® C++ Compiler v13.0 to compile the CPU implementations with optimization parameters -O3 -ipo -parallel -AVX -xhost. Our GPU programs were written in CUDA. The programs were compiled with nvcc compiler with parameters -O3 -gencode arch=compute_35,code=sm_35.

Implementations. We focus on four DP/DP-like problems: Floyd-Warshall's APSP (FW-APSP), Gaussian elimination without pivoting [21], parenthesis problem [17,31], and sequence alignment with gap penalty (gap problem) [30,31].

For all problems we consider the following two implementations where cpu and gpu prefixes are used to indicate programs written for CPUs and GPUs, respectively.

For FW-APSP, we also consider: (*iii*) gpu-tidp-harish: Harish and Narayanan's [34] tiled-iterative code, (*iv*) gpu-tidp-lund: Lund and Smith's [47] tiled-iterative code, (*v*) gpu-tidp-katz: Katz and Kider's [40] tiled-iterative code, (*vi*) gpu-rec-buluc: Buluc et al.'s implementation of the 2-way R-Kleene algorithm with Volkov and Demmel's optimization [72] for the matrix multiplication (MM) kernel, and (*vii*) gpu-rdp-opt: r-way $\mathcal{R}\text{-}\mathcal{DP}$ replaced with Buluc et al.'s MM-like kernel for MM-like functions (i.e., functions reading from and writing to disjoint matrices).

For the other three problems (i.e., parenthesis, Gaussian elimination w/o pivoting, and gap) we could not find any publicly available GPU codes for comparison.

Optimizations. We list below the optimizations we applied on various programs in addition to the compiler optimizations enabled by the optimization flags we used.

Major optimizations applied on gpu-rdp and gpu-rdp-opt are as follows.

(*i*) We used GPU shared memory by setting BLOCK_SIZE $= 32$ so that 1024 threads could work on matrices of size 32×32 simultaneously. Also, two blocks with 1024 threads each were run in parallel. But since NVIDIA K20 can run up to 2496 hardware threads at a time, 448 threads remained unused. Use of more than 2048 threads required dropping to 16×16 or some non-power-of-2 size, and then either run into extra overhead for launching jobs or be way under the 48KB shared memory limit per block. This ended up being the bigger bottleneck on the system and our preliminary experiments showed that even with 256 more threads 16×16 was worse than 32×32.

(ii) All our DP applications have very predictable data access patterns, and so a user-managed shared-memory seems more appropriate for them than an L1 cache. But we tried both Shared Memory/L1 cache configurations and also tried varying threads, and the best configuration was 48KB shared memory with 2048 threads. Our most memory-hungry computations access three disjoint matrices. Hence, a block with BLOCK_SIZE $= 32$ and single precision floats uses $3 \times \frac{32 \times 32 \times 4}{1024} = 12$ KB of the shared memory and with double precision floats uses 24KB. Though BLOCK_SIZE $= 64$ with single precision floats will fill up the 48KB shared memory, we won't have enough threads to compute all $64 \times 64 = 4096$ output cells in parallel. Our preliminary experiments showed that 32 was a better choice for BLOCK_SIZE than 64.

(iii) If a function kernel reads only from submatrices it is not writing to, then we do not synchronize inside it.

(iv) Row-major order was used for all submatrices. Flipping a submatrix to column-major degrades performance. Row-major was used for the grid and inside each block.

(v) GRID_SIZE was set to min $\{n, 16384\}$, where 16384 was the maximum size such that our subproblems can exactly fit in the 5 GB of global memory.

(vi) Allocating memory using gpuMalloc() on GPU global memory is slow. Instead we simply malloc once and then copy the submatrices to the respective regions.

(vii) We allocate directly in the host's pinned memory using cudaMallocHost(). This reduces the block transfers between pageable host memory and pinned memory.

With more aggressive optimizations gpu-rdp and gpu-rdp-opt are likely to perform even better than what we report in this paper. However, we want to show that GPU algorithms designed based on recursive divide-and-conquer are I/O-efficient and remain compute-bound for modern GPUs even when the data is in external-memory. Once that goal is reached, additional optimizations will only improve the results.

Additional optimizations used for cpu-rdp include:

(i) #pragma parallel, #pragma ivdep, and min loop count(B),

(ii) 64 byte-aligned matrices,

(iii) write optimization in the basecase – if an innermost loop updates the same DP table cell repeatedly we apply all of them on a register instead of the DP cell, and update that cell only once at the end of the loop using the value in the updated register,

(iv) copy optimization in the basecase – copying the transpose of a column-major input matrix to a local array in order to access it in unit stride during computation,

(v) pointer arithmetic, and

(vi) Z-morton layout (only for the gap problem). Each of our DP applications in this paper runs in $\Theta\left(n^3\right)$ time which asymptotically dominates the $\Theta\left(n^2\right)$ time needed for layout conversion of the input matrix. Indeed, we have found that the layout conversion time has very little impact on the actual running times.

The three tiled-iterative implementations of FW APSP used 32×32 tiles.

Internal-Memory Results. Figure 5 shows the speedup of various programs w.r.t. cpu-rdp for four DP problems. For each program, the DP table dimension n is varied from 2^{10} to 2^{15}. For single precision floats $n = 2^{15}$ is the largest power of 2 for which an $n \times n$ DP table (using 4 GB space) completely fits inside the 5 GB GPU global memory.

For FW-APSP, gpu-rdp-opt was the second fastest running program with gpu-rec-buluc running 1.5 times faster for $n = 2^{15}$. This is because unlike gpu-rec-buluc, all kernels of gpu-rdp-opt were not MM-like and hence it ran slower than Buluc et al.'s implementation. While our gpu-rdp and gpu-rdp-opt continued to run for $n = 2^{16}$ and beyond, none of the other GPU implementations did as they did not have mechanisms to expand beyond the GPU global memory.

When $n = 2^{15}$, our gpu-rdp programs for the Gaussian elimination, parenthesis and gap problems ran $1.3\times$, $11\times$, and $2.8\times$ faster, respectively, than their cpu-rdp counterparts. The speedup factors achieved by the GPU algorithms for the parenthesis and gap problems are higher than that for FW-APSP/Gaussian elimination because gpu-rdp for the former two problems have higher parallelism than the latter two.

External-Memory Results. It is easy to extend our algorithms to work for DP tables that are too large to fit in the CPU RAM and hence must be stored in external-memory (or disks). We can use either a 2-way or an r-way $\mathcal{R}$-$\mathcal{DP}$ for external-memory until a subproblem fits in the GPU global memory, after which we use an r-way $\mathcal{R}$-$\mathcal{DP}$ between GPU global memory and GPU shared memory. When an r-way $\mathcal{R}$-$\mathcal{DP}$ is used between two levels of memory, r is chosen as the smallest integer such that if an $m \times m$ DP (sub-)table is stored in the larger memory dividing it into tiles of size $(m/r) \times (m/r)$ each will make sure that $1 + s$ such tiles completely fit in the smaller memory, where s is the maximum number of additional tiles one must read from to update one tile. Using a 2-way $\mathcal{R}$-$\mathcal{DP}$ between the external-memory and the GPU global memory makes our algorithm oblivious of the CPU RAM size provided an appropriate automatic page replacement protocol is functional between the external-memory and the CPU RAM.

We use Standard Template Library for Extra Large Data Sets (STXXL) [1] 1.4.1 to implement our algorithms for external-memory. STXXL is a C++ library for implementing containers and algorithms that process vast amounts of disk data. In STXXL, we set the external block size as 4 MB, #pages as 1024, and #blocks per page as 1. This gives us a RAM of size 4 GB. STXXL maintains the CPU RAM as a fully associative memory with an automatic LRU page replacement policy.

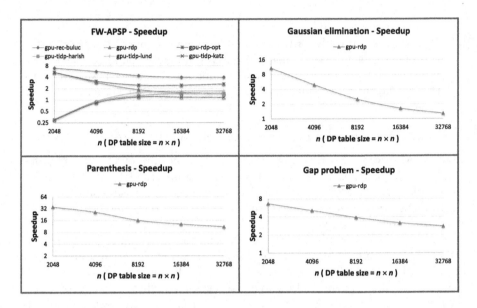

Fig. 5. Speedup of gpu-rdp programs over cpu-rdp for various dynamic programs. For FW-APSP, gpu-buluc-rec and gpu-rdp-opt are also included.

For each of the four DP problems we compare: (*a*) cpu-rdp-1: serial $\mathcal{R}\text{-}\mathcal{DP}$ running on CPU, (*b*) cpu-rdp-128: parallel $\mathcal{R}\text{-}\mathcal{DP}$ running on a CPU with 128 cores (details will follow), and (*c*) gpu-rdp: parallel $\mathcal{R}\text{-}\mathcal{DP}$ running on a GPU machine.

For gpu-rdp we store the input DP table in Z-Morton layout in the external-memory until we reach a submatrix size that fits in the GPU global memory at which point it is stored in row-major order. While the input problem accesses a single matrix in external-memory, a subproblem may access multiple submatrices of the DP table and they all have to fit in the GPU global memory. Once we compute a submatrix, we write the output to the same location in the DP table in the external-memory.

For cpu-rdp-1 and cpu-rdp-128, the base case dimension length is set to 256 and we run iterative kernels inside each base case. Since these two programs take too long to run, we approximate their running times as follows (instead of measuring time during real runs). The DP table is stored as a grid of blocks of size 16 K × 16 K each and it is stored in Z-Morton order. We use r-way $\mathcal{R}\text{-}\mathcal{DP}$ in external-memory and whenever a subproblem is brought to RAM, we use 2-way $\mathcal{R}\text{-}\mathcal{DP}$ to execute it on CPU. Observe that unlike our GPU program gpu-rdp, the two CPU programs are kept aware of the CPU RAM size in order to get faster running times. Let n_{base}, n_{base}^{128}, n_{chunk}, t_{base}, and t_{chunk} represent the number of invocations of base case kernels, number of parallel steps of execution of the base case kernels when we assume 128 cores, number of times RAM (of size 16 K × 16 K) is loaded/unloaded, minimum time taken (among several runs) to execute a base case kernel, and time taken to copy data between external-memory and RAM as given in STXXL I/O statistics, respectively. Then the running time of cpu-rdp-1 is $(n_{base} \cdot t_{base} + n_{chunk} \cdot t_{chunk})$, and that of cpu-rdp-128 is $(n_{base}^{128} \cdot t_{base} + n_{chunk} \cdot t_{chunk})$.

When $n = 2^{17}$, in our experiments for FW-APSP, Gaussian elimination, parenthesis and gap problems gpu-rdp ran 3.1×, 1×, 3.5×, and 1.6× faster, respectively, than cpu-rdp-128.

4 Distributed-Memory Algorithms

4.1 Distributed-Memory r-way $\mathcal{R}\text{-}\mathcal{DP}$

Our r-way $\mathcal{R}\text{-}\mathcal{DP}$ algorithms can be easily modified to run efficiently on distributed-memory machines. We modify the top level of the recursion by setting r to an appropriate value based on the number of compute nodes

Table 1. Our distributed-memory r-way $\mathcal{R}\text{-}\mathcal{DP}$ algorithms.

DP	Work	Latency	Bandwidth
LCS/Edit distance	$\mathcal{O}\left(\frac{n^2}{p}\right)$	$\mathcal{O}\left(\sqrt{p}\right)$	$\mathcal{O}(n)$
Parenthesis, Floyd-Warshall's APSP, Gaussian elimination w/o pivoting, Gap, Protein accordion folding	$\mathcal{O}\left(\frac{n^3}{p}\right)$	$\mathcal{O}\left(\sqrt{p}\log p\right)$	$\mathcal{O}\left(\frac{n^2}{\sqrt{p}}\log p\right)$

available and adding appropriate communication instructions. Only the first level of recursion under function $\mathcal{A}$ (e.g., $\mathcal{A}_{par}$) will have a distributed-memory implementation. Every other function and every other level of recursion of $\mathcal{A}$ will run completely inside a compute node and thus will have either a multicore or a manycore implementation.

```
distributed_𝒜_par (X)

 1.  d ← 1
 2.  r ← tilesize[d]                    {assuming tilesize[1] = √p}
 3.  Split X into r × r submatrices of size n/r × n/r each. The submatrix
     of X at the i-th position from the top and the j-th position from the left
     is denoted by X_{i,j}, where i, j ∈ [1, r].
 4.  We assume that for 1 ≤ i, j ≤ r, initially X_{i,j} belongs to node P_{i,j}.
     STEP 1 (LINES 5–6): corresponds to Line 4 of 𝒜_par in Figure 2
 5.  parallel for i ← 1 to r do
 6.      P_{i,i} calls 𝒜_par(X_{i,i}, X_{i,i}, X_{i,i}, d + 1)
     STEP 2 (LINES 7–23): corresponds to Lines 5–8 of 𝒜_par in Figure 2
 7.  for k ← 1 to r − 1 do
     STEP 2.1 (LINES 8–13): corresponds to Line 6 of 𝒜_par in Figure 2
 8.      parallel for i ← 1 to r − k do
 9.          P_{i,i+k−1} broadcasts X_{i,i+k−1} to P_{i,i+k...i+min{2k−2,r−i}}
10.      parallel for i ← 1 to r − k do
11.          parallel for j ← i + k to i + min{2k − 2, r − i} do
12.              P_{i+k−1,j} sends X_{i+k−1,j} to P_{i,j}
13.              P_{i,j} calls 𝒞_par(X_{i,j}, X_{i,i+k−1}, X_{i+k−1,j}, d + 1)
     STEP 2.2 (LINES 14–19): corresponds to Line 7 of 𝒜_par in Figure 2
14.      parallel for j ← k + 1 to r do
15.          P_{j−k+1,j} broadcasts X_{j−k+1,j} to P_{j−min{2k−3,j−1}...j−k,j}
16.      parallel for j ← k + 1 to r do
17.          parallel for i ← j − min{2k − 3, j − 1} to j − k do
18.              P_{i,j−k+1} sends X_{i,j−k+1} to P_{i,j}
19.              P_{i,j} calls 𝒞_par(X_{i,j}, X_{i,j−k+1}, X_{j−k+1,j}, d + 1)
     STEP 2.3 (LINES 20–23): corresponds to Line 8 of 𝒜_par in Figure 2
20.      parallel for i ← 1 to r − k do
21.          j ← i + k
22.          P_{i,i} sends X_{i,i} to P_{i,j}, and P_{j,j} sends X_{j,j} to P_{i,j}
23.          P_{i,j} calls 𝐵_par(X_{i,j}, X_{i,i}, X_{j,j}, d + 1)
```

Fig. 6. Distributed-memory implementation of A_{par} from Fig. 2. Here, X is an $n \times n$ DP table and p is the number of compute nodes.

We explain our approach by applying it to $\mathcal{A}_{par}$ from Fig. 2. The modified function is shown in Fig. 6. We map the given p compute nodes onto the nodes of a $\sqrt{p} \times \sqrt{p}$ grid P. We set r to $\sqrt{p}$, and split the $n \times n$ input matrix X into $r \times r$ submatrices of size $\frac{n}{r} \times \frac{n}{r}$ each. The submatrix of X (resp. compute node of P) at the i-th position from the top and the j-th position from the left is denoted by $X_{i,j}$ (resp. $P_{i,j}$), where $i, j \in [1, r]$. For $1 \leq i, j \leq r$, initially only $P_{i,j}$ holds

$X_{i,j}$. Only $P_{i,j}$ updates $X_{i,j}$, and all other submatrices needed for the purpose are brought to $P_{i,j}$ through either broadcasts or direct sends. Steps 1, 2.1, 2.2 and 2.3 of distributed-$\mathcal{A}_{par}$ in Fig. 6 correspond respectively to lines 4, 6, 7 and 8 of $\mathcal{A}_{par}$.

We use the following three cost metrics [60] computed along the critical path to evaluate our algorithms: (*i*) *computational cost* (F): #flops executed, (*ii*) *latency cost* (S): #messages transferred, and (*iii*) *bandwidth cost* (W): #words transferred. For example, for Fig. 6, $F = \mathcal{O}\left(\left(n/\sqrt{p}\right)^3\right)$ (Step 1) + $\mathcal{O}\left(\sqrt{p} \times \left(n/\sqrt{p}\right)^3\right)$ (Step 2) $= \mathcal{O}\left(n^3/p\right)$. The latency cost is dominated by the cost of broadcasts in the loop of Step 2 which iterates $\sqrt{p}$ times, and hence $S = \mathcal{O}\left(\sqrt{p}\log p\right)$. Since each message is of size $\mathcal{O}\left(n^2/p\right)$ the bandwidth cost of each broadcast is $\mathcal{O}\left(\left(n^2/p\right)\log p\right)$. Taking into account that the loop in Step 2 iterates $\sqrt{p}$ times, the overall bandwidth cost of distributed-$\mathcal{A}_{par}$ is $W = \mathcal{O}\left(\sqrt{p}\left(n^2/p\right)\log p\right) = \mathcal{O}\left(\left(n^2/\sqrt{p}\right)\log p\right)$. Table 1 lists these cost metrics for a number of distributed-memory r-way $\mathcal{R}$-$\mathcal{DP}$ algorithms.

We have designed distributed-memory r-way $\mathcal{R}$-$\mathcal{DP}$s for Floyd-Warshall's APSP, Gaussian elimination w/o pivoting and the gap problem, too.

4.2   Bandwidth and Latency Lower Bounds

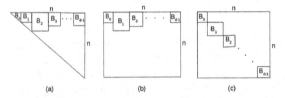

(a)   (b)   (c)

Fig. 7. Critical path in the (*a*) parenthesis DP evaluation, (*b*) GAP DP evaluation, and (*c*) APSP/GE DP evaluation.

In the parenthesis problem, we need to compute the cells in the triangle as shown in Fig. 7(*a*). The sequence of blocks $\langle B_0, B_1, B_2, .., B_{d-1}\rangle$ form a critical path as the values of the cells in a block depend on the cells of the block preceding it. Hence, unless B_i's values are computed, they can't be used for B_{i+1}. Let's assume that each block is computed by a single processor and there is no re-computation. As there are d blocks on the critical path, its latency is d. Let the block dimensions be $k_0, k_1, ..., k_{d-1}$, respectively. Then $W = \sum_{i=0}^{d-1}\Omega(k_i^2)$ and $F = \sum_{i=0}^{d-1}\Omega\left(k_i^3\right)$. We also know that $\sum_{i=0}^{d-1}k_i = n$. Hence, to minimize bandwidth and computation cost, we make each $k_i = k$ for some k. Thus $d = n/k$ which gives us $F = \sum_{i=0}^{d-1}\Omega\left(k_i^3\right) = \Omega\left(nk^2\right)$.

If $F = \mathcal{O}\left(n^3/p\right)$, then combining with $F = \Omega\left(nk^2\right)$, we get $k = \mathcal{O}\left(n/\sqrt{p}\right)$. Latency, $S = d = \Omega\left(\sqrt{p}\right)$, and bandwidth, $W = \sum_{i=0}^{d-1}\Omega\left(k_i^2\right) = \Omega\left(n^2/\sqrt{p}\right)$.

For other problems such as the Gaussian elimination without pivoting and the gap problem, similar arguments hold.

4.3   Related Work (Distributed Memory)

Communication lower bounds have been established for several linear algebra algorithms, including QR and LU decomposition [10,11,16,25,28,57,59,65–67].

Classical $2D$ distributed-memory matrix multiplication (MM) algorithms use only one copy of the input/output matrix which is distributed across all p processors (by making a $\sqrt{p} \times \sqrt{p}$ processor grid [15]). They have $\Theta\left(n^2/\sqrt{p}\right)$ bandwidth cost and $\Theta\left(\sqrt{p}\right)$ latency cost, while they balance the load ($F = \Theta\left(n^3/p\right)$) [8,10,36]. Our distributed-memory $\mathcal{R}\text{-}\mathcal{DP}$ algorithms also use only one copy of the input, and the ones that access $n \times n$ matrices also distribute them evenly across processors arranged in a $\sqrt{p} \times \sqrt{p}$ processor grid. While our algorithms also balance load they are a $\log p$ factor away from the bandwidth and latency costs of the best 2D MM algorithm.

There is a class of distributed-memory MM algorithms, called $3D$, where $p^{\frac{1}{3}}$ copies of the input matrix are spread across processors which make a $3D$ processor grid of $p^{\frac{1}{3}} \times p^{\frac{1}{3}} \times p^{\frac{1}{3}}$ [5,6,24,39]. These algorithms also load balance ($F = \Theta\left(n^3/p\right)$) as well as minimize the communication, with $\Theta\left(\log(p)\right)$ latency and $\Theta\left(n^2/p^{\frac{2}{3}}\right)$ bandwidth [10,36,60]. The third class of MM algorithms interpolate between the two classes where they take advantage of having c copies of the input matrix ($c \in \{1, 2, ..., p^{1/3}\}$) to build a $(p/c)^{1/2} \times (p/c)^{1/2} \times c$ processor grid, and hence they are called 2.5D. These algorithms have $\Theta\left(n^2/\sqrt{cp}\right)$ bandwidth and $\mathcal{O}\left(\sqrt{p/c^3} + \log(c)\right)$ latency. The same technique can be used for Gaussian-elimination style LU algorithm to obtain bandwidth cost of $\Theta\left(n^2/\sqrt{cp}\right)$ and a latency cost of $\mathcal{O}\left(\sqrt{cp}\log p\right)$ which is asymptotically optimal for any choice of c (modulo $\log(p)$ factor for latency). Ballard et al. [9] have extended the communication cost analysis of distributed memory algorithms to fast MM algorithms

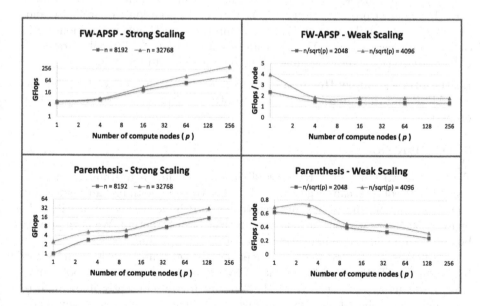

Fig. 8. Strong and weak scaling of our distributed-memory FW-APSP and parenthesis DP.

(Strassen's) and have proved that Communication-Avoiding Parallel Strassen (CAPS), running on a distributed-memory parallel machine meets the lower bounds on bandwidth and latency costs.

Distributed-memory graph algorithms [43,50] and DP algorithms also exist [33,35,38,42–44,63,68]. Solomonik et al. [58] presented a FW-APSP algorithm based on a block-cyclic approach which performs $\mathcal{O}\left(n^3/p\right)$ work and has $\mathcal{O}\left(n^2/\sqrt{p}\right)$ bandwidth and $\mathcal{O}\left(\sqrt{p}\log^2 p\right)$ latency. The 2.5D APSP algorithm given in [60] which builds on a recursive divide-and-conquer FW-APSP (Kleene) algorithm [7] has $\mathcal{O}\left(n^2/\sqrt{cp}\right)$ bandwidth and $\mathcal{O}\left(\sqrt{cp}\log^2 p\right)$ latency and performs $\mathcal{O}\left(n^3/p\right)$ work, where $c \in \{1, 2, ..., p^{1/3}\}$.

4.4 Distributed Memory Experimental Results

In this section, we present empirical results showing the performance benefits of our distributed memory algorithms that are based on r-way $\mathcal{R}$-$\mathcal{DP}$.

Setup. All experiments were performed on the SKX nodes of Stampede2 [3,70]. Each SKX node has dual-socket 24-core 2.1 GHz Intel Skylake processors ($2 \times 24 = 48$ cores in total) and 192 GB of DDR4 RAM. Each core is connected to a 32 KB L1 and a 1 MB L2 private caches. All 24 cores on a socket share one 33 MB L3 cache. Our Stampede2 allocation allowed us to use up to 128 SKX nodes simultaneously. We ran each MPI task on a separate socket, enabling us to run up to 256 MPI task for our experiments.

Implementations and Optimizations. All our algorithms (FW-APSP, parenthesis, gap) were implemented in C++. For distributed memory, we used intel MPI. Inside each process, we used Intel Cilk Plus extension to parallelize and Intel® C++ Compiler version 17.0.4 to compile the CPU implementations with optimization parameters -O3 -ipo -parallel -AVX -xhost. Additional intra-node CPU optimizations were the same as the ones explained in Sect. 3.5.

Distributed-Memory Results. Figure 8 shows the strong and weak scaling for FW-APSP and the parenthesis problem. Both algorithms show good scalability properties.

5 Conclusion

We have shown that 2-way recursive divide-and-conquer algorithms for a wide class of DP problems can be generalized so that they run with provable efficiency on shared-memory multicores and manycores (GPUs) as well as on distributed-memory machines without any changes in their basic structure. We have proved bounds on I/O and communication costs of these algorithms.

We believe that "Architecture-Independent Algorithms" holds promise for harnessing the full power of networks of hybrid compute nodes with both multicores and manycores because of their ability to run efficiently under multicore, manycore, shared-memory and distributed-memory settings. Many modern supercomputers already have such heterogeneous structures and exascale supercomputers in the near future are expected to look similar.

Acknowledgements. This work is supported in part by NSF grants CCF-1439084, CNS-1553510 and CCF-1725428. Part of this work used the Extreme Science and Engineering Discovery Environment (XSEDE) which is supported by NSF grant ACI-1053575. The authors would like to thank anonymous reviewers for valuable comments and suggestions that have significantly improved the paper.

References

1. Standard Template Library for Extra Large Data Sets (STXXL). http://stxxl. sourceforge.net/
2. The Stampede Supercomputing Cluster. https://www.tacc.utexas.edu/stampede/
3. The Stampede2 Supercomputing Cluster. https://www.tacc.utexas.edu/systems/ stampede2/
4. Top 500 Supercomputers of the World. https://www.top500.org/lists/2018/06/
5. Agarwal, R.C., Balle, S.M., Gustavson, F.G., Joshi, M., Palkar, P.: A three-dimensional approach to parallel matrix multiplication. IBM J. Res. Dev. **39**(5), 575–582 (1995)
6. Aggarwal, A., Chandra, A.K., Snir, M.: Communication complexity of PRAMs. Theor. Comput. Sci. **71**(1), 3–28 (1990)
7. Aho, A.V., Hopcroft, J.E.: The Design and Analysis of Computer Algorithms. Pearson Education India, Noida (1974)
8. Ballard, G., Carson, E., Demmel, J., Hoemmen, M., Knight, N., Schwartz, O.: Communication lower bounds and optimal algorithms for numerical linear algebra. Acta Numer. **23**, 1–155 (2014)
9. Ballard, G., Demmel, J., Holtz, O., Lipshitz, B., Schwartz, O.: Communication-optimal parallel algorithm for strassen's matrix multiplication. In: Proceedings of the Twenty-Fourth Annual ACM Symposium on Parallelism in Algorithms and Architectures, pp. 193–204. ACM (2012)
10. Ballard, G., Demmel, J., Holtz, O., Schwartz, O.: Minimizing communication in numerical linear algebra. SIAM J. Matrix Anal. Appl. **32**(3), 866–901 (2011)
11. Ballard, G., Demmel, J., Holtz, O., Schwartz, O.: Graph expansion and communication costs of fast matrix multiplication. J. ACM (JACM) **59**(6), 32 (2012)
12. Bellman, R.: Dynamic Programming. Princeton University Press, Princeton (1957)
13. Bender, M., Ebrahimi, R., Fineman, J., Ghasemiesfeh, G., Johnson, R., McCauley, S.: Cache-adaptive algorithms. In: SODA (2014)
14. Buluç, A., Gilbert, J.R., Budak, C.: Solving path problems on the GPU. Parallel Comput. **36**(5), 241–253 (2010)
15. Cannon, L.E.: A cellular computer to implement the Kalman filter algorithm. Technical report, Montana State University. Bozeman Engineering Research Labs (1969)
16. Carson, E., Knight, N., Demmel, J.: Avoiding communication in two-sided Krylov subspace methods. Technical report, EECS, UC Berkeley (2011)
17. Cherng, C., Ladner, R.: Cache efficient simple dynamic programming. In: AofA, pp. 49–58 (2005)
18. Chowdhury, R., Ganapathi, P., Tang, Y., Tithi, J.J.: Provably efficient scheduling of cache-oblivious wavefront algorithms. In: Proceedings of the 29th ACM Symposium on Parallelism in Algorithms and Architectures, pp. 339–350. ACM, July 2017

19. Chowdhury, R., et al.: AUTOGEN: automatic discovery of efficient recursive divide-&-conquer algorithms for solving dynamic programming problems. ACM Trans. Parallel Comput. **4**(1), 4 (2017). https://doi.org/10.1145/3125632

20. Chowdhury, R.A., Ramachandran, V.: Cache-efficient dynamic programming algorithms for multicores. In: SPAA, pp. 207–216 (2008)

21. Chowdhury, R.A., Ramachandran, V.: The cache-oblivious Gaussian elimination paradigm: theoretical framework, parallelization and experimental evaluation. Theory Comput. Syst. **47**(4), 878–919 (2010)

22. Cormen, T.H., Leiserson, C.E., Rivest, R.L., Stein, C.: Introduction to Algorithms, 3rd edn. The MIT Press, Cambridge (2009)

23. D'Alberto, P., Nicolau, A.: R-Kleene: a high-performance divide-and-conquer algorithm for the all-pair shortest path for densely connected networks. Algorithmica **47**(2), 203–213 (2007)

24. Dekel, E., Nassimi, D., Sahni, S.: Parallel matrix and graph algorithms. SIAM J. Comput. **10**(4), 657–675 (1981)

25. Demmel, J., Grigori, L., Hoemmen, M., Langou, J.: Communication-optimal parallel and sequential QR and LU factorizations. SIAM J. Sci. Comput. **34**(1), A206–A239 (2012)

26. Diament, B., Ferencz, A.: Comparison of parallel APSP algorithms (1999)

27. Djidjev, H., Thulasidasan, S., Chapuis, G., Andonov, R., Lavenier, D.: Efficient multi-GPU computation of all-pairs shortest paths. In: IPDPS, pp. 360–369 (2014)

28. Driscoll, M., Georganas, E., Koanantakool, P., Solomonik, E., Yelick, K.: A communication-optimal n-body algorithm for direct interactions. In: IPDPS, pp. 1075–1084. IEEE (2013)

29. Frigo, M., Leiserson, C.E., Prokop, H., Ramachandran, S.: Cache-oblivious algorithms. In: FOCS, pp. 285–297 (1999)

30. Galil, Z., Giancarlo, R.: Speeding up dynamic programming with applications to molecular biology. TCS **64**(1), 107–118 (1989)

31. Galil, Z., Park, K.: Parallel algorithms for dynamic programming recurrences with more than $O(1)$ dependency. JPDC **21**(2), 213–222 (1994)

32. Gusfield, D.: Algorithms on Strings, Trees and Sequences. Cambridge University Press, New York (1997)

33. Habbal, M.B., Koutsopoulos, H.N., Lerman, S.R.: A decomposition algorithm for the all-pairs shortest path problem on massively parallel computer architectures. Transp. Sci. **28**(4), 292–308 (1994)

34. Harish, P., Narayanan, P.: Accelerating large graph algorithms on the GPU using CUDA. In: HiPC, pp. 197–208 (2007)

35. Holzer, S., Wattenhofer, R.: Optimal distributed all pairs shortest paths and applications. In: PODC, pp. 355–364. ACM (2012)

36. Irony, D., Toledo, S., Tiskin, A.: Communication lower bounds for distributed-memory matrix multiplication. J. Parallel Distrib. Comput. **64**(9), 1017–1026 (2004)

37. Itzhaky, S., et al.: Deriving divide-and-conquer dynamic programming algorithms using solver-aided transformations. In: OOPSLA, pp. 145–164. ACM (2016)

38. Jenq, J.F., Sahni, S.: All pairs shortest paths on a hypercube multiprocessor (1987)

39. Johnsson, S.L.: Minimizing the communication time for matrix multiplication on multiprocessors. Parallel Comput. **19**(11), 1235–1257 (1993)

40. Katz, G.J., Kider Jr., J.T.: All-pairs shortest-paths for large graphs on the GPU. In: ACM SIGGRAPH/EUROGRAPHICS, pp. 47–55 (2008)

41. Kogge, P., Shalf, J.: Exascale computing trends: adjusting to the "new normal" for computer architecture. Comput. Sci. Eng. **15**(6), 16–26 (2013)

42. Krusche, P., Tiskin, A.: Efficient longest common subsequence computation using bulk-synchronous parallelism. In: Gavrilova, M.L., et al. (eds.) ICCSA 2006. LNCS, vol. 3984, pp. 165–174. Springer, Heidelberg (2006). https://doi.org/10.1007/11751649_18
43. Kumar, V., Grama, A., Gupta, A., Karypis, G.: Introduction to Parallel Computing: Design and Analysis of Algorithms, vol. 400. Benjamin/Cummings, Redwood City (1994)
44. Kumar, V., Singh, V.: Scalability of parallel algorithms for the all-pairs shortest-path problem. J. Parallel Distrib. Comput. **13**(2), 124–138 (1991)
45. Liu, W., Schmidt, B., Voss, G., Muller-Wittig, W.: Streaming algorithms for biological sequence alignment on GPUs. TPDS **18**(9), 1270–1281 (2007)
46. Liu, W., Schmidt, B., Voss, G., Schroder, A., Muller-Wittig, W.: Bio-sequence database scanning on a GPU. In: IPDPS, 8 pp. (2006)
47. Lund, B., Smith, J.W.: A multi-stage CUDA kernel for Floyd-Warshall. arXiv preprint arXiv:1001.4108 (2010)
48. Manavski, S.A., Valle, G.: CUDA compatible GPU cards as efficient hardware accelerators for Smith-Waterman sequence alignment. BMC Bioinform. **9**(2), 1 (2008)
49. Matsumoto, K., Nakasato, N., Sedukhin, S.G.: Blocked all-pairs shortest paths algorithm for hybrid CPU-GPU system. In: HPCC, pp. 145–152 (2011)
50. Meyerhenke, H., Sanders, P., Schulz, C.: Parallel graph partitioning for complex networks. IEEE Trans. Parallel Distrib. Syst. **28**(9), 2625–2638 (2017)
51. Nishida, K., Ito, Y., Nakano, K.: Accelerating the dynamic programming for the matrix chain product on the GPU. In: ICNC, pp. 320–326 (2011)
52. Nishida, K., Nakano, K., Ito, Y.: Accelerating the dynamic programming for the optimal polygon triangulation on the GPU. In: Xiang, Y., Stojmenovic, I., Apduhan, B.O., Wang, G., Nakano, K., Zomaya, A. (eds.) ICA3PP 2012. LNCS, vol. 7439, pp. 1–15. Springer, Heidelberg (2012). https://doi.org/10.1007/978-3-642-33078-0_1
53. Rizk, G., Lavenier, D.: GPU accelerated RNA folding algorithm. In: Allen, G., Nabrzyski, J., Seidel, E., van Albada, G.D., Dongarra, J., Sloot, P.M.A. (eds.) ICCS 2009. LNCS, vol. 5544, pp. 1004–1013. Springer, Heidelberg (2009). https://doi.org/10.1007/978-3-642-01970-8_101
54. Schulte, M.J., et al.: Achieving exascale capabilities through heterogeneous computing. IEEE Micro **35**(4), 26–36 (2015)
55. Sibeyn, J.F.: External matrix multiplication and all-pairs shortest path. IPL **91**(2), 99–106 (2004)
56. Solomon, S., Thulasiraman, P.: Performance study of mapping irregular computations on GPUs. In: IPDPS Workshops and PhD Forum, pp. 1–8 (2010)
57. Solomonik, E., Ballard, G., Demmel, J., Hoefler, T.: A communication-avoiding parallel algorithm for the symmetric eigenvalue problem. In: SPAA, pp. 111–121. ACM (2017)
58. Solomonik, E., Buluc, A., Demmel, J.: Minimizing communication in all-pairs shortest paths. In: IPDPS, pp. 548–559 (2013)
59. Solomonik, E., Carson, E., Knight, N., Demmel, J.: Trade-offs between synchronization, communication, and computation in parallel linear algebra computations. TOPC **3**(1), 3 (2016)
60. Solomonik, E., Demmel, J.: Communication-optimal parallel 2.5D matrix multiplication and LU factorization algorithms. In: Jeannot, E., Namyst, R., Roman, J. (eds.) Euro-Par 2011. LNCS, vol. 6853, pp. 90–109. Springer, Heidelberg (2011). https://doi.org/10.1007/978-3-642-23397-5_10

61. Steffen, P., Giegerich, R., Giraud, M.: GPU parallelization of algebraic dynamic programming. In: Wyrzykowski, R., Dongarra, J., Karczewski, K., Wasniewski, J. (eds.) PPAM 2009. LNCS, vol. 6068, pp. 290–299. Springer, Heidelberg (2010). https://doi.org/10.1007/978-3-642-14403-5_31
62. Striemer, G.M., Akoglu, A.: Sequence alignment with GPU: performance and design challenges. In: IPDPS, pp. 1–10 (2009)
63. Tan, G., Sun, N., Gao, G.R.: A parallel dynamic programming algorithm on a multi-core architecture. In: SPAA, pp. 135–144. ACM (2007)
64. Tang, Y., You, R., Kan, H., Tithi, J., Ganapathi, P., Chowdhury, R.: Improving parallelism of recursive stencil computations without sacrificing cache performance. In: WOSC, pp. 1–7 (2014)
65. Tiskin, A.: Bulk-synchronous parallel Gaussian elimination. J. Math. Sci. **108**(6), 977–991 (2002)
66. Tiskin, A.: Communication-efficient parallel gaussian elimination. In: Malyshkin, V.E. (ed.) PaCT 2003. LNCS, vol. 2763, pp. 369–383. Springer, Heidelberg (2003). https://doi.org/10.1007/978-3-540-45145-7_35
67. Tiskin, A.: Communication-efficient parallel generic pairwise elimination. Future Gener. Comput. Syst. **23**(2), 179–188 (2007)
68. Tiskin, A.: All-pairs shortest paths computation in the BSP model. In: Orejas, F., Spirakis, P.G., van Leeuwen, J. (eds.) ICALP 2001. LNCS, vol. 2076, pp. 178–189. Springer, Heidelberg (2001). https://doi.org/10.1007/3-540-48224-5_15
69. Tithi, J.J., Ganapathi, P., Talati, A., Aggarwal, S., Chowdhury, R.: High-performance energy-efficient recursive dynamic programming with matrix-multiplication-like flexible kernels. In: IPDPS, pp. 303–312 (2015)
70. Towns, J., et al.: XSEDE: accelerating scientific discovery. Comput. Sci. Eng. **16**(5), 62–74 (2014)
71. Venkataraman, G., Sahni, S., Mukhopadhyaya, S.: A blocked all-pairs shortest-paths algorithm. JEA **8**, 2–2 (2003)
72. Volkov, V., Demmel, J.: LU, QR and Cholesky factorizations using vector capabilities of GPUs. EECS, UC Berkeley, Technical report UCB/EECS-2008-49, May 2008
73. Waterman, M.S.: Introduction to Computational Biology: Maps. Sequences and Genomes. Chapman & Hall Ltd., New York (1995)
74. Wu, C.C., Wei, K.C., Lin, T.H.: Optimizing dynamic programming on graphics processing units via data reuse and data prefetch with inter-block barrier synchronization. In: ICPADS, pp. 45–52 (2012)
75. Xiao, S., Aji, A.M., Feng, W.c.: On the robust mapping of dynamic programming onto a graphics processing unit. In: ICPADS, pp. 26–33 (2009)

HPC Applications

Petaflop Seismic Simulations
in the Public Cloud

Alexander Breuer[1], Yifeng Cui[1], and Alexander Heinecke[2(✉)]

[1] UC San Diego, La Jolla, CA 92093, USA
{anbreuer,yfcui}@ucsd.edu
[2] Intel Corporation, Santa Clara, CA 95054, USA
alexander.heinecke@intel.com

Abstract. During the last decade cloud services and infrastructure as a service became a popular solution for diverse applications. Additionally, hardware support for virtualization closed performance gaps, compared to on-premises, bare-metal systems. This development is driven by offloaded hypervisors and full CPU virtualization. Today's cloud service providers, such as Amazon or Google, offer the ability to assemble application-tailored clusters to maximize performance. However, from an interconnect point of view, one has to tackle a 4–5× slow-down in terms of bandwidth and 25× in terms of latency, compared to latest high-speed and low-latency interconnects. Taking into account the high per-node and accelerator-driven performance of latest supercomputers, we observe that the network-bandwidth performance of recent cloud offerings is within 2× of large supercomputers. In order to address these challenges, we present a comprehensive application-centric approach for high-order seismic simulations utilizing the ADER discontinuous Galerkin finite element method, which exhibits excellent communication characteristics. This covers the tuning of the operating system, normally not possible on supercomputers, micro-benchmarking, and finally, the efficient execution of our solver in the public cloud. Due to this performance-oriented end-to-end workflow, we were able to achieve 1.09 PFLOPS on 768 AWS c5.18xlarge instances, offering 27,648 cores with 5 PFLOPS of theoretical computational power. This correlates to an achieved peak efficiency of over 20% and a close-to 90% parallel efficiency in a weak scaling setup. In terms of strong scalability, we were able to strong-scale a science scenario from 2 to 64 instances with 60% parallel efficiency. This work is, to the best of our knowledge, the first of its kind at such a large scale.

Keywords: High-order DG · Seismic simulations ·
Earthquake simulations · Cloud computing · Petascale computing

1 Introduction and Related Work

About 10 years after the introduction of cloud services, their 2018 worldwide revenue is estimated above 175 billion U.S. dollars, with a projected growth of

© Springer Nature Switzerland AG 2019
M. Weiland et al. (Eds.): ISC High Performance 2019, LNCS 11501, pp. 167–185, 2019.
https://doi.org/10.1007/978-3-030-20656-7_9

over 17% in 2019[1]. Further, recent enhancements of Cloud Service Providers (CSPs), e.g., the introduction of lightweight virtualizations and high-bandwidth networks, led to competitive solutions for the High Performance Computing (HPC) market. Yet, federal and institutional machines dominate the November 2018 Top500 List. This dominance is accompanied by an intense discussion of the HPC community, often questioning the feasibility of clusters, operating in the cloud [7,14,17,18]. Therefore, virtualized Infiniband solutions [15] or loosely coupled applications were proposed [8].

This work studies the Amazon Web Services (AWS) Elastic Compute Cloud (EC2) and the Google Compute Engine (GCE) of the Google Cloud Platform (GCP) in the context of large-scale HPC. First, we present thorough general-purpose performance benchmarking, explaining crucial HPC implications of the cloud providers' hardware settings. Next, we present a comprehensive study of high-order seismic simulations with the ADER discontinuous Galerkin finite element method. The method has been continuously and extensively optimized for extreme-scale performance (more than 10 PFLOPS) in the last five years [2–4,12,19,22]. However, respective advancements are limited to on-premises bare-metal machines. By exploiting the public cloud for the setup of tailored elastic supercomputers, we obtain a true end-to-end approach, starting at the machine setup, covering HPC optimizations, and reaching the full spectrum of modeling and simulation. Our contributions in this work are as follows:

(a) Section 2 motivates the need for fused forward simulations in earthquake science and summarizes the application EDGE, short for Extreme-scale Discontinuous Galerkin Environment. This section also introduces a new open source surface meshing tool and a new dynamic load balancing scheme for the solver's shared memory parallelization in noisier execution environments.

(b) Section 3 illustrates, that the open-source HPC ecosystem is well-prepared to operate high performance cloud computing solutions with latest hardware enhancements. Here, we describe the optimization of the CentOS7 Linux operating system for our cloud clusters, the preparation of custom machine images through system-wide setups of dependencies, and the use of the batch scheduling tools AWS ParallelCluster and Slurm GCP for elastic scalability.

(c) Section 4 assesses the theoretical performance of AWS EC2 and GCE through rigorous micro-benchmarking and shows that recent cloud-offerings are performance-comparable to bare-metal, on-premises systems.

(d) Section 5 analyzes the performance and scalability of the software EDGE in the cloud. We demonstrate that it is possible to achieve petascale performance for tightly coupled high-order DG simulations. This includes nearly matching the performance of an entire 2013 Top10 supercomputer (Super-MUC) for the same scientific workload, when using an elastic petascale cluster in the public cloud.

---

[1] Source: https://www.gartner.com/en/newsroom/press-releases/2018-09-12-gartner-forecasts-worldwide-public-cloud-revenue-to-grow-17-percent-in-2019.

We conclude our presentation by summarizing transferable observations and discussing implications for the future of HPC in Sect. 6.

2   Earthquake Simulations

High-dimensional challenges in earthquake science are common and have an inherently parallel inter-problem component. Important examples are Probabilistic Seismic Hazard Analysis (PSHA), the derivation of seismic velocity models through tomographic inversion, or seismic source inversions. Common approaches exploit the linearity of the used seismic wave propagation models. This enables reciprocity in the Strain Green's Tensors (SGTs) [5, 24], which, in simple words, allows us to exchange seismic sources with seismic receivers.

For example, CyberShake [11], the approach of the Southern California Earthquake Center to PSHA, discretizes the study area into hazard sites. Each site is a point of interest at the surface, where we quantify the seismic hazard, originating from potential fault ruptures in the vicinity of the site. We have two options to compute the ground shaking from the discretized high-dimensional space of uncertain ruptures: (a) Run one forward simulation for every fault rupture and sample the seismic wave field at each of the hazard sites, or (b) exploit reciprocity by running two (horizontal ground motion components only) or three forward simulations for every hazard site, and sample the seismic wave field at the surrounding faults. The latter case is preferable, if the number of hazard sites is much smaller than the number of considered ruptures, as in the case of PSHA.

In either case, the simulation setup of close-by ruptures in (a), or close-by hazard sites in (b) is, except for the used source discretization, typically identical. Shared parameters include the seismic velocity model, the mesh, the simulations' end time, and the output sampling of the wave field. From a computational perspective, this allows us to exploit inter-problem parallelism by fusing multiple forward simulations within one execution of the solver. The Extreme-scale Discontinuous Galerkin Environment (EDGE) is the first seismic solver, which integrates the idea of fused simulations into the entire modeling and simulation pipeline [4]. The remainder of this section describes a model setup, covering the San Andreas Fault's Parkfield section using EDGE. This fused setup is also used as the setting for our strong scaling study in Sect. 5.

2.1   Fused Forward Simulations

We use the Discontinuous Galerkin (DG) method in space and the ADER scheme in time to solve the elastic wave equations in velocity-stress formulation. The elastic wave equations are a linear system of hyperbolic partial differential equations:

$$q_t + Aq_x + Bq_y + Cq_z = S. \tag{1}$$

$x = (x, y, z) \in \mathbb{R}^3$ is the vector of Cartesian coordinates and $t \in \mathbb{R}^+$ time. Subscripts denote partial derivatives. The three normal stresses σ_{xx}, σ_{yy} and σ_{zz}, the three shear stresses σ_{xy}, σ_{xz} and σ_{yz}, and the three particle velocities in x-, y- and

z-direction, given as u, v and w, are summarized in the nine-dimensional vector of quantities $q(\boldsymbol{x},t) = (\sigma_{xx}, \sigma_{yy}, \sigma_{zz}, \sigma_{xy}, \sigma_{xz}, \sigma_{yz}, u, v, w) \in \mathbb{R}^9$. The three space-dependent Jacobians $A(\boldsymbol{x}), B(\boldsymbol{x}), C(\boldsymbol{x}) \in \mathbb{R}^{9 \times 9}$ depend on the seismic velocity model. The right-hand-side term, $S(x,t)$, accounts for seismic sources.

Application of the ADER-DG machinery leads to the discrete formulation. We use unstructured tetrahedral meshes for the spatial discretization of the computational domain. The discrete formulation consist of a series of small and sparse matrix-tensor products, which drive our computational single core performance. EDGE's fused approach allows us to execute these products as fully-vectorized sparse operators on cache-line-aligned degrees of freedom without artificial zero-padding [4]. More precisely, the LIBXSMM-library[2] is used to run-time generate and compile vectorized kernels, targeting Intel's AVX512 instruction set extensions. In the following, we use a fifth order ADER-DG scheme in space and time, and refer to [4] for further details on EDGE's discretization.

Previous versions of EDGE implemented the Standard Rupture Format[3] (SRF) for the source terms $S(x,t)$. The SRF discretizes kinematic ruptures as a collection of rupturing planar sub-faults, which act on the stress tensor. We replaced this implementation by a new and generic point source discretization in this work. Our new HDF5-based source format allows us to modify the particle velocities (not only the stresses) in the source terms, as required for the implementation of point forces at the surface. Surface point forces are, for example, used for forward simulations in PSHA. Additionally, EDGE's new source input reduces the modeling burden by projecting specified sources, outside of the computational domain, to the surface of the mesh.

2.2 Model Setup

Mesh: In the first step of our setup, we derived a surface triangulation from the 1/3rd arc-second Digital Elevation Models (DEMs) of the USGS National Map 3DEP Downloadable Data Collection[4] in the area of interest. For this purpose, we introduce the tool EDGEcut, based on the open-source library CGAL [1,23]. EDGEcut is able to automatically triangulate a projected DEM and to compute feature-preserving intersections of the discretized mountain topography with specified outflow boundaries. We used the transverse Mercator projection with center at 35.817°N, 120.365°W to project the DEM to a plane. The projection center coincides with the epicenter of the 2004 Parkfield event in [6]. Further, we introduced outflow boundaries at an 80 km epicentral distance in every cardinal direction and 40 km below sea level. EDGEcut supports problem-adapted surface meshing by following the attractor concept of the volume mesher Gmsh [9]. Here, we defined an attractor at $(-6\,\text{km}, 6\,\text{km}, 0)$ and linearly coarsened the surface mesh by eight times in an attractor-distance from 10 km to 50 km. We used a minimal edge length of 200 m and identical refinement specifications for the final volume meshing through Gmsh.

---

[2] LIBXSMM is available from: https://github.com/hfp/libxsmm.

[3] http://equake-rc.info/static/publish/paper/SRF-Description-Graves_2.0.pdf.

[4] https://catalog.data.gov/dataset/national-elevation-dataset-ned-1-3-arc-second-downloadable-data-collection-national-geospatial.

Velocity Model: We used a homogeneous velocity model with a density of $\rho = 2.8\,\text{g/cm}^3$, an s-wave velocity of $v_s = 1.2\,\text{km/s}$, and a p-wave velocity of $v_p = 3\,\text{km/s}$. Note, that EDGE's tool EDGE-V supports data-based mesh annotations via the Unified Community Velocity Model [20] and velocity-aware mesh refinement. However, as outlined below, our focus in this work is topography support for high-dimensional earthquake science.

Sources, Receivers and SGTs: Currently, most approaches to high-dimensional earthquake science use flat topography. The reason is often originated in the use of finite difference forward solvers, relying on regular meshes. As we are reaching higher resolved frequencies through the use of more powerful supercomputers, this lack of modeling complexity is getting more severe. Thus, for example in PSHA, adding topography to the forward solves is one of the most urgent model extensions. In this work, we benchmark the accuracy of three-dimensional reciprocal computations through SGTs, when using mountain topography in EDGE. For this purpose we placed eight sources at the surface. Our setup uses two configurations for each of the sources, a point force in x-direction (West-East), and a point force in y-direction (South-North). The source-time function of the point forces is given through the following Gaussian:

$$S(t) = \text{e}^{-60 \cdot t^2}. \tag{2}$$

In addition, we ran a single forward simulation with a single double-couple point source, located at $(0, 0, -7622.4\,\text{m})$. The source-time function of this source is a Ricker wavelet:

$$S(t) = \left(\frac{1}{2} - (1.92\pi)^2 \cdot t^2\right) \text{e}^{-(1.92\pi)^2 \cdot t^2}. \tag{3}$$

We obtained all simulation results in this section by using EDGE's fifth order ADER-DG scheme, 32-bit floating point precision, and by running in the Google Cloud Platform. Figure 1 illustrates our model setup, where the visualized wave fields correspond to the eight forward simulations with the point force in South-North direction. Further, similar to [24], Fig. 2 compares the synthetics of the single forward simulation to the SGT-derived synthetics of the point forces. Here, each of the signals was convolved with the Ricker wavelet as the new source-time function. We observe an almost perfect fit of the seismograms, which confirms the applicability of EDGE's reciprocal SGT pipeline within our modeling constraints. This procedure could now, for example, be extended to PSHA, where the insertion of rupture uncertainties reduces to a data-processing step w.r.t. source convolutions, once the forward simulations are completed.

2.3   Shared Memory Dynamic Load Balancing

EDGE is exposed to two sources of load imbalances in the shared memory domain: (a) Possibly runtime-dependent performance variations of the worker threads, and (b) diverse memory access patterns, caused by the unstructured mesh, when reading face-adjacent data in EDGE's neighboring kernel. Tasks of

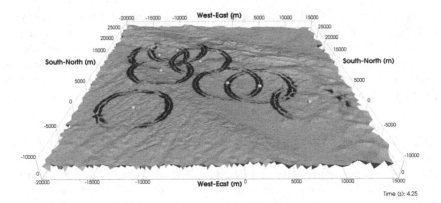

Fig. 1. Visualization of the surface point force forward simulations. The output require-ments were greatly reduced by only writing tetrahedrons at the surface and by limiting the output to the first and constant of the 35 modes of every fused simulation. The gray spheres indicate the locations of the surface point sources. Colors denote the South-North particle velocities of the eight South-North point forces after 4.25 simulated seconds. Warm colors denote positive velocities, cold colors negative ones. The entire run covered 16 fused settings and was executed in GCP. (Color figure online)

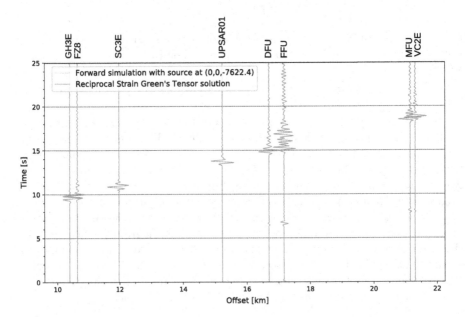

Fig. 2. Comparison of the post-processed point force simulations with the double-couple reference. Shown are the seismograms of the particle velocity in South-North direction for the eight stations at the surface. The x-axis reflects hypocentral distance. The convolved SGTs are largely indistinguishable from the reference. At the very begin-ning of each seismogram, a small and expected offset is visible, since we processed the raw signals without tapering.

the operating system can contribute background noise to the first case. Here, our core-specialization in Sect. 3 isolates most of the operating system's tasks to reserved cores, not used by any of EDGE's threads. However, within the preparation of this work, we additionally observed rare ($\approx 1\%$ probability per node and run) performance drops of isolated cores in our program execution. These drops appear to be independent of the Skylake-processor (bare-metal or virtualized) and the affected core seems to be random. They cannot be circumvented by using 1 GiB huge pages, as done in [16]. The impact on the overall runtime of EDGE without dynamic load balancing is severe, since we observed up to 20% slowdowns in our ADER-DG kernels.

We introduce a dynamic load balancing scheme to account for possible imbalances in EDGE's shared memory domain. Our load balancer is called, whenever EDGE reaches a synchronization point and the threads are joined. Synchronization automatically happens for wave field output at the free-surface or in the volume, whereas our point-wise sampling of the wave field at seismic receivers is entirely asynchronous. Thus, in settings using receivers only, e.g., in an SGT-only configuration, we enforce artificial synchronization for the purpose of load balancing. This synchronization interval is a runtime parameter, where all our scaling runs in this work used 5% of the simulation time, resulting in a total of 19 synchronization points for the duration of each run. Whenever we reach a synchronization point, we determine if re-balancing of any of our work regions is required. EDGE's seismic solver has four significant work regions: (1) the ADER time-prediction and local update of the send-elements, which computes data, required by other ranks, (2) the ADER time-prediction and local update of inner-elements, independent of communication within a time step, (3) the neighboring update of the send-elements, requiring data from other ranks, and (4) the neighboring update of inner-elements, not requiring any data of other ranks within a time step [4].

Let us assume a single work region, where worker w is responsible for N_w elements in a time step. This worker spent a total of t_w seconds in respective work packages from the previous synchronization point to the current one, where the load balancing is executed. Further, N_{all} is the number of all elements in the work region, $\max(t_w)$ is the maximum invested time of any worker, $\min(t_w)$ is the minimum spent time of any worker, and $\text{ave}(t_w)$ is the average time, spent by the workers. We define the element throughput T_w of a worker w, the element throughput T_{all} of all workers, the imbalance I of the work region, and the rebalancing R_w of worker w as follows:

$$T_w = \frac{N_w}{t_w}, \quad T_{\text{all}} = \sum_{w=1}^{W} T_w, \quad I = \frac{\max(t_w) - \min(t_w)}{\text{ave}(t_w)} \quad R_w = \frac{T_w \cdot N_{\text{all}}}{T_{\text{all}}}. \quad (4)$$

Now, whenever the imbalance I exceeds a given threshold, e.g., $I > 2.5\%$ in our case, we re-balance our work region by assigning R_w elements to each of the workers. If this does not lead to a worker for every element, we increase the number of elements per worker round-robin, until the N_{all} elements are distributed.

3   Cloud Setup

The cloud offers Infrastructure as a Service (IaaS). This allows us to customize the entire setup of our high-performance compute clusters to match EDGE's demands. Included are not only the choice of the underlying hardware, e.g., the CPU architecture, but also the entire software stack, for example, the operating system and its boot-options. This section describes the setup of our customized cloud-based compute clusters using the Amazon Web Services (AWS) and the Google Cloud Platform (GCP). The obtained single-application clusters are highly specialized to maximize the performance of EDGE (see Sect. 2). All used software and tools are freely available and open source. Thus, in contrast to commercial high performance cloud computing solutions, respective charges of our clusters solely originate from the used AWS and GCP resources.

The first software-related step of our cloud setup is the generation of customized cloud images, which are used for our login and compute instances. We base our AWS cloud image on the AWS ParallelCluster[5]-variant of CentOS7. Our GCP CentOS7 cloud image customizes the cloud-offered images of the GCP centos-7 family. Both cloud image setups share the same set of scripts, which first install all tools and libraries, required for building and executing our solver. For example, we install a recent version of the GNU compilers, OpenMPI, the libraries HDF5 and MOAB, or the performance monitoring tools Score-P and Scalasca. Once all software is installed system-wide, we customize the configuration of the operating system to maximize the instances' performance and to minimize possible interference with our solver. Using dual-socket instances, we reserve the first core of every socket for the operating system and instruct it through the GRUB2 bootloader to exclusively use these two cores. We complement this configuration in the job executions by pinning our applications' threads to all but the two set-aside cores. Upon completion of the setups, we store the images permanently in the cloud. We open-sourced the scripts, tuning our cluster, such that our findings can be transferred to other software.

We use the two tools AWS ParallelCluster and Slurm GCP[6] to generate our high performance computing clusters. AWS ParallelCluster and Slurm GCP use the clouds' APIs for this step, for example, by generating respective virtual private networks, or by using our machine images for the compute instances. Both tools offer a variety of configuration-options, where the most important ones are the used instance types, the used cloud images, and the instance placing. For maximum network performance, we use a dynamic AWS placement group and a single GCP zone for all of the clusters' instances. Further, since we are generating single-application clusters, we either generate clusters, exactly matching our instance requirements, or allocate no initial compute instances at all. In the latter case, if not used for computations, AWS ParallelCluster runs a single master instance, and our Slurm GCP configuration a single controller instance. The submission and monitoring of jobs on the generated clusters is similar to every

---

[5] AWS ParallelCluster is available from: https://aws-parallelcluster.readthedocs.io.

[6] Slurm GCP is available from: https://github.com/SchedMD/slurm-gcp.

other Slurm-based[7] on-premises solution. However, after job submission, the change in Slurm's node types triggers respective resume-scripts in background. These scripts elastically allocate instances from the cloud for use as Slurm nodes. Analogue, after completion of the job and a pre-defined idle time, the compute instances are released back to the cloud through suspend-scripts. Because our AWS and GCP charges are dominated by the number of allocated instances, the process of elastically allocating and releasing infrastructure minimizes costs.

4   Benchmarking the Cloud

This section summarizes important Key Performance Indicators (KPIs) of various cloud instance types on a per-node basis. We limit ourselves to Intel Xeon instances featuring Skylake-SP CPUs, as our application makes heavy use of 512-bit vector instructions, while maintaining a small memory footprint. CSPs use special versions of these processors and do not publish their processor-specifications. The same applies to the specifications of the physical memory population or network details. We mitigate this lack of documentation by studying a set of micro-benchmarks and a single-node setup of EDGE on various instance types. The obtained performance is then compared to runs on an on-premises bare-metal dual-socket Intel Xeon Platinum 8180 machine. The Xeon 8180 is the top-of-the-line processor, that is generally available and fully documented[8]. Apart from illustrating the actual performance of each instance type, we also set the micro-benchmarks' performance in relation to respective charges. This allows us to pick the best cloud solution for our application in terms of U.S. dollars ($) per simulation.

Table 1 summarizes all KPIs, we were able to gather from online documentation for our considered instance types. In the text of this section, we shorten notation by only using the lower-case names of the instance families, when referring to the considered instance models: **n1** for n1-highcpu-96, **c5** for c5.18xlarge, **c5n** for c5n.18xlarge, and **m5** for m5.24xlarge.

As instances are only described by their number of vCPUs (which are hardware threads) and the amount of available memory, it is hard to conclude how the actual underlying dual-socket platform is comprised. Let us take the vCPU count as an example. Here, the number of physical CPU cores could be higher and remaining "empty" cores could run the hypervisor. We found an indication in the AWS News Blog, that c5, c5n and m5 use the so-called Nitro Hypervisor, which provides nearly full hardware performance[9]. This indicates that no cores are set aside for additional management tasks. For Google's n1 we were not able to find a hint supporting one or the other assumption. A micro-benchmark could determine this detail by trying to determine Skylake's last level cache size, which

---

[7] AWS ParallelCluster supports further submission systems, e.g., AWS Batch or SGE.

[8] https://ark.intel.com/products/120496/Intel-Xeon-Platinum-8180-Processor-38-5M-Cache-2-50-GHz.

[9] AWS News Blog post: https://aws.amazon.com/blogs/aws/amazon-ec2-update-additional-instance-types-nitro-system-and-cpu-options/.

Table 1. Publicly available KPIs for various cloud instances of interest to our workload. Pricing is for US East at non-discount hours on Monday mornings (obtained on 3/25/19). *AWS CPU core name strings were retrieved using the "lscpu" command; **AWS physical cores are assumed from AWS's documentation, indicating that all cores are available to the user due to the Nitro Hypervisor; ***supported in multi-flow scenarios (means multiple communicating processes per host), each process is limited to 10 Gbps.

KPI	n1-highcpu-96	c5.18xlarge	c5n.18xlarge	m5.24xlarge	on-premises
CSP	Google	Amazon	Amazon	Amazon	N/A
CPU name	N/A	8124M*	8124M*	8175M*	8180
#vCPU (incl. SMT)	2 × 48	2 × 364	2 × 36	2 × 48	2 × 56
#physical cores	N/A	2 × 18**	2 × 18**	2 × 24**	2 × 28
AVX512 Frequency	≤2.0 GHz	≤3.0 GHz	≤3.0 GHz	≤2.5 GHz	2.3 GHz
DRAM [GB]	86.4	144	192	384	192
#DIMMs	N/A	2 × 10?	2 × 12?	2 × 12/24?	2 × 12
Preemptive $/h	$0.72	$0.7	$0.7	$0.96	N/A
On-demand $/h	$3.4	$3.1	$3.9	$4.6	N/A
Interconnect [Gbps]	16(eth)	25***(eth)	25***(eth)	25***(eth)	100(OPA)

is built as an aggregated cache of Cache-Home-Agent (CHA) slices. Normally, the number of cores matches the number of active CHAs. However, this is not important to our application EDGE, hence we did not perform such a test.

As the specifications of the cloud CPUs are not publicly available, also their frequencies are largely unknown, especially when running AVX(512) instructions. Therefore, the AVX512 Turbo frequencies are unknown, but given that they are normally lower than the regular base frequency, we can take the frequencies in the CSPs' online documentation[10,11] as an upper limit.

Similar educated guessing is needed, when studying the instances' memory configurations. In n1's case, 0.9 GB per core are offered, resulting in 86.4 GB for a two-socket machine. If the machine would be fully populated with 6 DIMMs per socket, this would mean 7.2 GB DIMMs. Therefore, we assume that the physical memory is (much) bigger, but still do not know if all DIMMs are plugged in. For the AWS instances the amount of available memory is at least matching with 16 GB populations, allowing the thesis, that c5 instances have 10 out of 12 slots in use, while c5n and m5 are fully populated. This theory is supported by AWS's recent announcement, that c5n instances can offer up to 19% higher memory bandwidth than c5 instances[12].

To shed more light on the instance types, we present micro-benchmarks with the goal to fill and/or refine some of the vague entries in Table 1. In particular, we test the floating point throughput, the memory throughput, the interconnects' capabilities and the full-application performance of a single instance.

[10] https://aws.amazon.com/ec2/instance-types/.
[11] https://cloud.google.com/compute/docs/cpu-platforms.
[12] https://aws.amazon.com/blogs/aws/new-c5n-instances-with-100-gbps-networking/.

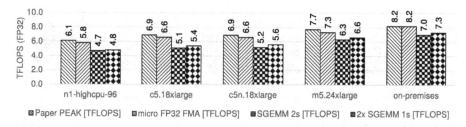

Fig. 3. Sustained FP32-TFLOPS of various instance types: (a) simple FMA instruction from register (micro FP32 FMA), (b) an MKL-SGEMM call, spanning both sockets (SGEMM 2s), and (c) two MKL-SGEMM calls, one per socket (SGEMM 1s). All numbers are compared to the expected AVX512 turbo performance (Paper PEAK).

4.1 Floating Point Throughput

Our first test studies the raw floating point performance. This is a key performance metric for EDGE, since the solver's local kernel is heavily flop-bound in order five. This kernel executes small FP32 sparse matrix-tensor operators. The results of our performance tests are shown in Fig. 3. Here, the first bar for each instance type is theoretical peak performance, derived from documented values (CSPs' websites, data sheet for bare-metal [13]). We see that our micro-benchmark, simply running FMA instructions through a sequence of 32 independent vfmadd231ps instructions, is able to reach close to the expected peak performance. While the bare-metal runs match our expectations, we observe about 5% lower values for the virtualized cloud instances. This can have several reasons: (a) the virtualization is adding a slight overhead, or (b) the AVX512 all-core turbo-frequencies are about 100 MHz lower than the CSP-specified frequencies in Table 1. In summary, we see that n1 is able to get 71% of the bare-metal system. The AWS instance models c5/c5n reach 80%, while m5 is at 90%. These numbers are aligned with the difference in peak performance, meaning that the cloud configurations are within 95% of the efficiency of the bare-metal system.

Further, we ran SGEMM across both sockets and two SGEMMs per socket. In the latter case, we obtained, compared to the bare-metal system, 66% for n1, 74% for c5, 77% for c5n, and 90% for m5. This indicates a difference in the memory subsystem between c5 and c5n, and a weaker subsystem for n1. Also, c5n seems to throttle the AVX512 frequency by 100–200 MHz, as the ratios drop to 77% from 80%. We observed a 50:50 frequency split on the bare-metal machine between 2.2 and 2.3 GHz, due to the TDP limit of the CPUs. Apart from small performance losses (≤10%), compared to our FMA benchmark, we conclude, that all instance types offer a solid performance relative to their peak. Thus, the instance type should be chosen by the pricing for flop-bound codes.

4.2 Memory

After analyzing the floating performance of heavily compute-bound kernels, we switch to the other extreme and investigate the offered memory bandwidth.

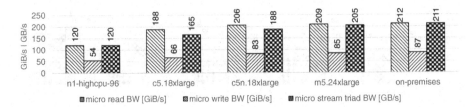

Fig. 4. Sustained bandwidth of various instance types: (a) a pure read-bandwidth benchmark (read BW), (b) a pure write-bandwidth benchmark (write BW), and (c) the classic STREAM triad with a 2:1 read-to-write mix (stream triad BW).

EDGE's unstructured accesses to data of the four faced-adjacent tetrahedrons in the neighboring update kernel ($4 \cdot 35 \cdot 9 \cdot 16 \cdot 4$ byte/float = 80,640 bytes) generate a significant pressure on the memory subsystem. Given Skylake-SP's FLOPS/bandwidth ratios, this operation runs at close-to full read bandwidth for order five. As shown in Fig. 4, the indication of the SGEMM tests in Sect. 4.1 is confirmed, since the n1 and c5 instances do not reach Skylake-SP's maximum memory performance. Since Goto's algorithm [10] has a high write bandwidth demand, due to blocking of the inner product, we can now explain the SGEMM performance drop. In the case of n1, the measured read bandwidth is very low, indicating either a multiplexed system among several VMs, a low physical DIMM population, and/or issues with the virtualization of the NUMA domains of the host system. For the STREAM triad, c5n is 14% faster than c5. m5 is an additionally 9% faster than c5n and very close to the bare-metal solution. This is aligned with Amazon's statement that c5n can provide up to 19% more memory performance over c5. Taking the memory sizes into account, this hints that c5 instances have only 10/12 DIMM sockets populated, whereas c5n and m5 should use all 6 memory channels per socket. A reduction of the populated memory channels for compute-optimized instances is explainable, since DRAM is a huge cost factor in a datacenter. In summary, the c5n and m5 instance models behave similar to the bare-metal machine. While c5 has an additional degradation, n1's read bandwidth is considerably lower. Section 4.4 studies how the memory bandwidth influences EDGE's full application performance.

4.3   Interconnect

We close our micro-benchmarking section of the cloud by examining the interconnect, when using AWS's c5 and GCP's n1 instance models. Here, we ran a subset of the latest OSU MPI micro-benchmarks[13]. Figure 5 depicts the following micro-benchmarks: point-to-point one process pair unidirectional bandwidth (osu_bw), point-to-point multiple processes pair unidirectional bandwidth (osu_mbw_mr), point-to-point one process pair bidirectional bandwidth (osu_bibw), point-to-point one process pair latency (osu_latency). osu_bw confirms our expectations

---

[13] http://mvapich.cse.ohio-state.edu/download/mvapich/osu-micro-benchmarks-5.5.tar.gz.

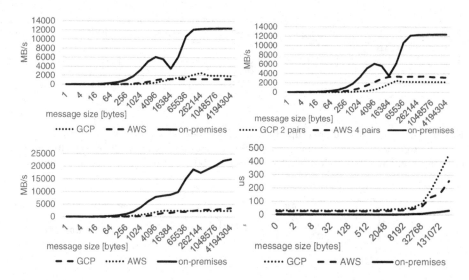

Fig. 5. Interconnect performance of n1-highcpu-96 (GCP), c5.18xlarge (AWS) and the on-premises, bare-metal system. Shown are results for the benchmarks osu_bw (top left), osu_mbw_mr (top right), osu_bibw (bottom left) and osu_latency (bottom right).

for all platforms: on the bare-metal system we get 12 GB/s for the Intel Omni-path 100 Gbps fabric, 1.8 GB/s (which is slightly short of 16 Gbps) for n1, and 1.2 GB/s for c5. As only one flow is active, the AWS performance is therefore limited to 10 Gbps. osu_bibw shows that all interconnects offer full-duplex transfers, however GCP's n1 instances need larger messages for full-duplex bandwidth. osu_mbw_mr, which runs multiple unidirectional channels through multiple ranks, does not offer an improvement when using Intel OPA. The n1 performance is now at full 16 Gbps for two processes. AWS's c5 peak is 25 Gbps with at most 10 Gbps per process, meaning that we require at least 3 process pairs for full bandwidth. For two pairs (not shown), the c5 interconnect achieves exactly 20 Gbps. Finally, osu_latency demonstrates that for message sizes below 16 KiB, both n1 and c5 exhibit 25× higher latencies (25us vs 1us), compared to Intel OPA. However, recall, that we send #modes · #variables · #fused runs · 4 byte/float ≈20 KiB for every communicating face, when using order 5 and FP32. Thus, the size of the messages in EDGE, comprised of the communicating tetrahedral faces, are in the MiB range, which shadows the higher latency. Sect. 5 shows in a simple model of a structured setup, that our solver is robust w.r.t. a network, offering 5× less bandwidth than latest supercomputing fabrics. This is due to the face-only stencil of the used high-order DG method.

4.4   Single-Node Application Performance

Finally, after deriving the flop, bandwidth and network performance through micro-benchmarking, we execute a single node scenario of EDGE with FP32, 16

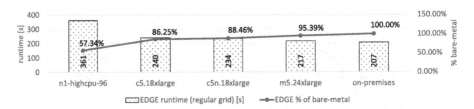

Fig. 6. Runtime of a regular setup of EDGE. As expected all cloud instances are slower than the top-bin bare-metal machine. AWS instances are within 85% of the bare-metal performance, the GCP instance achieves roughly 60% of the bare-metal performance.

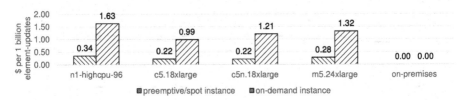

Fig. 7. US-Dollars ($) spent for one billion element-updates, when using pre-emptive/spot instances (interruptible by the CSP) and on-demand instances (uninterruptible).

fused runs and order 5 (35 · 9 degrees of freedom per element and simulation). Based on our micro-benchmarks, we expect, that the c5n and m5 instances reach a performance close to the bare-metal machine. While c5's performance should only be slightly lower, the degradation of GCP's n1 is expected to be most severe. Figure 6 confirms this estimate. Due to its higher flop performance, the m5 instance can get very close to the bare-metal machine (95%). c5 and c5n stay slightly under 90% of the bare-metal performance. n1 is still able to achieve 57% of the on-premises bare-metal solution with 70% of the flop and 57% of the STREAM performance.

However, when running in the cloud, one should also consider the instance pricing. Today's CSPs offer various types of instances, where we might utilize preemptive/spot instances for short-running or interruptible jobs. On-demand instances are best for uninterruptible long-running jobs. Table 1 provides the pricing for both types. We see, that the spot instances offer a huge discount. Figure 7 sets the measured full-application performance in relation to the instance price. We use the price in dollars per 1 billion element updates as a metric. For a given mesh, number of time steps, and by considering EDGE's scalability (see Sect. 5), this allows us to derive the costs of an execution upfront. Additionally, we are able to derive the most efficient cloud configuration: c5n is most cost-efficient, when using spot instances, whereas c5 leads for on-demand settings. Note, that other factors, e.g., the amount of available memory, the interconnect performance, the storage costs, or the availability of instance types should be considered in a final decision as well.

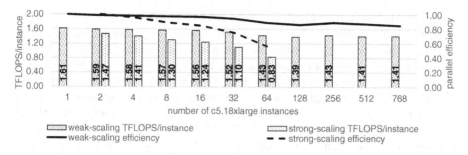

Fig. 8. Weak and strong scalability of EDGE in AWS EC2 on c5.18xlarge instances. We sustained 1.09 PFLOPS in weak-scaling on 768 instances. This elastic high performance cluster contained 27,648 Skylake-SP cores with a peak performance of 5 PFLOPS. The strong scaling setting on 64 instances had a performance of 53 TFLOPS.

5 Elastic Scalability

The previous section shows that, due latest hardware enhancements, single-instance public cloud executions can match the performance, provided by on-premises installations. In order to scale out, novel algorithms are needed to mitigate the 4–5× lower interconnect bandwidth. We address this by employing a high-order DG-solver with a high computation-to-communication ratio. As a side note, even latest on-premises systems can suffer from such an imbalance. A c5.18xlarge instance offers 6.6 TFLOPS with a bandwidth of 25 Gbps. In contrast to this, one node of the GPU-accelerated Summit supercomputer has 96 TFLOPS (also FP32) per node and offers 200 Gbps bandwidth[14]. Therefore, the cloud offers a FLOPS/bandwidth ratio, which is within 2× of Summit (of course the latency on Summit is still ∼25× better than in the cloud). This means, in order to run efficiently in the cloud and on Summit, similar approaches for communication avoidance and hiding are needed. In the following, we scale our application to 768 c5.18xlarge instances, having 27,648 Skylake-SP cores with a peak performance of 5 PFLOPS. This is a high instance count, considering that one normally has to wait in queues on a dedicated supercomputer. In all our tests the cloud was able to serve our requests within 2.5 h. That includes the largest setting, which required booting 768 instances with our custom machine image and registering them on the Slurm-controller.

We carried out two scaling tests, depicted in Fig. 8 (due to space limitations, we focussed on AWS for scaling and used GCP for the presented SGT runs). First, we executed a weak scaling scenario with two processes per instance to reach the benchmarked 20 Gbps bandwidth. Here, we took a regular five-fold subdivided hexahedral mesh with a total of 655,360 tetrahedral elements per instance for 1–512 instances. The 768 instance setting used $384 \cdot 512 \cdot 528 \cdot 5 = 675,840$ elements to provide a proper setting for our dimension-wise $8 \times 8 \times 24$ partitioning in this case. All boundary conditions were periodic, increasing the

---

[14] https://www.olcf.ornl.gov/olcf-resources/compute-systems/summit/.

communication footprint. Further, we did not exploit any of the structure, when running our unstructured solver, e.g., stored all adjacency information explicitly.

Taking the 768 instance setting as an example, we obtain $(48 \cdot 64 \cdot 2 + 48 \cdot 22 \cdot 2 + 64 \cdot 22 \cdot 2) \cdot 2 = 22,144$ tetrahedral faces for the six rectangular sides of each partition. For each face, data of the face-adjacent tetrahedrons has to be communicated to neighboring ranks. One y-z-side ($64 \cdot 22 \cdot 2$ faces) neighbors the second rank on the other socket of each instance. Thus, we obtain an uni-directional network-only communication volume of $19.6875\,\text{KiB} \cdot 19,328 \approx 371.6\,\text{MiB}$, when also considering the number of required bytes for the elements' degrees of freedom. With a single-instance average time of 0.81 s per timestep, we can estimate a bandwidth requirement of $\sim$460 MiB/s on the fabric in one direction and 920 MiB/s full duplex. This is also confirmed by our extensive Scalasca measurements. As AWS EC2 delivers 1.2 GB/s per process, the headroom is sufficient to account for efficiency losses due to congestion with other cloud jobs, using the fabric. This is important, as we cannot influence the instances' placement within the datacenter's placement group, e.g., schedule instances, which are all connected to the same Ethernet switch. For up to 32 instances we measured perfect weak scalability of 95% and for larger cluster sizes a slight decrease, staying above 86%. As comparison, our in-house 32-node Xeon 8180 cluster, connected by an Intel OPA fabric, achieved a parallel efficiency of 98% on all 32 nodes.

Second, in addition to weak-scaling a structured mesh, we ran the SGT scenario of Sect. 2, which includes topography and has an unstructured mesh, comprised of 3,861,780 tetrahedral elements. This setting fits well into 288 GB of memory, provided by two c5.18xlarge instances. In this case, the volume-to-surface ratio shrinks with an increased instance count and we expect the fabric to be limiting at larger scale. Figure 8 confirms this expectation. We can strong scale by 4× with close-to 90% efficiency. 60% are still possible, when using once again 8× more resources and strong scaling the original problem by 32×. While our elastic cloud cluster delivered 77% parallel efficiency on 32 instances, the 32 nodes bare-metal Intel OPA cluster achieved a parallel efficiency of 90%.

Last but not least, we want to highlight that for neither the weak- nor the strong-scaling case optimal placement in the datacenter or mesh-aware scheduling was exploited to keep results as generalizable as possible.

6   Discussion and Conclusion

This work demonstrates the efficient use of application-centric cloud clusters for modern and tightly-coupled scientific computing. Public cloud services offer elastic multi-petaflops machines, which were four years ago only available through on-premises supercomputing centers. In particular, we examined Google's and Amazon's cloud offerings. For a single instance, we observed a performance, matching that of a competitive on-premises bare-metal system. This is due to two recent hardware advancements: (a) offloaded hypervisors and (b) full virtualization support in CPUs for high performance VMs, allowing access to the underlying logical CPUs and NUMA domains. From an interconnect point of view, we observed a 4–5× slow-down in terms of bandwidth and ∼25× in terms of latency, compared to latest high-speed and low-latency interconnects. Taking into account the per-node performance of supercomputers, we see that recent cloud offerings are within ∼2× of latest accelerated supercomputers, when it comes to the per-node interconnect bandwidth. Therefore, no matter if one is running on an accelerated supercomputer or in the cloud, a bandwidth-efficient algorithm is needed. This work illustrates the cloud-specific end-to-end optimization of the high-order ADER-DG solver EDGE for seismic wave propagation problems, such as earthquake simulations. Due to EDGE's low communication volume, we were able to achieve 1.09 PFLOPS on 768 c5.18xlarge instances. These instances theoretically offer 5 PFLOPS, resulting in an application peak efficiency of more than 20% and a parallel efficiency of close-to 90% in a weak scaling setup.

This performance can be set into relation to previous work. In [3] a weak-scaling of another ADER-DG solver, SeisSol, is presented. The authors sustained 1.09 FP64 PFLOPS in hardware on the, at this time, Top500 #10-placed Super-MUC, an Intel Sandy Bridge system with 6.2 FP32 PFLOPS peak [21] (today this system is listed #64 in the Nov'18 edition of the Top500 list). The presented, application-relevant non-zero performance in [3] is 750 FP64-TFLOPS. In theory, this could double to 1.5 PFLOPS in a potential FP32 run[15]. Thus, five years later, public cloud clusters with 12 times less nodes and roughly five times less cores can replace a 2013 top 10 system.

This is due to three main factors: First, improvements in hardware (often associated with Moore's Law): instead of an 8-core CPU at 2.6 GHz, having two 256-bit VPUs without FMA, the current work uses an 18-core CPU at ≈3.0 GHz with two 512-bit FMA-VPUs per core. This means, that each Skylake core offers ∼4.5× higher capabilities than Sandy Bridge. Including the core-count, every socket in the cloud cluster is ∼10× more capable than a Super-MUC socket. Second, the efficient elimination of artificial zero-operations in the ADER-DG kernels through fused simulations, combined with runtime code-generation of sparse matrix-tensor kernels through the LIBXSMM library using single precision. And finally, third, an aggressive communication scheme, utilizing application-integrated MPI progression. Only the combination of all three aspects allows EDGE to reach high application-performance in the cloud.

In terms of strong scalability, we scaled a demanding setting from 2 to 64 instances with a parallel efficiency of 60%. This performance is a bit lower, compared to Intel OPA. For such scenarios, AWS announced the so-called EFA network, which provides lower latencies at up to 100 Gbps bandwidth.

Acknowledgements. EDGE, EDGEcut and the discussed cloud-related scripts are available under BSD-3 from the linked resources at: http://dial3343.org. We thank David Lenz for his contributions to EDGEcut. We thank the AWS Cloud Credits for Research and Academic Google Cloud program. At AWS we thank Walker Stem-

---

[15] Verification of FP32 for ADER-DG seismic wave propagation is recent work (see http://doi.org/10.17605/OSF.IO/H9G5N and http://opt.dial3343.org).

ple, Linda Hedges, Aaron Bucher, Heather Matson, Randy Ridgley and Pierre-Yves Aquilanti for their patient and very helpful support. This work was supported by the Southern California Earthquake Center through award #18211.

Optimization Notice. Software and workloads used in performance tests may have been optimized for performance only on Intel microprocessors. Performance tests, such as SYSmark and MobileMark, are measured using specific computer systems, components, software, operations and functions. Any change to any of those factors may cause the results to vary. You should consult other information and performance tests to assist you in fully evaluating your contemplated purchases, including the performance of that product when combined with other products. For more information go to http://www.intel.com/performance. Intel, Xeon, and Intel Xeon Phi are trademarks of Intel Corporation in the U.S. and/or other countries.

References

1. Alliez, P., et al.: 3D mesh generation. In: CGAL User and Reference Manual (2018)
2. Breuer, A., et al.: Petascale local time stepping for the ADER-DG finite element method. In: IPDPS 2016 (2016)
3. Breuer, A., Heinecke, A., Rettenberger, S., Bader, M., Gabriel, A.-A., Pelties, C.: Sustained petascale performance of seismic simulations with SeisSol on SuperMUC. In: Kunkel, J.M., Ludwig, T., Meuer, H.W. (eds.) ISC 2014. LNCS, vol. 8488, pp. 1–18. Springer, Cham (2014). https://doi.org/10.1007/978-3-319-07518-1_1
4. Breuer, A., Heinecke, A., Cui, Y.: EDGE: extreme scale fused seismic simulations with the discontinuous Galerkin method. In: Kunkel, J.M., Yokota, R., Balaji, P., Keyes, D. (eds.) ISC 2017. LNCS, vol. 10266, pp. 41–60. Springer, Cham (2017). https://doi.org/10.1007/978-3-319-58667-0_3
5. Chen, P., Lee, E.-J.: Full-3D Seismic Waveform Inversion: Theory, Software and Practice. SG. Springer, Cham (2015). https://doi.org/10.1007/978-3-319-16604-9
6. Custódio, S., et al.: The 2004 mw6.0 Parkfield, California, earthquake: inversion of near-source ground motion using multiple data sets. Geophys. Res. Lett. **32**(23) (2005)
7. Deelman, E., et al.: The cost of doing science on the cloud: the montage example. In: SC 2008 (2008)
8. Evangelinos, C., et al.: Cloud computing for parallel scientific HPC applications: feasibility of running coupled atmosphere-applications (2008)
9. Geuzaine, C., et al.: Gmsh: a 3-d finite element mesh generator with built-in pre- and post-processing facilities. Numer. Methods Eng. **79**(11), 1309 (2009)
10. Goto, K., et al.: Anatomy of high-performance matrix multiplication. ACM Trans. Math. Softw. **34**, 12 (2008)
11. Graves, R., et al.: Cybershake: a physics-based seismic hazard model for Southern California. Pure Appl. Geophys. **168**(3), 367–381 (2011)
12. Heinecke, A., et al.: Petascale high order dynamic rupture earthquake simulations on heterogeneous supercomputers. In: SC 2014 (2014)
13. Intel: Intel Xeon Processor Scalable Family Specification Update (2018)
14. Jackson, K.R., et al.: Performance analysis of high performance computing applications on the Amazon web services cloud. In: CCCTS 2010 (2010)

15. Mauch, V., et al.: High performance cloud computing. Future Gener. Comput. Syst. **29**, 1408 (2013)
16. McCalpin, J.D.: HPL and DGEMM performance variability on the Xeon Platinum 8160 processor. In: SC 2018, pp. 18:1–18:13. IEEE Press, Piscataway (2018)
17. Mohammadi, M., et al.: Comparative benchmarking of cloud computing vendors with high performance linpack. In: HPCCC 2018 (2018)
18. Napper, J., et al.: Can cloud computing reach the top500? In: UCHPC-MAW 2009 (2009)
19. Schoeder, S., et al.: Efficient explicit time stepping of high order discontinuous Galerkin schemes for waves. arXiv e-prints arXiv:1805.03981, May 2018
20. Small, P., et al.: The SCEC unified community velocity model software framework. Seismol. Res. Lett. **88**(6), 1539 (2017)
21. Top500 Authors: Top500 List, November 2013
22. Uphoff, C., et al.: Extreme scale multi-physics simulations of the tsunamigenic 2004 sumatra megathrust earthquake. In: SC 2017 (2017)
23. Yvinec, M.: 2D triangulation. In: CGAL User and Reference Manual (2018)
24. Zhao, L., et al.: Strain green's tensors, reciprocity, and their applications to seismic source and structure studies. Bull. Seismol. Soc. Am. **96**(5), 1753 (2006)

MaLTESE: Large-Scale Simulation-Driven Machine Learning for Transient Driving Cycles

Shashi M. Aithal and Prasanna Balaprakash[(✉)]

Argonne National Laboratory, Lemont, IL, USA
{aithal,pbalapra}@anl.gov

Abstract. Optimal engine operation during a transient driving cycle is the key to achieving greater fuel economy, engine efficiency, and reduced emissions. In order to achieve continuously optimal engine operation, engine calibration methods use a combination of static correlations obtained from dynamometer tests for steady-state operating points and road and/or track performance data. As the parameter space of control variables, design variable constraints, and objective functions increases, the cost and duration for optimal calibration become prohibitively large. In order to reduce the number of dynamometer tests required for calibrating modern engines, a large-scale simulation-driven machine learning approach is presented in this work. A parallel, fast, robust, physics-based reduced-order engine simulator is used to obtain performance and emission characteristics of engines over a wide range of control parameters under various transient driving conditions (drive cycles). We scale the simulation up to 3,906 nodes of the Theta supercomputer at the Argonne Leadership Computing Facility to generate data required to train a machine learning model. The trained model is then used to predict various engine parameters of interest, and the results are compared with those predicted by the engine simulator. Our results show that a deep-neural-network-based surrogate model achieves high accuracy: Pearson product-moment correlation values larger than 0.99 and mean absolute percentage error within 1.07% for various engine parameters such as exhaust temperature, exhaust pressure, nitric oxide, and engine torque. Once trained, the deep-neural-network-based surrogate model is fast for inference: it requires about $16\,\mu s$ for predicting the engine performance and emissions for a single design configuration compared with about $0.5\,s$ per configuration with the engine simulator. Moreover, we demonstrate that transfer learning and retraining can be leveraged to incrementally retrain the surrogate model to cope with new configurations that fall outside the training data space.

Keywords: Transient driving cycle modeling · Surrogate modeling · Machine learning · Deep learning · Deep neural networks

© Springer Nature Switzerland AG 2019
M. Weiland et al. (Eds.): ISC High Performance 2019, LNCS 11501, pp. 186–205, 2019.
https://doi.org/10.1007/978-3-030-20656-7_10

1   Introduction

In order to achieve the goals of increased fuel economy and performance while reducing emission, automotive manufacturers have implemented various strategies and parameter variables to control and optimize automotive engines. Engine calibration—the process of determining the optimal values of control variables such as spark/fuel injection timing, valve timing, exhaust gas recirculation (EGR) fraction is of paramount importance in achieving high engine performance and fuel economy while meeting emission standards. Currently, to make the problem tractable, automotive manufacturers optimize one or more engine performance indices (e.g., fuel economy, emissions, or engine torque) with respect to a given set of engine-controllable variables such as valve timing, EGR fraction, or ignition/injection timing, with all other conditions such as engine speed and load remaining the same. Optimal values of various engine operating points (speed and load) are obtained via dynamometer tests that are then used to generate engine maps. This procedure is called static calibration for steady-state conditions. These static calibration values are then interpolated to obtain optimal operating conditions for other operating points. The static calibration process, however, presents significant and unique challenges on account of the large design space and conflicting constraints. Over thirty independent design variables, including engine speed (i.e., RPM), torque, air-to-fuel ratio (AFR), and driving conditions (e.g., city or highway) influence the fuel economy, engine performance, and emissions. Moreover, most engines are operated in transient mode, especially during city drives. During the transient mode of operation, the engine speed and load change continuously and frequently (as opposed to a highway drive), and hence optimal operating conditions derived from static calibrations are not accurate. The lack of accuracy stems from the fact that there is a strong nonlinear correlation between various input parameters and outputs. For instance, a small change in the spark timing can increase the engine torque but also greatly increase the NO emission. In order to increase the accuracy for transient engine operation, more calibration tests have to be conducted over a wider range of input/controllable parameters to span the entire feasible engine operating domain. Hence, the cost and duration of the calibration process grow exponentially with the number of input/controllable parameters, greatly increasing the product design cycle/time to market. Even for engines with simple technologies, achievement of the optimal calibrations for the transient driving mode is impractical.

Harnessing the power of high-performance computing, one can perform optimal calibrations for the transient driving conditions using massively parallel computations. Conducting design, analyses, and optimization studies over such a large parameter space presents serious computational challenges, however. To span the entire engine operating range over the vast parameter space requires thousands of combinations of input conditions. For instance, if one were to consider just six different input control parameters with five parametric values for each input variable, one would have 15,625 (5^6) different input combinations for a single transient drive cycle (or commute of a single driver). Given the wide variability in the driving habits of individual drivers and different types of commutes, simulating the typical drives of a handful of drivers would yield over a 100,000 transient simulations. Each such simulation would produce vast amounts of output data, such as peak, average, and cumulative values of emissions, power, engine temperature, and exhaust gas temperature and pressure. Computational time for a typical city or highway drive is also a major barrier to the use of high-performance computing in large-scale transient drive cycle simulations. For instance, the computational time for a single engine cycle (one compression stroke followed by one expansion stroke of the piston) can range from a few hours to days at the strong-scaling limit (50–100 cores) of modern multidimensional simulation codes. A typical 25–30-min drive involves about 40–50,000 engine cycles. Thus, a single multidimensional drive cycle simulation would require well over a year, which precludes their use for such drive cycle simulations and optimization (calibration).

Given the need to simulate typical drive cycles of thousands of vehicles in real time (physical time taken to run engine dynamometer tests or dyno tests) while efficiently harvesting and learning useful design, development, and optimization data, we have developed a modeling framework called MaLTESE[1] (Machine Learning Tool for Engine Simulations and Experiments). It is a scalable simulation-driven machine learning (ML) framework that enables automotive design engineers to exploit the task parallelism inherent in simulating thousands of transient drive cycles and learning at real-time speeds. The framework also allows the coupling of experimental engine data in order to tune simulation constants and/or train the neural network and hence closely couples large-scale simulations, available engine data, and ML. This paper describes the use of MaLTESE to conduct the largest transient driving cycle simulation conducted on the Theta supercomputer at the Argonne Leadership Computing Facility. We also present an in-depth study of the use of ML methods to predict engine performance and emissions based on the training and test data obtained from the drive cycle simulations.

The MaLTESE framework consists of two main components: an engine simulator pMODES and a neural-network-based surrogate-modeling tool. Engine simulations of thousands of different typical transient city driving commutes, each approximately 25–30 min, were accomplished by using pMODES (parallel Multi-fuel Otto Diesel Engine Simulator). This is a parallel, robust, physics-based real-time engine simulator that can concurrently compute the performance and emissions for thousands of transient drive cycles. The simulator can perform engine simulations for either gasoline (Otto) or diesel engines with any combination of over thirty user-defined input/control variables. Given a set of driving conditions (wind speed, friction, gear-shift/transmission strategy, etc), one can obtain detailed information about over twenty engine outputs, such as fuel consumption, engine performance (power/torque), emissions (carbon dioxide, carbon monoxide, nitric oxide, soot), exhaust gas temperatures and pressures, and maximum engine temperature and pressure. The engine simulator produces the

---

[1] Aptly named after a small, intelligent dog that loves to learn new tricks.

same data as an engine being tested on a dynamometer. Since thousands of driving commutes can be simulated simultaneously, accurate input/output correlations (transient calibration) over a wide range of input parameters can be accomplished without the prohibitive testing costs. Furthermore, since the drive cycle simulations can be conducted at speeds faster than real time, a typical drive cycle simulation can be conducted in less than 30 min, hence making it practical for the design and development of fleets of cars. A subset of the large calibration data is then input to the neural-network-based surrogate modeling tool. Based on the calibration data, a surrogate model is trained to capture the relationship between the multiple inputs and outputs. The trained surrogate model can then be used to predict expected calibration values of other driving conditions and can be a part of the engine control unit. Large computing clusters with thousands of cores greatly reduce the wall time and effort by concurrently simulating thousands of driving cycles. A subset of the large data set was generated from over 300 million engine operating points in a typical commute of 250,000 different drivers. Finding the optimum operating condition for a given engine operation (speed, load, driving condition) can improve engine efficiency, reduce emissions, reduce engine wear and tear, and improve fuel economy. Use of large-scale computing and data analytics for drive cycle analyses enables engine designers to reduce the cost and time required for engine dyno tests, hence reducing the product design cycle and cost to consumers.

The main goal of this paper is to use MaLTESE to demonstrate the following:

1. Concurrent simulation of thousands of driving cycles with the engine simulator (pMODES) for a typical 25-min commute at faster-than-real-time speed.
2. Ability of deep neural networks to use a small subset of the parameter space to train a model and predict engine output characteristics of any arbitrary driving cycle in the parameter space.
3. Inference time of a deep-neural-network-based surrogate model being considerably lower than simulations with near 1% error in prediction accuracy.

This paper is organized as follows. Section 2 describes the method of solution for the engine simulation and the training and testing of the neural-network-based ML predictions. Section 3 presents the numerical experiments using various ML methods. Section 4 discusses related work. The main conclusions of the paper are presented in Sect. 5.

2 Surrogate Modeling for Transient Drive Cycle Simulation

In this section, we discuss the engine simulator and the ML approach for surrogate modeling. We also describe the parameters of the drive cycle simulations and the choice of the parameter subspace to train the neural network.

2.1   Engine Simulator

The engine simulator pMODES [2, 3] is used to compute the temporal variation of various engine parameters such as pressure, temperature, and mixture composition for each CAD over an entire drive cycle. The energy equation shown in Eq. (1) describes the relationship between the engine crank angle θ and instantaneous pressure $(P(\theta))$.

$$\frac{dP(\theta)}{d\theta} = \frac{\gamma - 1}{V(\theta)}(Q_{in} - Q_{loss}) - \gamma \frac{P(\theta)}{V(\theta)}\frac{dV}{d\theta} \qquad (1)$$

Here, Q_{in} is the heat input due to fuel combustion, Q_{loss} is the heat lost from the engine, γ is the ratio of specific heats of the working fluid, and $V(\theta)$ is the instantaneous volume of the cylinder. Solution of this equation yields the temporal variation of cylinder pressure for a given set of operating conditions (such as load, combustion duration, fuel type, and engine RPM). The instantaneous values of temperature and composition of the burned and unburned gas zones can be obtained from the instantaneous value of computed pressure. Knowing the instantaneous temperature, pressure, and composition of the burned zone, one can compute emissions such as nitric oxide, carbon monoxide, soot, and unburned hydrocarbons using simplified reduced chemistry models. Details of these models and the solution procedure are discussed in Ref. [4]. Instantaneous values of equilibrium concentrations of the combustion products are needed in order to compute various emissions. Computation of these equilibrium concentrations poses serious numerical challenges because of the stiffness of the system of nonlinear equations describing the formation of combustion products. References [2, 3] discuss the details of the computation procedure and steps taken to ensure a fast, robust solution. Following the solution procedure discussed above, one can obtain a temporal variation of output quantities such as emissions (NO, CO), engine exhaust temperature and pressure, and torque as a function of time. Figure 1 in Ref. [5] shows the temporal variation of NO and CO for a given fuel injection pattern.

   In this work we considered sixteen driving cycles. Each transient cycle had 1,500 data points corresponding to a typical 25-min commute, with data sampled every second (25 * 60). For each drive cycle, we considered five values for six independent engine parameters—spark timing, engine rpm (depends on gear ratio), ambient air temperature, air humidity, internal EGR fraction (proportional to valve timing), and compression ratio (engine size)—thus yielding 15,625 cases (5^6) with different input conditions for each drive cycle and 250,000 for all sixteen drive cycles considered. This number of 250,000 drive cycles is representative of the rush-hour traffic on four major freeways in a typical large city.

2.2   ML-Based Surrogate Modeling

A class of ML approaches used for surrogate modeling is supervised learning [6]. Typically, it is used to model the relationship between the output variables and several independent input variables. In this work, we seek to find a surrogate model that captures the relationship between the five output variables (exhaust temperature, exhaust pressure, NO, CO, and engine torque) and the ten input variables (ambient air temperature, air humidity, valve timing, engine size, spark timing, gear ratio, fuel injection rate, air-fuel ratio, engine inlet pressure, and intake air mass). A supervised learning method takes as input a set $\mathcal{T}$ of N training points of the form $\{(x_1, y_1), \ldots, (x_N, y_N)\}$, where x_i and y_i are the input and output vectors of the ith training point, respectively. The training procedure of the supervised learning method seeks to find a surrogate function h for $f : X \to Y$, where f is an unknown function that maps the multidimensional input space X to the multidimensional output space Y, respectively, such that the difference between $f(x_i)$ and $h(x_i)$ is minimal for all $x_i \in \mathcal{T} \subset \mathcal{D}$, where $\mathcal{D}$ is the full data set.

Arguably, classical ML methods are limited in their ability to learn directly from raw data. For decades, the development of ML surrogate models required considerable domain expertise to transform raw input data into a suitable internal representation from which the system could try to learn the relationship between inputs and outputs. Recently, representation learning methods have been developed to automatically discover representations that are best for learning the relationship between inputs and outputs [14]. Deep learning approaches [18] are representation learning methods with multiple levels of representation. They are obtained by composing simple nonlinear computational units that transform the representation at one level into a representation at a higher, slightly more abstract level. These approaches have dramatically improved the state of the art in many ML tasks, such as speech recognition, visual object recognition, drug discovery, and genomics [14,18].

Deep neural network (dnn) [18] systems are a prominent class of deep learning approaches. A dnn comprises a stack of computational layers organized in a hierarchical way, with the layers connected through a system of weighted connections. Each layer has a number of simple computational units, each with a nonlinear transformation operation called an activation function. The input layer of the dnn receives a batch of input data, which is transformed into higher-level representations through the stack of computational layers and weighted connections. The output layer of the dnn gives the predicted values of the outputs. During the training phase, the weights of the connections in the network are adjusted to minimize prediction errors. This adjustment is achieved efficiently by using a back propagation method that calculates the gradient of the error with respect to all the weights in the network and uses it in a stochastic gradient-based optimization to adjust the connection weights.

While there exists a standard dnn configuration for traditional ML tasks such as image and text classification, there is no default or general-purpose dnn configuration for surrogate modeling of engineering applications and in particular transient drive cycle modeling. Designing a suitable dnn for a given modeling task is a key research challenge for many nontraditional ML tasks.

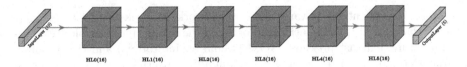

Fig. 1. The dnn configuration obtained for transient drive cycle surrogate modeling

We carried out an exploratory study and developed a relatively simple multi-layered feed-forward neural network. Figure 1 shows the obtained network used in this work: the input layer of size $|X| = 10$ is connected to a dense hidden layer with 16 units (HL0) and a rectified linear activation function (not shown in the figure). This configuration is repeated six times (HL1, ..., HL5), where the output of the previous layer is given as the input for the next layer. Consequently, the 16 units of the jth layer are connected to each of the 16 units in the $(j + 1)$th layer. The last layer is the output layer of size $|Y| = 5$ that gives predicted values.

3   Experimental Results

In this section, we first describe the setup that we used to assess the efficacy of the proposed dnn method. We then describe the training data generation and prediction accuracy results.

3.1   Setup

In addition to dnn, many classical ML methods (sometimes referred to as shallow learning methods) for surrogate modeling exist in the literature. Based on the algorithmic similarity and functionality, they can be grouped as regularization, instance-based, recursive partitioning, kernel-based, bagging, and boosting methods. For comparison with dnn, we selected several classical ML methods to cover different groups: ridge regression (rg) [16], k-nearest-neighbor regression (knn) [6], support vector machine (svm) [25], decision tree (dt) [19], random forest (rfr) [8], extremely randomized trees (etr) [13], ADA-boosting regression (abr) [11], bagging regression (br) [7,20], gradient boosting regression (gbr) [12], and eXtreme gradient boosting (xgb) [9]. As a baseline, we also included the simplest regression method, multivariate linear regression (lm).

The ML training and inference experiments were run on a single-node hardware platform with a 3.4 GHz Intel Xeon E5-2687W processor (8 cores per CPU), 64 GB RAM, with an NVIDIA Tesla P100, 16 GB GPU RAM. The dnn training and inference leveraged GPUs, whereas the classical ML methods used only the host CPU processors.

We used Python (Intel distribution, version 3.6.3) and the scikit-learn library [23] (version 0.19.0) to implement all the classical ML methods. We used the default hyperparameters provided by the scikit-learn library for the ML methods. For dnn, we used Keras [10] (version 2.0.8), a high-level neural network Python library that runs on the top of the TensorFlow library [1] (version 1.3.0). We used the following hyperparameter settings for dnn training: epochs = 50, batch size = 16, loss = mean squared error, and optimizer = adam. While dnn natively supports multioutput regression, where we can build a single model with multiple outputs, the classical ML methods considered in our study do not support multioutput regression. Therefore, we built one model for each output. We leveraged the MultiOutputRegressor interface in the scikit-learn library to build the multioutput regression models.

Given the different ranges for inputs and outputs, ML methods benefit from preprocessing the training and the testing data set. For each input and output, we applied MinMaxScaler and StandardScaler transformations in the scikit-learn library. The former scales the values between 0 and 1, and the latter removes the mean and scales the values to unit variance. We applied the two transformations before training and applied the inverse of StandardScaler and MinMaxScaler transformations after inference so that evaluation metrics were computed on the original scale. Note that the inverse transformations are required only for the predicted output values.

We adopted two evaluation metrics to assess the accuracy of the ML models on the test data and to compare them. The first metric is the Pearson product-moment correlation coefficient (r), which we use to measure the strength of a linear association between observed and predicted values on the test data. This metric ranges from -1 to $+1$. A value of 1 indicates a perfect linear relationship between observed and predicted values. A value of 0 indicates that no linear correlation exists between observed and predicted values and thus the prediction accuracy of the model is poor. A value of less than 0 means that as the value of observed (predicted) values increases, the value of the predicted (observed) values decreases. While this metric does not capture the absolute error, it is particularly useful when engineers build ML models for optimization as an end goal, where the relative ordering of the predicted values is sufficient to choose the best configurations. The second metric is the mean absolute percentage error (MAPE) given by the mean of $100 \times \frac{|y^i - \hat{y}^i|}{y_i}\%$ for $i \in 1, \ldots, n$, where y_i and $\hat{y}_i$ are observed and predicted values of the test data point i, respectively. We used this metric to assess the prediction error for each output.

3.2 Training Data Generation at Scale

As explained earlier, 250,000 different transient drive cycles were simulated concurrently by using the engine simulator pMODES to generate the training and test data for the ML algorithms. The simulations were conducted on Theta—a 4,392-node, 11.69-petaflop Cray XC40–based leadership-class supercomputer at the Argonne Leadership Computing Facility (ALCF). Each node of Theta is a 64-core Intel Xeon Phi processor with 16 gigabytes of high-bandwidth in-package memory, 192 GB of DDR4 memory, and a 128 GB SSD. The nodes of Theta are interconnected by an Aries fabric. Theta has a total file system capacity of 10 petabytes.

In this work, large-scale computing was used to exploit the inherent task parallelism in the simulation of a large number of drive cycles. In such applications, it is important to demonstrate that the overall size of the problem (number of drive cycles considered) does not adversely affect the total wall time for simulation. In order to test the weak-scaling characteristics of the simulation, three different tests were run, with 62,500, 12,5000, and 250,000 cases run concurrently, corresponding to 1/4, 1/2, and near-full-machine simulation (3,906 nodes out of 4,392 nodes). Since each drive cycle was run concurrently on a single processor, the total wall time for each of these cases should be nearly constant. Within each set of runs, the simulation time for an individual drive cycles depends on the computations required for the emissions, which can vary depending on the case being considered. Table 1 shows the minimum and maximum time required for computing an individual drive cycle.

Table 1. Weak scaling on Theta

Nodes (cases)	Min time (sec)	Max time (sec)
1024 (62500)	728	1157
2048 (125000)	740	1252
3906 (250000)	720	947

The runtime for a typical 25-min drive cycle was about 12–15 min (faster than real time) on the Intel Knights Landing (KNL) cores on Theta. From Table 1, we can see that the minimum simulation time is nearly constant for all the cases considered. We also can see that the maximum simulation time is nearly constant for the 1/4 and 1/2 machine size cases, whereas the near-full-machine simulation is about 20% lower. The system load from other jobs on the machine seems to have a greater impact on the simulation time for cases 1 & 2 compared with case 3, where there is less interference from other jobs on the system. These results demonstrate that one can simulate drive cycles of various sizes—even thousands—on a large-scale production cluster such as Theta without a serious penalty on overall wall time for computation as the size of the drive cycle simulations increases. Such a capability might be required if one were to use physics-based models to develop the acceleration and braking strategies for connected vehicles in order to optimize fuel efficiency, reduce emissions, and reduce engine wear and tear.

The discussion also shows that conducting a drive cycle simulation of a large parameter space requires considerable computational resources. To minimize the use of large-scale computing for drive cycle analyses, we investigated the possibility of using machine learning techniques wherein a small subset of the large parameter space is used as training data. We explored the possibility of using a trained model in predicting the characteristics of other drive cycles without the need for conducting simulations or gathering engine data with acceptable accuracy. In this work, we generated the following data sets for training and testing.

1. **train-data-1**: From the complete parametric study of 250,000 different drive cycles, a representative set of 64 different drive cycles, spanning the input parameter range, was chosen for training data. We used Latin hypercube sampling [21], a statistical method on the input space to select the 64 representative sets. Since each drive cycle had 1,500 data points for fuel flow rate, a total of 96,000 data points were used for training.
2. **test-data-1a**: To test the accuracy of prediction from the training set, we used two different test data sets from the entire set of 250,000 (excluding those used in the training). The first set comprised four different drive cycles, which had the same fuel flow rate but for which the other input parameters were different, for a total of 6,000 data points.
3. **test-data-1b**: In addition to this test data set, a random set of four drive cycles (for a total of 6,000 points) was chosen for the 250,000 cases (excluding those used to train the model). By random, unlike the **test-data-1a** case, no parameter was intentionally kept constant.
4. **test-data-2**: Both the test cases **test-data-1a** and **test-data-1b** were drive cycles wherein the range of input parameters of the test drive cycles was the same as that for the training model. In order to test the efficacy of the ML methods wherein the test data might have parameters beyond the bounds of the trained data, a third data set was generated. This data set had a fuel flow rate that was 20% higher than the corresponding fuel flow rate used in **test-data-1a**. Furthermore, the engine RPM was lower than that used in **test-data-1a** by 17%.

3.3   Comparison of ML Methods

In this section, we compare the different ML methods that were trained on **train-data-1** and tested on **test-data-1a** and **test-data-1b**. We use parallel coordinate plots to visualize the accuracy metrics obtained by the ML methods on the five outputs. In the plot, each output is given an axis; the five axes are placed parallel to each other. Each axis can have a different scale because each output can have a different range of values. Given an ML method, its accuracy value on each axis is connected and visualized through a line.

The parallel coordinate plots for Pearson product-moment correlation coefficients are shown in Figs. 2a and b. On both testing data sets, all ML methods obtain correlation coefficients larger than 0.92. On **test-data-1a**, dnn outperforms other ML methods, obtaining correlation coefficient values larger than 0.99 for exhaust temperature, exhaust pressure, NO, CO, and engine torque, respectively. The trend is similar on **test-data-1b**, where dnn achieves larger correlation coefficient values than those of the classical ML methods. An exception is for exhaust temperature, where the correlation coefficient of xgb is slightly larger than dnn.

Figures 2c and d show the MAPE values on **test-data-1a** and **test-data-1b**, respectively. The range of error percentages for exhaust temperature, exhaust pressure, NO, and engine torque is between 0.2% and 2.5%; but for CO the error goes up to 10.39% and 7.23% on **test-data-1a** and **test-data-1b**,

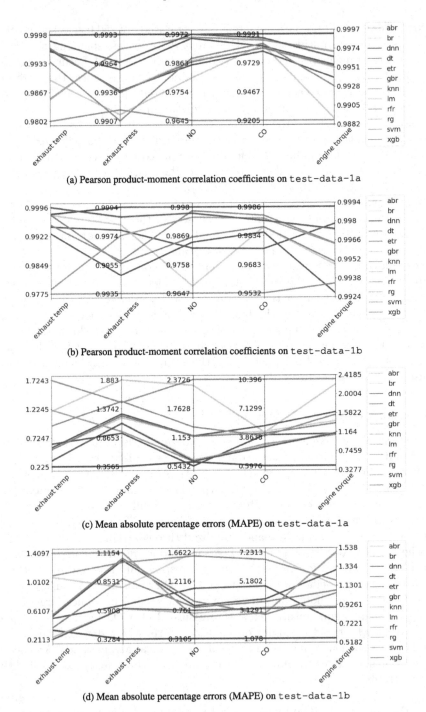

(a) Pearson product-moment correlation coefficients on test-data-1a

(b) Pearson product-moment correlation coefficients on test-data-1b

(c) Mean absolute percentage errors (MAPE) on test-data-1a

(d) Mean absolute percentage errors (MAPE) on test-data-1b

Fig. 2. Parallel coordinate plot showing the accuracy metrics obtained by different ML methods

respectively. This indicates that prediction of CO is more difficult than prediction of exhaust temperature, exhaust pressure, NO, and engine torque. The MAPE values obtained by dnn are smaller than those of other ML methods. In particular, dnn achieves significantly smaller MAPE values for the outputs; exhaust pressure, CO, and engine torque. Overall, MAPE values of dnn are not more than 0.59% and 1.07% on test-data-1a and test-data-1b, respectively. The scatter plots of observed and predicted values from dnn for the five outputs on test-data-1a and test-data-1b are given in Appendix A.

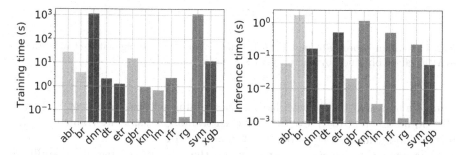

(a) Time required for training different ML methods with train-data-1 (96000 training points)

(b) Time required for inference using different ML methods on test-data-1a (6000 testing points)

Fig. 3. Bar plots showing the training and inference times of the different ML methods

Figure 3 shows the training and inference times of the different ML methods on train-data-1 and test-data-1a, respectively. From Fig. 3a, we observe that dnn requires approximately 1,000 s for training. On the other hand, the training times of classical ML methods range between 0.1 and 10 s. An exception is svm, which requires a training time similar to that of dnn. Even though dnn leverages P100 GPUs, it is more computationally expensive than other ML methods. This difference can be attributed to the cubic algorithmic time complexity. The bagging and boosting methods typically have a time complexity of $O(N \log N)$ in the training set size N. Figure 3b shows the time required for inference on test-data-1a. To predict 6,000 points, dnn requires approximately 0.1 s (16 microseconds/configuration), which is lower than that of several sophisticated classical ML methods such as br, etr, rfr, and svm. Simple ML methods such as lm, rg, and dt require less than 0.01 s, but their accuracy values are not as high. We observed a similar trend on test-data-1b.

3.4   Impact of Training Set Size

We studied the impact of the training data size on the accuracy of the dnn method by varying the number of training points. In addition to the default training data size of 96,000, we considered training set sizes of 1,500, 3,000, 6,000, 12,000, 24,000 and 48,000 data points (1,500 data points represent one

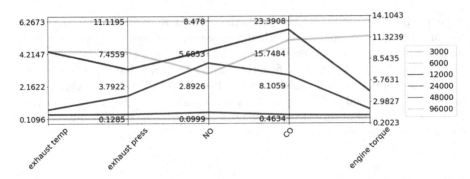

Fig. 4. Parallel coordinate plot showing the impact of training data set size on the MAPE values obtained by **dnn** on **test-data-1a**

complete transient drive cycle; hence, the training set sizes represent 1, 2, 4, 8, 16, and 32 different drive cycles). For each training set size, we trained the **dnn** method and evaluated the model on **test-data-1a**.

The results are shown in Fig. 4, where the lines in the parallel coordinate plot correspond to the training data set sizes. We observe that an increase in the training set size decreases the MAPE values. We did not include the MAPE values for 1,500 because the error values are too high (greater than 100%), which results in skewed axes ranges. The **dnn** model trained with 3,000 points yields MAPE values between 6.26% and 23.39%. While the MAPE values for training set size to 6,000 and 12,000 are lower than that of 3,000, to achieve MAPE values within 1% for all the outputs, the **dnn** model requires at least 48,000 training points.

3.5   Model Adaptation Using Transfer Learning and Retraining

We evaluated the efficacy of the ML models when the test data falls outside the training data regime. We took the ML models trained on **train-data-1** and tested them on **test-data-2**. The results are shown in Fig. 5a. The ranges of MAPE values for all ML models are large: [1.71%, 20.24%] for exhaust temperature, [10.21%, 22.73%] for exhaust pressure, [1.83%, 15.25%] for NO, [10.61%, 269.43%] for CO, [5.34%, 46.86%] for engine torque. This range can be attributed to the fact that while ML methods can generalize the learned functional relationship inside the input space spanned by the training points, outside that space their prediction power decreases significantly.

A promising approach to adapt ML models for new test cases such as **test-data-2** involves calibrating the trained model by using transfer learning, where a model trained on one task can be adapted to a similar task with limited training data. In our case, a small subset of data from **test-data-2** can be used to retrain the model. Nevertheless, not all ML methods offer that transfer learning capability. Among the ML methods considered in our study only **dnn** can be

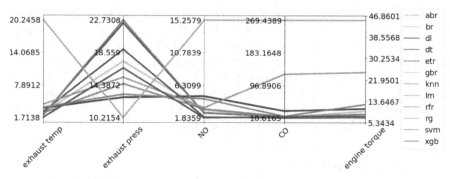

(a) MAPE values obtained by the ML methods on `test-data-2`

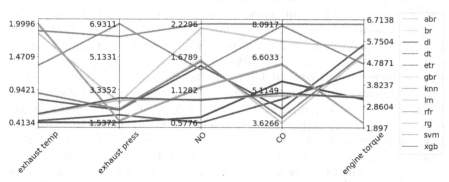

(b) MAPE values obtained by the ML methods on `test-data-2` with retraining and transfer learning

Fig. 5. Parallel coordinate plots showing the impact of retraining and transfer learning on the ML methods

used for transfer learning. All other methods require complete retraining, where one needs to add the new data to the training data and train from scratch.

We used 1,500 points from `test-data-2` for transfer learning and retraining from scratch. We note that the training data set size of 1,500 points alone resulted in poor prediction accuracy on `train-data-1`. Our hypothesis is that using the ideas of transfer learning and retraining but with the same limited data setting, we can significantly improve the prediction accuracy of the ML models.

For **dnn**, we took the model trained on `train-data-1`. To enable transfer learning, we froze the weights of HiddenLayer0, HiddenLayer1, and Hidden-Layer2 layers (see Fig. 1); used 1,500 points from `test-data-2`; and retrained the **dnn** model, where the weights of HiddenLayer3, HiddenLayer4, and Hidden-Layer5 layers were adjusted. The retrained **dnn** model was then used to predict the outputs in `test-data-2`. For other ML models, we used the retraining-from-scratch approach, where we added 1,500 points from `test-data-2` to 96,000 points of `train-data-1` and trained the ML models.

The results are shown in Fig. 5b. We observe that both the transfer learning method and training from scratch for other ML methods significantly reduce error values for all the outputs. The ranges of MAPE values are [0.41%, 1.99%] for exhaust temperature, [1.53%, 6.93%] for exhaust pressure, [0.57%, 2.22%] for NO, [3.62%, 8.09%] for CO, and [1.89%, 6.71%] for engine torque. The dnn method obtains smaller MAPE values for three outputs: 0.41% for exhaust temperature, 1.53% for exhaust pressure, and 0.58% for NO. Only for CO and engine torque are the MAPE values larger. Overall, however, MAPE is within 5.5%.

4   Related Work

Given the importance of internal combustion (IC) engines in transportation and power generation, considerable work has been conducted in the area of predicting their performance and emissions, including the use of soft computing techniques such as artificial neutral networks (ANNs). Some of the earliest attempts to use ANNs to predict the NO emissions during the transient operation of a diesel engine were reported by Ref. [17]. Similar attempts were reported in Refs. [15, 22]. Reference [24] provides an exhaustive review of the use of soft computing techniques in automotive engines. All the reported results with these techniques for IC engines are for a single engine/transient operation. Most of these reported results use experimental data from an engine operation with a small set of input parameters (two to three input variables) to predict a specific output quantity such as NO or exhaust temperature. None of the papers have attempted to use machine learning techniques to predict the performance and emissions of a fleet of cars with a large set of input parameters, each of which was varied over a large operating range, as reported in this work.

To the best of our knowledge, this is the single largest drive cycle simulation (250,000 different cases) conducted by using a well-validated, physics-based reduced-order model at faster-than-real-time computing speeds. This is also the first demonstration of the ability to apply ML methods to such large-scale engine data to predict performance and emissions.

5   Conclusion

We developed MaLTESE, a simulation-driven machine learning modeling framework that couples massively parallel simulations of thousands of engine drive cycles at real-time speeds and a machine-learning-based surrogate modeling approach. We scaled the simulation up to 3,906 nodes on the Theta supercomputer at the Argonne Leadership Computing Facility to generate data for training the surrogate model. We developed a deep-neural-network-based surrogate model and compared it with several classical machine learning methods. From our numerical experiments we observed that all learning methods yielded reasonably good prediction accuracy. We demonstrated that the deep neural network is a promising method: it outperforms other classical machine learning techniques and achieves correlation coefficient values larger than 0.99 and a mean absolute percentage error within 1.07% for exhaust temperature, exhaust pressure, nitric oxide, carbon monoxide, and engine torque. Our comparative study of machine learning methods provides valuable input to design engineers who can make an informed decision about the use of machine learning methods for their design and development assessments.

In addition to the prediction accuracy of various machine learning methods, we studied the training and inference times for the various learning methods. We observed that the training time for deep neural networks was about two to four orders of magnitude higher than that for classical machine learning methods: 0.1–10 s for classical methods vs 1000 s for deep neural networks. Once the model is trained, however, the interference time required by the deep neural network to predict the output characteristics 6,000 data points (4 different drive cycles) is about 0.1 s (16 microseconds/configuration). As shown earlier, concurrent simulation of four different drive cycles on four KNL processors would take over 700 s. These inference timing studies show that the deep-neural-network-based surrogate-model can be used for real-time control using the emerging low-cost and relatively low-powered on-board deep learning chips.

The parametric study of the size of the training set showed that for predicting all output variables within 1% accuracy, 48,000 data points (corresponding to 32 different representative drive cycles) were required. This study shows that a small subset of well-chosen representative drive-cycles (64 drive cycles in this case) can be used to predict the output of other drive cycles without having to simulate the entire parametric range (250,000 drive cycles). Based on the transfer learning studies, we have demonstrated the possibility of using machine learning methods to yield high-accuracy prediction even when the input parameter space is considerably different from the parameter range used for training.

Acknowledgment. This research used resources of the Argonne Leadership Computing Facility, which is a DOE Office of Science User Facility supported under Contract DE-AC02-06CH11357. This material was based upon work supported by the U.S. Department of Energy, Office of Science, under Contract DE-AC02-06CH11357.

A   Appendix

See Figs. 6, 7, 8, 9 and 10.

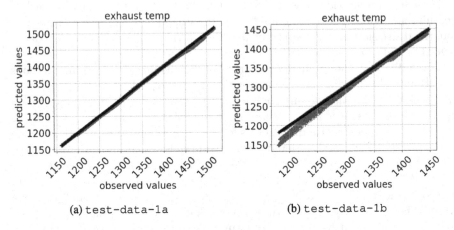

(a) test-data-1a

(b) test-data-1b

Fig. 6. Scatter plot of observed and predicted values from **dnn** for exhaust temperature on **test-data-1a** and **test-data-1b**

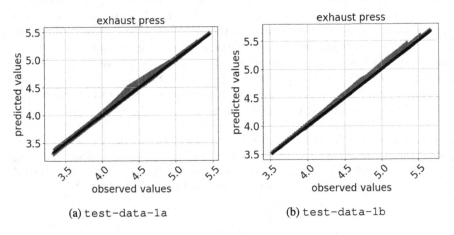

(a) test-data-1a

(b) test-data-1b

Fig. 7. Scatter plot of observed and predicted values from **dnn** for exhaust pressure on **test-data-1a** and **test-data-1b**

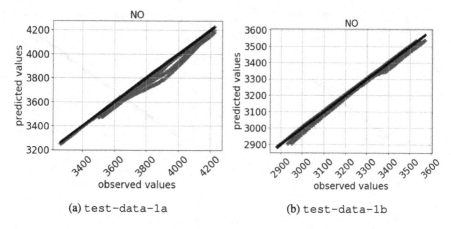

Fig. 8. Scatter plot of observed and predicted values from **dnn** for NO on **test-data-1a** and **test-data-1b**

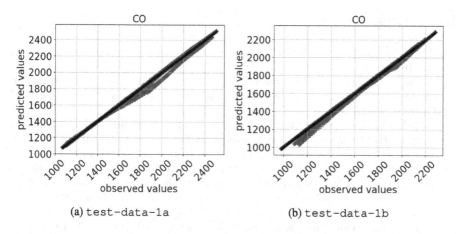

Fig. 9. Scatter plot of observed and predicted values from **dnn** for CO on **test-data-1a** and **test-data-1b**

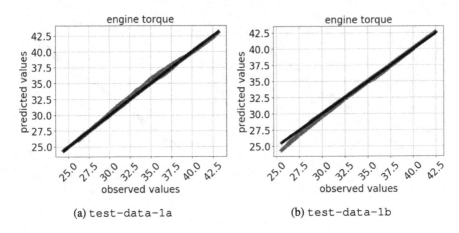

Fig. 10. Scatter plot of observed and predicted values from **dnn** for engine torque on `test-data-1a` and `test-data-1b`

References

1. Abadi, M., et al.: Tensorflow: a system for large-scale machine learning. In: OSDI, vol. 16, pp. 265–283 (2016)
2. Aithal, S.M.: Analysis of the current signature in a constant-volume combustion chamber. Combust. Sci. Technol. **185**(2), 336–349 (2013). https://doi.org/10.1080/00102202.2012.718297
3. Aithal, S.M.: Prediction of voltage signature in a homogeneous charge compression ignition (HCCI) engine fueled with propane and acetylene. Combust. Sci. Technol. **185**(8), 1184–1201 (2013). https://doi.org/10.1080/00102202.2013.781593
4. Aithal, S.M.: Development of an integrated design tool for real-time analyses of performance and emissions in engines powered by alternative fuels. In: Proceedings of SAE 11th International Conference on Engines & Vehicles. SAE (2013)
5. Aithal, S.M., Wild, S.M.: ACCOLADES: a scalable workflow framework for large-scale simulation and analyses of automotive engines. In: Kunkel, J.M., Ludwig, T. (eds.) ISC High Performance 2015. LNCS, vol. 9137, pp. 87–95. Springer, Cham (2015). https://doi.org/10.1007/978-3-319-20119-1_7
6. Bishop, C.M.: Pattern Recognition and Machine Learning, vol. 1. Springer, New York (2006). https://doi.org/10.1007/978-1-4615-7566-5
7. Breiman, L.: Bagging predictors. Mach. Learn. **24**(2), 123–140 (1996)
8. Breiman, L.: Random forests. Mach. Learn. **45**(1), 5–32 (2001)
9. Chen, T., Guestrin, C.: Xgboost: a scalable tree boosting system. arXiv preprint arXiv:1603.02754 (2016)
10. Chollet, F., et al.: Keras (2015). https://keras.io
11. Drucker, H.: Improving regressors using boosting techniques. In: ICML, vol. 97, pp. 107–115 (1997)
12. Friedman, J.H.: Stochastic gradient boosting. Comput. Stat. Data Anal. **38**(4), 367–378 (2002)
13. Geurts, P., Ernst, D., Wehenkel, L.: Extremely randomized trees. Mach. Learn. **63**(1), 3–42 (2006)

14. Goodfellow, I., Bengio, Y., Courville, A., Bengio, Y.: Deep Learning, vol. 1. MIT press, Cambridge (2016)

15. Hashemi, N., Clark, N.: Artificial neural network as a predictive tool for emissions from heavy-duty diesel vehicles in Southern California. Int. J. Eng. Res. **8**(4), 321–336 (2007)

16. Hoerl, A.E., Kennard, R.W.: Ridge regression: biased estimation for nonorthogonal problems. Technometrics **12**(1), 55–67 (1970)

17. Krijnsen, H.C., van Kooten, W.E., Calis, H.P.A., Verbeek, R.P., Bleek, C.M.: Prediction of NOx emissions from a transiently operating diesel engine using an artificial neural network. Chem. Eng. Technol. Industr. Chem. Plant Equip. Process Eng. Biotechnol. **22**(7), 601–607 (1999)

18. LeCun, Y., Bengio, Y., Hinton, G.: Deep learning. Nature **521**(7553), 436–444 (2015)

19. Loh, W.Y.: Classification and regression trees. Wiley Interdisc. Rev. Data Min. Knowl. Discov. **1**(1), 14–23 (2011)

20. Louppe, G., Geurts, P.: Ensembles on random patches. In: Flach, P.A., De Bie, T., Cristianini, N. (eds.) ECML PKDD 2012. LNCS (LNAI), vol. 7523, pp. 346–361. Springer, Heidelberg (2012). https://doi.org/10.1007/978-3-642-33460-3_28

21. McKay, M., Beckman, R., Conover, W.: Comparison the three methods for selecting values of input variable in the analysis of output from a computer code. Technometrics; (United States). https://doi.org/10.1080/00401706.1979.10489755

22. Parlak, A., Islamoglu, Y., Yasar, H., Egrisogut, A.: Application of artificial neural network to predict specific fuel consumption and exhaust temperature for a diesel engine. Appl. Therm. Eng. **26**(8–9), 824–828 (2006)

23. Pedregosa, F., et al.: Scikit-learn: machine learning in Python. J. Mach. Learn. Res. **12**, 2825–2830 (2011)

24. Shrivastava, N., Khan, Z.M.: Application of soft computing in the field of internal combustion engines: a review. Arch. Comput. Meth. Eng. **25**(3), 707–726 (2018)

25. Smola, A.J., Schölkopf, B.: A tutorial on support vector regression. Stat. Comput. **14**(3), 199–222 (2004)

Performance Modeling and
Measurement

PerfMemPlus: A Tool for Automatic Discovery of Memory Performance Problems

Christian Helm$^{(\boxtimes)}$ and Kenjiro Taura

The University of Tokyo, Tokyo, Japan
{christian,tau}@eidos.ic.i.u-tokyo.ac.jp

Abstract. In high-performance computing many performance problems are caused by the memory system. Because such performance bugs are hard to identify, analysis tools play an important role in performance optimization. Today's processors offer feature-rich performance monitoring units with support for instruction sampling. But existing tools only partially use this data. Previously, performance counters were used to measure the memory bandwidth. But the attribution of high bandwidth to source code has been difficult and imprecise. We introduce a novel method for identifying performance degrading bandwidth usage and attributing it to specific objects and source code lines. This paper also introduces a new method for false sharing detection. It can differentiate false and true sharing, identify objects and source code lines where the accesses to falsely shared objects are happening. It can uncover false sharing, which has been overlooked by previous tools. PerfMemPlus automatically reports those issues by using instruction sampling data captured with a single profiling run. This simplifies the tedious search for the location of performance problems in complex code. The tool design is simple, provides support for many existing and upcoming processors and the recorded data can be easily used in future research. We show that PerfMemPlus can automatically report performance problems without producing false positives. Additionally, we present case studies that show how PerfMemPlus can pinpoint memory performance problems in the PARSEC benchmarks and machine learning applications.

Keywords: Performance analysis · Memory bandwidth ·
False sharing · Instruction sampling

1 Introduction

If an application shows unsatisfactory performance or bad parallel scaling the often tedious process of performance optimization starts. Many potential performance problems are caused by the interactions of hardware and software.

This work is partially supported by a project commissioned by the New Energy and Industrial Technology Development Organization (NEDO).

© Springer Nature Switzerland AG 2019
M. Weiland et al. (Eds.): ISC High Performance 2019, LNCS 11501, pp. 209–226, 2019.
https://doi.org/10.1007/978-3-030-20656-7_11

Especially the memory system, with its complex architecture and shared resources is the bottleneck for many applications.

Simple execution time profiles, like gprof [10] cannot identify if there is a performance problem and what kind of performance problem it is. Specialized parallelism profilers like Delay Spotter [12] or Aftermath [5] can identify a lack of parallelism or inefficient scheduling. A tool specialized for analyzing memory accesses, such as the one we are introducing here can be helpful because it can identify the exact location (Function, Object, Source code line) where the problem is occurring. Modern processors have a performance monitoring unit (PMU) that can record information about the interaction of software and hardware. Instruction sampling is one of the features offered by the PMU. AMD calls this method Instruction Based Sampling (IBS). Intel calls it Precise Event Based Sampling (PEBS). Performance analysis tools use the recorded data, analyze it and can help to uncover performance problems.

Some previously developed tools became unusable on current hardware and require large efforts to keep them running on current hardware [16,29]. Existing tools do not enable researchers to easily explore and reuse instruction sampling data for the development of new performance analysis methods [8,9,15,16,24,35]. Instruction sampling does not provide information about the consumed DRAM bandwidth. Performance counters, which do provide this information, cannot be attributed precisely to source code lines and objects. Even when knowing the exact consumed memory bandwidth, it is difficult to decide if the used bandwidth is hurting performance or if it is within the supported limits of a system. False sharing is still a problem that is difficult to detect and existing tools [4,15] failed to detect cases of false sharing as we show in this paper. Tools that present performance data [9,14] are helpful but it is still time-consuming to check for specific problems using those tools. Automatic discovery and reporting reduce the required time and effort. Previous tools, that support automated discovery are specialized on the detection of one specific problem [15,18,19,23,35]. They use different methods and rely on different data that needs to be captured with individual recording tools. Using several completely different tools is not the preferred solution to find different kinds of memory-related performance problems. To address these issues, we make the following contributions:

- An algorithm that automatically discovers memory-related performance problems and attributes them to source code lines and objects using instruction sampling data, that is captured with a single profiling run. The discoverable problems include:
  - Performance degrading memory bandwidth consumption on remote and local DRAMs.
  - False sharing and differentiation from true sharing.
- A future-proof tool, which implements the algorithm and can record instruction sampling data with low overhead. It also enables users to explore all aspects of instruction sampling data and provides visualizations.
- Case studies that demonstrate how instruction sampling data and PerfMemPlus can be used to locate different kinds of performance problems.

2 Related Work

In the past tools that present performance data and allow manual exploration were introduced. In addition, there are analysis tools which are designed for specific problems and come with automated detection features.

Specialized tools for specific performance problems can detect only a certain kind of performance problem. In contrast, PerfMemPlus can automatically detect different performance problems with data captured by a single tool with a single profiling run. ScaAnalyzer [24] uses metrics to quantify the scalability loss to find the most promising optimization opportunities. The reported metrics help the user to identify remote memory accesses and the cache level in which a problem occurs. Liu et al. [21] introduce a data centric profiler. It helps to identify high latency memory accesses in the source code. It can also identify variables with a high number of remote memory accesses. HPCToolkit-NUMA [22] enhances this by introducing metrics to quantify the severity of remote memory accesses. It also adds a method to detect an actual place where the allocation in a NUMA system is happening. Memprof [16] is another profiler for NUMA multicore systems. It detects remote memory accesses by looking at thread and object interactions. Identification of remote memory accesses is one of the major features of the tools introduced above. They all require a manual interpretation of the reported metrics. Our approach can automatically identify these performance degrading main memory accesses. DProf [29] is a specialized tool to locate cache performance bottlenecks. DProf can show a cache miss based object profile and classify misses. It can also indicate when an object is accessed from multiple cores. It only supports object-based analysis and cannot provide information about functions and source code lines. Memprof and DProf both implement their own low-level hardware interface. Both only support outdated AMD processors. In contrast, PerfMemPlus benefits from an existing and well maintained low level interface. DR-BW [35] is a tool which can detect remote memory bandwidth contention in NUMA Systems. It is based on machine learning using features extracted from the performance monitoring unit. It is limited to the remote DRAM bandwidth contention on NUMA systems. In contrast, our approach can be applied to local and remote DRAM and can even be used on single socket systems. ParaTools ThreadSpotter [28] is a tool that can give suggestions on potential performance problems. It does not have an object-based view. Because it uses software instrumentation and cache simulation, it has a higher overhead compared to PerfMemPlus and cannot collect information directly from the hardware. Instruction sampling based tools, such as PerfMemPlus, can collect data with less overhead.

False sharing detection based on machine learning using PMU data is introduced by Jayasena et al. [15]. But their approach could not detect the case of false sharing in Freqmine which we found using PerfMemPlus. Our approach does not require a training phase. A detection method that uses samples of accessed addresses is introduced by Liu et al. [18,19] and by Chabbi et al. [4] as an on-the-fly method. These approaches are all based on analyzing the address access patterns. In contrast, our approach avoids this by using data about modified cache lines from the hardware. Chabbi et al. also examined the Freqmine benchmark but could not detect the false sharing with their approach.

Tools for manual exploration usually cover a wider range of memory-related performance problems, but come with no or little automated detection. Linux Perf is a general purpose profiler not limited to memory performance. Perf is well maintained and offers the best support for different and new hardware architectures out of all considered tools. It is a powerful tool, but it requires knowledge about the hardware and its potential bottlenecks to configure the right events. Dynamically allocated data cannot be resolved. Analysis features are mostly designed for a general purpose profiler with few features for memory performance analysis. PerfMemPlus is built on those good features of Perf and adds specialized features for recording and analyzing memory accesses. MemAxes [8,9] introduces new visualizations for data gathered through instruction sampling and annotation of the code. It uses a latency profile to point out significant functions and objects and a clustering mechanism to find interesting subsets in the data. The authors demonstrate that their visualizations are suitable for identifying unbalanced hardware utilization. In order to spot problems, the user needs to interpret the visualizations and draw conclusions regarding what type of performance problem is the limiting factor. It does not come with any automatic detection features. Intel VTune Amplifier XE is a general purpose profiling tool, but it also has some specialized memory performance features [14]. Using this tool it is possible to explore many aspects of the data, including relevant data for finding false sharing [13]. It does not have automated detection of false sharing. Main memory bandwidth can be measured and attributed to the source code. But this tool cannot make a decision whether there is bandwidth contention or not. Which level of bandwidth usage is regarded as too high has to be set by the user.

3   Automatic Discovery of Performance Problems

The automatic detection of performance problems consists of two steps. First, it selects function and object combinations as candidates. Second, these candidates are checked for signs of memory performance problems using the algorithms introduced in this section. A candidate is a pair of a function accessing an object. Objects are identified by a common allocation call stack. All function and object pairs are considered as candidates. Except for those functions that contribute less than 1% to the total execution time. Excluded functions can at most bring a one percent speedup if their execution time was fully eliminated, which is not possible in practice.

3.1   False Sharing

False sharing is hard to detect manually because its occurrence depends on the data layout and cache line size. Despite numerous previous efforts [4,15,18–20] detecting false sharing is still difficult and previous tools could not identify some cases of false sharing as we show in Sect. 5. The previous tools are specialized tools for false sharing detection and cannot find any other performance problems. Our approach can be applied to instruction sampling data, which can also be used to detect other types of performance problems.

Instruction sampling provides data about the coherency status of accessed cache lines. The hit modified flag (HITM) indicates that the cache line, in which the requested data resides, is shared with another core and has been previously modified. By using this hardware feature, we avoid expensive cache simulation or analysis of access patterns. The idea to use the hit modified flag was proposed before [26]. But no concrete algorithm to identify false sharing and differentiate it from true sharing is given in this earlier publication and objects cannot be pointed out. We add such a differentiation and can give a clear answer whether there is false sharing or not without any further manual interpretation. We can also report the objects affected by false sharing.

The algorithm is applied to a candidate as described in Sect. 3. Objects can be identified by a common allocation call stack or as individual allocations. The algorithm counts the number of threads that write a certain address in a shared cache line. If only one thread writes it, there is false sharing. If multiple threads write this address, it is true sharing. Additionally, we make sure to consider only addresses within the same object and not just reused addresses. The proposed algorithm consists of the following steps:

1. Check all access samples for the HITM flag. If the HITM flag is set in at least one sample, mark it as "modified cache line" and continue with step two.
2. Check if the object (identified by common call stack) is written by multiple threads to confirm that it is an actual shared object. If the object is written by multiple threads, then continue with step three.
3. Check if addresses within the object are shared. Select all addresses that have the HITM flag set for a specific object. In this step, individual objects are used even if they have the same allocation call stack. Then see how many different threads write this location. If it is more than one, there is true sharing. If it is only one, then it is false sharing.

After this confirmation, the source code locations of readers and writers, thread ids and the allocation call stack of the object can be taken from the samples. The report of this performance problem contains the location and how many percents out of all accesses have the HITM flag set to judge how severe the problem is.

3.2 Main Memory Bandwidth

The performance monitoring unit in processors contains counters for the number of DRAM requests. Using those counters the memory bandwidth can be measured. Because those counters exist for each socket and count globally for the whole socket, they cannot be directly attributed to a specific core, object or function. In contrast, instruction sampling data can be precisely attributed to code and data, but it has no direct way of measuring the memory bandwidth. We introduce an approach to use instruction sampling, identify performance degrading bandwidth usage and attribute it to source code lines and objects.

This section describes the approach for the local DRAM. The same method can be applied to the remote DRAM. We use the latency of load instructions that hit the local DRAM as an indicator for memory bandwidth saturation. The basic idea is that loading data from a memory can be done with a fixed latency. If other issues, like bandwidth saturation, occur the load request is delayed and the total latency to complete the load instruction increases. Figure 1 shows the increase in latency when increasing the main memory bandwidth. The data was generated with the Intel memory latency checker [34] on the systems which are introduced in Sect. 5. It shows that the latency stays low with only a small increase until the bandwidth gets close to the hardware limit. At this point, when the system reaches its throughput limit, there is a sharp increase in latency. This relationship is well known in queuing theory. When the arrival rate (bandwidth requirement of the application) is higher than what the system can process in a certain time (maximum hardware memory bandwidth) the time required for queuing and processing (latency) of the requests will increase. We do not know all details about the internal operations in the processor and there might be unknown effects that cause latency spikes. However, our method uses a large number of samples, considers only accesses that actually hit the DRAM and excludes samples that have other known problems such as a TLB miss. We conclude that if there is a high latency in all the captured samples, the reason is most likely DRAM bandwidth contention. Our experiments in Sect. 5 have not raised any false positives.

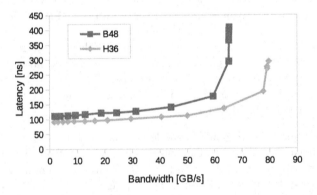

Fig. 1. Latency change of DRAM accesses with increased required memory bandwidth of the benchmark. B48 and H36 are two different hardware platforms described in Sect. 5.

For measuring the base latency of a DRAM access we use the ScanRad64-IndexUnrollLoop benchmark [3]. It is a pointer chasing benchmark. Elements in an array are accessed in random order and only after a load is completed the address of the next element is known. Only one access at a time is executed and the processor cannot predict the access pattern. It is the worst case of a local DRAM accesses without contention effects. We execute this benchmark on a single core with an array size of 2 GB. The benchmark execution is profiled with PerfMemPlus. This microbenchmark causes TLB misses due to the large array size and random access of array elements. To obtain the latency threshold, we exclude all DRAM accesses samples that have caused a TLB miss. This is easily possible because a flag in the instruction sampling data is set if there was a TLB miss. The median latency of load accesses from the local DRAM becomes the threshold for identifying memory bandwidth related performance problems. If this performance problem is detected the report contains how much the limit was exceeded in percent. When applying this algorithm for detection and there are less than 10 samples hitting the local DRAM a warning is printed that indicates that the sample count is too low. This limit avoids drawing wrong conclusions from an insufficient number of samples. The actual value for this limit is not critical since it is just used to guarantee that the detection works on large enough data. Running the analysis again with a higher samplerate can solve this problem.

4   PerfMemPlus Implementation

Performance monitoring hardware changes between processor generations. Previous tools [16,29], which implement a custom hardware interface, require code changes for new hardware. The data that is collected through instruction sampling can be huge and previously it was stored in binary formats which make it hard to explore the data for interesting features. To process the large data efficiently a scalable storage format is required. Because of their monolithic design existing tools [9,24,35] are hard to extend and modify.

The following key ideas in our tool design address these issues. The central component in PerfMemPlus is Linux Perf. Perf is available as part of the Linux kernel and can be run on a variety of Linux based operating system without modifications and it comes with regular updates for new hardware. We add a few other software components around Perf to make its use easier and tailored to the analysis of memory accesses. Figure 2 shows the software components. Perf cannot resolve dynamically allocated objects so we add an allocation tracker to provide this capability and merge the captured data based on timestamps. Perf stores the recorded sampling data in a binary, Perf specific format. Through a scripting interface we export the data into an SQLite database. The advantage of SQLite is that it is an easily usable data format and separates the recording tool from the analysis tool. Because the instruction sampling data on its own does not provide insights to software developers, we supply a GUI viewer tool with PerfMemPlus. The viewer executes the automatic detection of performance problems as described in Sect. 3 and displays the findings. The viewer also supports manual exploration of the data. It has a unique approach to guide the user through the data step by step without overwhelming the user with too much information at a time. The following sections describe the details

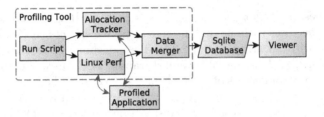

Fig. 2. Components of the PerfMemPlus implementation.

of our tool design and the challenges we had to solve for implementing this tool. The PerfMemPlus source code is available at https://github.com/helchr/perfMemPlus.

4.1 Profiling Tool

Because Linux Perf is maintained through the Linux kernel development community, we expect this tool to provide support for the upcoming years. We can update the underlying Perf without modifications to PerfMemPlus as long as the interface remains stable. We do not use the perf_event_open syscall interface, because using the command line interface provided by the Perf tools makes the implementation simpler and better isolates the individual components. We do not modify Perf itself because we would have to maintain a forked version of the original Perf. Instruction sampling has the advantage that it can analyze an application without modification of the source code of the application. Only debug information needs to be available in the binary and fully optimized binaries are supported. Perf already provides all those capabilities.

Because of the SQLite-based data format, is possible to keep the profiling tool and use another custom tool for visualization of the data and vice versa. The relational data model and SQL are suitable for instruction sampling data. Aggregations to specific functions or objects, sorting by certain attributes and selecting ranges can be done using SQL queries. Researchers can easily access the data and extract performance relevant information. Unlike binary formats, where parsing data structures, iterating through them and manually aggregating them to useful views is necessary. The implementation of the viewer component of PerfMemPlus serves as an example. It is essentially a set of predefined SQL queries that have proven to show useful views for performance analysis. SQLite as data format gives scalability with little implementation effort. Big trace files can be stored on disk and indexes enable quick lookups to find the required data. Any other relational database would also satisfy these requirements. But we chose the file-based SQLite database because it does not require the installation of databases and file-based operations are familiar to most users.

Because of Perf lacks some of the required features, we use two independent tools to profile an application. Perf does the instruction sampling and the allocation tracker records data about the dynamic memory allocations. To attribute accessed addresses to objects the data needs to be merged. Dynamic memory allocations are only valid for a certain time period. To make a lookup from a given accessed data address to an allocation call stack the time information has to be considered. Both tools individually record a timestamp for samples and allocations. In order to have comparable timestamps from both sources, both must rely on the same clock source. We use the CLOCK_MONOTONIC clock source which returns a timestamp counted in nanoseconds from the startup of the system. This counter needs to be in sync between multiple cores and sockets of the same system. The CLOCK_MONOTONIC is internally based on the Time Stamp Counter (TSC). The TSC is not affected by power management and it is synchronized at startup with all cores across all sockets. The support for those features can be verified by checking the presence of the constant_tsc and nonstop_tsc flags. By correlating the process id, timestamp and address Perf-MemPlus can find the corresponding data object for a given address. Because SQLite already provides methods for efficiently selecting an address and timestamp within ranges our simple implementation is entirely based on SQL queries.

4.2   Viewer

The auto analysis results view (Fig. 3) contains the function, accessed object and identified performance problem. Complete allocation call stacks of indicated objects and exact source code lines, where the problems are caused, can be displayed. The view also includes metrics to judge the severity of the problem in the application. First, the contribution of a function to the total execution time Second, the latency contribution of accesses to the reported object within this function. Third, a problem specific value which is explained in Sects. 3.1 and 3.2. If many problems are reported this value is useful to decide which problems to tackle first.

In the manual exploration view, the user can first check if there is a memory-related problem. The memory access latency of functions and objects is a good indicator for performance problems. Because inefficient use of the memory system (cache miss, remote memory access, TLB miss) will increase the latency. The second step is to identify offending functions and objects. PerfMemPlus extends the common execution time profile with a latency profile as shown in Fig. 7. This helps to identify the most offending functions and objects in terms of memory access. Figure 8 shows a call stack after selecting one of the functions. This call stack shows from where the selected function is called. It uses the latency metric, instead of the execution time, to identify the source of the most expensive memory accesses. Once a function has been selected, it is possible to explore the objects it accesses. This view, which is shown in Fig. 5, also comes with a profile to select the most offending objects within a previously selected function. It is also possible to explore the data in the same way starting from the objects. Finally, the investigation for the cause of the performance problem can be done considering only the previously selected functions and objects. Possibilities to find performance problems include views of cache hit rates and latencies in different cache levels (Fig. 6), cache coherency statistics, access patterns (Fig. 4) and data sharing between threads. All these views are placed in separate windows to limit the amount of information a user has to process at a time.

5   Evaluation

We used two different systems for the evaluation. Both are NUMA systems with two sockets. They are denoted as B48 (Intel Broadwell with a total of 48 physical cores) and H36 (Intel Haswell with a total of 36 physical cores). The details are listed in Table 1. Both systems run Ubuntu 16.04 and we used the gcc compiler version 5.4. In order to apply the bandwidth limit detection, it is required to first characterize the systems. We determined the latency threshold for both systems with the method described in Sect. 3.2 and the peak memory bandwidth measured with STREAM triad [27].

Table 1. Hardware used for the evaluation.

System	CPU	Peak bandwidth	Latency threshold
B48	2x E7-8890v4@2.2 Ghz	62 GB/s	371 cycles
H36	2x E5-2699v3@2.3 Ghz	76 GB/s	208 cycles

5.1   The PARSEC Benchmarks

We evaluated the automatic discovery using all the 13 PARSEC [2] benchmarks. All PARSEC benchmarks were executed with the native input set and the speedup results are based on the time required for the region of interest (ROI). All reported numbers are the average of ten repetitions. On the H36 system, we used 36 threads. On the B48 system, we used 48 threads. Except for Facesim and Fluidaniamate where we used 32 threads due to limitations in the benchmark. In this paper, we present the results for the pthreads version of all benchmarks except for Freqmine, which only has an OpenMP version. PerfMemPlus supports other parallelization methods such as Intel TBB but we omit the results in this paper because it does not provide any relevant insights.

The PARSEC benchmarks were analyzed in several previous studies [1,2,6, 7,16,19,25,31,32] so that we can draw conclusions about the ground truth of the performance problems from the existing literature. Only two benchmarks have known memory-related performance issues. In Canneal memory issues [7] contribute to the slowdown and it has the second highest bandwidth requirement [2] of all PARSEC benchmarks. Streamcluster is sensitive to DRAM speed [1] and has the highest main memory bandwidth requirement of all PARSEC benchmarks [2]. There are also NUMA issues due to the allocation of the main array to one node and accesses from both nodes [16]. The benchmark also suffers from false sharing [15,19]. Data locality is worsened by shuffling pointers to data between algorithm iterations [25]. In Freqmine no false sharing has been detected in previous work [4,15] but we found a previously unknown case of false sharing. Table 2 shows a summary of the known memory performance problems and the detected memory performance problems. PerfMemPlus was able to correctly identify false sharing and main memory bandwidth limitations in Streamcluster. It also detected the memory bandwidth issue in Canneal. It found a previously unknown case of false sharing in Freqmine. In the other 10 benchmarks, PerfMemPlus has not reported cases of false sharing and main memory bandwidth limitation. Thus, it reported no false positives.

Table 2. Known and detected memory performance problems in PARSEC.

Benchmark	Memory performance problem	
	Actual	Detected
Canneal	Memory bandwidth	Memory bandwidth
Streamcluster	Memory bandwidth, False sharing, Bad locality	Memory bandwidth, False sharing
Freqmine	False sharing (Previously unknown)	False sharing
Others	None	None

5.2 Canneal

The automatic discovery reported two instances of memory bandwidth limitation on the B48 and H36 system. Both occur in the function netlist_elem::swap_cost. The first one when accessing the std::vector elements. The second one when accessing the std::vector locations. The objects are allocated to one of the two nodes but later accessed from both nodes. We applied interleaved allocation to those two objects. Table 3 shows the performance improvement and change in DRAM access latency. For both systems, the initial latencies were above the latency limit. However, on the H36 system, the reported latencies are only slightly above the threshold. But the performance gain on this system was only 6.0%. The Canneal benchmark issues more memory request when increasing the number of threads and the main memory bandwidth is also lower on the B48 system. Thus, we already expected main memory bandwidth limitations to be more severe on the B48 system.

Table 3. Optimization results of the Canneal benchmark. The two different cycle values represent the access to the two different reported objects.

System	Speedup	Initial latency [cycles]	Optimized latency [cycles]
B48	11.8%	539 ± 45.9, 403 ± 43.6	312 ± 13.6, 310 ± 20.0
H36	6.0%	218 ± 17.4, 224 ± 20.2	201 ± 11.4, 215 ± 11.9

5.3 Streamcluster

In Streamcluster PerfMemPlus reported a memory bandwidth limitation and false sharing on both systems. The report is shown in Fig. 3. In the function pgain accesses to the array block exceed the available bandwidth. The object is allocated to one of the two nodes but later accessed from both nodes. We applied interleaved allocation to the array block. Table 4 shows the speedup and latency.

Performance Problems	Severity
▼ Function: pgain	Execution time contribution: 87.5%
▼ Object id 9 alloced at: streamcluster.orig.cpp:1880	Latency contribution in function: 99.4%
Main memory bandwidth limit	Latency limit exceeded by 31.0%
▼ Object id 26 allocated at: streamcluster.orig.cpp:1017	Latency contribution in function: 0.2%
False Sharing	HITM Accesses: 28.2%

Fig. 3. Auto analysis results view of Streamcluster. It lists the detected performance problems, their location and severity metric.

Table 4. Speedup and DRAM latencies of the Streamcluster benchmark when applying interleaved allocation to the array block.

System	Speedup	Initial latency [cycles]	Optimized latency [cycles]
B48	45.2%	496 ± 16.0	226 ± 11.7
H36	14.5%	253 ± 25.6	231 ± 17.1

Additionally, false sharing occurs in the function pgain accessing an array called work_mem. When we checked the source code at the indicated location we found that there is already padding to prevent false sharing in this application. But it assumes a cache line size of 32 bytes. We set the padding to match the real cache line size of 64 bytes and we achieved a speedup of 5.7% and the HITM accesses in the function pgain disappeared. PerfMemPlus detected false sharing in all of the 10 repetitions of the experiment.

The third problem of bad locality cannot be detected by our automated approach. However, it can be diagnosed using visualizations created by PerfMemPlus. The function pgain accessing the array block was identified as the main offender from the function and object profiles. We focused the analysis on this function and object. Figure 4(a) shows the addresses within the array block that are accessed over time. This diagram shows one specific thread, but it looks similar for other threads. Each point represents one access sample. The figure shows no clear structure and addresses are accessed randomly. Moreover, every thread accesses the whole range of the array.

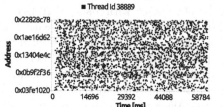

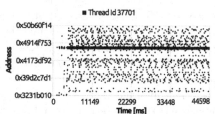

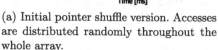

(a) Initial pointer shuffle version. Accesses are distributed randomly throughout the whole array.

(b) Optimized copy shuffle version. Accesses concentrate on a small space of the array indicated by the thick horizontal line.

Fig. 4. Access pattern of the array block in the function pgain in one thread of the Streamcluster benchmark.

The reason for this random access is that the clustering part is repeatedly executed and data needs to be processed multiple times in different orders for this algorithm to work correctly. In this implementation not the data itself is shuffled, but pointers to the data are shuffled. Consequently, in every iteration different addresses are accessed by every thread. A comment in the source code indicates that it was done to avoid copying the large data elements and to increase performance. We changed it to a copy based shuffle operation that copies the actual data and does not change the pointers as already suggested by Majo et al. [25]. The accessed addresses stay the same even though the underlying data changes. By using PerfMemPlus to display the access patterns such problems can be discovered easier compared to manual examination, which was used in the previous publication. In the optimized version, we saw that a thread mostly accesses the same part of the array throughout the execution. This is indicated by the horizontal line in Fig. 4(b). The diagrams for other threads look similar with the horizontal line shifted on the vertical axis because they access a different part of the array. This optimization resulted in an improved L1 hit rate in the concerned functions and objects from 72% to 94% and a speedup of 45.2% on B48 and 36.7% on H36.

5.4 Freqmine

We found a case of false sharing in Freqmine. PerfMemPlus detected false sharing in all of the 10 repetitions of the experiment. It was not found by specialized false sharing detection tools [4,15]. The studies were done in a similar software and hardware environment. We suspect that the first tool could not detect false sharing due to the machine learning approach and insufficient training data. The second tool needs to work with a limited amount of debug registers and can only cover a part of the addresses. The amount HITM accesses in Freqmine is lower than in Streamcluster where false sharing was discovered by the previous tool. The sparse occurrence of false sharing in Freqmine makes it more difficult to detect. We verified that it is an actual case of false sharing by reading the source code. The falsely shared object is the class stack with a size of 20 bytes. There is an array named list, which is defined defined in fp_tree.cpp, with one element of type stack for each thread. If the stack objects are placed right next to each other, false sharing occurs. Write accesses happen at multiple lines inside the parallel section of the FP_tree::FP_growth function. Perf c2c [26] does also detect modified cache lines. However it cannot identify the object and cannot confirm whether there is true or false sharing. We added padding to the struct so that each struct is placed in its own cache line. This optimization led to a speedup of 4.6% on B48 and 4.8% on H36.

5.5   Mnist

The application called Mnist [33] is a neural network implemented in plain C++ without using any specialized libraries. It performs handwritten digit recognition on the Mnist [17] dataset. It is a single threaded application. The function profile showed that the operator*<1000, 100, 784> has a higher latency than any other function. The objects accessed by this function are shown in Fig. 5. All high latency accesses go to one object with id 3. The allocation call stack showed that object 3 is a matrix. Figure 6 shows the cache hit rates of the function operator*<1000, 100, 784> when it accesses the object 3. Most accesses hit in the L2 cache. Other functions and objects have good L1 hit rates. Only this one function, processing one type of matrix has bad cache hit rates.

Memory Level	Count	Average Latency	Hit Rate
L1	74	19.5541	0
LFB	240	30.5417	2
L2	8497	21.756	91
L3	435	45.8092	4
Local DRAM	1	261	0

Selected functions: operator*<1000, 100, 784>

	Object ▲	Samples %	Average Latency	Latency %
1	3	50	20.9531	73

Fig. 5. The object profile of objects accessed by operator*<1000, 100, 784>. The screenshot is cut to show only the most significant object.

Fig. 6. Cache hit rates and latencies of the operator*<1000, 100, 784> function accessing one specific matrix with id 3.

We implemented cache blocking in the operator*<1000, 100, 784> function. We only changed the one template specialization that processes the identified matrix type and did not modify other functions that multiply matrices of different sizes. PerfMemPlus pointed out only the function and object where modification was necessary and did not report cases where no optimization was necessary. The performance was increased by 12.8% on B48 and 7.7% on H36. L1 cache hit rates of the specific function and object were increased to 99.8%.

5.6 N3LP

N3LP [30] is a neural machine translation application. It is implemented using the Eigen library [11] for arithmetic operations. This library is fairly complex and relies on C++ template metaprogramming to implement optimizations at compile time. Despite that, using PerfMemPlus it is possible to find the memory access hotspots and analyze the interaction of user program and library.

First, the auto analysis showed that memory bandwidth is exceeded by many functions. To take a more detailed look, we used the function profile that is shown in Fig. 7. It shows all functions with a significant contribution to the execution time. It also shows that those functions cause most of the latency and average latencies are high.

Function	Execution Time %	Average Latency	Latency %	Latency Factor
SoftMax::backward	18.48	617.47	26.17	3.77
Eigen::internal::general_matrix_vector_product<long, float, Eigen::internal::const_bla...	16.36	94.12	20.56	0.57
Eigen::internal::outer_product_selector_run<Eigen::Matrix<float, -1, -1, 0, -1, -1>, Eige...	15.52	241.25	14.51	1.47
Eigen::internal::outer_product_selector_run<Eigen::Matrix<float, -1, -1, 0, -1, -1>, Eige...	15.51	242.32	14.51	1.48
Eigen::internal::general_matrix_vector_product<long, float, Eigen::internal::const_bla...	15.15	178.79	18.01	1.09
Eigen::internal::outer_product_selector_run<Eigen::Matrix<float, -1, -1, 0, -1, -1>, Eige...	11.79	100.08	3.22	0.61

Fig. 7. Function profile which shows the functions contributing to the latency in N3LP. This profile combines traditional metrics, like execution time, with latency based metrics for memory performance analysis.

To get more details, we looked at inlined functions, callstacks and source code lines of the reported functions, which is possible due to the precision of the instruction sampling. Almost all the latency of the function SoftMax::backward is produced by the source code line *grad.weight += delta*input.transpose();* Where delta and input are two vectors. Assuming that the Eigen library already does as much optimization as possible we suspected that the culprit must be in the way it is used. We resolved the call stacks to each of the other reported functions to find out from where in the user code they are called. Figure 8 shows one of those callstacks. Normal profilers use the fraction of the execution time to sort functions. Whereas PerfMemPlus shows the latency contribution, coming from each calling function. In summary, we identified that mainly the functions LSTM::backward and SoftMax::backward are calling the Eigen operations with high latency.

Function	Latency
▾ Eigen::internal::general_matrix_vector_product<long, fl...	99.9999
▾ Eigen::internal::gemv_dense_selector<2, 1, true>::ru...	99.9979
▸ LSTM::backward	82.9066
▸ SoftMax::backward	17.0913

Fig. 8. Callstack of one of the reported functions in the Eigen library. The percentage of total latency is shown in the right column.

The cache and memory details window of PerfMemPlus showed that the average L1 cache hit rate in those six functions is only 40% and only 15% in SoftMax::backward. We focused our optimization on improving the data locality. In our optimization, the single vectors are merged into a matrix. This way Eigen can execute a matrix multiplication instead of multiple vector multiplications and Eigen is able to apply better optimizations such as cache blocking. This optimization strategy was first proposed by Qiao et al. [30]. We achieved higher cache hit rates and performance improvements of 229.9% on the B48 system and 194.2% on the H36 system.

5.7 Overhead

We individually chose samplerates for each benchmark to keep the overhead low and to provide enough samples to correctly execute the automated detection without warnings. Because the overhead was similar on both systems we report the average overhead on both systems in Table 5.

Table 5. Overhead of PerfMemPlus in the analyzed benchmarks.

Application	Samplerate	Overhead
Canneal	6000	4.9%
Streamcluster	16000	22.5%
Freqmine	64000	10.3%
Mnist	6000	3.8%
N3LP	8000	6.3%

6   Conclusion and Future Work

Performance analysis is still a challenging task even with tool support. PerfMemPlus can simplify the process by automatically discovering false sharing and main memory bandwidth limitations. PerfMemPlus points out the exact location of performance problems making it easy to fix them. In the case studies, covering all PARSEC benchmarks, we demonstrated that problems are reliably detected. The manual analysis methods of PerfMemPlus helped to find performance problems in machine learning applications. The data format and design of PerfMemPlus allows researchers to easily modify the tool and explore all aspects of instruction sampling data. We plan to apply the automatic discovery method to detect other kinds of performance problems.

References

1. Bhadauria, M., Weaver, V.M., Mckee, S.A.: Understanding parsec performance on contemporary CMPS. In: Proceedings of the 2009 IEEE International Symposium on Workload Characterization, IISWC 2009, pp. 98–107 (2009)
2. Bienia, C.: Benchmarking Modern Multiprocessors. Ph.D. thesis, Princeton University (2011)
3. Bingmann, T.: Parallel Memory Bandwidth Benchmark (2013). https://panthema.net/2013/pmbw/
4. Chabbi, M., Wen, S., Liu, X.: Featherlight on-the-fly false-sharing detection. In: Proceedings of the 23rd ACM SIGPLAN Symposium on Principles and Practice of Parallel Programming, pp. 152–167 (2018)
5. Drebes, A., Pop, A., Heydemann, K., Cohen, A., Drachtemam, N.: Aftermath: a graphical tool for performance analysis and debugging of fine-grained task-parallel programs and run-time systems. In: 7th Workshop on Programmability Issues for Heterogeneous Multicores (2014)
6. Eklov, D., Nikoleris, N., Hagersten, E.: A software based profiling method for obtaining speedup stacks on commodity multi-cores. In: ISPASS 2014 - IEEE International Symposium on Performance Analysis of Systems and Software (2014)
7. Eyerman, S., Du Bois, K., Eeckhout, L.: Speedup stacks: identifying scaling bottlenecks in multi-threaded applications. In: ISPASS 2012 - IEEE International Symposium on Performance Analysis of Systems and Software, pp. 145–155 (2012)
8. Gimenez, A., et al.: MemAxes: visualization and analytics for characterizing complex memory performance behaviors. IEEE Trans. Vis. Comput. Graph. 27(5), 2180–2193 (2017)
9. Giménez, A., et al.: Dissecting on-node memory access performance: a semantic approach. In: International Conference for High Performance Computing, Networking, Storage and Analysis, SC, pp. 166–176 (2014)
10. GNU: gprof (2018). https://sourceware.org/binutils/docs/gprof/
11. Guennebaud, G., Jacob, B., et al.: Eigen v3 (2010). http://eigen.tuxfamily.org
12. Huynh, A., Taura, K.: Delay Spotter: a tool for spotting scheduler-caused delays in task parallel runtime systems. In: IEEE International Conference on Cluster Computing, ICCC, pp. 114–125 (2017)
13. Intel Corporation: Avoiding and identifying false sharing among threads (2012). https://software.intel.com/en-us/articles/avoiding-and-identifying-false-sharing-among-threads
14. Intel Corporation: Finding your memory access performance bottlenecks (2016). https://software.intel.com/en-us/articles/finding-your-memory-access-performance-bottlenecks
15. Jayasena, S., et al.: Detection of false sharing using machine learning. In: Proceedings of the International Conference for High Performance Computing, Networking, Storage and Analysis - SC 2013 (2013)
16. Lachaize, R., Lepers, B., Quéma, V.: MemProf: a memory profiler for NUMA multicore systems. In: Proceedings of the 2012 USENIX Conference on Annual Technical Conference, p. 5 (2012)

17. LeCun, Y., Cortes, C., Burges, C.: The Mnist Database of Handwritten Digits (2016). http://yann.lecun.com/exdb/mnist/

18. Liu, T., Berger, E.D.: SHERIFF: precise detection and automatic mitigation of false sharing. In: Proceedings of the 2011 ACM International Conference on Object Oriented Programming Systems Languages and Applications, pp. 3–18 (2011)

19. Liu, T., Liu, X.: Cheetah: detecting false sharing efficiently and effectively. In: Proceedings of the International Symposium on Code Generation and Optimization (2016)

20. Liu, T., Tian, C., Hu, Z., Berger, E.D.: PREDATOR: predictive false sharing detection. In: Proceedings of the 19th ACM SIGPLAN Symposium on Principles and Practice of Parallel Programming (2014)

21. Liu, X., Mellor-Crummey, J.: A data-centric profiler for parallel programs. In: Proceedings of the International Conference for High Performance Computing, Networking, Storage and Analysis - SC 2013 (2013)

22. Liu, X., Mellor-Crummey, J.: A tool to analyze the performance of multithreaded programs on NUMA architectures. In: ACM SIGPLAN Symposium on Principles and Practice of Parallel Programming (PPoPP), pp. 259–272 (2014)

23. Liu, X., Sharma, K., Mellor-Crummey, J.: ArrayTool: a lightweight profiler to guide array regrouping. In: Proceedings of the 23rd International Conference on Parallel Architectures and Compilation, pp. 405–416 (2014)

24. Liu, X., Wu, B.: ScaAnalyzer: a tool to identify memory scalability bottlenecks in parallel programs. In: Proceedings of the International Conference for High Performance Computing, Networking, Storage and Analysis - SC 2015 (2015)

25. Majo, Z., Gross, T.R.: (Mis) Understanding the NUMA memory system performance of multithreaded workloads. In: IEEE International Symposium on Workload Characterization (IISWC), pp. 11–22 (2013)

26. Mario, J.: C2C - False Sharing Detection in Linux Perf (2016). https://joemario.github.io/blog/2016/09/01/c2c-blog

27. McCalpin, J.D.: STREAM benchmark (1995). http://www.cs.virginia.edu/stream/

28. Paratools: Threadspotter (2018). http://threadspotter.paratools.com

29. Pesterev, A., Zeldovich, N., Morris, R.T., Orlando, T.P.: Locating cache performance bottlenecks using data profiling. In: Proceedings of the 5th European Conference on Computer Systems EuroSys 2010, p. 335 (2010)

30. Qiao, Y., et al.: Parallelizing and optimizing neural Encoder Decoder models without padding on multi-core architecture. Future Gener. Comput. Syst. (2018)

31. Roth, M., Best, M.J., Mustard, C., Fedorova, A.: Deconstructing the overhead in parallel applications. In: Proceedings - 2012 IEEE International Symposium on Workload Characterization, IISWC 2012 1, pp. 59–68 (2012)

32. Southern, G., Renau, J.: Deconstructing PARSEC scalability. In: 11th Annual Workshop on Duplicating, Deconstructing and Debunking, p. 10 (2015)

33. Taura, K.: Mnist application (2016). https://www.eidos.ic.i.u-tokyo.ac.jp/~tau/lecture/paralleldistributed/2016/examples/18mnist/

34. Viswanathan, V., Kumar, K., Willhalm, T., Lu, P., Filipiak, B., Sakthivelu, S.: Intel memory latency checker (2018). https://software.intel.com/en-us/articles/intelr-memory-latency-checker

35. Xu, H., Wen, S., Gimenez, A., Gamblin, T., Liu, X.: DR-BW: identifying bandwidth contention in NUMA architectures with supervised learning. In: IEEE International Parallel and Distributed Processing Symposium, IPDPS (2017)

GPUMixer: Performance-Driven Floating-Point Tuning for GPU Scientific Applications

Ignacio Laguna[1]([✉]), Paul C. Wood[2], Ranvijay Singh[3], and Saurabh Bagchi[4]

[1] Lawrence Livermore National Laboratory, Livermore, CA 94550, USA
ilaguna@llnl.gov
[2] Johns Hopkins Applied Physics Lab, Laurel, MD 20723, USA
[3] NVIDIA Corporation, Santa Clara, CA 95051, USA
[4] Purdue University, West Lafayette, IN 47907, USA

Abstract. We present GPUMixer, a tool to perform mixed-precision floating-point tuning on scientific GPU applications. While precision tuning techniques are available, they are designed for serial programs and are accuracy-driven, i.e., they consider configurations that satisfy accuracy constraints, but these configurations may degrade performance. GPUMixer, in contrast, presents a *performance-driven* approach for tuning. We introduce a novel static analysis that finds *Fast Imprecise Sets (FISets)*, sets of operations on low precision that minimize type conversions, which often yield performance speedups. To estimate the relative error introduced by GPU mixed-precision, we propose shadow computations analysis for GPUs, the first of this class for multi-threaded applications. GPUMixer obtains performance improvements of up to 46.4% of the ideal speedup in comparison to only 20.7% found by state-of-the-art methods.

1 Introduction

GPU accelerated computing has reached a tipping point in the high-performance computing (HPC) market. As HPC scientific applications increasingly rely on GPU accelerators to perform floating-point arithmetic, tools to extract the maximum performance out of floating-point intensive computations are also becoming increasingly important.

This paper presents GPUMixer, the first tool to tune floating-point mixed-precision scientific applications on GPUs. While most mission-critical scientific applications use double-precision floating-point arithmetic (FP64) because of accuracy requirements, current generations of GPU architectures have higher peak computation rates in single-precision floating-point arithmetic (FP32) or lower precision [19]. To take advantage of the performance that lower precision

---

This work was performed when P. C. Wood and R. Singh were at Purdue University.

M. Weiland et al. (Eds.): ISC High Performance 2019, LNCS 11501, pp. 227–246, 2019.
https://doi.org/10.1007/978-3-030-20656-7_12

offers, programmers can use mixed-precision computing to perform some computations in high precision (e.g., FP64) and some in low precision (e.g., FP32, or lower). GPUMixer provides a practical method to select the computations to be performed on FP32 or FP64 precision so that (a) user-defined accuracy constraints are maintained and (b) performance is significantly improved.

Tuning mixed-precision programs is challenging. Programmers are interested in finding mixed-precision *configurations*, i.e., sets of operations on more than one precision, that satisfy both accuracy and performance demands. However, because the number of possible configurations is very large, manually exploring all configurations is impractical, even in small programs. For FP64/FP32 mixed-precision programs, for example, the number of possible configurations is 2^N, where N is the number of floating-point arithmetic operations.

In the domain of serial applications, a number of techniques for automatic tuning have been proposed to address this problem [3,4,6,7,11,13,16,22,23], however, practical and efficient tuning tools for multi-threaded applications are scarce, making mixed-precision programming for GPUs hard.

Irrespective of their architectural focus, a limitation of the majority of these methods is that they focus on mixed-precision tuning with accuracy as a target. That is, the configuration space search is driven by accuracy constraints in the program solution. We call this methods *accuracy-driven* approaches. Because performance is not explicitly modeled, these approaches have the disadvantage of suggesting configurations that provide *no performance guarantees*, and in many cases configurations that degrade performance.

GPUMixer, on the other hand, is designed as a *performance-driven* approach. We introduce the concept of *Fast Imprecise Sets (FISets)*, a set of arithmetic operations in a GPU kernel on which the data that enters and that leaves the set is in high precision, but on which the operations of the set are in low precision (hence an *imprecise* set). A FISet has the property that the ratio of arithmetic operations to cast operations is high; thus, an *FISet* is a configuration that, almost always, yields performance speedups (hence a *fast* set).

We demonstrate that *FISets* can be found via static analysis, which eliminates the need for running configurations to determine whether they provide performance speedup or not, as existing techniques do (e.g., [7,16]). Our algorithm for finding *FISets* locally maximizes the number of low-precision arithmetic operations while it minimizes the number of type cast operations in input/output boundaries of operation sets.

To find the *FISets* that also satisfy accuracy requirements, we perform *shadow computations*, a dynamic analysis that calculates an approximation of the relative error introduced when the precision is decreased from FP64 to FP32 in GPU kernels. While previous shadow computations techniques exist to tune serial programs [13,22], to the best of our knowledge, we present the first shadow computations framework for multi-threaded/GPU programs.

The contributions of this paper are:

1. We introduce the concept of *FISets*, floating-point configurations that provide performance speedups, and present an algorithm to find them statically.

2. We describe an implementation of our algorithm in the LLVM compiler [14] for the NVIDIA CUDA programing model. We show that our method can be applied efficiently to realistic multi-kernel GPU programs.
3. We implement the first GPU shadow computations framework for mixed-precision tuning, a dynamic analysis to compute the relative error introduced when the precision of FP64 operations is decreased to FP32.
4. We evaluate our implementation in three computationally intensive CUDA programs. We show that our approach finds configurations that are always faster than the default (all in FP64) for a given error threshold and input.

We compare our approach to the Precimonious approach [22,23], a state-of-the-art method for mixed-precision tuning on serial programs. On our evaluation, our approach finds performance speedups that can vary between 9.8%–46.4% of the ideal speedup, whereas the comparison approach finds speedups of only 1.4%–20.7%.

2   Related Work

Formal Methods. FPTuner [3] is a rigorous approach for precision tuning based on Symbolic Taylor Expansions and interval functions; FPTuner meets error thresholds across all program inputs, however it has been demonstrated only on small programs and it has limitations handling conditional expressions. Rosa [6] is a source-to-source compiler that uses an SMT solver to annotate a program with mixed-precision types; the compiler operates on the Scala programming language. Paganelli and Ahrendt [21] present an approach that formally proves that an increased precision in a variable causes only a limited change of the result; it uses SMT solvers and is demonstrated on FPhile, a toy sequential imperative language. Other formal methods include Salsa [5] and S3FP [4].

Although these methods perform rigorous analysis and can verify properties for all inputs, they scale poorly and/or do not support common HPC programing languages (C/C++) and coding patterns (branches and loops), thus their applicability to realistic HPC applications is limited.

Heuristics for Automated Search. These methods cannot prove properties but they are able to scale to real-world programs, and as a result have broader practical utility. Our approach falls in this category.

CRAFT [11,12] performs an automated search of a program's instruction space, determining the level of precision necessary in the result of each instruction to pass a user-provided verification routine assuming all other operations are done in high precision, i.e., FP64. While it uses heuristics to sample a fraction of the search space, it can be very time consuming even for very small programs (worst case complexity is $O(2^N)$). Precimonious [23] uses the delta-debugging algorithm to search for configurations. While this algorithm helps in speeding up the search, this can still lead to a high number of builds and runs of the program. Blame Analysis [22] finds configurations that satisfy user-given error constraints, using a *single execution of the program*. The analysis finds a set of variables that can be in single precision, while the rest of the variables are in double precision; however, the output configurations may or may not improve performance, so to use the analysis in practice one must perform runs of the program to determine which configurations actually improve performance. The experiments in [22] use Precimonious to perform the program runs in a guided manner. ADAPT [16] uses algorithmic differentiation to provide estimates about the final output error, which can be used for mixed-precision tuning.

The above techniques are *accuracy-driven* approaches, i.e., the configuration space search is driven by accuracy constraints in the program solution. Because performance is not explicitly modeled—the cost of operations is seen as a black box—these approaches may suggest configurations that provide no performance guarantees. GPUMixer, in contrast, is driven by performance gains.

A recent approach, HiFPTuner [7], considers performance by avoiding frequent precision casts on program variables. This approach, however, focuses on serial programs and is not available on GPUs and/or CUDA. Another difference is that [7] requires dynamic profiling to build a weighted dependence graph of the program, which is non-trivial to build efficiently on CUDA. One of the challenges to gather the per-instruction error introduced on multi-threaded code is to do it with reasonable overhead (one of the problems that we solve partially in our shadow computation framework). Because of the above limitations, we compare our method to the Precimonious method [22,23] instead of comparing it to [7]. The Precimonious approach (via delta debugging) is a more generic approach that can be easily adapted to GPUs (see Sect. 5.1 for more details).

3   Background and Overview

3.1   Example of Mixed-Precision Tuning

To illustrate the problem of mixed-precision tuning, we present an example using a CUDA kernel from an N-body simulation [18]. Listing 1.1 shows an implementation of the force calculation in an n-body simulation obtained from [8]. After the kernel calculates the forces and velocities of particles, the positions of the particles, x, y, and z, are updated in the main function.

Table 1. Error and speedup for different configurations of Listing 1.1 on a NVIDIA Tesla P100 GPU

Case	x	y	z	Error	Speedup (%)
1	−0.599775587166981	−0.906326702752302	−0.217694232807352		
2	−0.508669376373291	−0.906326711177825	−0.217694222927093	15.19	53.70
3	−0.575293909888785	−0.906326702752302	−0.217694232807352	4.08	5.78
4	−0.611327409124778	−0.906326702752302	−0.217694232807352	1.93	−43.35
5	−0.588951610438680	−0.906326702752302	−0.217694232807352	1.80	11.69

We perform mixed-precision tuning on the kernel variable declarations to find a configuration that yield both accurate results and a performance speedups. The *baseline* configuration is where all variables are declared as FP64, i.e., as double, the one shown in Listing 1.1. To illustrate the calculation of the error introduced by mixed-precision, we focus on the error introduced to the particle positions (x, y, and z) for a single particle (i=0). Programmers of scientific codes may define their own metric for error, however, for this illustrative case, we define the relative error introduced by mixed-precision as: $error = (|(x - x_0)/x| + |(y - y_0)/y| + |(z - z_0)/z|) * 100.0$, where x, y, z are the particle positions for the baseline, and x_0, y_0, z_0 are the particle positions for a new configuration.

```
1  __global__ void bodyForce(double *x, double *y,
2  double *z, double *vx, double *vy, double *vz,
3  double dt, int n)
4  {
5    int i = blockDim.x * blockIdx.x + threadIdx.x;
6    if (i < n) {
7      double Fx=0.0; double Fy=0.0; double Fz=0.0;
8      for (int j = 0; j < n; j++) {
9        double dx = x[j] - x[i];
10       double dy = y[j] - y[i];
11       double dz = z[j] - z[i];
12       double distSqr = dx*dx + dy*dy + dz*dz + 1e-9;
13       double invDist = rsqrt(distSqr);
14       double invDist3 = invDist * invDist * invDist;
15       Fx += dx*invDist3; Fy += dy*invDist3; Fz += dz*invDist3;
16     }
17     vx[i] += dt*Fx; vy[i] += dt*Fy; vz[i] += dt*Fz;
18   }
19 }
```

Listing 1.1. Force computation in an N-body simulation

Table 1 shows the particle values, error, and performance speedup of four configuration with respect to the baseline, case 1. Case 2 shows the configuration where all variables in the kernel are declared as FP32, i.e., as float. We observe that while the speedup is significant, 53%, the error is high, 15.19. Case 3 shows the case where only variable invDist3 is declared as FP32 and the rest as FP64— in this case the error decreases, but the speedup is not too high, only 5%. Case 4 shows an interesting case: when the variable invDist3 is the only one declared as FP32, the error is very low, but the speedup is negative, i.e., performance degrades. Case 5 shows the best we found when the distSqr,invDist, and invDist3 variables are declared as FP32: the error is lower than as in case 4 while the speedup is about 11%. This example illustrates that some configurations can produce low performance speedup or even performance degradation; the goal of our approach is to find via static analysis configurations such as 3 and 5 that improve performance and discard cases such as 4.

3.2 Configurations

While mixed-precision configurations can be expressed in terms of the precision of variable declarations (as in the previous example), a more precise approach is to express configurations in terms of the precision of floating-point operations. The reason behind this is that a variable can be used in multiple floating-point operations; the precision of each of these operations can be decreased/increased.

More formally, given a program with N floating-point arithmetic operations and two classes of floating-point precision, e.g., FP32 and FP64, a *configuration* is a set of operations on which a subset of n_1 operations are executed in one precision and a subset of n_2 operations are executed in another precision, such that $n_1 + n_2 = N$. For k classes of floating-point precision, subsets of operations can be executed on different precision, such that $n_1 + n_2 + \ldots + n_k = N$. Table 2 shows the four possible classes of mixed-precision configurations. The goal is to automatically find configurations that belong to class A.

Table 2. Classes of configurations of a program

Satisfy accuracy constraints	Improve performance	Class
Yes	**Yes**	**A**
Yes	No	B
No	Yes	C
No	No	D

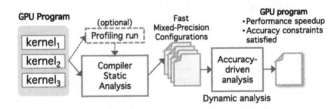

Fig. 1. Workflow of the approach.

3.3   Overview of Our Approach

Figure 1 shows the overview of our approach. Given a GPU program, we optionally run a profiling run to determine kernels on which precision reduction can potentially give the highest performance benefits, e.g., by analyzing the kernels where the application spends most of its time or kernels that are computationally intensive. Note that this step is **optional**—if the programmer is not interested in profiling the application, our method analyzes all kernels.

Next, the compiler transforms kernels into an intermediate representation and searches for code regions where precision reduction could speedup the program execution, i.e., *FISets*. For each identified case, the compiler automatically performs code transformations and generate a program configuration. This configuration will likely yield a performance speedup when executed, thus it belongs to $\mathcal{P} = A \cup C$ (see Table 2).

Finally, since some of the configurations in $\mathcal{P}$ may not satisfy the user accuracy constraints, configurations must be analyzed to identify those that satisfy such constraints. Note that the user is free to use any existing accuracy-driven tuning method that is available in conjunction with *FISets*. However, since there is no accuracy-driven analysis available for GPUs, we develop our own method (shadow computations for GPUs), to fill this gap.

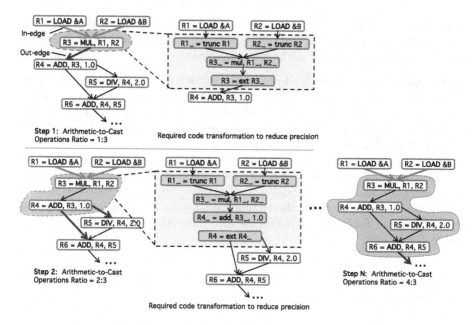

Fig. 2. Illustration of the algorithm to find *FISets*.

4 Approach

We describe our approach to model performance of mixed-precision code regions via static analysis with *FISets*, and our shadow computations approach to compute the error of mixed-precision configurations in GPUs.

4.1 Kernel Intermediate Representation

We use the NVVM IR [17] as the intermediate representation for GPU kernels. This representation is based on the LLVM IR and allows us to use high-level language front-ends, such as Clang to generate NVVM IR. Our approach performs transformation on the NVVM IR, a binary format to represent CUDA kernels.

4.2 *FISet* Design

The base working abstraction of *FISets* is a *data dependence graph* $G = (V, E)$. This is a directed graph whose nodes V represent NVVM IR instructions whose edges E represent dependencies between nodes. We assume that the compiler (in our case, LLVM) generates a data dependence graph for each kernel.

Roughly speaking, a *FISet*, which we denote as Φ, is a group of operations $v \in V$ on which the data that enters and that leaves the group is in high precision, i.e., FP64, and on which the operations that compose the group are in low precision, i.e., FP32. A *FISet* can contain both arithmetic floating-point operations and non-arithmetic operations, such as comparison or select operations, that join together groups of arithmetic operations.

Type Conversions. Any mixed-precision approach incurs type conversion operations, or *casting*, to transform data from one precision to another. Type conversions are expensive in GPU architectures. Our algorithm to find a Φ in a kernel attempts to minimize the number of conversion operations and to maximize the number of floating-point operations in the set.

A key idea of the algorithm is that if we can perform conversions only *at the beginning and at the end* of a large sequence of floating-point operations that have high degree of dependence among them, we can increase the ratio of arithmetic-to-cast operations, therefore increasing the arithmetic throughput of the code region. Formally, we define the arithmetic-to-cast operations ratio for a code region as

$$r_{ac} = O/C, \tag{1}$$

where O is the number of floating-point operations and C is the number of casting operations.

4.3   *FISet* Illustration

Consider a portion of a graph as shown in the beginning of Fig. 2, where two data values are loaded and stored into registers R1 and R2, which are then used by a multiplication. In step 1, the algorithm considers the code transformations that are required to lower the precision of the multiplication operation. In this example, we use a three-input instruction format with operations in FP64 denoted in upper case (e.g., MUL), and operations in FP32 in lower case (e.g., mul).

The second column of step 1 in the figure shows the required transformation to reduce the precision. Since data in registers R1 and R2 is in FP64, we need to perform two type conversions to truncate their data to FP32. After the multiplication in FP32 is performed, we need to extend the result to FP64, incurring another conversion (from FP32 to FP64). In this step, $r_{ac} = 1/3$. This ratio will likely not improve performance; in fact, it will degrade performance since for the same MUL operation we are performing three additional instructions, i.e., type conversion operations. The goal of the algorithm is to find cases where $r_{ac} > 1.0$.

In step 2 (second row of the figure), we consider the *neighbors* of the previous MUL operation. Here, neighbors are operations that depend on MUL and operations that influence MUL. Since the only operations that influence MUL are load operations, we do not consider them (they are not arithmetic floating-point operations); however, we consider the ADD operation that depends on the result of MUL. The second column of step 2 shows the required transformation to reduce the precision, which would produce $r_{ac} = 2/3$; this can be easily seen by noticing that there would be two arithmetic operations and three type conversions, $r_{ac} = O/C = 2/3$ after the corresponding transformation. Since $r_{ac} < 1.0$, the algorithm keeps expanding the neighbors set and performs the same estimations.

Finally in step N we find a set with $r_{ac} > 1.0$, i.e., $r_{ac} = 4/3$ (see last part of Fig. 2). Here we declare this set a Φ.

4.4 *FISet* Properties and Algorithm

Loops. If all nodes of a *FISet* are in the same loop (or loop level), or there is no loop in the kernel, we do not do anything special because all the instructions will be executed the same number of times, which will not affect r_{ac}; this is the common case for most kernels. When this is not the case, we consider the following two cases—we assume kernels can have nesting loops, $L_0 > L_1 > L_2 > ...$, where L_0 encloses L_1, L_1 encloses L_2, and so on:

- *Arithmetic operation nodes are in loop level L_x and conversions are in loop level L_y, where $L_x > L_y$.* We assume that the arithmetic operations will be executed equal or more times than the conversions so we do not do anything special. Note that this applies even for $L_x \geq L_y$, for a given input. In this case, r_{ac} may be higher than expected, which is fine for performance speedups.
- *Arithmetic operation nodes are in loop level L_x and conversions are in loop level L_y, where $L_y > L_x$.* In this case, conversions may be executed more times than arithmetic operations. We use a heuristic to handle this case: if we find the same number of arithmetic operations as the number of conversions in the loop that contains the conversions, we allow this to be a *FISet*; otherwise, we discard this case, and the algorithm proceeds.

Algorithm. The *FISet* search algorithm is shown in Algorithm 1. The algorithm starts by taking a node from the dependence graph and by calculating the number of in/out edges, which is then used to calculate r_{ac}. If $r_{ac} > 1.0$, it adds it to the list of *FISet*. Next, it increases the set to explore by adding the neighbors of the node, which are then used to calculate r_{ac} like in the previous step. The nodes to be explored are added to the *neighborsList*. It does not add neighbors to the list if the node is a *terminating node*, i.e., it is a load/store operation or a function call since these operations do not have lower precision versions. For GPU kernels with very large dependence graphs, the algorithm can find many *FISets*. In those cases, we allow the user to specify the maximum number of *FISets* that the algorithm return, using the parameter ϕ.

Multiple *FISets*. Algorithm 1 can identify multiple disjoint *FISets* in the same kernel. If two *FISets* overlap, i.e., they have instructions in common, the algorithm will return the union of the two. If *FISets* do not overlap, multiple configurations combining these *FISets* are considered. In practice, however, we found that a single *FISet* per kernel typically gives reasonable speedups.

Compilation Process. Once CUDA modules are transformed to NNVM IR (by the clang front-end), the *FISets* search is performed in the NVVM IR representation. After this, the kernel is transformed to PTX, which is then assembled into object files. Finally the NVIDIA nvcc compiler is used to link objects.

4.5   Shadow Computations

FISets per se give no information about the error introduced by lower precision arithmetic. To calculate this error we use dynamic *shadow computations*. Shadow computations analysis for mixed-precision tuning has been used before [13, 22]; however, none of the previous frameworks handle multi-threaded programs, so, as far as we know, ours is the first.

```
input  : Dependence graph DG
output: FISets: list of FISets found
1  for node n ∈ DG do
2      if n is not arithmetic op then
3          continue
4      else
5          currentSet = [n]
6          neighborsList = [n]
7          while neighborsList is not empty do
8              tmp = neighborsList.getFirstElement()
9              for node m ∈ neighbors(tmp) do
10                 if m is not load/store or function call then
11                     numConversions += numInEdgesOfNode(m) +
                           numOutEdgesOfNode(m) - numFloatingPointConstants(m) - 1
12                     numOperations += 1
13                     add neighbors of m to neighborsList
14                     remove m from neighborsList
15                     add m to currentSet
16                 if numOperations/numConversions > 1.0 then
17                     add currentSet to FISets
```

Algorithm 1. *FISet* Search Algorithm. Symbols and operation definitions: *neighborsList* is the list of nodes to visit; *currentSet* is the set of nodes we have visited and may become a *FISet*; *neighbors()* returns the in- and out-edges of a node that have not been visited; *numInEdgesOfNode()* and *numOutEdgesOfNode()* return the number of in- and out-edges of a node respectively; *numFloatingPointConstants()* returns the number of constant input parameters of an operation (they do not require conversion). Note that line 11 subtracts 1 because we need to subtract the edge that connects m to the *currentSet*, otherwise it would be counted twice when we calculate *numInEdgesOfNode()* or *numOutEdgesOfNode()*.

The idea of shadow analysis is that, for each floating-point arithmetic operation in high precision, e.g., FP64, a similar operation is performed side-by-side on lower precision, e.g., FP32. By comparing the result of the operation in low precision with the result of the operation in high precision, we calculate the relative error that the low-precision operation would introduce.

Calculating the Kernel Total Error. We compute an approximation of the total error that is introduced in the kernel when the precision of portion of the kernel (a *FISet*) is downgraded. This allows us to guide the search for *FISet* configurations that introduce low total error.

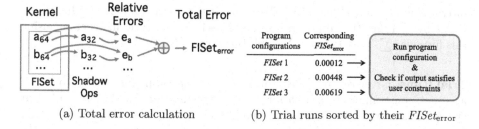

(a) Total error calculation   (b) Trial runs sorted by their $FISet_{error}$

Fig. 3. Shadow computations used to calculate the mixed-precision error

More formally, let us say that a kernel comprises FP64 operations $\{a_{64}, b_{64}, c_{64}\}$. Operations are of the form $[x_{64} = OP, y_{64}, z_{64}]$, and $OP \in \{+, -, *, /, <, >, =, \neq\}$. When an operation is transformed to FP32, its operands y_{64}, z_{64} must be truncated to FP32. Both the truncations and the operation performed to lower precision introduce errors. Shadow computations analysis computes an approximation of the total error introduced by these transformations. The word *total* means that the contribution to the error of **all** the GPU threads is considered.

Kernel Instrumentation. We start with a kernel with all its instructions in FP64. Each FP64 operation is instrumented with a callback function. The function takes as input the operands of the FP64 operation (in FP64 precision) and truncates them to FP32 precision. It then computes two values: v_{64} and v_{32}. v_{64} corresponds to the result of the operation as if the operation is performed in FP64 precision; v_{32} corresponds to the result of the operation as if the operation is performed in FP32 precision. The following calculates the relative error:

$$e = abs((v_{64} - v_{32})/v_{64}), \qquad (2)$$

where $abs()$ is the absolute value function. The result of e is stored in FP64 precision. Because of the SIMT execution model of GPUs, all threads in a warp in the kernel block execute the same callback function.

GPU In-Memory Structure. We keep a structure in the GPU global memory of the form:

$$total\_error[INST][THREADS],$$

where $INST$ is the number of static instructions of the kernel, and $THREADS$ is the maximum number of threads that the kernel can use. This keeps track of the error values for all static instructions and for all the threads that execute the instruction. Since a thread can execute a static instruction multiple times, each calculated e is aggregated (added) into a single e for the static instruction—this allows us to calculate a total relative error for the instruction (see Fig. 3a).

Assigning an Error Value to a FISet. We run the GPU program once with a set of inputs from the user to obtain a total error value for each static instruction. Given a *FISet* with N instructions, we assign an error value to the *FISet* by merging the *total_error* value of each *FISet* static instruction, using this formula: $\sum_i^N total\_error_i$. We call this error $FISet_{\mathrm{error}}$.

Trial Runs. Given several *FISets*, and their corresponding $FISet_{\mathrm{error}}$, to satisfy accuracy constraints, we search for *FISets* configurations in the order of their error, starting with those with the smallest $FISet_{\mathrm{error}}$ (see Fig. 3b). Searching for configurations means that we run the program to determine its output. We call this a *trial run*. Trial runs are independent of the shadow computations run.

Putting It All Together Error and Performance Thresholds. To search for configurations, the user provides two independent parameters: *error threshold* and *performance threshold*. *Error threshold* specifies the number of digits of accuracy that is expected in the program output with respect to the baseline FP64 precision case. For example, if the output of the FP64 case is 3.1415 and the output of the mixed-precision case is 3.1479, we say that the latter is accurate up to 3 digits (i.e., from left to right, digits 3, 1 and 4).

Performance threshold specifies the minimum performance speedup that is expected. Here, performance speedup is defined with respect to the maximum ideal speedup, i.e., the performance of the program when it is compiled using fully FP32. We use the figure of merit (FOM), which represents the metric of performance of the program. Specifically, we define the speedup of the mixed-precision case as:

$$s = ((p_{\mathrm{mixed}} - p_{64})/(p_{32} - p_{64})) * 100, \tag{3}$$

where p_{mixed} is the performance of the mixed-precision case, p_{64} is the performance of the FP64 case, and p_{32} is the performance of the FP32 case. Thus, $s = 100\%$ when the mixed-precision case performs as the FP32 case, i.e., when all instructions are converted from FP64 to FP32.

Modes of Operation. Our approach has three modes of operation to search for configurations:

- **Mode 1:** the user cares only about the output error and does not care about the magnitude of performance speedup (as long as there is some performance speedup). In this case, the user provides only an error threshold. The search is based on the *FISets* total error value—we start running the *FISet* configuration with the smallest total error, then continue with the configuration with the second smallest total error, and so on. The search ends when the output error meets the error threshold.
- **Mode 2:** the user cares about both output error and performance speedup, *but output error has priority*. Here, the search is performed like in Mode 1, but it ends when both the output error meets the error threshold and the performance speedup meets the performance threshold.

– **Mode 3:** the user cares about both output error and performance speedup, *but performance speedup has priority.* Here, the search is based on the ratio r_{ac} of the *FISets* (high r_{ac} implies high chances of performance improvements)— we start by running the *FISet* configuration with the largest r_{ac}, then continue with the configuration with the second largest r_{ac}, and so on. The search ends when both the output error meets the error threshold and the performance speedup meets the performance threshold.

4.6   Limitations

Accuracy of Ratio r_{ac}. A limitation of r_{ac} is that it does not consider the actual cost of operation types. Unfortunately, we are limited by the fact that the NVIDIA CUDA C Programming Guide [20] does not specify the cost of all GPU operations—it specifies the throughput of add and multiply operations but it lacks throughput specs for other common operations, such as division and math operations, e.g., sqrt. We believe that per-instruction costs could be empirically estimated for specific GPU architectures, but it requires significant benchmarking that is out of the scope of this paper. Nevertheless, we have found that r_{ac} is practical for most cases.

Register Pressure. Mixed-precision programs can incur register pressure because new type conversions introduce additional instructions, thus more registers may be required. Registers, along with other resources, are scarce in GPU Streaming Multiprocessors (SM). There is a maximum number of available registers in an SM—255 per thread for NVIDIA compute capability 6.0. If a kernel uses more registers than the hardware limit, the excess registers will *spill* over to local memory impacting performance. *FISets* can increase registers usage by a small amount. This may be a problem only on kernels with a register usage that is close to the limit. In such cases, a configuration may not yield any speedup. In our experiments, however, we only saw one kernel in this category.

5   Evaluation

We present our evaluation of GPUMixer. We implement GPUMixer in the Clang/L-LVM compiler [14] 4.0, using the CUDA ToolKit 8.0. Experiments are conducted in a cluster with IBM Power8 CPU Core nodes, 256 GB of memory, and NVIDIA Tesla P100 GPUs (compute capability 6.0), running Linux.

5.1   Comparison Approach: *Precimonious*

While none of the existing mixed-precision tuning methods handle multi-threaded and/or CUDA codes, the Precimonious technique [22,23] uses a generic search algorithm, *delta debugging*, that can be implemented for CUDA programs (the original version in the paper works on CPU-base serial programs). This algorithm is considered the state-of-the-art on automatic mixed-precision tuning and it is also used as a comparison baseline in several works [7,22]. We implement the delta debugging tuning algorithm as described in [23] as a comparison framework for our approach as well, which we call `Precimonious-GPU`.

As described in [23], our implementation finds a 1-minimal configuration, i.e., a configuration for which lowering the precision of any one additional variable would cause the program to compute an insufficiently accurate answer or violate the performance threshold. To generate program variants, we use static changes to the source code to modify the declarations of variables from FP64 to FP32.

Table 3. Profile of Top Kernels in LULESH

Kernel	Time	r_{ac}	Registers usage	
			FP64	Mixed
CalcVolumeForceForElems	25.21%	8.13	254	255
ApplyMaterialPropertiesAndUpdateVolume	24.62%	1.01	62	65
CalcKinematicsAndMonotonicQGradient	18.87%	3.45	128	128

Mode of Operation. Since Precimonious does not perform a search separately driven by error or by performance, we only use one mode of operation: once both the error and performance constraints are met, the algorithm stops.

5.2 CUDA Programs

We evaluate our approach on three scientific computing CUDA programs: LULESH [10], CoMD [1], and CFD [2]. LULESH is a proxy application that solves a Sedov blast problem. This simulation is useful in a variety of science and engineering problems that require modeling hydrodynamics. CoMD is a reference implementation of typical classical molecular dynamics algorithms and workloads. CFD (from Rodinia benchmarks) is an unstructured grid finite volume solver for the three-dimensional Euler equations for compressible flow. We use -O2 optimization in all programs. As inputs we use: -s 50 for LULESH, N=20, nx=25,ny=25,nz=25, for CoMD, and fvcorr.domn.193K for CFD.

Output. For LULESH, we consider the TotalAbsDiff as the main output, a symmetry value for the final origin energy of the simulation. For configuration, we also perform other correctness checks, including making sure that the final energy and iterations count is the same as in the FP64 version. For CoMD, we use the simulation final energy as the main output since this is one of the key interesting final results for molecular dynamics simulations. For CFD, we use the total density energy as the output.

Figure of Merit (FOM). For LULESH, we use zones per second as the FOM; for CoMD we use the average atom rate, i.e., processed atoms per time (atoms/usec); for CFD we use execution time in seconds. Note that for LULESH and CoMD, higher FOM is better, while for CFD, lower is better.

5.3 Overhead of Shadow Computations

The overhead of shadow computations analysis is on average 24× (61× for LULESH, 1.5× for CoMD, and 11.12× for CFD), which is comparable to the overhead of static and binary instrumentation tools [9,15]. Note that shadow computations analysis is run only once with a given input and is independent of the trial runs (see Sect. 4.5).

5.4 Threshold Settings

We present results for three levels of accuracy (3, 6, and 9 digits of accuracy) with respect to the baseline FP64 precision case, and four performance thresholds (5%, 10%, 15%, and 20%). We experimented with higher digits of accuracy and higher performance thresholds, however, none of the approaches found solutions in such cases, so we limit the results in the paper to 9 digits of accuracy and 20% of performance threshold. Note that for CFD, where lower FOM is better, speedup is $-s$. We set the maximum number of *FISets*, ϕ, to 100 in all experiments. In practice, the number of trial runs is always less than this value.

5.5 Case 1: LULESH

Table 3 shows the result of LULESH's profile. The first and second columns show the three kernels that consume most of the execution time and the percentage of time, respectively. Since time in the remaining kernels is small (less than 5%), we do not consider them in the rest of the analysis as they are unlikely to yield high speedups when using mixed-precision. The third column shows the average arithmetic-to-cast operations ratio, r_{ac}, for the kernel *FISets*.

As we observe in the table, `CalcVolumeForceForElems` has a high average r_{ac}, which means that the *FISets* of this kernel could potentially give high speedups. As we observe in the fourth and fifth columns of the table, which show the register usage for the baseline (FP64) and mixed precision versions,

Table 4. Results of using *FISets* and shadow computations: performance speedup (% of maximum ideal speedup) for three error thresholds, four performance thresholds and tree modes of operation; number of runs in parenthesis.

	Error thold. (digits)	Mode 1	Mode 2				Mode 3			
			Performance threshold				Performance threshold			
			5%	10%	15%	20%	5%	10%	15%	20%
LULESH	3	9.8% (1)	9.8% (1)	30.4% (2)	30.4% (2)	30.4% (2)	46.4% (1)	46.4% (1)	46.4% (1)	46.4% (1)
	6	0.3% (12)	8.4% (79)	–	–	–	–	–	–	–
	9	0.3% (12)	–	–	–	–	–	–	–	–
CoMD	3	24.2% (1)	24.2% (1)	24.2% (1)	24.2% (1)	24.2% (1)	10.9% (1)	10.9% (1)	37.5% (7)	37.5% (7)
	6	24.2% (1)	24.2% (1)	24.2% (1)	24.2% (1)	24.2% (1)	10.9% (1)	10.9% (1)	37.5% (7)	37.5% (7)
	0	2.3% (3)	19.7% (62)	19.7% (62)	19.7% (62)	–	19.3% (8)	19.3% (8)	19.3% (8)	–
CFD	3	8.3% (1)	8.3% (1)	13.3% (3)	15.3% (35)	–	5.1% (9)	12.6% (15)	15.1% (39)	–
	6	8.34% (1)	8.3% (1)	13.3% (3)	15.3% (35)	–	5.1% (9)	12.6% (15)	15.1% (39)	–
	9	–	–	–	–	–	–	–	–	–

242   I. Laguna et al.

Table 5. `Precimonious-GPU` results: performance speedup (% of maximum ideal speedup) for the error thresholds and performance thresholds; number of runs are in parenthesis. See Fig. 4 for the maximum speedup reported for each approach.

	Error Thold. (digits)	Performance threshold			
		5%	10%	15%	20%
LULESH	3	11.6% (11)	11.4% (11)	17.4% (32)	20.7% (34)
	6	11.5% (11)	11.4 (11)	–	–
	9	–	–	–	–
CoMD	3	12.6% (2)	12.9% (2)	–	–
	6	13.6% (2)	12.7% (2)	–	–
	9	5.4% (24)	–	–	–
CFD	3	–	–	–	–
	6	–	–	–	–
	9	–	–	–	–

the register usage of this kernel is very close to the limit, i.e., 254 out of a maximum of 255 registers per thread in this GPU. The average register usage for the mixed-precision version is 255, which indicates that this is kernel is not a good candidate for mixed-precision, therefore, we discard this kernel in the analysis.

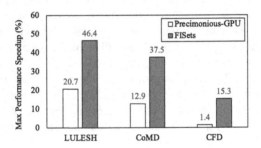

Fig. 4. Maximum performance speedup (% of the ideal speedup) reported by `Precimonious-GPU` and the *FISets* approach.

`ApplyMaterialPropertiesAndUpdateVolume` is the next kernel that we consider (second in the table). While the algorithm found a few *FISets* in it (4), the average r_{ac} of these *FISets* is quite low: only 1.01. This indicates that there is almost no potential for performance improvements in this kernel, thus, we also discard this kernel in the analysis.

`CalcKinematicsAndMonotonicQGradient`, the third kernel is next considered. This kernel has the appropriate characteristics: the average *FISets* r_{ac} is 3.45 and its average register usage is 125, even when *FISets* are used, i.e., for this kernel *FISets do not increase register usage*. Therefore, we focus on this kernel in the rest of the analysis and experiments.

Table 4 (first section) shows the performance results for LULESH, for the error thresholds, performance thresholds and the three modes of operation; the number of trial runs are shown in parenthesis. For Mode 1, we find a configuration with 3 digits of accuracy and 9.8% of speedup with a single trial run; the cases for 6 and 9 accuracy digits do not produce significant performance improvements.

Except for the 6-digit case in Mode 2 (5% of performance threshold), which requires 79 runs, Mode 1 and Mode 2 both generally find configurations with high performance improvement (up to 46%) with *only a few runs* (1–2 runs). We did not find configurations for the 9-digit case in Modes 2–3.

Precimonious. The `Precimonious-GPU` results are shown in Table 5. We observe that the maximum speedup found is about 20.7% for the 3-digit case. Like in our approach, it cannot find good solutions for the 9-digit case.

Input Sensitivity. We measure the performance speedup (using Eq. 3) for multiple LULESH inputs. We use two *FISet* configurations: one with a low r_{ac} of 2.08 (case 1), and another one with a high r_{ac} of 6.90 (case 2). Figure 5 shows the results; digits of accuracy are shown as labels. We observe that for case 1, the speedup for a small input (20) is small, but it increases for larger inputs. For case 2, the speedup for a small input is large and it decreases for larger input. In both cases the speedup stays almost the same for several large inputs, 50–80. The digits of accuracy for case 1 tend to be higher than for case 2 because case 1 has less FP32 operations than case 2 (its *FISet* is smaller) and as a result it incurs smaller error.

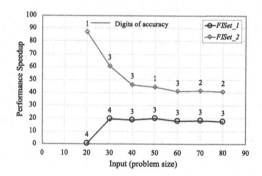

Fig. 5. Performance speedup for multiple LULESH inputs for two *FISet* configurations. Labels are the digits of accuracy.

5.6   Case 2: CoMD

CoMD is a compute-intensive workload, where a large portion of time is spent computing forces between particles—these operations involve several addition and multiplication operations versus a few load/store operations. This code is a good candidate for *FISets* and mixed-precision in general.

We follow a profiling phase that is similar to the one we did for LULESH. Out of the top four time-consuming kernels, `SortAtomsByGlobalId`,

LoadAtomsBufferPacked, fill, and LJ_Force_thread_atom, our algorithm only
found *FISets* in LJ_Force_thread_atom. Thus, this was the only candidate
for performance improvements for our technique. The average *FISets* r_{ac} for
this kernel was 3.10. By inspecting the code more carefully, we found that
LJ_Force_thread_atom is where particle force calculations is done, so this finding makes sense. We did not find any kernel with high register pressure in this
code.

Table 4 (mid section) shows the performance results for CoMD. As expected,
the algorithm finds configurations that meet both error and performance thresholds for all modes of operation, in many cases with a single trial run. The best
case in terms of performance was about 37% for 6 digits of accuracy with only
7 runs. As shown in Table 5, while it can find solutions with a few trial runs,
Precimonious-GPU finds a maximum speedup of about 12.9%.

5.7   Case 3: CFD

CFD presents high potential for performance improvements via mixed-precision
since the code core computations, flux computations, involve a number of
compute-intensive operations. While this program is smaller than the LULESH
and CoMD, it challenges our approach because its main kernel is relatively large,
potentially causing *FISets* to put pressure on register usage.

After profiling the code, we find that 67% of the time is spent in
cuda_compute_flux, while the rest of time is spent mostly on cuda_time_step
(22%). Our algorithm did not find *FISets* in cuda_time_step; so we focus on
cuda_compute_flux on which the average r_{ac} of *FISets* is 3.56. Note that we did
not find any kernel on which *FISets* causes a register pressure in this code.

Table 4 (third section) shows the performance results for CFD. We find configurations of up to 15.1% with up to 6 digits of accuracy running the code 39
times. It can also find a case for 8% of speedup on 6 digits of accuracy with a
single trial run. Precimonious-GPU is, however, unable to find solutions for the
target error and performance thresholds—the maximum performance speedup
ever reported during the search was about 1.4% as shown in Fig. 4.

6   Conclusions

While floating-point mixed-precision tuning techniques exist, they are accuracy-
driven and do not provide significant performance speedups to GPU programs.
We introduce and evaluate GPUMixer, a new tool to tune floating-point precision on GPU programs with a focus on performance improvements. GPUMixer
is engineered on novel concepts, such as *FISets* to statically identify regions
that yield performance, and shadow computations analysis to compute the error
introduced by mixed-precision. Our evaluation shows that our approach can be
used in realistic GPU applications, and that it can find configurations that produce higher speedups (up to 46% of the ideal speedup) than those of current
state-of-the-art techniques.

Acknowledgments. We thank the anonymous reviewers for their suggestions and comments on the paper. This work was performed under the auspices of the U.S. Department of Energy by Lawrence Livermore National Laboratory under contract DEAC52-07NA27344 (LLNL-CONF-748618).

References

1. CoMD-CUDA (2017). https://github.com/NVIDIA/CoMD-CUDA
2. Che, S., et al.: Rodinia: a benchmark suite for heterogeneous computing. In: IEEE International Symposium on Workload Characterization (IISWC 2009), pp. 44–54. IEEE (2009)
3. Chiang, W.F., Baranowski, M., Briggs, I., Solovyev, A., Gopalakrishnan, G., Rakamarić, Z.: Rigorous floating-point mixed-precision tuning. In: 44th ACM SIG-PLAN Symposium on Principles of Programming Languages, POPL 2017. Association for Computing Machinery (2017)
4. Chiang, W.-F., Gopalakrishnan, G., Rakamaric, Z., Solovyev, A.: Efficient search for inputs causing high floating-point errors. In: Proceedings of the 19th ACM SIGPLAN Symposium on Principles and Practice of Parallel Programming, PPoPP 2014, pp. 43–52. ACM, New York (2014)
5. Damouche, N., Martel, M., Chapoutot, A.: Intra-procedural optimization of the numerical accuracy of programs. In: Núñez, M., Güdemann, M. (eds.) FMICS 2015. LNCS, vol. 9128, pp. 31–46. Springer, Cham (2015). https://doi.org/10.1007/978-3-319-19458-5_3
6. Darulova, E., Kuncak, V.: Towards a compiler for reals. ACM Trans. Program. Lang. Syst. (TOPLAS) **39**(2), 8 (2017)
7. Guo, H., Rubio-González, C.: Exploiting community structure for floating-point precision tuning. In: Proceedings of the 27th ACM SIGSOFT International Symposium on Software Testing and Analysis, pp. 333–343. ACM (2018)
8. Harris, M.: Mini-nbody: a simple N-body code (2014). https://github.com/harrism/mini-nbody
9. Iskhodzhanov, T., Potapenko, A., Samsonov, A., Serebryany, K., Stepanov, E., Vyukov, D.: ThreadSanitizer, MemorySanitizer, 8 November 2012. https://urldefense.proofpoint.com/v2/url?u=http-3A__www.llvm.org_devmtg_2012-2D11_Serebryany-5FTSan-2DMSan.pdf&d=DwIF-g&c=vh6FgFnduejNhPPD0fl_yRaSf Zy8CWbWnIf4XJhSqx8&r=UyK1_569d50MjVlUSODJYRW2epEY0RveVNq0Y CmePcDz4DQHW-CkWcttrwneZ0md&m=QbB1B0a55LgDuuwoFrE3U3GhMpM GOKghlpBLKQdmd1A&s=XadD1efiG2KOXnZcaadrIMuS10vDECEVJu__ wnFtYQU&e=
10. Karlin, I., Keasler, J., Neely, R.: Lulesh 2.0 updates and changes. Technical report LLNL-TR-641973, August 2013
11. Lam, M.O., Hollingsworth, J.K.: Fine-grained floating-point precision analysis. Int. J. High Perform. Comput. Appl. **32**, 231 (2016). 1094342016652462
12. Lam, M.O., Hollingsworth, J.K., de Supinski, B.R., LeGendre, M.P.: Automatically adapting programs for mixed-precision floating-point computation. In: Proceedings of the 27th International ACM Conference on Supercomputing, pp. 369–378. ACM (2013)
13. Lam, M.O., Rountree, B.L.: Floating-point shadow value analysis. In: Proceedings of the 5th Workshop on Extreme-Scale Programming Tools, pp. 18–25. IEEE Press (2016)

14. Lattner, C., Adve, V.: LLVM: a compilation framework for lifelong program analysis & transformation. In: Proceedings of the International Symposium on Code Generation and Optimization: Feedback-Directed and Runtime Optimization, p. 75. IEEE Computer Society (2004)
15. Luk, C.-K., et al.: Pin: building customized program analysis tools with dynamic instrumentation. ACM SIGPLAN Not. **40**, 190–200 (2005)
16. Menon, H., et al.: ADAPT: algorithmic differentiation applied to floating-point precision tuning. In: Proceedings of the International Conference for High Performance Computing, Networking, Storage, and Analysis, p. 48. IEEE Press (2018)
17. NDIDIA. CUDA ToolKit Documentation - NVVM IR Specification 1.5 (2018). https://docs.nvidia.com/cuda/nvvm-ir-spec/index.html
18. Nguyen, H.: GPU Gems 3, pp. 677–694. Addison-Wesley Professional, Reading (2007). chapter 31
19. Nvidia. Nvidia Tesla P100 GPU. Pascal Architecture White Paper (2016)
20. Nvidia. CUDA C Programming Guide, v9.0 (2018). http://docs.nvidia.com/cuda/cuda-c-programming-guide/index.html
21. Paganelli, G., Ahrendt, W.: Verifying (in-) stability in floating-point programs by increasing precision, using SMT solving. In: 2013 15th International Symposium on Symbolic and Numeric Algorithms for Scientific Computing (SYNASC), pp. 209–216. IEEE (2013)
22. Rubio-González, C., et al.: Floating-point precision tuning using blame analysis. In: Proceedings of the 38th International Conference on Software Engineering, ICSE 2016, pp. 1074–1085. ACM, New York (2016)
23. Rubio-González, C., et al.: Precimonious: tuning assistant for floating-point precision. In: Proceedings of the International Conference on High Performance Computing, Networking, Storage and Analysis, p. 27. ACM (2013)

Performance Exploration Through Optimistic Static Program Annotations

Johannes Doerfert$^{(\boxtimes)}$ (ID), Brian Homerding (ID), and Hal Finkel (ID)

Argonne National Laboratory, Lemont, IL, USA
{jdoerfert,bhomerding,hfinkel}@anl.gov

Abstract. Compilers are limited by the static information directly or indirectly encoded in the program. Low-level languages, such as C/C++, are considered problematic as their weak type system and relaxed memory semantic allows for various, sometimes non-obvious, behaviors. Since compilers have to preserve the program semantics for all program executions, the existence of exceptional behavior can prevent optimizations that the developer would consider valid and might expect. Analyses to guarantee the absence of disruptive and unlikely situations are consequently an indispensable part of an optimizing compiler. However, such analyses have to be approximative and limited in scope as global and exact solutions are infeasible for any non-trivial program.

In this paper, we present an automated tool to measure the effect missing static information has on the optimizations applied to a given program. The approach generates an optimistically optimized program version which, compared to the original, defines a performance gap that can be closed by better compiler analyses and selective static program annotations.

Our evaluation on six already tuned proxy applications for high-performance codes shows speedups of up to 20.6%. This clearly indicates that static uncertainty limits performance. At the same time, we observed that compilers are often unable to utilize additional static information. Thus, manual annotation of all correct static information is therefore not only error prone but also mostly redundant.

Keywords: Compiler guided auto tuning · Performance gap · LLVM

1 Introduction

Programs in the high-performance computing domain are often subject to fine-grained tuning and therefore developed in low-level programming languages such as Fortran or C/C++. However, this tuning potential can cut both ways. Without proper annotations, low-level languages allow various behaviors that are uncommon to occur during a normal program execution. These "corner case behaviors" include, for example, potentially aliasing pointers and possibly overflowing integer operations. While performance can increase if such corner case behaviors are exploited properly, performance can also be limited if beneficial compiler transformations are prevented by their presence.

© Springer Nature Switzerland AG 2019
M. Weiland et al. (Eds.): ISC High Performance 2019, LNCS 11501, pp. 247–268, 2019.
https://doi.org/10.1007/978-3-030-20656-7_13

Figure 1 illustrates how corner case behaviors can prevent desired optimizations. The call to the `external` function might cause arbitrary side effects and changes to the values passed as arguments. After the call, `sum` might not be zero and `locP` is not guaranteed to be {5, 11}. Additionally, the address of `sum` or `locP` could escape, creating aliasing issues if one is stored in `globalPtr`. As a result, compilers cannot assume the access to `globalPtr` is invariant in the loop.

Finally, the loop iteration counter u may overflow. Thus, the loop can iterate either UB - LB iterations, if LB <= UB, or alternatively 256 - UB + LB iterations, if LB > UB. Due to this uncertainty, most compilers will struggle to optimize the loop, e.g., to replace it by a closed form expression. As discussed in Sect. 2, all these optimizations would be possible *if* better static information on the effects of the `external` function and the values of LB and UB were available.

```
int *globalPtr;
void external(int*, std::pair<int>&);

int foo(uint8_t LB, uint8_t UB) {
  int sum = 0;
  std::pair<int> locP = {5, 11};
  external(&sum, locP);
  for (uint8_t u = LB; u != UB; u++)
    sum += *globalPtr + locP.first;
  return sum;
}
```

Fig. 1. Low-level code that allows for various unexpected behaviors which prevent performance critical transformations.

In this work we identify and optimistically eliminate situations in which static information is missing, e.g., due to the low-level nature of the program. In particular, we determined 20 opportunities for which skilled, performance-minded developers, or improved compiler analyses, could enhance conservatively sound compiler assumptions. For these, our tool automatically explore the performance impact if perfect information would have been provided by optimistically providing it, followed by an application specific verification step. In other words, we automatically accumulate optimistic static program annotations under which the program remains valid on user specified inputs. After this tuning process, the last successfully verified version defines a performance gap which can be minimized through manual annotations.

It is important to note that optimistic optimization is not meant to be used in production because it gives up on total correctness, the foundation of the compilation process. Instead, it should be seen as a compiler guided development tool. It directs performance minded programmers towards static information both *required and usable* by the compiler, consequently minimizing manual effort while effectively increasing performance.

The paper is organized as follows: Sect. 2 explains how static annotations restrict the set of defined program behaviors, potentially enabling program optimizations. In Sect. 3, we detail the exploited opportunities for additional static information. We explain the corner case behaviors which annotation can exclude, the transformations that could be enabled, and how static information can be provided in the source. Before we present an elaborate evaluation of our approach on six high-performance proxy applications in Sect. 5, we list implementation choices in Sect. 4. After related work is discussed in Sect. 6, we conclude in Sect. 7.

2   Static Program Annotation

Programming languages, including the intermediate representations used inside a compiler, allow to encode additional information directly in the program code. Such information can improve later analyses and enable optimizations, regardless of how the information came to be. This is especially important for performance aware developers that use program annotations to encode their domain knowledge, e.g., the shapes of possible inputs or the contexts in which code will be used. Encoded information lifts a burden from the compiler as it limits the set of defined program behaviors. The only (purely static) alternative is running complex analyses at compile time. Given that some program properties, e.g., pointer aliasing, are in their general form undecidable [20], programmer annotated knowledge is often irreplaceable.

```
int *globalPtr;                          int *globalPtr;
void external(int*, std::pair<int>&)     void external(int*,std::pair<int>&);
  __attribute__((pure));
int foo(uint8_t LB, uint8_t UB) {        int foo(uint8_t LB, uint8_t UB) {
  int sum = 0;                             int sum = 0;
  std::pair<int> locP = {5, 11};           std::pair<int> locP = {5, 11};
  external(&sum, locP);                     external(&sum, locP);
  __builtin_assume(LB <= UB);
  for (uint8_t u = LB; u != UB; u++)
    sum += *globalPtr + locP.first;        int gPVal = *globalPtr;
  return sum;                              return (UB - LB) * (gPVal+5);
}                                        }
```

Fig. 2. Left: The code shown in Fig. 1 statically annotated with optimistic information. Right: The same code after annotation enabled compiler optimizations eliminated the loop.

Section 1 lists problems and missed transformations for the code in Fig. 1. To overcome these problems, and thereby enable optimizations that lead to the version shown in Fig. 2 (right), the problematic corner case behaviors need to be eliminated through program annotations. The first was the potential for the external function call to manipulate the arguments as well as globalPtr. While our implementation in the LLVM [16] compiler can encode this in different ways, programming languages like C/C++ generally offer less possibilities. In this situation it is *sufficient* to annotate the external function as pure, as shown in the left part of Fig. 2. Pure functions may not alter outside state, preventing the escape of the argument pointers and thereby also potentially aliasing accesses. Consequently, the compiler can hoist the load of globalPtr out of the loop. Also the access to locP.first can be hoisted which leaves a loop that accumulates an unknown but *fixed* value. If we additionally ensure the compiler that the loop iteration variable u is not going to wrap around, e.g., through the `__builtin_assume(LB <= UB)` annotation, the loop is replaced by a closed form expression that directly computes the result. Note that the absence of memory writes in the external function, the consequent absence of aliasing pointers, and the lifetime of sum allow to simplify the closed form expression even further.

As manual exploration of such annotations is tedious, and most are superfluous, we provide an automated way. It allows developers to periodically determine the impact of some, or all, static uncertainty sources in application hotspots and, depending on the results, manually verify and manifest the most important annotations in the code.

3 Optimistic Optimization Opportunities

Optimistic optimization opportunities arise whenever the semantic of the program allows different behaviors to manifest at runtime. While this is the essence of any input-dependent, non-trivial program, there are various situations for which the runtime behavior for all inputs, or at least the ones the user is interested in, is actually the same. While the purpose of compiler analyses is to identify which behaviors cannot occur at runtime, optimistic optimization opportunities allow to explore the space of the ones we need to allow. Thus, program analyses find a potentially conservative, but sound approximation of the actual runtime behaviors while optimistic optimization opportunities enable us to explore less conservative, potentially unsound approximations. Figure 3 lists the optimistic optimization opportunity kinds our approach can identify and exploit.

Whenever one of these situations is encountered in the program, our compiler extension generates an optimistic choice, which, if taken, results in a program annotation that limits the behaviors the rest of the compiler will assume to be legal.

In the remainder of this section, identified and exploited opportunity kinds and their source annotations are detailed together with a discussion how subsequent transformations may be enabled by seized optimistic opportunities.

Description	Section
pot. overflowing computations	3.1
pot. parallel loops	3.2
unknown control flow choices	3.3
pot undefined behavior in functions	3.4.1
unknown function side-effects	3.4.2
pot runtime exceptions in functions	3.4.3
unknown function return values	3.4.4
externally visible functions	3.4.5
pot. aliasing pointers	3.5.1
pot. escaping pointers	3.5.2
unknown pointer usage	3.5.3
unknown pointer alignment	3.5.4
pot. non-dereferenceable pointers	3.5.5
pot. invariant memory locations	3.5.6

Fig. 3. Identified and exploited opportunities.

3.1   Potentially Overflowing Computations

Binary computations in low-level languages, such as C/C++ and LLVM intermediate representation (LLVM-IR), have multiple evaluation semantics that differ for overflowing operations. In C/C++, the signedness of the operands determines if operations are computed with *wrapping* or *undefined* semantics. For the former, the result of the operation is computed modulo the largest value representable in the target type bit-width. For the latter, the value is undefined if the mathematically exact result would require more bits than provided by the target type. In LLVM-IR, values do not have an associated signedness but operations carry annotations to determine the semantics. If none are present, *wrapping* semantic is used. While it is an implementation of *undefinied* semantic, it is more restrictive when it comes to the possibility of integer overflows. Only if operations are tagged with no-(un)signed-wrap (nsw/nuw), LLVM is allowed to assume the more lenient *undefinied* semantic. Thus, the result, if interpreted as signed or unsigned value respectively, will either be mathematically exact or undefined. Similarly, C/C++ compilers allow to enforce *wrapping* or *undefined* semantic for potentially overflowing computations regardless of the operands signedness through the command line options -fwrapv and -fno-strict-overflow.

Potentially overflowing arithmetic operations, including address computations, offer an opportunity for optimistic annotation. If the program semantic did not imply nsw/nuw for a computation, or if transformations applied by the compiler could not prove these properties for newly introduced or modified code, a potential overflow is well-defined and has to be taken into consideration. As integer overflows rarely happen (on purpose) in practice, especially in loop heavy computation hot-spots [1,9], the missing nsw/nuw flags provide a perfect opportunity for optimistic optimization.

Our optimistic code annotator can add missing annotations, e.g., nsw and nuw, to potentially overflowing operations. We distinguish thereby between annotations for signed, unsigned, and address computations which can be enabled separately.

3.2   Potentially Parallel Loops

Detecting parallelism in sequential programs has been a major challenge for decades. Especially for low-level languages there are various caveats including, but not limited to: potentially overflowing computations (ref. Sect. 3.1), potentially aliasing pointers (ref. Sect. 3.5.1), and unknown side-effects of function calls (ref. Sect. 3.4.2). Even if all of these issues are tamed, powerful dependence analyses are needed to identify parallelism in non-trivial loops [5,11,19].

In the context of LLVM, parallelism is usually exploited by the loop vectorizer and the polyhedral loop optimizer Polly [13]. While both employ runtime checks to deal with some of the aforementioned low-level issues [3,9], these come with their own set of limitations. As our approach shifts the soundness liability to the expert developer, we can optimistically annotate loops as parallel.

LLVM currently encodes parallelism as metadata annotations on non-pure instructions inside of loops. The annotations are only exploited in two ways, both related to the loop vectorizer: First, the dependency legality check for vectorization is skipped, and, second, in case if-conversion [2] is necessary, it is assumed to be legal.

3.3   Control Flow Speculation

Programs, especially in high-performance computing, often interleave various operating modes that result in variations in the executed program path. In the benchmarks we evaluated, input flags determined for example which energy transfer function and output method is used. In case we are only interested in a subset of these modes, we can specialize the program based on the content of variables which determine the executed path. Thus, if a variable is used as a control condition, we can optimistically assume that only one control flow target is always executed next. To embed this information in the program, we place an assumptions intrinsics call (`llvm.assume`) which is LLVM's counterpart of Clang's `__builtin_assume`. Other C/C++ compilers have similar functionality.

Similar to general value specialization, which could also be done through this scheme, unguided control flow speculation is unlikely to succeed. We therefore restrict ourselves to the control flow conditions that depend on global variables, parameters, and function return values. Additionally, we do not speculate for loop exit or latch branches, and we require a non-relational control flow condition with one constant operand. While this already reduces the possibilities significantly, we additionally try to use a single optimistic optimization choice variable to represent all opportunities induced by the same a global variable, function return value, or function parameter. This will synchronize all speculative choices as described in Sect. 4.1.

3.4   Function Behavior

A compiler has to treat calls to unknown functions as optimization barriers because the callee can not only cause arbitrary side-effects, but it could also never return control to the caller. Even if the called function is known, its definition might not necessarily be available in the current translation unit. If a definition is available but the language semantic allows a different one to be chosen at link time or run-time, it is not allowed to deduce information from this *potential* definition. Finally, if the definition is available and known to be executed, the compiler has to employ inter-procedural analyses. From an algorithmic standpoint such inter-procedural analyses are often less precise, due to uncertainty stemming from unknown outside callers. From an implementation standpoint they are also less interesting than their intra-procedural counterparts because the latter are predominantly needed after (aggressive) inlining was performed.

In LLVM, intra-procedural analyses are dominating in numbers and potential. The existing inter-procedural analyses mostly try to limit the possible effects of function calls and simplify the caller-callee interface through propagation of constants. However, all of the above mentioned issues will limit the information that can be deduced from, and the transformations than can be applied to, functions.

Since function call can generally cause various possible behaviors at runtime, especially if the called function is unknown or not inlined, they provide different optimistic optimization opportunities discussed in the following.

3.4.1   Undefined Behavior

Functions might not only cause side-effects and raise exceptions, they can also cause undefined behavior, e.g., a division by zero. While compilers generally take advantage of undefined behavior, they shall never introduce it on a path on which it would not manifest anyway. Consequently, unconditionally hoisting of calls out of a loop is unsound, even if the call is to a *constant* function (ref. Sect. 3.4.2) not raising exceptions (ref. Sect. 3.4.3). Doing so is only valid if the callee does either not cause undefined behavior, or it would have been executed anyway.

To enable control dependence changes for calls, we provide an optimistic optimization opportunity for the `speculatable` LLVM-IR function attribute[1]. Since `speculatable` does imply the absence of undefined behavior and also other side-effects, we combined this opportunity with the side-effect encoding described in Sect. 3.4.2.

3.4.2 Side-Effects

Conservatively, a function might read or write any accessible memory location. Thus, everything transitively reachable through global variables or pointer arguments is potentially accessed. Since this generally includes locations to which pointers might have escaped earlier (ref. Sect. 3.5.2), the set of *known invariant locations* is often quite limited. Consequently,

1. `speculatable` (and `readnone`[1], ref. Section 3.4.1)
2. `readnone`
3. `readonly` and `inaccessiblememonly`
4. `readonly` and `argmemonly`
5. `readonly` and `inaccessiblemem_or_argmemonly`
6. `readonly`
7. `writeonly` and `inaccessiblememonly`
8. `writeonly` and `argmemonly`
9. `writeonly` and `inaccessiblemem_or_argmemonly`
10. `writeonly`
11. `inaccessiblememonly`
12. `argmemonly`
13. `inaccessiblemem_or_argmemonly`

Fig. 4. Optimistic function side-effect choices.

transformations involving memory are severely restricted as they could potentially interact with the called function. To restrict the possibly accessed locations, low-level languages provide function and parameter annotations. The function level is discussed here and parameters in Sect. 3.5. In C/C++, functions can be marked as *pure* and *constant* via `__attribute__((pure/const))`. The pure annotation guarantees that the function will at most *read* global variables and not *access* any other location. The `const` annotation also disallows global reads. In LLVM-IR,

---

[1] The `speculatable` annotation is fairly new so we add the implied `readnone` explicitly.

similar annotations exist. A function can be marked as readnone, to indicate that no memory is accessed, as readonly if there is no memory write, or as writeonly if there is no memory read. In addition, LLVM uses inaccessiblememonly to indicate that all accessed locations are not directly accessible from the user code, argmemonly to indicate that all memory accesses are based on pointer arguments, and inaccessiblemem_or_argmemonly to combine the two[2]. To exploit actual, not potential, behaviors, we generate optimistic opportunities with the optimistic choices listed in Fig. 4. During the search space exploration (ref. Sect. 4.2), the choices are tried in order, thereby gradually decreasing the optimism.

3.4.3   Runtime Exceptions

A function invocation can return to its respective call site, not terminate at all, or it can return to a point higher up the call chain. The latter, referred to as stack unwinding, is most often associated with runtime exceptions. Thus, if the called function raises an exception which is not caught inside that function invocation, the exception will traverse the call chain until a suitable handler is found. Since the code succeeding the in-between invocations would then be skipped, the compiler has to ensure the integrity of the program state prior to a potentially unwinding call. Hence, all non-local memory effects preceding an invocation that might transitively raise an exception have to be visible, and the side-effects after the invocation shall not be visible. As this severely limits the code movement and combination abilities only to preserve the semantics in case an exception is actually raised, it offers a perfect optimistic optimization opportunity for all programs, and program runs, that will not raise exceptions.

Compilers often allow to disable exceptions through options, e.g., -fno-exceptions. Additionally, C++ has the keyword noexcept, and the nothrow attribute is often supported. However, runtime exceptions are not the only cause for stack unwinding. We therefore use the LLVM-IR nounwind function attribute to guarantee each call site will either return control to its successor instruction, or not at all.

3.4.4   Return Values

In addition to the side-effects, functions return values. While speculation on values opens up a far too large search space, there are common idioms that we optimize for. In particular, functions that return a value with the same type as one or multiple of their parameters might always return one of them.

To limit the number of optimistic opportunities, we only consider functions that return a pointer type. The number of optimistic choices is then equal to the number of parameters with the same type. The LLVM-IR parameter attribute returned is used to indicate that the return value is equal to the argument passed for this parameter. During the search space exploration (ref. Sect. 4.2),

---

[2] GCC's attribute leaf is similar to inaccessiblemem_or_argmemonly in LLVM-IR.

the suitable parameters are tried from the first one declared to the last. This is preferable because class methods take an implicit "this" object pointer, which is often returned.

3.4.5   Visibility

To write modular and maintainable programs, most programming languages allow to choose different scopes for a symbol declaration. In particular, functions can be, among others, declared with a global or local scope. In C/C++, the former is the default while the latter, i.e., translation unit local, requires the function to be declared as static. Only if that is the case, the compiler can reason about *all* call sites prior to link time[3]. This can then justify more aggressive inlining as well as inter-procedural information propagation from call sites to the function definition[4].

To limit the visibility, or scope, of a function declaration optimistically, we change the linkage type of external functions to internal. This is valid if, at link time, there are no users outside the current translation unit. If there are, the linking process, and thereby the verification, will automatically fail. Changing the linkage type of a function declaration in LLVM-IR to internal has a similar effect as the static keyword in C/C++.

3.5   Pointer Attributes

Pointers and the associated memory accesses, are arguably the most complicated part of a program. Especially in low-level languages, such as a compiler's intermediate representation, there are various caveats that have to be considered. Two memory accesses can for example alias, hence they might access (partially) the same memory locations. An access can be invalid at runtime if the accessed location is not dereferenceable, e.g., if the access pointer is "dangling". Similarly, the access can be invalid if the alignment of the access pointer violates the requirements of the assembly instruction that was chosen to implement it. As a consequence, potentially aliasing accesses induce dependences that have to be preserve similar to the control conditions of potentially invalid accesses.

3.5.1   Aliasing

Since the use of unrestricted pointers is a major source of uncertainty during program optimization, compilers employ various forms of context-, flow-, type- and field-sensitive alias analyses [7,10,14,17,22,23]. Alias analyses, as well as the dependence analyses built on top, are tasked to identify and classify the dependence between side-effects. Only due to this information, transformations can decide if it is sound to alter the execution order of accesses, substitute them with already available values, or eliminate them all together. However, identifying aliasing pointers is on its own an undecidable problem [20]. Even if it is decidable for a

---

[3] Link time optimizations [12,15] are discussed in more detail in Sect. 5 and Sect. 6.

[4] While not in LLVM, a prototype for such a pass has been proposed already [8].

given program, it is complex and consequently unrealistic to expect pointer related uncertainties to be resolved through static analyses alone [3].

Programming languages for which pointers by default alias commonly provide annotations to *restrict* the set of objects a pointer can alias with. While these annotations, e.g., `restrict`/`__restrict__` in C/C++, and `noalias` in LLVM-IR, are coarse-grained tools, they already allow to handle a common case: *Two pointers that do not originate in the same "restrict" qualified declarations cannot alias.*

We introduce the `noalias` annotation to function parameters and return values with pointer type. As the support for otherwise scoped restrict qualified pointers in LLVM is preliminary, we did not investigate this possibility for now.

3.5.2   Capturing

Compilers try to determine the provenance, or the source object, of a pointer to rule out aliasing. Aliasing is impossible if a pointer is based on an object another pointer cannot be based on. An example are stack allocated objects that, *initially*, cannot alias with any pointer loaded from memory or provided from the outside. However, as soon as a pointer to the stack object *escapes*, i.e., the address of the object is potentially duplicated and made available to the rest of the program, this guarantee is void. A pointer conservatively escapes if it is passed to a function or stored in memory.

We augment the results of the already performed inter-procedural capture analyses in LLVM, which derives `nocapture` function parameter annotations, with optimistic annotations if they were not derived. For C/C++, Clang allows the programmer to achieve the same effect through `__attribute__((noescape))`.

3.5.3   Usage

As a fine-grained supplement to the function side-effects described in Sect. 3.4.2, LLVM allows to annotate pointer parameters with access information. The choices again include `readnone`, to express that the pointer is not dereferenced during the execution of the function, `readonly`, to guarantee the absence of stores through the pointer, and `writeonly`, which rules out read accesses to the pointer.

The optimistic opportunity generated for each pointer parameter includes all three optimistic alternatives and is, again as the function side-effect equivalent, explored from the most optimistic one to the least. As before, if no optimistic choice could be successfully verified a pessimistic choice is taken, thus the pointer is not annotated.

3.5.4   Alignment

There are different ways pointer alignment is exploited by a compiler. A very important one is the ability to utilize specialized instructions on machines that distinguish between aligned and unaligned memory accesses. Especially for vector code (SIMD) this can cause a significant performance difference.

For C/C++, compilers offer various ways to add alignment information including `__attribute__((aligned(N)))` qualifier, and the `__builtin_assume_aligned` (P, N) call. In this work, we introduced three different alignment annotations into the LLVM-IR. First, for memory accesses to describe their individual alignment, then for pointer parameters, and finally for pointers loaded from memory. In each case we provided two optimistic choices, cache line alignment and pointer alignment.

3.5.5 Dereferenceability

Pointers might or might not point to a memory address that can be accessed at a certain program point. If they do not when accessed, the behavior is undefined. Consequently, compilers have to be especially careful when they move memory accesses which can easily prevent powerful optimizations such as loop hoisting or argument promotion.

As pointers most often point to memory that is in fact accessible, we can optimistically introduce the corresponding LLVM-IR annotation `dereferenceable(N_Bytes)`. It is used for function parameters and return values with pointer type, as well as to annotate pointers loaded from memory. In all three situations we have two optimistic choices, dereferenceability of a single element, or, alternatively, 64 consecutive elements. To achieve a similar effect for returned pointers in C/C++, i.e., to guarantee a certain number of accessible bytes *if the returned pointer is non-null*, GCC and Clang provide the `__attribute__((alloc_size(...)))` function annotation.

3.5.6 Memory Invariance

The `const` keyword in C/C++ can be circumvented by a `const_cast` except for uses in certain variable declarations. Even though LLVM does not generally retain `const` information, it allows to annotate accesses as *invariant* which states that all executions will result in the same value.

To improve optimizations of memory loads, we use the LLVM-IR `invariant.load` annotation optimistically. It can act as an alternative to fine-grained alias annotations and as such enable load coalescing and load hoisting out of loops.

3.6 Overlapping and Inconsistent Annotations

The various annotations we introduce are not disjoint. In fact, it is possible that the optimistically annotated program contains logical inconsistencies. As an example take a function which we optimistically declared as *constant* (ref. Sect. 3.4.2), thus which can be assumed to be completely free of memory side-effects. While this annotation already provides a tight guarantee on the overall side-effects the function shall induce, our algorithm might still not be able to annotate all pointer parameter of this function as "read-only" or "not-accessed" (ref. Sect. 3.5.3). While such inconsistencies can potentially violate implicit pre-conditions of the optimization pipeline, they might also allow to enable optimistic transformations that would otherwise not have been possible. This is partially due to the granularity of the annotations and partially due to the multitude of ways analysis and optimization passes can query information.

4   Implementation Details

Our implementation[5] is split into three components. The first, thought to be provided by the application developer, is a benchmark description. It consists of benchmark specific information, for example the compilation flags, and instructions to verify the result, e.g., the invocation of the test suite. Additionally, the source files, or individual functions, chosen for optimistic optimization are identified. The second component is a transformation pass in the LLVM compiler. It is run at 14 locations in the otherwise original -O2/-O3 pipeline. Every time it will identify optimistic annotation opportunities and, depending on the command line flags provided, either ignore them, act on them, or report them to the outside. The brains of our approach is located in a dedicated and external driver script. It will interpret benchmark description files, request optimistic opportunities from the compiler pass, and explore the space of optimistic choices until a timeout is reached or all opportunities have been resolved. Since early decision can impact the code and thereby change the opportunities available at a later point in the pipeline, it is important to perform the exploration iteratively, one annotation insertion point at a time. Not all opportunities described in Sect. 3 are exploited at every location. Instead, easily droppable annotations, e.g., for parallel loops (ref. Sect. 3.2), are placed only before they are used, e.g., prior to the loop vectorizer. Invariable annotations, e.g., for functions visibility (ref. Sect. 3.4.5), are introduced only once in the very beginning.

4.1   Granularity of Optimistic Opportunities

Optimistic information can often be added in different, potentially nested, granularities. As an example we can annotate a function declaration as a whole, all pointer arguments individually, or, as implemented, do both. While we choose a fine granularity for declarations, we did not yet investigate annotations on individual call sites. Depending on the compiler, finer-grained annotations, i.e., parameter vs. function annotation, and call site vs. declaration annotation, can improve the result. However, they can also easily cause overlapping and inconsistent annotations (ref. Sect. 3.6), increase tuning time, and lead to results that are harder to replicate through source code annotations.

To limit tuning time we eliminated opportunities early on. This means, (1) we do not add annotations if *any* of the possible optimistic choices is already present in the code, and (2) we accumulate opportunities into a single pick based on the kind and name of the value involved. Hence, every time an opportunity arises for a variable, we check if we can reuse the choice made earlier for the same opportunity kind and variable name. For example, all function parameters with the same name in a single translation unit are annotated the same. While this is especially useful for the control flow speculation explained in Sect. 3.3, it generally reduces the number of opportunities we explore.

---

[5] Please see https://github.com/jdoerfert/PETOSPA for the code and benchmarks.

4.2   Search Space Exploration

The space of potential choices for optimistic optimization opportunities is often too large to be searched exhaustively. This is partially because the order in which opportunities are resolved is important, e.g., earlier choices may interact with new ones, and because different optimistic opportunities are non-binary choices, e.g., the function side-effects explained in Sect. 3.4.2. Consequently, a globally optimal solution, measured for example by the number of optimistically resolved opportunities or the final performance, is unrealistic for any real program. Instead, we find a locally optimal solution where opportunity kinds are explored in a fixed order. This order is empirically chosen to allow our exploration algorithm to optimistically resolve many opportunities at once. When the verification failed, the number of optimistically resolved opportunities is split in half. If an opportunity is already tested in isolation, the optimism of the choice is decreased. After a less optimistic choice was fixed, we increase the number of tested opportunities again to potentially allow many choices at once.

5   Evaluation

We evaluated our approach on six proxy applications for high-performance codes described in Fig. 5. While these codes are simplified, they retain much of the original complexity, making them authentic benchmarks for our approach. They especially already contain manual annotations, though, they are, as any production code would be, too complicated to provide *all valid annotations* manually. Several of the codes have few important kernels which encompass the vast majority of the runtime. Others have a long flat profile which is similarly common in practise. We also have variety within our annotated sections with large and small kernels, along with stand alone kernels and kernels with deep call paths. Beyond the code details, the benchmarks exhibit a variety of run time profiles, providing a range from compute to memory bound proxy applications.

The experiments were performed on an Intel(R) Xeon(R) CPU E5-2699 v3 (Haswell), running at 2.30 GHz with 72 threads and 36 cores across two sockets. For each generated executable we collected 20 timings for a medium problem definition. The following discussion is based on the results shown in Fig. 7.

5.1   RSBench (A)

RSBench simulates resonance representation cross sections lookups for nuclear reactor core Monte Carlo particle transport. It is a compute bound alternative to the XSBench kernel (ref. Sect. 5.2), the algorithm that is currently in use. RSBench heavily relies on the standard math library. As shown in Fig. 7, we compiled RSBench 99 times during the tuning. It took 497 s to finish with all 240 optimistic opportunities and we achieved 20.6% speedup compared to the original.

Benchmark	ID	Description	# Threads	Base Time	Compilations All	Succ.	New Vers.
RSBench	(A)	Multipole resonance representation cross section lookup	72	8.56s	99	32	9 (28.1%)
XSBench	(B)	Macroscopic cross section lookups	1	75.13s	96	47	5 (10.6%)
PathFinder	(C)	Searches for 'signatures' within graph	1	363.50s	257	62	22 (35.5%)
CoMD	(D)	Classical molecular dynamics algorithms	72	44.70s	129	49	13 (26.5%)
Pennant	(E)	Unstructured mesh with radiation-hydro physics	1	33.66s	530	69	12 (17.4%)
MiniGMG	(F)	Geometric multigrid solver	1	6.10s	16	16	4 (25.0%)

Fig. 5. Benchmark name, identifier, and description are shown first, followed by the number of threads executing the optimized hotspots and the baseline execution time. Column six describe how often the benchmark was compiled during tuning, column seven shows how often the result was successfully verified, and the last column specifies how many of these verified versions were not bit-wise identical to the last one created before.

Sec.	3.1	3.1	3.1	3.2	3.3	3.4.2	3.4.3	3.4.4	3.4.5	3.5.1	3.5.2	3.5.3	3.5.4	3.5.5	3.5.1	3.5.4	3.5.4	3.5.4	3.5.5	3.5.6	Total
Det.	nsw	nuw	gep			function behavior				pointer argument					ret. ptr	mem	mem	ptr	mem	load	
(A)	0	12	3	1		5/7	2	0	4	19	0	11	11	19	0	0	63/64	20/21	21	34/45	225/240
(B)	0	16/22	3	1		4	0	0	1/3	1/2	0	1/2	11	11	0	0	33/34	9/10	10	28	129/141
(C)	0	0	4	8/27		15/23	14	0	2	16	15	12	16	16	4	4	29/30	37/41	38	34/37	264/299
(D)	2	16	6	0/2		3/4	1	0	0	2	0	2	1/2	2	0	0	61/71	25/26	26	32	179/194
(E)	0	18/19	0	0		18/37	9/14	8	33/37	66/78	71	77/79	53/85	46	10	2	91/92	37	36/37	35/37	610/689
(F)	47	132	18	3		3	3	1	0	2	5	0	4	5	5	0	132	44	44	25	479/479

Fig. 6. Annotation opportunities identified and successfully exploited for the tested benchmarks (ref. Fig.5). The numbers denote how often optimistic choices were used for opportunities in the final program version (first value), as well as the total number of opportunities identified (second value). A single number is shown if both would be equal.

During the tuning, we see two significant speedups, each $\approx 10\%$ compared to the baseline, both while working on the earliest of the 14 annotation points. The first improvement happened after alias (Sect. 3.5.1), wrapping (Sect. 3.1), exception (Sect. 3.4.3), visibility (Sect. 3.4.5), dereferenceability (Sect. 3.5.5), and alignment (Sect. 3.5.4) annotations were added in a single step. The second one while annotating function side-effects (Sect. 3.4.2), the last annotation kind at each insertion point.

For this compute heavy code the first significant speedup is visible after 15 compilations (of 99) which together took 98 s (of 497 s) to explore.

5.2   XSBench (B)

XSBench simulates the macroscopic cross section lookups that are the primary performance concern for nuclear reactor core Monte Carlo particle transport simulations. It is a memory intensive, semi random memory access code. Our evaluation focused on a serial run of the XSBench proxy application as the code is memory latency bound and the limitation of our memory system hides any performance changes in parallel runs. After 96 compilations, 422 s, and 141 optimistically annotated opportunities, the final executable shows a 15.6% speedup over the baseline.

The first optimistically annotated version performed even $\approx 18.13\%$ better than the baseline. It contained 23 optimistic choices for alias and wrapping opportunities. The next three versions internalized functions and forfeited the speedup. It is not until 54 annotations later that we regain most of the performance gains. These 54 choices are spread over dereferenceability, alignment, and control flow (Sect. 3.3) annotations.

For this memory latency sensitive code, we find our best version in the middle of our optimistic annotation tuning after only 28 compilation (of 96) and 88 s. XSBench has many successful compilations that make no change in the resulting binary (marked as ○), especially in the second half of the tuning. This is interesting as evidence of the compilers inability to utilize the additional information.

5.3   PathFinder (C)

PathFinder is a memory latency sensitive graph traversal and search. We see a 17.3% speedup with 299 annotations after 257 compilations taking a total of 4259 s.

PathFinder is the code that has the most "new" versions (shown as ♦), i.e., successfully verified binaries that differ from the last. In total, 35% of all successful builds are (new) versions. Over all versions, a relatively steady performance increase is visible. There are two smaller drops that happen, and recover, while annotating a single opportunity kind, first memory invariance (Sect. 3.5.6), and then function side-effects. For PathFinder we make the least optimistic choices, totaling 11.7% of all opportunities, but additional information is consistently changing the executable.

After 96 compilations, taking 1194 out of the 4259 total seconds, the maximum speedup was almost reached. While the most significant improvement happens for an early insertion point, gains are made throughout the entire tuning.

5.4   CoMD (D)

CoMD is a molecular dynamics code which uses the Lennard-Jones potential. It is another compute heavy proxy application and shows a 4.6% speedup. Tuning introduces 194 annotations in 2614 s and spread over 129 compilations.

While the final result is faster than the baseline, we see slowdowns for intermediate versions. The first happens after annotating alias, wrapping, exception, dereferenceability, and alignment opportunities. The next version, still working on alignment, abruptly regains the loss. Later we experience a similar drop below the base line, again after annotating alignment and wrapping information. The majority of the optimistic opportunities are concerned with memory operations in this compute intensive code.

The final and best version is 4.62% faster than the baseline, but a speedup of 3.92% is already achieved after 21 compilations and 404 out of 2614 s.

5.5   Pennant (E)

Pennant is an unstructured mesh physics application using radiation–hydro code. Pennant's runtime has a long tail of small functions which limits (due to time) our ability to annotate more of the application. Our tuning is unable to make any performance gain despite adding 689 annotations over the course of 530 compilations.

While no speedup was achieved, we discovered an intermediate version with a significant slowdown. This version has only five additional optimistic annotations compared to the one before. The slowdown, as well as the subsequent recover, happens while we annotate function memory effects, an opportunity with 13 different optimistic choices. The five annotations which cause the slowdown, along with the five that recover it again, are annotated through 119 compilations. Thus, our search algorithm was forced to reduce the optimism of the individual choices until verification succeeded.

The Pennant code is unable to capitalize on the additional information despite 610 optimistic choices made for 689 opportunities. During most of the tuning (observe the logarithmic axis) additional annotations did not change the binary.

5.6   MiniGMG (F)

MiniGMG is a benchmark for geometric multigrid solvers. It is designed to stress both the compute and memory subsystem of the hardware. MiniGMG has shown no performance changes after annotating all 479 opportunities optimistically.

MiniGMG has the most regular results. Each of the four versions was followed by three successful compilations, which did not change the binary. None of the version showed any significant change in performance. The two opportunity kinds wrapping and alignment account for over half of all opportunities.

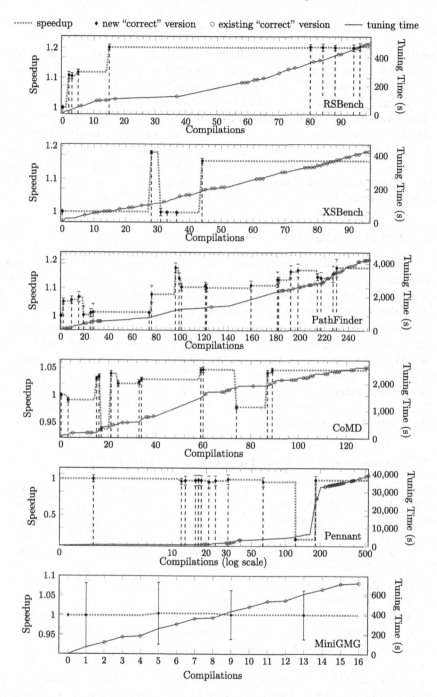

Fig. 7. Performance and optimization results for the six high-performance proxy applications described in Fig. 5. Each plot shows the speedup (left) relative to the original version, and the tuning time (right), both with regards to the number of compilations (=tries) performed. If annotations yielded a successfully verified executable we mark it as ♦, if it was different from the last one, or as ○, if it was not.

5.7 Successfully Verified Annotations

The dots ○ in Fig. 7 indicate successfully verified builds that contain more annotations but do not change the resulting binary. Depending on the benchmark, between 10.6% and 35.5% of valid builds resulted in a new binary which we had to verify. The other cases were versions bit-equal to the last which were not verified. XSBench (B) only produces five different versions despite 47 successful builds with new annotations. In contrast, PathFinder (C) creates 22 different binaries in 62 successful builds. XSBench and Pennant (E) both have substantial successful compilations after the final version is first compiled. PathFinder is the only benchmark that continues to make improvements late, however these are only regaining lost performance from earlier optimistic versions.

5.8 Optimistic Choices

Over all benchmarks, a large percent (>88%) of opportunities result in optimistic choices (see Total in Fig. 6). This holds to the understanding that there is a great deal of information that the compiler is not aware of. The hope is to help the developer understand what information will most likely generate a positive effect on the application. At the same time we need to remedy limitations in current compilers to make profitable use of additional knowledge. The annotation pass run first in the optimization pipeline discovers the majority of the optimistic opportunities (always >70%). This is not surprising as optimistic information is often maintained throughout the pipeline. As a consequence, we will, for example, explore function interface specific opportunities only at the first (of the 14) insertion points.

5.9 Comparison with Link Time Optimization (LTO)

We also collected data for both (monolithic) LTO and thin-LTO [15]. Figure 8 show the performance gap determined by our technique with LTO/thin-LTO as a baseline. While the difference is smaller than for non-LTO builds, it remains significant, i.a., our optimistically annotated XSBench shows a 14% speedup compared to a full monolithic LTO build.

Proxy	LTO	thin-LTO
(A)	2.86%	5.68%
(B)	14.03%	41.23%
(C)	3.67%	4.79%
(D)	4.75%	4.48%
(E)	-1.13%	-1.14%
(F)	0.73%	0.79%

Fig. 8. Performance compared to monolithic and thin-LTO.

Compile time over the original source increased through monolithic LTO by 5.5% to 18.5%. With (sequential) thin-LTO the increase was between 3.6% and 17.3% (expect for MiniGMG (F) which showed a compile decrease of 15.6%). For the optimistically annotated benchmarks compile time decreased by 0.3% to 2.5%.

6 Related Work

While we are not aware of exiting work that makes similar use of additional optimistic static information to identify performance gaps through the optimizations in an exiting compiler, there are various related research fields.

Autotuning. Given our moderate knowledge in the area of autotuning we restricted ourselves to the most important files and functions in the evaluated benchmarks. Consequently, it was sufficient to use ad-hoc search space reductions and a custom search space exploration to determine optimistic choices. To allow the approach to scale in the future we need to incorporate elaborate tuning mechanism as offered through tools like OpenTuner [4] or BOAT [6]. The latter seems explicitly interesting as we can integrate domain knowledge, e.g., we could leverage information such as the expected benefit based on the opportunity kind.

Link Time Optimization. Certain inter-procedural uncertainties are already resolvable through link time optimization (LTO). While existing LTO implementations in GCC [12] and LLVM [15] have shown great success, it is unrealistic to assume they will ever reach the same level of inter-procedural information that can be provided through optimistic annotations. There are two main reason. First, only where LTO compilation was used, link time inter-procedural information can be collected. Thus, system or third party library calls will often limit the analyses results as external functions call do it in non-LTO compilation. Second, LTO enabled compilation suffers still from input and context dependent uncertainties. Even if we assume we could inline all function calls or derive perfect caller-callee information statically, nine of the 20 optimistic opportunities we collected would still be needed. Finally, LTO approaches induce a constant compile time penalty as discussed in Sect. 5.9.

Super Optimization. Our technique shares ideas and goals with super optimization approaches [21,25] as well as other aggressive optimization techniques [18,24] developed outside of a classic compilation toolchain. While these techniques are often focused on correctness first, e.g., through semantic encodings or rewrite systems, and performance second, we relaxed the correctness criterion and put the user in charge of verification. We also do not introduce or explore new transformations but instead try to enable existing ones. An interesting future direction is the combination of the reasoning capabilities common to super optimizations with an optimistic approach to identify the most promising opportunities. Even if complete static verification might be out of reach, runtime check based verification has shown great success in the LLVM loop vectorizer and polyhedral optimizer Polly [3,9].

7   Conclusion and Future Work

Our findings show that there is extensive knowledge, which may be apparent to the developer, that the compiler is unable to discover statically. This information, once exposed to the compiler, can significantly improve performance. However, additional information will most often not result in better performance or even a different executable, either because it is unusable or unneeded for optimizations, suitable optimizations are simply missing, or later analyses would have determined it as well.

Beyond the integration of new opportunities, we plan to isolate interesting optimistic choices automatically. Those with the most significant performance impact, the ones without any impact at all, as well as those causing a regression, may all provide valuable information. Optimally, we want to predict what informational will be used, and what annotations are necessary to achieve a performance gain. In addition, we want to hone in on annotations producing a performance loss because these indicate compiler flaws.

Acknowledgments. We would like to thank the reviewers for their extensive and helpful comments.

This research was supported by the Exascale Computing Project (17-SC-20-SC), a collaborative effort of two U.S. Department of Energy organizations (Office of Science and the National Nuclear Security Administration) responsible for the planning and preparation of a capable exascale ecosystem, including software, applications, hardware, advanced system engineering, and early testbed platforms, in support of the nation's exascale computing imperative.

References

1. Ahmad, D.: The rising threat of vulnerabilities due to integer errors. IEEE Secur. Priv. **1**(4) (2003). https://doi.org/10.1109/MSECP.2003.1219077
2. Allen, J., Kennedy, K., Porterfield, C., Warren, J.: Conversion of control dependence to data dependence. In: ACM Symposium on Principles of Programming Languages, Austin, Texas, USA (1983). https://doi.org/10.1145/567067.567085
3. Alves, P., et al.: Runtime pointer disambiguation. In: ACM SIGPLAN International Conference on Object-Oriented Programming, Systems, Languages, and Applications, OOPSLA (2015). https://doi.org/10.1145/2814270.2814285
4. Ansel, J., et al.: OpenTuner: an extensible framework for program autotuning. In: International Conference on Parallel Architectures and Compilation, PACT. ACM (2014). https://doi.org/10.1145/2628071.2628092
5. Collard, J., Barthou, D., Feautrier, P.: Fuzzy array dataflow analysis. In: ACM SIGPLAN Symposium on Principles & Practice of Parallel Programming (PPOPP) (1995). https://doi.org/10.1145/209936.209947
6. Dalibard, V., Schaarschmidt, M., Yoneki, E.: BOAT: building auto-tuners with structured bayesian optimization. In: International Conference on World Wide Web, WWW. ACM (2017). https://doi.org/10.1145/3038912.3052662

7. Diwan, A., McKinley, K.S., Moss, J.E.B.: Type-based alias analysis. In: Conference on Programming Language Design and Implementation (PLDI) (1998). https://doi.org/10.1145/277650.277670

8. Doerfert, J., Finkel, H.: Compiler optimizations for OpenMP. In: International Workshop on OpenMP (IWOMP) (2018). https://doi.org/10.1007/978-3-319-98521-3_8

9. Doerfert, J., Grosser, T., Hack, S.: Optimistic loop optimization. In: International Symposium on Code Generation and Optimization, CGO (2017). http://dl.acm.org/citation.cfm?id=3049864

10. Emami, M., Ghiya, R., Hendren, L.J.: Context-sensitive interprocedural points-to analysis in the presence of function pointers. In: Conference on Programming Language Design and Implementation (PLDI) (1994). http://doi.acm.org/10.1145/178243.178264

11. Feautrier, P.: Dataflow analysis of array and scalar references. Int. J. Parallel Prog. (1991). https://doi.org/10.1007/BF01407931

12. Glek, T., Hubicka, J.: Optimizing real world applications with GCC link time optimization. CoRR (2010). http://arxiv.org/abs/1010.2196

13. Grosser, T., Größlinger, A., Lengauer, C.: Polly - performing polyhedral optimizations on a low-level intermediate representation. Parallel Process. Lett. (2012). https://doi.org/10.1142/S0129626412500107

14. Jeong, S., Jeon, M., Cha, S.D., Oh, H.: Data-driven context-sensitivity for points-to analysis. PACMPL (2017). https://doi.org/10.1145/3133924

15. Johnson, T., Amini, M., Li, D.X.: ThinLTO: scalable and incremental LTO. In: International Symposium on Code Generation and Optimization, CGO (2017). http://dl.acm.org/citation.cfm?id=3049845

16. Lattner, C., Adve, V.S.: LLVM: a compilation framework for lifelong program analysis & transformation. In: International Symposium on Code Generation and Optimization CGO (2004). https://doi.org/10.1109/CGO.2004.1281665

17. Lattner, C., Lenharth, A., Adve, V.S.: Making context-sensitive points-to analysis with heap cloning practical for the real world. In: Conference on Programming Language Design and Implementation (PLDI) (2007). https://doi.org/10.1145/1250734.1250766

18. Lopes, N.P., Menendez, D., Nagarakatte, S., Regehr, J.: Provably correct peephole optimizations with alive. In: Conference on Programming Language Design and Implementation (PLDI) (2015). https://doi.org/10.1145/2737924.2737965

19. Pugh, W.: The Omega test: a fast and practical integer programming algorithm for dependence analysis. In: Conference on Supercomputing (SC) (1991). https://doi.org/10.1145/125826.125848

20. Ramalingam, G.: The undecidability of aliasing. Trans. Program. Lang. Syst. (1994). https://doi.org/10.1145/186025.186041

21. Sasnauskas, R., Chen, Y., Collingbourne, P., Ketema, J., Taneja, J., Regehr, J.: Souper: a synthesizing superoptimizer. CoRR (2017). http://arxiv.org/abs/1711.0442

22. Shapiro, M., Horwitz, S.: Fast and accurate flow-insensitive points-to analysis. In: ACM SIGPLAN-SIGACT Symposium on Principles of Programming Languages (POPL) (1997). https://doi.org/10.1145/263699.263703

23. Steensgaard, B.: Points-to analysis in almost linear time. In: ACM SIGPLAN-SIGACT Symposium on Principles of Programming Languages (POPL) (1996). https://doi.org/10.1145/237721.237727

24. Tate, R., Stepp, M., Lerner, S.: Generating compiler optimizations from proofs. In: Proceedings of the 37th ACM SIGPLAN-SIGACT Symposium on Principles of Programming Languages, POPL 2010, Madrid, Spain, 17–23 January 2010, pp. 389–402. ACM (2010), https://doi.org/10.1145/1706299.1706345

25. Tate, R., Stepp, M., Tatlock, Z., Lerner, S.: Equality saturation: a new approach to optimization. In: ACM SIGPLAN-SIGACT Symposium on Principles of Programming Languages (POPL) (2009). https://doi.org/10.1145/1480881.1480915

Programming Models and Systems Software

End-to-End Resilience for HPC Applications

Arash Rezaei[1], Harsh Khetawat[1], Onkar Patil[1], Frank Mueller[1(✉)]🔾,
Paul Hargrove[2], and Eric Roman[2]

[1] Department of Computer Science, North Carolina State University,
Raleigh, NC 27695-8206, USA
mueller@cs.ncsu.edu
[2] Lawrence Berkeley National Laboratory, Berkeley, CA 94730, USA
{phhargrove,ERoman}@lbl.gov

Abstract. A plethora of resilience techniques have been investigated to protect application kernels. If, however, such techniques are combined and they interact across kernels, new vulnerability windows are created. This work contributes the idea of end-to-end resilience by protecting windows of vulnerability **between** kernels guarded by different resilience techniques. It introduces the live vulnerability factor (LVF), a new metric that quantifies any lack of end-to-end protection for a given data structure. The work further promotes end-to-end application protection across kernels via a pragma-based specification for diverse resilience schemes with minimal programming effort. This lifts the data protection burden from application programmers allowing them to focus solely on algorithms and performance while resilience is specified and subsequently embedded into the code through the compiler/library and supported by the runtime system. In experiments with case studies and benchmarks, end-to-end resilience has an overhead over kernel-specific resilience of less than 3% on average and increases protection against bit flips by a factor of three to four.

Keywords: Resilience · Silent data corruption · Pragma programming

1 Introduction

In large-scale parallel systems, faults are not an exception but rather the norm [18,29]. Faults such as bit flips or hardware faults may result in application or operating system failures. Hardware and software techniques have been

This work was supported in part by a subcontract from Lawrence Berkeley National Laboratory and NSF grants 1525609, 1058779, and 0958311. This manuscript has three authors of Lawrence Berkeley National Laboratory under Contract No. DE-AC02-05CH11231 with the U.S. Department of Energy. The U.S. Government retains, and the publisher, by accepting the article for publication, acknowledges, that the U.S. Government retains a non-exclusive, paid-up, irrevocable, world-wide license to publish or reproduce the published form of this manuscript, or allow others to do so, for U.S. Government purposes.

© Springer Nature Switzerland AG 2019
M. Weiland et al. (Eds.): ISC High Performance 2019, LNCS 11501, pp. 271–290, 2019.
https://doi.org/10.1007/978-3-030-20656-7_14

devised to make such systems more resilient to failures. But future exascale systems are projected to see an increase in the frequency of faults, which would require 20% more circuitry and energy to counter them [33]. However, hardware vendors tend to design and build general-purpose, and not exascale-specific hardware due to manufacturing costs. As a result, the future systems will be likely built with off-the-shelf components while delegating a significant part of the resilience responsibility to the software layer.

The significance of resilience in future HPC systems has been emphasized in prior research, e.g., [33]. In particular, multiple challenges arise in HPC systems from the size (millions of cores) and the programming model (tightly coupled). Intuitively, larger numbers of components result in a higher probability of failures. What's more, a tightly coupled programming model may result in fast fault propagation after just one node has been hit [17]. Hence, resilience is considered a major roadblock on the path to next-generation HPC systems.

In practice, hardware protection is complemented by software resilience. A variety of software techniques exist, such as checkpoint/restart (CR), redundancy, and algorithm-based fault tolerance (ABFT), each with their own benefits and limitations in terms of applicability and cost. CR has high storage overheads and requires backward recovery via re-execution, which limits scalability [16]. Redundancy requires either only extra memory or both extra memory and processing resources, which is costly [17]. ABFT results in low overheads and supports forward execution, but each numerical algorithm has to be customized [12,15,19]. A choice of a low-cost resilience scheme is best made per numerical kernel rather than for an entire application. The composition of different resilience techniques, however, results in a generally overlooked problem: It creates windows of vulnerability. Consider kernel K1 with redundant execution followed by kernel K2 with ABFT protection. K1's result is consumed by K2, yet the result's integrity is no longer checked after K1 has finished. This leaves variables storing K1's result vulnerable until K2 has consumed all of them. In contrast, by protecting both K1 and K2 with redundancy, intermediate and final results can be compared (dual redundancy) or even corrected (triple redundancy with voting).

We introduce *end-to-end resilience* to allow the selection of different low-cost resilience techniques across different application phases. End-to-end resilience composes protection spaces of kernels with disjoint resilience techniques such that windows of vulnerability are avoided. Another problem is that programmers are often forced to clutter numerical methods with tangential resilience concerns making codes hard to maintain. Resilience APIs try to reduce this clutter but cannot eliminate it, e.g., Containment Domains [9], GVR [39], Charm++ [21], etc. Also, transparent resilience techniques, such as BLCR [13], tend to impose much higher overhead than application-specific resilience via CR [26] or ABFT [15]. But the interleaving of algorithmic and resilience concerns makes it hard to maintain such programs. End-to-end resilience is realized elegantly via pragmas at the program level, which provides the benefits of the aspect-oriented programming (AOP) paradigm [22] as it increases modularity by allowing the separation of algorithmic and resilience concerns at no extra cost while still meshing with a variety of execution paradigms and resilience methods.

This work makes the following contributions:

- We identify the vulnerabilities between protected kernels and offer a systematic solution via end-to-end resilience.
- We propose a metric to quantify vulnerability *across* protected kernels.
- We design and implement a resilience pragma to support separation of the resilience aspects from the algorithms to increase portability and modularity imposing minimal programming effort.
- We show that, in contrast to prior work, auto-generated protection provides full end-to-end protection at less than 3% additional time overhead on average.

2   Background

Hardware faults can be persistent or transient. Persistent faults are typically due to aging or operation beyond temperature thresholds. If a persistent faults results in a failure, re-execution will not help, i.e., an HPC job of thousands of processes is rendered useless. Transient hardware errors, also called soft errors, are often due to cosmic radiation. They allow the application to continue execution, albeit with tainted data. Such faults manifest as bit flips in the data in memory or anywhere in the data path (e.g., caches, data bus). Although CPU registers, caches, and main memory are often equipped with ECC, only single bit flips are correctable while double-flips generally are not (by SEC-DED ECC while chipkill can correct some multi-bit errors depending on their device locality).[1] Jaguar's 360TB of DRAM experienced a double bit flip every 24 h [18]. Some soft faults may remain undetectable and may result in so-called Silent Data Corruption (SDC). SDCs may manifest at application completion by producing wrong results or, prior to that, wrong interim results. It is known that SDC rates are orders of magnitude larger than manufacture specifications [27,30,35].

Resilience methods usually compensate for the computation/state loss by performing a backward or forward recovery. Backward recovery recreates an older state of an application through classic rollback recovery methods, such as system-level or application-level checkpoint/restart (CR) [26]. Forward recovery typically handles errors by repairing the affected data structures. A correction procedure is invoked that may recover the intended values from a peer replica (redundant computing) [17], or via Algorithm-Based Fault Tolerance (ABFT) from checksums or solver properties [8,12,15,19,31].

Many HPC applications are comprised of multiple kernels that form a multi-phase pipeline. The above-mentioned methods are resilient to one or multiple types of faults with different overhead. Intuitively, there is no single solution that fits all scenarios while providing the best performance. Thus, a combination of methods enables the selection of the best resilience mechanism per application phase considering factors such as computation time and size of data that needs protection. End-to-end data integrity is a goal explicitly cited in exascale reports [33]. Our end-to-end resilience fills this very gap.

---

[1] Bit flips in code (instruction bits) create unpredictable outcomes (most of the time segmentation faults or crashes but sometimes also incorrect but legal jumps) and are out of the scope of this work.

3 Assumptions

Our fault model considers soft errors/SDCs that materialize in memory in a fault agnostic manner, i.e., SDCs may occur in unprotected DRAM (no ECC) due to cosmic rays or may result from bit flips in the processor core during calculations, unprotected register files, or caches. Hence, results of (faulty) calculation are subsequently written to memory, which creates an SDC even if memory is protected with ECC/chipkill. This is consistent with findings of past work [30,35] indicating that undetected errors in SECDED ECC-protected DRAM present a problem today, and that some SRAM structures remain unprotected.

On the software side, we assume that the correctness of a *data structure* can be verified (through a *Checker* method) and the stored values can be recovered through a *Recover* method should an inconsistency be detected. Many algorithms commonly used in HPC, such as numeric solvers, have approximation methods based on convergence tests. These convergence tests could be used as the *Checker*. If an algorithm lacks a simple checking method or invariant, the *Checker* can be provided through comparison with a checksum over the data that was computed beforehand and stored in a safe region.[2] The *Recover* method is given by the forward recovery phase in ABFT methods, or simply by restoring a light-weight deduplicated [2] or compressed [20] checkpoint of the data.

We further assume that the computation is (or can be made) idem-potent *with respect to the encapsulated region*, i.e., if globals are changed inside the region, they have to be restored by the recovery method. In other words, if a method/region is called twice in a row, the result would be the same as the inputs (or global variables) remain unmodified by the computation (no side effects).[3] CR and redundant computing already ensure idem-potency since identical state is restored in the former while redundant state exists for the latter. ABFT methods have to be analyzed to ensure that dynamic live ranges are encapsulated by end-to-end resilience, while any other global side effects need to capture/restore globals at region boundaries. Existing solutions to I/O idem-potency are required as well [4]. We can then retry a computation if needed, i.e., when no other recovery methods exist (or if the other recovery methods have failed). Notice that we do allow the side effects of communication inside regions (see Sect. 4). Application kernels, e.g., the ones studied, were found to be already compliant with these constraints, and frameworks have similar constraints, e.g., DAG-based HPC tasks and map-reduce [1,7].

---

[2] Extra checks are added to guarantee the correctness of data stored in a safe region. A safe region is assumed to neither be subject to bit flips nor data corruption from the application viewpoint—yet, the techniques to make the region safe remain transparent to the programmer. In other words, a safe region is simply one subject to data protection/verification via checking.

[3] Inputs are read from disk and stored in globals or on the heap, but may be recovered by re-reading from disk. Globals are calculated in the program and can only be recovered by re-calculation or ABFT schemes.

4   End-to-End Resilience

Live Vulnerability Factor: We introduce a new metric, the term Live Vulnerability Factor (LVF): $LVF = L_v \times S_v,$
where L_v is the length of the *dynamic* live range of an arbitrary (incl. non-scalar array) data structure/variable v (vulnerability window), and S_v is the space required to hold the related data in memory. Length is measured as wall-clock time from first set to last use (dynamic live range) of a variable during execution.

Protection Across Scopes: Applications are typically composed of phases during which different algorithmic computations are being performed. Intermediate results are created and passed from phase to phase before the final result is generated. Our core idea is to exploit the *dynamic live range* of predominantly non-scalar variables within and across phases, and to immediately perform a correctness check after the last use of any given variable. *Scalar* live range analysis is a well-understood technique employed by compilers during code optimizations, such as register allocation (among others), while *dynamic* live ranges are rarely analyzed but can, in part, be inferred from escape analysis. Figure 1 outlines the idea for our running example, a sequence of two matrix multiplications, enhanced by an extra checksum row and column per matrix for resilience (see Huang et al. [19]). Huang's method provides protection for result matrices C and E *within* a single matmult kernel (arrows on left side) while end-to-end resilience protects all matrices during their *entire live time across kernels* (arrows on right side). If an error strikes during the lifetime of phase-dependent variables, single-kernel protection methods cannot provide any assistance as they are locally constrained to region boundaries. This is precisely where our end-to-end protection comes to the rescue. In fact, Fig. 1 concisely illustrates that *single-kernel protection misses out on more than half of the lifetime of variables compared to end-to-end protection* even if 99% of execution time is spent inside the two matmult kernels.

When a live range ends, data is checked for correctness. If correct, no action is taken, otherwise correct values are recovered (if detected as erroneous), or re-computation is performed (if erroneous but direct recovery has failed). The intuition here is to avoid the high overhead of frequent checks (e.g., after every variable redefinition or use inside the live range) while providing a guaranteed end-to-end correctness of the computation.

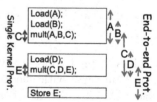

Fig. 1. Matrix multiplication, range of live variables

The Protect Pragma: We propose a pragma-based resilience scheme and show how the corresponding code is expanded to provide the extra end-to-end protection. This allows us to cover the vulnerability window of different variables by automatically expanding codes through the compiler. The expanded code performs check and recovery actions on the vulnerable data. We incorporate end-to-end resilience into OpenMP-like pragmas to facilitate adoption and code maintenance with a potential of future synergy between thread parallelism and resilience (beyond the scope of this paper). The pragma has a simple, yet powerful and extendable interface with the following syntax:

#**pragma** *protect* $[M][Check(f_1, .., f_n)][Recover(g_1, .., g_m)][Comm][Continue]$

The resilience method, M, which can be CR or **Redundancy (2/3)** (dual/triple), is an optional argument. The integration of both resilience approaches is discussed in a latter example. Check and Recover receive a list of functions parameterized by each variable that needs protection. We use f to denote a checker, and g for a recovery methods. By default, f and g are a checksum calculation and checksum-based correction, respectively. A user may overwrite f/g to supply more efficient checking/recovery. A region that contains MPI communication is annotated with the Comm keyword. The Continue keyword indicates that data is live beyond the current region, i.e., crossing phases/kernels, and requires end-to-end protection. Figure 2 depicts the source code of our running example with the protect pragmas with the "Continue" keyword to protect live matrices across kernels.

```
1   Matrix A, B, C, D, E;
2   Load(A);
3   Load(B);
4   #pragma protect Check(Checker(A),Checker(B)) \
5                   Recover(Correct(A),Load(A),  \
6                           Correct(B),Load(B))  \
7               Continue
8     mmult(A,B,C); // parallelized
9   Load(D);
10  #pragma protect Check(Checker(C),Checker(D)) \
11                  Recover(Correct(C),Correct(D),Load(D))  \
12              Continue
13    mmult(C,D,E); // parallelized
14  #pragma protect Check(Checker(E))
15                  Recover(Correct(E))
16    Store (E);
```

Fig. 2. Matrix multiplication with protect pragma

In the final code, every region is contained within a while loop (protection boundary) with checking and recovery code after the computation. After mmult(A,B,D), a Check is invoked followed by Recover if the check fails inside the loop. (Both are called via function pointers.)

Code resulting from chaining of regions with the Continue keyword are highlighted and described as follows. A boolean array of size 3 named completed and a flag first are maintained for the 3 chained regions in this code, which indicates the correct completion of regions 0, 1, and 2. At the end of region 0/1/2, the corresponding flag is set. Matrix D is only loaded once due to the conditional on the flag. Additional loads may be triggered inside the Recover() calls for matrices A, B, and D if they cannot be repaired using checksums.

Recovery from regions that involve MPI communication with other processes requires coordination among these processes. The `Comm` option of the pragma indicates that such communication exists inside that pragma region. It results in generating code for a global reduction of check() return codes indicating if any checks have failed, in which case recovery with recomputation is required where all peer MPI tasks participate in recomputation.

Notice that pragmas cannot easily be replaced by macros. First, variable number of check and recover routines may be specified, one per data structure, which cannot be expressed by a macro. Second, a begin and end macro would be required per pragma, but all three begins would have to be placed on line 4 of Fig. 2 while the ends would follow after lines 8, 13, and 16, respectively. This would make the source code significantly less legible. The compiler also has the ability to perform semantic checks to ensure that the live range of protected variables under the `Continue` keyword extends to the end of the scope spanning multiple pragmas and to capture/restore globals via live range analysis.

Source code changes in terms of added pragmas are only needed at the top level of computations (e.g., timestep loop for most HPC codes), and most notably not in libraries. `Continue` creates an orphaned semantics (in OpenMP terminology) that continues the lexical extent from scope-to-scope (transitively) in the current compilation unit, where each pragma in such a chain expands the live range for the current set of protected variables. For the enclosing scope, the resulting chain results in one checkpoint per pragma in the absence of faults. In the presence of a fault, selective recovery from the last valid data is only performed at the inner-most scope that stored this data.

Task-Based Resilience: An alternative to the pragma approach is to design a task-based programming scheme that implicitly provides end-to-end resilience. Tasking libraries are becoming more popular in the HPC community due to their more graceful load balancing and potentially asynchronous execution models, e.g., PaRSEC [5], OmpSs [14], the UPC Task library [25], and Cilk [3].

Resilience has been added to PaRSEC [6] and OmpSs [24]. Other work focuses on soft faults [6], i.e., they take advantage of the algorithmic properties of ABFT methods to detect and recover from failures at a fine grain (task level) and utilize periodic checkpointing at a coarse grain (application). Yet others uses CR and message logging at the task granularity to tolerate faults with re-execution [24].

Instead of focusing on a specific resilience approach, we target a more complex problem. We propose a tasking system that allows for different resilience methods to interact in an easily understandable and extendable manner. A resilient task class is provided with two methods that are called before and after the actual execution of a task, namely `resilience_pre`, `resilience_post`. In `resilience_pre`, depending on the resilience type of the task, CR or Redundancy, the `checkpoint` method or `wakeup_shadow` is called, respectively. In `resilience_post`, first the shadow process is put to sleep under redundant execution. Then data structures with their last use in the task are checked and corrected if needed. If correction fails, a set of tasks is put into the scheduling queue to recompute the tainted data structures.

5   Implementation Details

The resilience pragma API is implemented as a transform pass in the Cetus compiler [10] via source-to-source transformation (i.e., no need for more complex frameworks like LLVM as the IR is never used). Source-to-source compilation using Cetus allows us to transform an input C program to a modified C program as output. Cetus uses Antlr [28] in order to parse C programs into an Intermediate Representation (IR). The compiler passes are then run on the IR in order to generate the output source code. Each pass iterates over the IR and is capable of modifying it by adding, removing, or editing the input source. New code is added as Cetus IR objects, equivalent to building an IR tree from its leaves. Similarly, a complex IR can be generated by extending these trees. Cetus allows iterating over the IR in a depth-first manner, which is utilized here.

ProtectPragmaParser Class: We added the ProtectPragmaParser class, a transform pass that implements our pragma. Each pragma directive in the input program is represented as an object of the ProtectPragmaParser class. The ProtectPragmaParser class is run in order to transform the generated parse tree to an equivalent parse tree structure, which contains our protection boundaries, checker functionality, and recovery mechanisms. We traverse the input parse tree in a depth-first manner looking for the protect pragma directives. On finding the pragma, we parse the directive to populate the checker and recovery functions associated with this particular pragma. We also generate the necessary protection boundary, checking, and recovery code required in the current context and track the variables defined at these protection boundaries. As part of the ProtectPragmaParser object creation, we check if the current directive is chained to a previously encountered directive via the Continue keyword. If chained, we can recompute these resilient variables in case their recovery methods fail, and the ProtectPragmaParser object of the current context is added to the list of chained pragmas of the directive it is chained to. Otherwise, it is added as an independent (root) pragma. When chaining is found in the input IR, we extend the protection boundaries of the current pragma around that of the following pragma. When the input source code has been completely parsed, a logical structure of these chained (or unchained) directives is created (see pragmas in Fig. 2).

Once the entire input source code has been traversed and the logical structure of pragmas is created, a recursive function that emits transformed code is invoked on the root objects. This, in turn, invokes the function on each of its chained pragmas. It is at this stage that checking and recovery code for non-last-use variables is removed so as to reduce the checking overhead. This function uses the chaining information to correctly emit the nested while loop structure as part of the output source code. As part of the code emitting process, if a particular directive had the CR or Redundancy clause, then the compiler emits the appropriate function calls to wake_shadow and sleep_shadow in case of the Redundancy clause, and create_ckpt in case of the CR clause.

The Cetus compiler infrastructure along with our ProtectPragmaParser functionality allows us to transform our input source code in this manner to support end-to-end resilience. While these transformations could be performed manually by the programmer for simple examples, it quickly becomes tedious and error-prone for more complicated program structures or even chained regions. Our Cetus implementation transforms the input source in a single pass through the IR tree, emitting code recursively even for complicated, inter-leaving dependencies between resilient variables. This allows for the development of powerful software that has end-to-end resilience while off-loading the repetitive and sometimes non-trivial task of code expansion to the compiler.

6 Experimental Results

All experiments were conducted on a cluster of 108 nodes, each with two AMD Opteron 6128 processors (16 cores total) and 32GB RAM running CentOS 7.3 and Linux 4.10 (except for TF-IDF, which uses CentOS 5.5, Linux kernel 2.6.32 and Open MPI 1.6.1 due to BLCR [13] and RedMPI [17] requirements). ABFT resilience is realized via protecting critical data with checksums so that we can attempt to recover (repair) results, or, if recovery fails, resort to CR and reload data from disk. Redundancy is realized via Red-MPI of which we obtained a copy [17]. These techniques, referred to as *conventional* resilience in the following, are compared to their equivalent version with end-to-end resilience guarantees.

We present examples of pragma- and task-based end-to-end resilience for two variants of matrix multiplication and a page ranking program, with experimental results for these codes as well as the NAS Parallel benchmark codes. To this end, we already discussed end-to-end resilience for two successive matmult kernels in Fig. 2. The same kernels can also be refactored using fine-grained tasking as discussed next.

The task-based resilience class/capabilities (Sect. 4) plus a task-based runtime system are utilized to implement a blocked matrix multiplication utilizing POSIX threads. We add checksums per block of a matrix. The checksum elements are colored in the 2 examples of Fig. 3.

For a matrix of size 4×4, if the block size k is 2, then 20 extra elements are needed to hold the checksums. For a 6×6 matrix, 45 extra elements are needed. In practice, the size of a block (configured to fit into L1 cache with other data) is much larger than the extra space overhead for checksums.

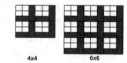

Fig. 3. Blocks (white) with checksums (blue) (Color figure online)

6.1 Matrix Multiplication

We use 5 input sizes for square matrices from 512×512 to 2560×2560. The size of last level cache (L3) is 12 MB, and only the first experiment ($N = 512$) completely fits in the L3 data cache. Thus, data is repeatedly loaded from main memory (DRAM) in all other experiments. We use 16 OpenMP threads that perform matrix multiplications in a blocked manner with a tile/block size of 32×32. Each thread needs 3 blocks to perform the multiplication. Thus, the block size is selected as number of elements that can be accommodated in $\frac{1}{4}$th of the L1 data cache size of 64 KB.

Figure 4 contrasts the performance evaluation of sequentially composed matrix multiplication with conventional resilience (left bar) with our end-to-end resilience (right bar). For the pragma-based solution (left half), fault-free execution ranges from 0.88 ($n = 512$) to 35 s ($n = 2560$) when no correction needs to be triggered. In this case, end-to-end resilience has a 0.99% overhead at $n = 512$; for larger matrix sizes, this overhead is also negligible (around 0.69%). Task-based execution (right half) results in slightly higher execution times and overheads that are between 1.4% (for large matrices) and -0.64% (for small ones) and varies between 4.6% and -6.5% due cache artifacts with unaligned (1536) and aligned (2048) cache lines resulting in more/fewer cache conflicts, respectively. The alignment can be attributed to the implementation of per-block checksums in task-based matrix multiplication. Overall, more computation is performed during the multiplications and check operations.

Observation 1: End-to-end resilience across kernels results in the same cost as conventional resilience only protecting single kernels.

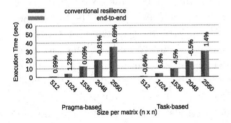

Fig. 4. Time of conventional/end-to-end resilience

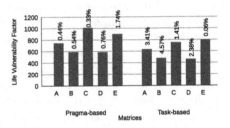

Fig. 5. Live Vulnerability Factor (bars) and % increase (above bars)

Performance Under Faults and Resulting Failures: We next investigate the correlation between LVF and the likelihood of failures in matrices. The LVF is computed from the vulnerability window of data structures (see Sect. 4). Figure 5 depicts the LVF as bars of each matrix under failure-free execution of the application. The vulnerability size is 50.03 MB and the vulnerability window depends on the live range of each matrix. C has the highest LVF, next comes E and then A. B and D have the same LVF, the smallest among the 5 matrices. This reflects the live ranges of the respective (same size) data structures during program execution (see Fig. 1). Notice that conventional resilience would only protect matrices C and E within, but not across kernels, i.e., they would only protect about 50% of our LVF for C/E and none for A/B/D (see Fig. 1). Furthermore, end-to-end resilience adds overhead that increases the LVF by only 0–5%, as depicted by the labels above bars in Fig. 5, but, unlike previous work, checks/corrects SDCs even *across* kernels that are otherwise only locally protected. Since these matrices comprise 99% of the program's data, the LVF per program is the average of weighted per-data LVFs, where weights are 1 (same size and range), except for matrix C with weight 2 (same size, twice the range).

Observation 2: End-to-end resilience protects data over significantly larger execution ranges at less than 1% increased LVF for pragma-based and 2.2% for task-based execution.

We also developed a program variant that injects faults (single bit flips) in uniformly randomized locations over the matrices (all 5 matrices, each sized at 2560×2560) and also at uniformly randomized times in a time window according to a given rate (configurable). This allows us study the effect of fault injections in real life and compare the results to the LVF metric. We randomly inject faults during runtime with fault rates from 25 to 45 s for pragma-based execution. Such high fault rates may be unlikely, but the point is to assess overhead and to illustrate the robustness of our technique: A second fault may be injected before the first one has been mitigated, yet end-to-end resilience is capable of making forward progress. (Solar flares are actually reported to result in multiple SDCs in rapid succession.) The y axis of Fig. 6 shows the number of faults. Using conventional resilience, only the faults in the lower-most shaded region of matrices C and E can be corrected by conventional resilience methods that are limited to a given scope/kernel, such as [11]. For end-to-end resilience, faults resulting in detectable errors in the lower portion of all matrices (errors across and in kernels, i.e., including the shaded regions of C/E) are *all subsequently corrected by end-to-end resilience*, even though they cross scope/kernel boundaries. This is the most significant result of our work as it demonstrates how much more fault coverage end-to-end resilience has compared to conventional resilience schemes. This covers cases where injections hit data while it is *live*. In fact, it shows that the majority of faults occurs *outside* of ABFT kernel protection, which is exactly what end-to-end resilience protects.

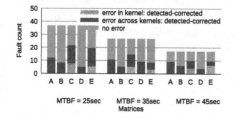

Fig. 6. Fault injection over 100 runs (pragma-based)

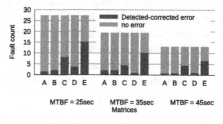

Fig. 7. Fault injection over 100 runs (task-based)

Other injections do not result in a failure as they hit stale data (uppermost portion per bar). In other words, end-to-end resilience never resulted in erroneous results while conventional ABFT misses errors across kernels, which are dominant. Furthermore, the distribution of corrected injection counts over matrices resembles the distribution of the LVF across matrices in Fig. 5. This is significant as injection experiments and LVF analysis thus validate each other. Slight differences can be attributed to the fact the LVF is based on failure-free execution while Fig. 6 is based on repeated executions for some corrections for certain detected errors (e.g., in the input matrices).

Observation 3: End-to-end resilience corrected all SDCs, i.e., 3 to 4 times as many as single-kernel conventional techniques.

Figure 7 depicts the corresponding results for task-based end-to-end resilience. We observe a similar distribution across matrices to Fig. 6, yet the number of faults lower since the task-based approach requires less time to execute. Consequently, fewer faults are injected at the same MTTF rate. Task-based injection counts that were corrected also loosely resemble the LVF in Fig. 5 for the same reasons as before, only that E is now indicated to be more prone to faults than C due to observed error corrections.

Observation 4: The LVF (without error injection) indicates the relative vulnerability of data structures.

Figure 8 depicts the average completion times after fault injection. All faults that resulted in an error were detected and corrected by end-to-end resilience. The pragma-based approach (left half) resulted in 8%–15% overhead for a fault rate from 45 to 25 s. Notice that such a high fault rate results

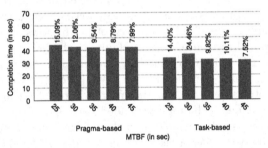

Fig. 8. Completion time with faults

in one or more faults per execution, some of which result in detectable errors that are subsequently corrected at the expense of executing recovery code. Again, such high SDC rates are not realistic, but they allow us to compare the *relative* overhead between pragma- and task-based. For the task-based case, overhead ranged from 8%–14%, nearly the same as pragma-based. The absolute time (y-axis) indicates that task-based is more efficient since tiling results in higher data reuse in caches on one hand and due to less overhead for corrections limited to a single tile on the other hand.

Observation 5: Overall, pragma- and task-based resilience result in comparable overheads for matmult.

6.2   TF-IDF

We further assessed the resilience capabilities for an MPI-based benchmark. We ported a term frequency/inverse document frequency (TF-IDF) benchmark for document clustering based on prior work [38]. TF-IDF is a classification technique designed to distinguish important terms in a large collection of text documents, which is the basis for page ranking with applications in data mining and search engines. The classification is broken into two steps. (1) TF calculates the frequency of a term on a per document basis. (2) DF counts the number of occurrences of a given term (document frequency). The final result is $tfidf = TF \times log\frac{N}{DF}$. Note that TF is a local computation while DF is global across all documents. As a result, the DFs need to be aggregated.

Figure 9 depicts the steps in the TF-IDF benchmark. At first, the names of files are loaded. Then the term frequency (TF) method is called with `filenames` as input and `tfs` as output. Next, the document frequency (DF) is called with `tfs` as input and `dfs` as output. Finally, the $tfidf$ value is computed for every term with a `TFIDF` call with `tfs` and `dfs` as input parameters. Figure 9 also depicts single kernel protection areas (arrows on left) and the vulnerability windows (live ranges) of variables protected by end-to-end resilience (arrows on right). The DF method contains MPI communication for the aggregation of document frequencies across all MPI ranks.

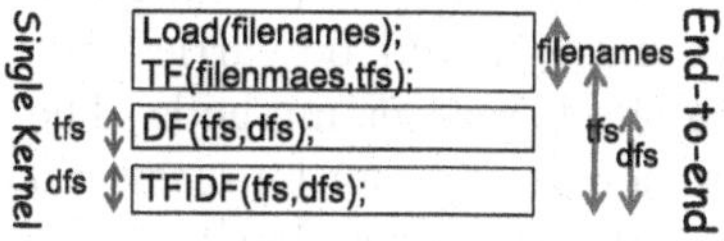

Table 1. Compiler-derived resilience info

Fig. 9. Vulnerability windows in TF-IDF

Region	Variable Name	Check method	Recover method
0	fn	Checker(fn)	Load(fn)
1	tfs	–	–
2	tfs	Checker(tfs)	Recover(tfs), Region(0)
	dfs	Checker(dfs)	Region(1)

Check and Recover Methods: TF-IDF does not have any check provided by the algorithm. Thus, we compute a checksum over the data. To demonstrate the capabilities of end-to-end resilience, we use a combination of redundancy and CR in this case study. CR provides a restore function, which we use as a recovery method.

Pragma Expansion: End-to-end resilience for TF-IDF can be provided by augmenting the code with three pragmas over as many regions (see Fig. 10). The first region is executed under redundancy with the default of dual redundancy to check if the filename is correct and, as recovery, reload the filename if this check fails. (Triple redundancy is optional and may allow the filename to be recovered, but this overhead is not justified just for protecting a filename.) The second region is protected with CR. The data of `tfs` is live across all three regions, while `dfs` is live across the last two pragma regions (`Continue` keyword).

```
1    vector<string> filenames;// input
2    vector<Dictionary> tfs;
     // output of Region 1
3    map <string,int> dfs;
     // output of Region 2

4
5    Load(filenames);
6    #pragma protect Redundancy Check(Checker(filenames))\
7                              Recover(Load(filenames)) \
8                              Continue
9      TF(filenames, tfs);
10   #pragma protect CR Check(Checker(tfs)) Comm Continue
11     DF(tfs, dfs); //contains MPI calls
12   #pragma protect Check(Checker(tfs), Checker(dfs))
13     TFIDF(tfs,dfs);
```

Fig. 10. TF-IDF with protect pragma

Inside the DF method, MPI communication is used and, consequently, the Comm keyword is added to the second pragma. Table 1 depicts the regions, the input variable(s) to each region and the check and recover method per variable. Note that tfs is still live in region 2. Thus, no check should be carried out on tfs in region 1. Thus, region 1 does not have check/recover methods. The chaining of regions is also shown in Table 1. In region 2, tfs can be recovered by recomputing region 0. Similarly, dfs can be calculated from region 1.

We perform the code transformation in two steps. At first, the function calls for the CR or Redundancy schemes are added to the source code, followed by expansion of the pragma regions which provide end-to-end resilience. (final code omitted due to space).

Experimental Results of TF-IDF: We used 750 text books with a total size of 500 MB for the TF-IDF benchmark with 4 MPI ranks. We performed the evaluation with 4 input sizes: 125 MB, 250 MB, 375 MB, and 500 MB, which were protected by checksums.

Figure 11 depicts the time for conventional per-kernel resilience of TF-IDF and compares that to our end-to-end resilience. Execution times are averaged over 30 runs with small standard deviations (0.01–0.22). The overheads are almost the same, fluctuations of higher/lower execution by 0.25% or less are insignificant for input sizes of 125 MB to 16.2% for 500 MB. *This confirms observation 1.*

Figure 13 depicts the LVF metric on a logarithmic scale (y-axis) for the three kernels filenames (filen), tfs, and dfs and an input of 500 MB. The tfs data has the highest vulnerability. This reflects a combination of data size (tfs is larger than filenames/dfs) and live range of tfs during program execution (see Fig. 9). The other two kernels operate on smaller data and live ranges, and while this data still critical for resilience (e.g., names of files that will be opened), they add little overhead and are less prone to corruption (lower LVF). We observe again significantly increased protection ranges with end-to-end resilience at virtually unchanged overheads (0.01% to 2.71%). *This confirms observation 2.*

Similar to the fault injection code for matrix multiplication, we inject faults uniformly across the 3 data structures with fault rates from 25 to 45 s for TF-IDF. Figure 14 depicts the faults normalized against the respective data structure sizes.

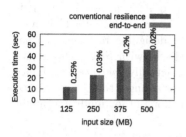
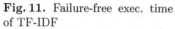

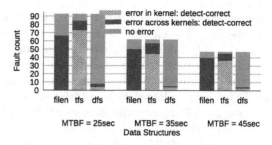

Fig. 11. Failure-free exec. time of TF-IDF

Fig. 12. Fault injection, various fault rates, 100 actual runs

The filenames data structure is small compared to the tfs and dfs structures, i.e., fewer faults are injected into filenames even though it has a larger life range than dfs. Similarly, tfs has the most injections as it is the largest data structure and is also live for the longest period of time. Finally, dfs is live for the shortest period of time, but because of its larger data footprint we see several injections into it. The shape of the fault distribution of Fig. 14 for actual injections closely resembles that of the modeling via the LVF metric in Fig. 13. *This confirms observation 4.*

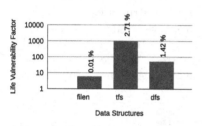

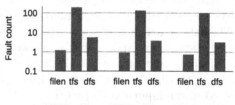

Fig. 13. Live Vulnerability Factor (bars) and % increase (above bars) for TF-IDF

Fig. 14. Fault injection normalized to respective data structure sizes

Results indicating different fault handling classes are presented in Fig. 12. As with the matrix multiplication example, only the faults in the lower-most shaded regions of the tfs and dfs data structures can be corrected by conventional resilience methods while end-to-end resilience manages to detect and correct *all* errors, even those crossing scope/kernel boundaries. Furthermore, tfs was benefiting the most from end-to-end resilience while conventional resilience in a single kernel left many SDCs in tfs and some in dfs undetected (reflecting the vulnerability per data structure expressed by the LVF in Fig. 13). *This confirms observation 3.*

Discussion: We also experimented with a XOR hash to protect the data structures of TF-IDF. To produce a plain text as input for XOR, key/value strings of the tfs data structure were concatenated per file before they could be hashed. Due to string concatenation, this resulted in an additional 10% performance overhead for a total increase in LVF by 13% compared to no protection. This increase in LVF is clearly inferior to the simple checksums with 2.71% LVF overhead (Fig. 13), which underlines the importance of designing resilience mechanisms that require *small* metadata and perform checks with *little* performance overhead. Otherwise, resilience mechanisms might actually *increase* the chance of SDCs (due to a larger data footprint vulnerable for a longer time), i.e., a 100% increase in LVF doubles the chance of SDCs (even though they might be caught and fixed with end-to-end resilience).

Observation 6: The LVF indicates (without error injection) that The change in LVF (in %) reveals if protection was effective or counter-productive.

6.3   NAS Parallel Benchmarks

We apply our resilience pragma to the NAS parallel benchmark (NPB) suite to calculate the overhead of our scheme. We use the C port of the OpenMP version of the NPB suite. We annotate each iteration of the benchmarks with a pragma that protects the input data structures. Notice that only four of the NPB benchmarks of this C-based OpenMP version compile correctly for input class C, i.e., we cannot report results for the remaining ones, because data structures that remain unmodified between iteration boundaries are too small for end-to-end resilience to be effective. The input data structures are verified with a simple scheme that calculates a checksum over the entire data structure.

The data structure is checked for correctness inside the resilience region specified by the pragma and control is allowed to move to the next iteration only when the input data structures are verified to be correct. Via checkpointing, one can revert the data structures to a previously saved state in case a soft error is detected in the input data structures.

Figure 15 shows the execution time (in seconds) of the different benchmarks with and without the resilience pragma. The results are averaged over 10 runs of the benchmark and run for up to 30 min. We observe that the incurred overhead in case of a fault-free execution is between 0.63%–2.61%. The standard deviation for the executions ranges from 0.983 for FT to 9.957 for SP (too small to show in the plots).

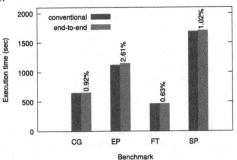

Fig. 15. Time of NPB codes (input class C) with/without pragma

Observation 7: Correctness of program-protected data structures can be guaranteed with a small penalty on performance of less than 3%.

7   Related Work

LVF differs from other metrics that assess resilience. The Failures in Time (FIT) rate is defined as a failure rate of 1 per billion hours. FIT is inverse proportional to MTBF (Mean Time Between Failures). The Architectural Vulnerability Factor (AVF) [35] is the probability that a fault (in microprocessor architecture) leads to a failure (in the program), defined over the fraction of time that data is vulnerable. The Program Vulnerability Factor (PVF) [34] allows insight into the vulnerability of a software resource with respect to hardware faults in a micro-architecture independent way by providing a comparison among programs with relative reliability. The Data Vulnerability Factor (DVF) [37] considers data spaces and the fraction of time that a fault in data will result in a failure. DVF takes into account the number of accesses as a contributor to fault occurrence. Past work has taken value live ranges into account to design a fault injection framework and measure CPU vs. GPU vulnerabilities in terms of PVF in Hauberk [36] and to protect critical data for GPU kernels [23]. Value live ranges encapsulate the live time of variables promoted to *registers* for short program segments while our variable live range captures the live time of compound structures/arrays over the entire program (from first define to last use) irrespective of register promotion. This is necessary as a singular structure/array element cannot be checked in isolation as required by end-to-end resilience (see next section), it can only be checked in conjunction with a subset of structure/arrays elements. Our LVF metric captures this difference and is thus different from AVF, PVF, and DVF. Furthermore, LVF takes into account time × space, which covers the effect of soft errors. Our metric is agnostic to architectural aspects of a processor (covered by AVF) and their impacts on programs (see PVF). It is also agnostic of the number of references (unlike DVF) as it considers both (a) written, incorrect results and (b) SDCs that may occur, even in the absence of write instructions (which other work does not). Simon et al. [32] use a Poisson distribution over a task's lifetime to determine the probability of task failures and derive from it the need for task-based replication. Unlike our work, they do not address the issue of data vulnerability when applications mix *multiple* resilience techniques. Diniz et al. [11] propose a resilience pragma to protect a *single* kernel. In contrast, our work contributes protection for end-to-end resilience *across* kernels.

8   Conclusion

We proposed an annotation-based approach for building highly modular and resilient applications such that resilience concerns are separated from algorithms. Our approach requires a minimal effort by application programmers and is highly portable. We introduced and investigated the significance of the live vulnerability factor, which takes into account the live range of a data structure and its storage space to provide insight into the likelihood of failures. We introduced an effective set of building blocks for detection and correction of soft faults through *Check* and *Recover* methods for arbitrary data structures. We provided two approaches, pragma- and task-based, to implement end-to-end resilience. We showed the effectiveness of end-to-end resilience for two variants of sequentially composed matrix multiplications and TF-IDF under failure-free execution and fault scenarios in detail. We further assessed the overhead of our method for NPB codes operating at input size C. End-to-end resilience incurred less than 3% overhead on average compared to conventional single-kernel resilience and increased protection against bit flips by a factor of three to four. The LVF metric helped in guiding which data structures to protect and assessing if protection meta-data and checking algorithms were effective (or counter-productive) in providing resilience.

References

1. Anderson, J.H., Calandrino, J.M.: Parallel task scheduling on multicore platforms. SIGBED Rev. **3**(1), 1–6 (2006)
2. Biswas, S., Supinski, B.R.D., Schulz, M., Franklin, D., Sherwood, T., Chong, F.T.: Exploiting data similarity to reduce memory footprints. In: IPDPS, pp. 152–163 (2011)
3. Blumofe, R.D., Joerg, C.F., Kuszmaul, B.C., Leiserson, C.E., Randall, K.H., Zhou, Y.: Cilk: an efficient multithreaded runtime system. In: PPoPP, pp. 207–216 (1995)
4. Böhm, S., Engelmann, C.: File I/O for MPI applications in redundant execution scenarios. In: Parallel, Distributed, and Network-Based Processing, February 2012
5. Bosilca, G., Bouteiller, A., Danalis, A., Faverge, M., Herault, T., Dongarra, J.: PaRSEC: exploiting heterogeneity to enhance scalability. Comput. Sci. Eng. **15**(6), 36–45 (2013)
6. Cao, C., Herault, T., Bosilca, G., Dongarra, J.: Design for a soft error resilient dynamic task-based runtime. In: IPDPS, pp. 765–774, May 2015
7. Chen, S., et al.: Scheduling threads for constructive cache sharing on CMPs. In: SPAA, pp. 105–115 (2007)
8. Chen, Z., Wu, P.: Fail-stop failure algorithm-based fault tolerance for cholesky decomposition. IEEE TPDS **99**(PrePrints), 1 (2014)
9. Chung, J., et al.: Containment domains: a scalable, efficient, and flexible resilience scheme for exascale systems. In: Supercomputing, pp. 58:1–58:11 (2012)
10. Dave, C., Bae, H., Min, S.J., Lee, S., Eigenmann, R., Midkiff, S.: Cetus: a source-to-source compiler infrastructure for multicores. Computer **42**(12), 36–42 (2009)
11. Diniz, P.C., Liao, C., Quinlan, D.J., Lucas, R.F.: Pragma-controlled source-to-source code transformations for robust application execution. In: Desprez, F., et al. (eds.) Euro-Par 2016. LNCS, vol. 10104, pp. 660–670. Springer, Cham (2017). https://doi.org/10.1007/978-3-319-58943-5_53
12. Du, P., Bouteiller, A., Bosilca, G., Herault, T., Dongarra, J.: Algorithm-based fault tolerance for dense matrix factorizations. In: PPoPP, pp. 225–234 (2012)
13. Duell, J.: The design and implementation of Berkeley Labs Linux Checkpoint/Restart. Technical report, LBNL (2003)
14. Duran, A., et al.: OmpSs: a proposal for programming heterogeneous multi-core architectures. Parall. Process. Lett. **21**(2), 173–193 (2011)
15. Elliott, J., Hoemmen, M., Mueller, F.: Evaluating the impact of SDC on the GMRES iterative solver. In: IPDPS, pp. 1193–1202 (2014)

16. Elliott, J., Kharbas, K., Fiala, D., Mueller, F., Ferreira, K., Engelmann, C.: Combining partial redundancy and checkpointing for HPC. In: ICDCS, 18–21 June 2012
17. Fiala, D., Mueller, F., Engelmann, C., Ferreira, K., Brightwell, R.: Detection and correction of silent data corruption for large-scale high-performance computing. In: Supercomputing (2012)
18. Geist, A.: How to kill a supercomputer: dirty power, cosmic rays, and bad solder. In: IEEE Spectrum, February 2016
19. Huang, K.H., Abraham, J.: Algorithm-based fault tolerance for matrix operations. IEEE Trans. Comput. **C–33**(6), 518–528 (1984)
20. Islam, T.Z., Mohror, K., Bagchi, S., Moody, A., de Supinski, B.R., Eigenmann, R.: MCREngine: a scalable checkpointing system using data-aware aggregation and compression. In: Supercomputing, pp. 17:1–17:11 (2012)
21. Kale, L.V., Krishnan, S.: Charm++: a portable concurrent object oriented system based on c++. In: OOPSLA, pp. 91–108 (1993)
22. Kiczales, G., et al.: Aspect-oriented programming. In: ECOOP, pp. 220–242 (1997)
23. Li, S., Sridharan, V., Gurumurthi, S., Yalamanchili, S.: Software-based dynamic reliability management for GPU applications. In: Workshop in Silicon Errors in Logic System Effects (2015)
24. Martsinkevich, T., Subasi, O., Unsal, O., Cappello, F., Labarta, J.: Fault-tolerant protocol for hybrid task-parallel message-passing applications. In: Cluster Computing, pp. 563–570, September 2015
25. Min, S., Iancu, C., Yelick, K.: Hierarchical work stealing on manycore clusters. In: Partitioned Global Address Space Programming Models (2011)
26. Moody, A., Bronevetsky, G., Mohror, K., Supinski, B.R.D.: Design, modeling, and evaluation of a scalable multi-level checkpointing system. In: Supercomputing, pp. 1–11 (2010)
27. Panzer-Steindel, B.: Data integrity. Technical report, 1.3, CERN (2007)
28. Parr, T., Quong, R.: ANTLR: a predicated. Softw. Pract. Exp. **25**(7), 789–810 (1995)
29. Schroeder, B., Gibson, G.A.: A large-scale study of failures in high-performance computing systems. In: DSN, pp. 249–258 (2006)
30. Schroeder, B., Pinheiro, E., Weber, W.D.: Dram errors in the wild: a large-scale field study. SIGMETRICS Perform. Eval. Rev. **37**(1), 193–204 (2009)
31. Shantharam, M., Srinivasmurthy, S., Raghavan, P.: Fault tolerant preconditioned conjugate gradient for sparse linear system solution. In: Supercomputing, pp. 69–78 (2012)
32. Simon, T.A., Dorband, J.: Improving application resilience through probabilistic task replication. In: Workshop on Algorithmic and Application Error Resilience, June 2013
33. Snir, M., et al.: Addressing failures in exascale computing. Int. J. High Perform. Comput. (2013)
34. Sridharan, V., Kaeli, D.: Eliminating microarchitectural dependency from Architectural Vulnerability. In: HPCA, pp. 117–128, February 2009
35. Sridharan, V., et al.: Memory errors in modern systems: the good, the bad, and the ugly. In: ASPLOS, pp. 297–310 (2015)
36. Yim, K.S., Pham, C., Saleheen, M., Kalbarczyk, Z., Iyer, R.: Hauberk: lightweight silent data corruption error detector for GPGPU. In: IPDPS, pp. 287–300 (2011)
37. Yu, L., Li, D., Mittal, S., Vetter, J.S.: Quantitatively modeling application resilience with the data vulnerability factor. In: Supercomputing, pp. 695–706 (2014)

38. Zhang, Y., Mueller, F., Cui, X., Potok, T.: Large-scale multi-dimensional document clustering on GPU clusters. In: IPDPS, pp. 1–10, April 2010

39. Zheng, Z., Chien, A.A., Teranishi, K.: Fault tolerance in an inner-outer solver: a GVR-enabled case study. In: Daydé, M., Marques, O., Nakajima, K. (eds.) VEC-PAR 2014. LNCS, vol. 8969, pp. 124–132. Springer, Cham (2015). https://doi.org/10.1007/978-3-319-17353-5_11

Resilient Optimistic Termination Detection for the Async-Finish Model

Sara S. Hamouda[1,2]([⊠]) [iD] and Josh Milthorpe[1] [iD]

[1] Australian National University, Canberra, Australia
josh.milthorpe@anu.edu.au
[2] Inria, Paris, France
sara.hamouda@inria.fr

Abstract. Driven by increasing core count and decreasing mean-time-to-failure in supercomputers, HPC runtime systems must improve support for dynamic task-parallel execution and resilience to failures. The async-finish task model, adapted for distributed systems as the asynchronous partitioned global address space programming model, provides a simple way to decompose a computation into nested task groups, each managed by a 'finish' that signals the termination of all tasks within the group.

For distributed termination detection, maintaining a consistent view of task state across multiple unreliable processes requires additional book-keeping when creating or completing tasks and finish-scopes. Runtime systems which perform this book-keeping *pessimistically*, i.e. synchronously with task state changes, add a high communication overhead compared to non-resilient protocols. In this paper, we propose *optimistic finish*, the first message-optimal resilient termination detection protocol for the async-finish model. By avoiding the communication of certain task and finish events, this protocol allows uncertainty about the global structure of the computation which can be resolved correctly at failure time, thereby reducing the overhead for failure-free execution.

Performance results using micro-benchmarks and the LULESH hydrodynamics proxy application show significant reductions in resilience overhead with optimistic finish compared to pessimistic finish. Our optimistic finish protocol is applicable to any task-based runtime system offering automatic termination detection for dynamic graphs of non-migratable tasks.

Keywords: Async-finish · Termination detection · Resilience

1 Introduction

Recent advances in high-performance computing (HPC) systems have greatly increased parallelism, with both larger numbers of nodes, and larger core counts

S. S. Hamouda—Research performed during PhD studies at the Australian National University

M. Weiland et al. (Eds.): ISC High Performance 2019, LNCS 11501, pp. 291–311, 2019.
https://doi.org/10.1007/978-3-030-20656-7_15

within each node. With increased system size and complexity comes an increase in the expected rate of failures. Programmers of HPC systems must therefore address the twin challenges of efficiently exploiting available parallelism and ensuring resilience to component failures. As more industrial and scientific communities rely on HPC to drive innovation, there is a need for productive programming models for scalable resilient applications.

Many productive HPC programming models support nested task parallelism via composable task-parallel constructs, which simplify the expression of arbitrary task graphs to efficiently exploit available hardware parallelism. Termination detection (TD) – determining when all tasks in a subgraph are complete – is a key requirement for dynamic task graphs. In an unreliable system, additional work is required for correct termination detection in the presence of component failures. Task-based models for use in HPC must therefore support resilience through efficient fault-tolerant TD protocols.

The async-finish task model is a productive task parallelism model adopted by many asynchronous partitioned global address space (APGAS) languages. It represents a computation as a global task graph composed of nested sub-graphs, each managed by a `finish` construct. Finish embodies a TD protocol to track the termination of the asynchronous tasks spawned directly or transitively within its scope.

The first resilient TD protocol for the async-finish model was designed by Cunningham et al. [3] as part of the Resilient X10 project. Resilient X10 provides user-level fault tolerance support by extending the async-finish model with failure awareness. Failure awareness enables an application to be notified of process failures impacting the computation's task graph to adopt a suitable recovery procedure. Unsurprisingly, adding failure awareness to the async-finish model entails a cost; it requires the runtime system to perform additional book-keeping activities to correctly detect termination despite the gaps created in the computation's task graph.

Cunningham et al. TD protocol for Resilient X10 tracks all state transitions of remote tasks in order to maintain a consistent view of the computation's control flow. While this ensures a simple failure recovery process, it adds more termination signals than are strictly necessary during normal failure-free execution. Since it favors failure recovery over normal execution, we describe this protocol as 'pessimistic'.

In this paper, we review the pessimistic finish protocol, and demonstrate that the requirement for a consistent view results in a high performance overhead for failure-free execution. We propose the 'optimistic finish' protocol, an alternative message-optimal protocol that relaxes the consistency requirement, resulting in faster failure-free execution with a moderate increase in recovery cost.

The remainder of the paper is organized as follows. Sections 2−3 review the nested task parallelism models, the X10 programming language, and related work. Section 4 proves the optimal number of messages required for correct async-finish termination detection. Section 5 describes the failure model and the challenges of recovering async-finish task graphs. Sections 6−8 describe the non-resilient finish protocol, the pessimistic finish protocol, and the optimistic finish protocol using an abstract TD framework. Section 9 describes a scalable resilient finish store. Sections 10–11 present the performance evaluations and the conclusion.

2 Background

2.1 Nested Task Parallelism Models

Computations that entail nested termination scopes are generally classified as fully-strict or terminally-strict. Blumofe and Leiserson [2] describe a fully-strict task graph as one that has fork edges from a task to its children and join edges from each child to its direct parent. A task can only wait for other tasks it directly forked (see Fig. 1-a). In contrast, a terminally-strict task graph allows a join edge to connect a child to any of its ancestor tasks, including its direct parent, which means a task can wait for other tasks it directly or transitively created (see Fig. 1-b). Cilk's spawn-sync programming model and X10's async-finish programming model are the most prominent representatives of fully-strict and terminally-strict computations, respectively. For dynamic irregular task trees, the async-finish model avoids unnecessary synchronization by relaxing the requirement to have each task to wait for its direct successors.

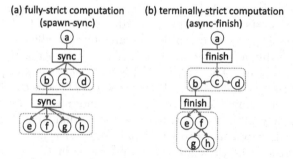

Fig. 1. Nested parallelism models. Dotted boxes are termination scopes; circles are tasks.

When failures occur, nodes in the computation tree are lost, resulting in sub-trees of the failed nodes breaking off the computation structure. Fault-tolerant termination detection protocols aim to reattach those sub-trees to the remaining computation to facilitate termination detection. Although in this paper we focus on the async-finish model, the described resilient protocols are also applicable to the spawn-sync model.

2.2 The X10 Programming Model

We used the APGAS language X10 as a basis for our study of the termination detection protocols of the async-finish model. X10 models a parallel computation as a global address space partitioned among places. Each place is a multi-threaded process with threads cooperating to execute tasks spawned locally or received from other places. A task is spawned at a particular place and cannot migrate to other places.

An X10 program dynamically generates an arbitrary task graph by nesting `async`, `at`, and `finish` constructs. The `async` construct spawns a new task at the current place. To spawn an asynchronous task at a remote place p, `at` is used with `async` as follows: (`at (p) async S;`). The `finish` construct is used for synchronization; it defines a scope of coherent tasks and waits for their termination. Each task belongs to one finish scope, and finish scopes can be nested. Exceptions thrown from any of the tasks are collected at the finish, and are wrapped in a `MultipleExceptions` object after finish terminates. A place may hold references to objects hosted at remote places using the `x10.lang.GlobalRef` type. To access a remote object using its global ref `gr`, a task must shift to the object's home as follows: (`at(gr) gr().doSomething();`).

3 Related Work

Dijkstra and Scholten (DS) [4] proposed one of the earliest and best-studied TD protocols for the so-called 'diffusing computation' model. In this model, the computation starts by activating a coordinator process that is responsible for signaling termination. Other processes are initially idle and can only be activated by receiving a message from an active process. An active process can become idle at any time. The DS protocol is a *message-optimal* protocol such that for a computation that sends M basic messages, DS adds exactly M control messages to detect termination. It requires each intermediate process to signal its termination only after its successor processes terminate. This termination detection model is very similar to Cilk's fully-strict spawn-sync model. Fault-tolerant extensions of the DS algorithm are presented in [6,7].

Lai and Wu [6] describe a resilient protocol that can tolerate the failure of almost the entire system without adding any overhead for failure-free execution. The idea is that each process (idle or active) detecting a failure must detach from its parent, adopt the coordinator as its new parent, and share its local failure knowledge with its parent and the coordinator. On detecting a failure, the coordinator expects all processes to send termination signals directly to it. The protocol introduces a sequential bottleneck at the coordinator process, which limits its applicability to large-scale HPC applications.

Lifflander et al. [7] took a practical approach for resilient TD of a fully-strict diffusing computation. Based on the assumption that multi-node failures are rare in practice, and that the probability of a k-node failure decreases as k increases, they designed three variants of the DS protocol that can tolerate most but not all failures. The INDEP protocol tolerates the failure of a single process, or multiple unrelated processes. It requires each parent to identify its successors and their successors. Therefore, each process notifies its parent of its potential successor before activating it. Two protocols were proposed to address related failures, however, they cannot tolerate the failure of an interior (non-leaf) node and its parent.

To the best of our knowledge, the only prior work addressing resilient TD for the terminally-strict async-finish model was done in the context of the X10 language. Cunningham et al. [3] enhanced X10 to allow a program to detect the failure of a place through a `DeadPlaceException` from the `finish` constructs that control tasks running at that place. The TD protocol extends `finish` with an adoption mechanism that enables it to detect orphan tasks of its dead children and to wait for their termination before reporting a `DPE` to the application. This adoption mechanism ensures that failures will not leave behind hidden tasks at surviving places that may silently corrupt the application's state after recovery. However, it requires additional book-keeping activities for tracking the control flow of the computation, which results in high resilience overhead for failure-free execution. Our work extends [3] to provide a low-overhead resilient termination detection protocol for the async-finish model. Assuming failures are rare events, we designed a message-optimal 'optimistic' TD protocol that aims to optimize the failure-free execution performance of resilient applications.

Resilient distributed work-stealing runtime systems use fault tolerant protocols for tracking task migration under failure [5,9]. Our work focuses on the APGAS model, in which tasks are explicitly assigned to places, hence they are not migratable.

4   Message-Optimal Async-Finish Termination Detection

In this section, we consider the optimal number of control messages required for correct async-finish termination detection in both non-resilient and resilient implementations.

We assume a finish block which includes nested async statements that create distributed tasks, such that each task and its parent (task or finish) are located at different places. Messages sent to fork these tasks at their intended locations are referred to as *basic messages*. For example, in the task graphs in Fig. 2, three basic messages are sent to fork tasks a, b, and c. The additional messages used by the system for the purpose of termination detection are referred to as *control messages* (shown as dotted lines in the figures). We consider the basic messages as the baseline for any termination detection protocol, thus an optimal protocol will add the minimum number of control messages as overhead. In resilient mode, we build on Cunningham et al.'s design [3] in which the TD metadata of the `finish` constructs are maintained safely in a *resilient store*. A `finish` and the resilient store exchange two signals: the `PUBLISH` signal is sent from the `finish` to the store to create a corresponding `ResilientFinish` object, and the `RELEASE` signal flows in the other direction when the finish scope terminates (see Fig. 2-b).

As a finish scope evolves by existing tasks forking new tasks, finish needs to update its knowledge of the total number of active tasks so that it can wait for

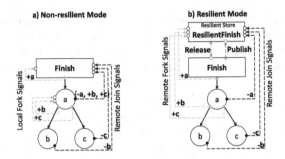

Fig. 2. Message-optimal async-finish TD protocols.

their termination. We refer to this number as the *global count* or gc. Finish forks the first task and sets gc = 1. A task must notify finish when it forks a successor task to allow finish to increase the number of active tasks (by incrementing gc). When a task terminates, it must notify finish to allow it to decrease the number of active tasks (by decrementing gc). When the last task terminates, gc reaches zero and finish is released. We use the terms FORK and JOIN to refer to the control signals used to notify finish when a new task is forked and when a running task terminates. Multiple signals from the same source may be packed in one message for better performance.

Lemma 1. *A correct non-resilient finish requires one TD control message per task.*

Proof. Finish detects termination only after all forked tasks terminate. Thus sending a JOIN signal when a task terminates is unavoidable for correct termination detection. During execution, a parent task may fork N successor tasks, and therefore, it must notify finish with N FORK signals for these tasks. Assuming that failures do not occur, each task must eventually terminate and send its own JOIN signal. A task can buffer the FORK signals of its successor tasks locally and send them with its JOIN signal in the same message. Thus, with only one message per task, finish will eventually receive a FORK signal and a JOIN signal for each task, which guarantees correct termination detection.

Figure 2-a illustrates this method of non-resilient termination detection. When task a forks tasks b and c, it delays sending their FORK signals (+b, +c) until it joins. At this point, it packs its JOIN signal (-a) with the delayed FORK signals and sends one message containing the three signals (-a, +b, +c). Note that delaying the fork signals may result in tasks joining before their FORK signals are received by finish. A correct implementation must delay termination until each FORK is matched by a JOIN and each JOIN is matched by a FORK.

Lemma 2. *A correct resilient finish requires two TD control messages per task.*

Proof. In the presence of failures, tasks may fail at arbitrary times during execution. For correct termination detection, finish must be aware of the existence of each forked task. If a parent task fails in between forking a successor task and sending the FORK signal of this task to finish, finish will not track the successor task since it is not aware of its existence, and termination detection will be incorrect. Therefore, a parent task must eagerly send the FORK signal of a successor task before forking the task, and may not buffer the FORK signals locally. For correct termination detection, each task must also send a JOIN signal when it terminates. As a result, correct termination detection in the presence of failures requires two separate TD messages per task – a message for the task's FORK signal, and a message for the task's JOIN signal. The absence of either message makes termination detection incorrect.

Figure 2-b demonstrates this method of resilient termination detection, which ensures that a resilient finish is tracking every forked task. Assuming that a resilient finish can detect the failure of any node in the system, it can cancel forked tasks located at failed nodes to avoid waiting for them indefinitely. Note that in counting the messages, we do not consider the messages that the resilient store may generate internally to guarantee reliable storage of resilient finish objects. While a centralized resilient store may not introduce any additional communication, a replication-based store will introduce communication to replicate the objects consistently.

Lemma 3. *Optimistic resilient finish is a message-optimal TD protocol.*

Proof. Our proposed optimistic finish protocol (Sect. 8) uses exactly two messages per task to notify task forking and termination. Since both messages are necessary for correct termination detection, the optimistic finish protocol is message-optimal.

5   Async-Finish Termination Detection Under Failure

In this section, we use the following sample program to illustrate the challenges of async-finish TD under failure and the possible solutions. In Sect. 7 and Sect. 8, we describe how these challenges are addressed by the pessimistic protocol and the optimistic protocol, respectively.

```
1 finish /*F1*/ {
2    at (p2) async { /*a*/ at (p3) async { /*c*/ } }
3    at (p4) async { /*b*/ finish /*F2*/ at (p5) async { /*d*/ } }
4 }
```

Failure Model: We focus on process (i.e. place) fail-stop failures. A failed place permanently terminates, and its data and tasks are immediately lost. We assume that each place will eventually detect the failure of any other place, and that a corrupted message due to the failure of its source will be dropped either by the network module or the deserialization module of the destination place. We assume non-byzantine behavior.

298   S. S. Hamouda and J. Milthorpe

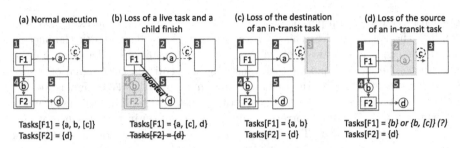

Fig. 3. Task tracking under failure. The square brackets mark in-transit tasks.

Challenge 1 - Loss of Termination Detection Metadata: As a computation evolves, finish objects are created at different places to maintain the TD metadata (e.g. the active tasks of each finish). Losing one of these objects impairs the control flow and prevents correct termination detection. To address this challenge, Cunningham et al. [3] proposed using a *resilient store* that can save the data reliably and survive failures. The design of the resilient store is orthogonal to the termination detection protocol, thus different stores (i.e. centralized/distributed, disk-based/memory-based, native/out-of-process) can be used. However, the survivability of the protocol implementation is limited by the survivability of the store. For the above program, we assume that F1 and F2 have corresponding resilient finish objects in the resilient store.

Challenge 2 - Adopting Orphan Tasks: When the finish home place fails, the finish may leave behind active tasks that require tracking. We refer to these tasks as orphan tasks. According to the semantics of the async-finish model, a parent finish can only terminate after its nested (children) finishes terminate. A parent finish can maintain this rule by adopting the orphan tasks of its dead children to wait for their termination. Figure 3-b shows the adoption of task d by F1 after the home place of F2 failed.

Challenge 3 - Loss of In-Transit and Live Tasks: Each task has a source place and a destination (home) place, which are the same for locally generated tasks. The active (non-terminated) tasks of the computation can be either running at their home place (live tasks) or transiting from a source place towards their home place (in-transit tasks).

The *failure of the destination place* has the same impact on live and in-transit tasks. For both categories, the tasks are lost and their parent finish must exclude them from its global task count. For example, the failure of place 4 in Fig. 3-b results in losing the live task b, and the failure of place 3 in Fig. 3-c results in losing the in-transit task c, because its target place is no longer available.

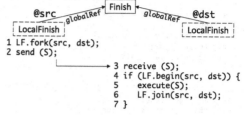

Listing 1.1. Finish TD API.

```
1  abstract class Finish(id:Id) {
2    val latch:Latch;
3    val parent:Finish;
4    def wait() { latch.wait(); }
5    def release() { latch.release(); }
6  }
7  abstract class LocalFinish(id:Id) {
8    val gr:GlobalRef[Finish];
9    def fork(src, dst):void;
10   def join(src, dst):void;
11   def begin(src, dst):bool;
12 }
```

```
finish { ... @src at (dst) async { S; } ... }
```

```
1 LF.fork(src, dst);
2 send (S);
         └─────────────→ 3 receive (S);
                         4 if (LF.begin(src, dst)) {
                         5   execute(S);
                         6   LF.join(src, dst);
                         7 }
```

Fig. 4. Tracking remote task creation.

The *failure of the source place* has a different impact on live and in-transit tasks. Live tasks proceed normally regardless of the failure, because they already started execution at their destinations. However, in-transit tasks are more difficult to handle (Fig. 3-d). Based on Lemma 2, in resilient mode, a source place must notify its finish of a potential remote task before sending the task to its destination. If the source place died after the finish received the notification, the finish cannot determine whether the potential task was: (1) never transmitted, (2) fully transmitted and will eventually be received by the destination, or (3) partially transmitted and will be dropped at the destination due to message corruption. A unified rule that allows finish to tolerate this uncertainty is to consider any in-transit task whose source place has died as a lost task and exclude it from the global task count. The finish must also direct the destination place to drop the task in case it is successfully received in the future.

To summarize, recovering the control flow requires the following: (1) adopting orphan tasks, (2) excluding live tasks whose destination place is dead, (3) excluding in-transit tasks whose source place or destination place is dead, and (4) preventing a destination place from executing an in-transit task whose source place is dead. The optimistic finish protocol achieves these goals using the optimal number of TD messages per task, unlike the pessimistic protocol which uses one additional message per task.

6 Distributed Task Tracking

In this section, we describe an abstract framework that can be used to implement termination detection protocols, based on the X10 runtime implementation. The essence of the framework is presented as pseudocode in Listing 1.1, and Fig. 4. In Sects. 6.3, 7, and 8, we will describe three termination detection protocols based on this framework.

6.1 Finish and LocalFinish Objects

A termination detection protocol is defined by providing concrete implementations of the abstract classes Finish and LocalFinish shown in Listing 1.1. For each finish block, an instance of Finish with a globally unique id is created to maintain a global view of the distributed task graph. When the task that

Listing 1.2. Non-resilient Finish

```
1  class NR_Finish(id) extends Finish {
2    gc:int=0; // global count
3    def terminate(live:int[places]) {
4      for (p in places) gc += live[p];
5      if (gc == 0) release();
6    }
7  }
8  class NR_LocalFinish(id) extends LocalFinish {
9    live:int[places]={0}; //signals buffer
10   def fork(src, dst) { live[dst]++; }
11   def begin(src, dst) { return true; }
12   def join(src, dst) { live[dst]--; @F[id].terminate(live); }
13 }
```

created the finish reaches the end of the block, it calls the function wait to block on the latch until all the tasks that were created by the finish block have terminated. When all tasks (direct and transitive) terminate, the runtime system calls the function release to release the blocked task. The runtime system links each finish object to its parent in a tree structure.

Each visited place within a finish block will create an instance of type LocalFinish to track task activities done locally. It holds a global reference to the global Finish object to notify it when changes in the task graph occur so that the Finish has an up-to-date view of the global control structure.

6.2 Task Events

LocalFinish defines three interfaces to track task events: fork, begin, and join. Figure 4 shows the invocation of the three task events when a source place src spawns a task at a destination place dst. On forking a new task, the source place calls fork to notify finish of a potential new task, then it sends the task to the destination place. On receiving a task, the destination place calls begin to determine whether or not the task is valid for execution. If the task is valid, the destination place executes it, then calls join to notify task termination. If the task is invalid, the destination place drops it.

We describe the protocols in terms of the variables of the Finish and LocalFinish objects, and the implementations of the three task events fork, begin, and join. In the included pseudocode, we use the notation @F[id], @LF[id], and @RF[id] to refer to a remote Finish object, LocalFinish object and ResilientFinish object, respectively.

6.3 Non-resilient Finish Protocol

Listing 1.2 describes a message-optimal implementation of a non-resilient finish. The finish object maintains a global count, gc, representing the number of active tasks. The LocalFinish maintains a live array to buffer the FORK and JOIN signal of its task and the FORK signals of successor tasks to other places. The begin event

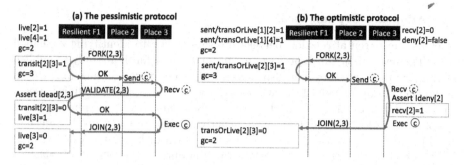

Fig. 5. The task tracking events as task c transitions from place 2 to place 3, based on Fig. 3-a.

accepts all incoming tasks, because this non-resilient protocol is not prepared for receiving invalid tasks due to failures. The `join` event passes the signals buffer `live` to the finish object. Finish updates `gc` according to the passed signals and releases itself when `gc` reaches zero.

7   Resilient Pessimistic Finish

The pessimistic resilient finish protocol requires the resilient finish objects to track the tasks and *independently* repair their state when a failure occurs. Independent repair requires advance knowledge of the status of each active task (whether it is in-transit or live) and the set of children of each finish for adoption purposes.

Classifying active tasks into in-transit and live is necessary for failure recovery, because the two types of tasks are treated differently with respect to the failure of their source, as described in Sect. 5. Using only the FORK and the JOIN signals (see Sect. 4), a resilient finish can track a task as it transitions between the not-existing, active, and terminated states. However, these two signals are not sufficient to distinguish between in-transit or live tasks. The pessimistic protocol adds a third task signal that we call VALIDATE to perform this classification. Although the classification is only needed for recovery, the application pays the added communication cost even in failure-free executions.

The resilient finish object uses three variables for task tracking: `gc` to count the active tasks, `live[]` to count the live tasks at a certain place, and `trans[][]` to count the in-transit tasks between any two places. On receiving a FORK signal for a task moving from place s to place d, the resilient finish object increments the variable `trans[s][d]` and the global count `gc`. When the destination place receives a task, it sends a VALIDATE message to resilient finish to check if the task is valid for execution. If both the source and the destination of the task are active, resilient finish declares the task as valid and transforms it from the transit state to the live state. That is done by decrementing `trans[s][d]` and incrementing `live[d]`. On receiving a JOIN signal for a task that lived at place d, the resilient finish decrements the variables `live[d]` and `gc` (see Fig. 5-a).

7.1 Adopting Orphan Tasks

Tracking the parental relation between finishes is key to identifying orphaned tasks. The pessimistic finish protocol requires each new finish not only to publish itself in the resilient store, but also to link itself to its parent. Thus, in addition to the PUBLISH and the RELEASE signals (see Sect. 4), a pessimistic finish uses a third signal ADD_CHILD to connect a new resilient finish to its parent. When a parent finish adopts a child finish, it deactivates the resilient finish object of the child and adds the child's task counts to its own task counts. A deactivated finish forwards the received task signals to its adopter. The FORWARD_TO_ADOPTER directive in Listing 1.3 refers to this forwarding procedure.

7.2 Excluding Lost Tasks

When place P fails, the live tasks at P and the in-transit tasks from P and to P are considered lost. The number of lost tasks is the summation of live[P], trans[*][P], and trans[P][*]. After calculating the summation, the pessimistic finish object resets these counters and deducts the summation from the global count gc (see the recover method in Listing 1.3). If the source place of an in-transit task fails, the finish requests the destination place to drop the task using the response of the VALIDATE signal.

8 Our Proposed Protocol: Resilient Optimistic Finish

The optimistic finish protocol aims to provide reliable execution of async-finish computations using the minimum number of TD messages. It optimizes over the pessimistic protocol by removing from the critical path of task execution any communication that is needed only for failure recovery. In particular, it removes the VALIDATE signal which classifies active tasks into in-transit and live, and removes the ADD_CHILD signal which synchronously tracks the children of each finish. It compensates for the missing information due to removing these signals by empowering the places with additional metadata that can complete the knowledge of the resilient store at failure recovery time.

A resilient optimistic finish object uses the following variables for task tracking: gc to count the active tasks, transOrLive[][] to count the active tasks, which may be in-transit or live, given their source and destination, and sent[][] to count the total number of sent tasks between any two places, which includes active and terminated tasks. Each visited place within a finish scope records the following variables in its LocalFinish object: recv[] to count the number of received tasks from a certain place, and deny[] to check whether it can accept in-transit tasks from a certain place. Initially, tasks can be accepted from any place.

When a source place s forks a task to a destination place d, transOrLive[s][d], sent[s][d] and the global count gc are incremented (see Listing 1.4-Line 32). When the destination place receives the task, it *locally* determines whether or not the task is valid for execution using its `deny` table (see Listing 1.4-Line 19). If the task is valid, the place executes it and sends a `JOIN` signal when the task terminates. The `JOIN` signal carries both the source and the destination of the task and results in decrementing `transOrLive[s][d]` and `gc` (see Fig. 5-b). Note that `sent[][]` and `recv[]` are never decremented. We will show in Sect. 8.2 how the `sent[][]` and the `recv[]` tables are used for resolving the number of lost in-transit tasks due to the failure of their source.

8.1   Adopting Orphan Tasks

The optimistic protocol does not use the `ADD_CHILD` signal, but rather calculates the set of children needing adoption at failure recovery time.

Each resilient finish object records the id of its parent, which was given in the `PUBLISH` signal that created the object. The protocol relies on the fact that a child finish at place x will be created by one of the living tasks at place x governed by the parent finish. When a place P dies, each resilient finish object checks the value of `transOrLive[*][P]` to determine whether it has any active tasks at that place. If there are no active tasks at P, then there are no children needing adoption due to the failure of place P. Otherwise, it consults the resilient store to retrieve the list of children whose home place is P, and therefore require adoption. The parent finish records these children in a set called `ghosts`. Termination is detected when `gc` reaches zero and the `ghosts` set is empty (see the condition of `tryRelease()` in Listing 1.4). A valid resilient store implementation of the optimistic finish protocol must implement the `FIND_CHILDREN` function. This function is reduced to a search in a local set of resilient finish objects in a centralized resilient store, or a query to the backup of the dead place in a replication-based resilient store.

The reason why we refer to the adopted children as 'ghosts' in this protocol is because we keep them active after their corresponding `finish` dies. The ghost finishes continue to govern their own tasks as normal, unlike the pessimistic finish protocol which deactivates the adopted children. When a ghost finish determines that all its tasks have terminated, it sends a `REMOVE_CHILD` signal to its parent (Line 50 in Listing 1.4). When the parent receives this signal, it removes the child finish from its `ghosts` set and checks for the possibility of releasing its corresponding finish.

8.2   Excluding Lost Tasks

Like the pessimistic protocol, we aim to exclude all transiting tasks from and to a dead place, and all live tasks at a dead place. However, because transiting and live tasks are not distinguished in our protocol, more work is required for identifying lost tasks.

Listing 1.3. Pessimistic Finish.

```
1  abstract class P_ResilientStore {
2    def PUBLISH(id):void;
3    def ADD_CHILD(parentId, childId):void;
4  }
5  class P_Finish(id:Id) extends Finish {
6    def make(parent:Finish) {
7      @store.ADD_CHILD(parent.id, id);
8      @store.PUBLISH(id);
9    }
10 }
11 class P_LocalFinish(id:Id) extends LocalFinish {
12   def fork(src, dst) {
13     @RF[id].FORK(src, dst);
14   }
15   def join(src, dst){
16     @RF[id].JOIN(src, dst);
17   }
18   def begin(src, dst) {
19     return @RF[id].VALIDATE(src, dst);
20   }
21 }
22 class P_ResilientFinish(id:Id) {
23   gc:int=0;
24   live:int[places];
25   trans:int[places][places];
26   children:Set[Id];
27   adopter:Id;
28   def FORK(src, dst){
29     FORWARD_TO_ADOPTER;
30     if (bothAlive(src, dst)) {
31       trans[src][dst]++; gc++;
32     }
33   }
34   def JOIN(src, dst) {
35     FORWARD_TO_ADOPTER;
36     if (!dst.isDead()) {
37       live[dst]--; gc--;
38       if (gc == 0) @F[id].release();
39     }
40   }
41   def VALIDATE(src, dst) {
42     FORWARD_TO_ADOPTER;
43     if (bothAlive(src, dst)) {
44       trans[src][dst]--;
45       live[dst]++;
46       return true;
47     }
48     else return false;
49   }
50   def addChild(cId) {
51     children.add(cId);
52   }
53   def recover(dead) {
54     // adopt orphaned tasks
55     for (c in children) {
56       if (c.home == dead) {
57         trans += @RF[c].trans;
58         live += @RF[c].live;
59         gc += @RF[c].gc;
60         @RF[c].adopter = id;
61       }
62     }
63     // exclude lost tasks
64     gc -= trans[dead][*] + trans[*][dead] +
         live[dead];
65     trans[dead][*] = 0;
66     trans[*][dead] = 0;
67     live[dead] = 0;
68     if (gc == 0) @F[id].release();
69   }
70 }
```

Listing 1.4. Optimistic Finish.

```
1  abstract class O_ResilientStore {
2    def PUBLISH(id, parentId):void;
3    def FIND_CHILDREN(id, place):Set[Id];
4  }
5  class O_Finish(id:Id) extends Finish {
6    def make(parent:Finish) {
7      @store.PUBLISH(id, parent.id);
8    }
9  }
10 class O_LocalFinish(id:Id) extends LocalFinish {
11   deny:bool[places]; recv:int[places];
12   def fork(src, dst) {
13     @RF[id].FORK(src, dst);
14   }
15   def join(src, dst){
16     @RF[id].JOIN(src, dst);
17   }
18   def begin(src, dst) {
19     if (deny[src]) return false;
20     else { recv[src]++; return true; }
21   }
22   def COUNT_TRANSIT(nSent, dead) {
23     deny[dead] = true;
24     return nSent - recv[dead];
25   }
26 }
27 class O_ResilientFinish(id:Id) {
28   gc:int=0; parent:Id;
29   transOrLive:int[places][places];
30   sent:int[places][places];
31   ghosts:Set[Id]; isGhost:bool;
32   def FORK(src, dst){
33     if (bothAlive(src, dst)){
34       transOrLive[src][dst]++; gc++;
35       sent[src][dst]++;
36     }
37   }
38   def JOIN(src, dst){
39     if (!dst.isDead()){
40       transOrLive[src][dst]--; gc--;
41       tryRelease();
42     }
43   }
44   def removeChild(ghostId) {
45     ghosts.remove(ghostId); tryRelease();
46   }
47   def tryRelease() {
48     if (gc == 0 && ghosts.empty())
49       if (isGhost)
50         @RF[parent].removeChild(id);
51       else @F[id].release();
52   }
53   def recover(dead) {
54     if (transOrLive[*][dead] > 0) {
55       val c = @store.FIND_CHILDREN(id, dead);
56       ghosts.addAll(c);
57       for (g in c) @RF[g].isGhost = true;
58     }
59     gc -= transOrLive[*][dead];
60     transOrLive[*][dead] = 0;
61     for (p in places) {
62       if ( transOrLive[dead][p] > 0) {
63         val s = sent[dead][p];
64         val t = @LF[id].COUNT_TRANSIT(s, dead);
65         transOrLive[dead][p] -= t;
66         gc -= t;
67       }
68     }
69     tryRelease();
70   }
71 }
```

For a destination place P, transOrLive[s][P] is the number of the in-transit tasks from s to P and the live tasks executing at P. If P failed, both categories of tasks are lost and must be excluded from the global count. After determining the ghost children (as described in Sect. 8.1), the resilient finish object can deduct transOrLive[*][P] from the global count, and reset transOrLive[*][P] for each failed place P. Any termination messages received from the dead place P must be discarded, otherwise they may incorrectly alter the global count. Handling the failure of both the source and the destination reduces to handling the failure of the destination.

For a source place P, transOrLive[P][d] is the number of the in-transit tasks from P to d and the live tasks sent by P and are executing at d. If P failed, only the in-transit tasks are lost and must be excluded from the global count; the live tasks proceed normally. An optimistic resilient finish can only identify the number of in-transit tasks through communication with the destination place d. Place d records the total number of received tasks from P in recv[P]. At the same time, the resilient finish object records the total number of sent tasks from P to d in sent[P][d]. The difference between sent[P][d] and recv[P] is the number of transiting tasks from P to d. The resilient finish object relies on a new signal COUNT_TRANSIT to calculate this difference and to stop place d from receiving future tasks from place P by setting deny[P] = true (see the COUNT_TRANSIT method in Listing 1.4, and its call in Listing 1.4-Line 64).

8.3   Optimistic Finish TLA Specification

TLA (Temporal Logic of Actions) [10] is a specification language for documentation and automatic verification of software systems. The system's specification includes an initial state, a set of actions that can update the system's state, and a set of safety and liveness properties that describe the correctness constraints of the system. The TLA model checker tool, named TLC, tests all possible combinations of actions and reports any detected violations of the system's properties.

We developed a formal model for the optimistic finish protocol using TLA to verify the protocols correctness. Using 22 TLA actions, the model can simulate all possible n-level task graphs that can be created on a p-place system, where each node of the task graph has at most c children. It can also simulate the occurrence of one or more place failures as the task graph evolves. The model specification is available at [11].

The distributed TLC tool currently cannot validate liveness properties, such as 'the system must eventually terminate', which we needed to guarantee in our protocol. Using the centralized TLC tool, it was infeasible for us to simulate large graph structures without getting out-of-memory errors due to the large number of actions in our model. Therefore, we decided to use a small graph configuration that can simulate all scenarios of our optimistic protocol. In order to verify the case when a parent finish adopts the tasks of a dead child, we need at least a 3-level graph, such that the finish at the top level can adopt the tasks at the third level that belong to a lost finish at the second level. In our protocol, separate cases handle the failure of the source place of a task, and the failure of the destination place of a task. With one place failure we can simulate either case. The case when a task loses both its source and destination requires killing two places, however, in our protocol handling the failure of both the source and destination is equivalent to handling the failure of the destination alone. Therefore, one place failure is sufficient to verify all rules of our protocol. Because we use the top finish to detect the full termination of the graph, we do not kill the place of the top finish. Therefore, we need two places or more in order to test the correctness of the failure scenarios.

Testing was performed using TLC version 1.5.6 on an 8-core Intel i7-3770 3.40 GHz system running Ubuntu 14.04 operating system. It took a total of 2 h and 59 min to verify the correctness of our protocol over a 3-level task tree with a branching factor of 2 using 3 places, with one place failure at any point in the execution.

9   Finish Resilient Store Implementations

Cunningham et al. [3] described three resilient store implementations, of which only two are suitable for HPC environments. One is a centralized store that holds all resilient finish objects at place-zero, assuming that it will survive all failures. The centralized nature of this store makes it a performance bottleneck for large numbers of concurrent finish objects and tasks. The other store is a distributed store that replicates each finish object at two places – the home place of the finish, which holds the master replica, and the next place, which holds a backup replica. Unfortunately, this scalable implementation was later removed from the code base of Resilient X10 due to its complexity and instability. As a result, users of Resilient X10 are currently limited to using the non-scalable centralized place-zero finish store for HPC simulations.

9.1   Reviving the Distributed Finish Store

Because a centralized place-zero finish store can significantly limit the performance of Resilient X10, we decided to reimplement a distributed finish store for Resilient X10 for both optimistic and pessimistic protocols. Using TLA's model checker, we identified a serious bug in the replication protocol described in [3] for synchronizing the master and the backup replicas of a finish. The problem in their implementation is that the master replica is in charge of forwarding task signals to the backup replica on behalf of the tasks. If the master dies, a task handles this failure by sending its signal directly to the backup. In cases when the master fails after forwarding the signal to the backup, the backup receives the same signal twice – one time from the dead master and one time from the task itself. This mistake corrupts the task counters at the backup and results in incorrect termination detection.

Using TLA, we designed a replication protocol (available in [11]) that requires each task to communicate directly with the master and the backup. The protocol ensures that each signal will be processed only once by each replica in failure-free and failure scenarios. When one replica detects the failure of the other replica, it recreates the lost replica on another place using its state. The protocol ensures that if both replicas are lost before a recovery is performed, the active tasks will reliably detect this catastrophic failure, which should lead the Resilient X10 runtime to terminate. Otherwise, the distributed store can successfully handle failures of multiple unrelated places. Because the failure of place-zero is unrecoverable in the X10 runtime system, our distributed finish implementations do not replicate the finish constructs of place zero.

10   Performance Evaluation

We conducted experiments on the Raijin supercomputer at NCI, the Australian National Computing Infrastructure. Each compute node in Raijin has a dual 8-core Intel Xeon (Sandy Bridge 2.6 GHz) processors and uses an Infiniband FDR network. We statically bound each place to a separate core. The X10 compiler and runtime were built from source revision 36ca628 of the optimistic branch of our repository https://github.com/shamouda/x10.git, which is based on release 2.6.1 of the X10 language. The experiments use the Native (C++ backend) version of X10 compiled using gcc 4.4.7 and use MPI-ULFM [1] for inter-place communication. MPI-ULFM is a fault tolerant MPI implementation that provides efficient fault tolerant point-to-point and collective communication interfaces over Infiniband and other networks. We built MPI-ULFM from revision e87f595 of the master branch of the repository https://bitbucket.org/icldistcomp/ulfm2.git.

10.1   Microbenchmarks

Cunningham et al. [3] designed the BenchMicro program to measure the overhead introduced by resilient finish in various distributed computational patterns, such as fan-out, all-to-all (or fan-out fan-out), and tree fan-out. We modified Bench-Micro to start all patterns from the middle place, rather than from place-zero. This avoids giving an unfair advantage to the centralized implementations by allowing them to handle most of the signals locally.

Table 1. Slowdown factor versus non-resilient finish with 1024 places. Slowdown factor = (time resilient/time non-resilient). The "Opt. %" columns show the percentage of performance improvement credited to the optimistic finish protocol.

Pattern	Finish count	Tasks/Finish	P-p0	O-p0	Opt. %	P-dist	O-dist	Opt. %
1 Fan out	1	1024	2.3	0.9	59%	9.2	7.9	14%
2 Fan out message back	1	2048	1.4	1.2	15%	22.3	7.2	68%
3 Fan out fan out	1	1024^2	51.4	23.9	53%	95.6	39.2	59%
4 Fan out fan out with nested finish	1025	1024	90.9	80.8	11%	4.1	3.8	7%
5 Binary tree fan out	512	2	8.6	8.5	2%	1.4	1.1	27%
6 Synchronous ring around	1024	1	1.8	1.7	1%	1.8	1.8	0%

We measured the time to execute each pattern using 256, 512 and 1024 places, with one place per core. Each configuration was executed 30 times. Figure 6 shows the median with error bars representing the range between the 25th percentile, and the 75th percentile. **P-p0**, **O-p0**, **P-dist**, and **O-dist** refer to pessimistic-centralized, optimistic-centralized, pessimistic-distributed and optimistic-distributed implementations, respectively. Table 1 summarizes the performance results with 1024 places.

From the results, we observe: (1) our proposed optimistic protocol reduces the resilience overhead of the async-finish model for all patterns. (2) the improvement with the optimistic protocol is greater as the number of remote tasks managed by a finish increases. (3) the more concurrent and distributed the finish scopes are in the program, the greater the improvement observed with the resilient distributed finish implementations.

10.2 LULESH

X10 provides a resilient implementation of the LULESH shock hydrodynamics proxy application [8] based on rollback-recovery. It is an iterative SPMD application that executes a series of stencil computations on an evenly-partitioned grid and exchanges ghost regions between neighboring places at each step.

We evaluated LULESH with a problem size of 30^3 elements per place for 60 iterations. In resilient modes, checkpointing is performed every 10 iterations. In the failure scenarios, we start three spare places and kill a victim place every 20 iterations – exactly at iterations 5, 35, and 55. Therefore, a total of 75 iterations are executed, because each failure causes the application to re-execute 5 iterations. The victim places are $N/4$, $N/2$, and $3N/4$, where N is the number of places. Both failure and checkpoint rates are chosen to be orders of magnitude higher than would be expected in a real HPC system, to allow checkpoint and recovery costs to be accurately measured. Table 2 and Fig. 7 show the weak scaling performance results using different TD implementations.

LULESH uses the fan-out finish pattern multiple times for creating the application's distributed data structures and for spawning a coarse-grain task at each place to compute on the local domain. These remote tasks do not add a resilience overhead, because the fan-out finishes start from place zero. The initialization kernel is highly communication-intensive – each place interacts with all its 26 neighbors to obtain access to remote buffers used for ghost cell exchange. This kernel is re-executed after each failure to reinitialize the references to the ghost regions. The optimistic finish protocol is highly effective in reducing the resilience overhead of this kernel and speeding up recovery.

Each LULESH step performs point-to-point communication between neighboring places for exchanging ghost regions, as well as collective functions. However, the collectives map directly to native MPI-ULFM calls, hence do not use finish. Ghost exchange is performed using finish blocks that manage a small number of tasks. With 1000 places, the measured resilience overhead of a single step is: 13% for P-p0, 8% for O-p0, 10% for P-dist, and only 4% for O-dist.

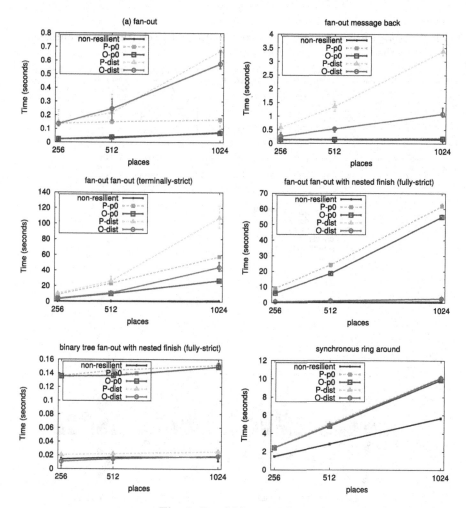

Fig. 6. BenchMicro results.

The application applies in-memory checkpointing by saving a copy of its state locally and another copy at the next place. Each copy is saved within a finish block that controls a single remote task; hence the advantage of the optimistic protocol is minimal.

The reported failure detection time is the time between killing a place and the time when the fan-out finish that controls the execution of the algorithm reports a `DeadPlaceException`. This occurs only after all its tasks terminate with errors due to the failure of the victim (global failure propagation is achieved by ULFM's communicator invalidation mechanism). Reducing the runtime's tracking activities for termination detection accelerates task processing as well as failure detection using optimistic finish.

Table 2. Average execution time for different LULESH kernels (times in seconds, finish resilience overhead shown in parentheses).

Places	Mode	Init.		Step		Ckpt	Detect.	Reinit.	Total time 60 steps (0 ckpt+0 fail)		Total time 60 steps (6 ckpt+0 fail)	Total time 75 steps (6 ckpt+3 fail)
	non-res.	0.97		0.073					5.33			
	P-p0	6.22	(539%)	0.091	(26%)	0.16	0.57	7.21	11.70	(119%)	12.64	37.35
343	O-p0	4.15	(326%)	0.092	(27%)	0.15	0.47	5.12	9.69	(82%)	10.58	28.75
	P-dist	2.02	(107%)	0.085	(17%)	0.05	0.23	1.93	7.12	(33%)	7.44	15.20
	O-dist	1.36	(39%)	0.082	(12%)	0.05	0.12	1.40	6.26	(17%)	6.58	12.36
	non-res.	1.72		0.085					6.82			
	P-p0	10.01	(482%)	0.096	(13%)	0.20	1.28	10.68	15.75	(131%)	16.92	54.25
1000	O-p0	7.49	(335%)	0.092	(8%)	0.18	0.66	8.54	12.99	(90%)	14.09	43.07
	P-dist	2.50	(45%)	0.094	(10%)	0.06	0.53	2.55	8.12	(19%)	8.46	19.07
	O-dist	2.41	(40%)	0.089	(4%)	0.06	0.36	2.50	7.73	(13%)	8.08	18.01

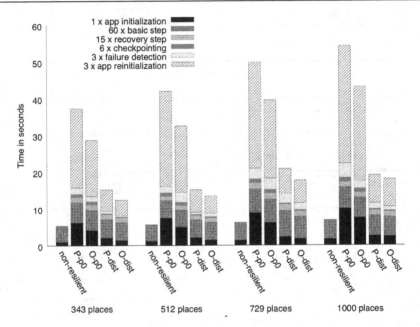

Fig. 7. LULESH weak scaling performance (1 core per place; this application requires a perfect cube number of places)

The computational pattern of LULESH is widely represented in the HPC domain. Overall, the optimistic finish protocol is successful in reducing the resilience overhead of the application in failure-free and failure scenarios. The frequent use of concurrent finish scopes demonstrates the scalability advantage of the distributed finish store.

11   Conclusion

We described *optimistic finish*, a resilient message-optimal termination detection protocol for the productive task model, async-finish. By reducing the signals required for tracking tasks and finish scopes, our protocol significantly reduces the resilience overhead of overly decomposed parallel computations and enables them to reliably recover from failures.

Acknowledgements. We would like to thank David Grove and Olivier Tardieu of IBM T. J. Watson Research Center and Peter Strazdins of the Australian National University for their valuable comments on this work. The research used resources from the National Computational Infrastructure and NECTAR cloud, which are supported by the Australian Government.

References

1. Bland, W., Bouteiller, A., Herault, T., Hursey, J., Bosilca, G., Dongarra, J.J.: An evaluation of user-level failure mitigation support in MPI. In: Träff, J.L., Benkner, S., Dongarra, J.J. (eds.) EuroMPI 2012. LNCS, vol. 7490, pp. 193–203. Springer, Heidelberg (2012). https://doi.org/10.1007/978-3-642-33518-1_24
2. Blumofe, R.D., Leiserson, C.E.: Scheduling multithreaded computations by work stealing. J. ACM **46**(5), 720–748 (1999)
3. Cunningham, D., et al.: Resilient X10: efficient failure-aware programming. In: ACM SIGPLAN Symposium on Principles and Practice of Parallel Programming (PPoPP), pp. 67–80 (2014)
4. Dijkstra, E.W., Scholten, C.S.: Termination detection for diffusing computations. Inf. Process. Lett. **11**(1), 1–4 (1980)
5. Kestor, G., Krishnamoorthy, S., Ma, W.: Localized fault recovery for nested fork-join programs. In: 2017 IEEE International Parallel and Distributed Processing Symposium (IPDPS), pp. 397–408. IEEE (2017)
6. Lai, T.H., Wu, L.F.: An (n-1)-resilient algorithm for distributed termination detection. IEEE Trans. Parallel Distrib. Syst. **6**(1), 63–78 (1995)
7. Lifflander, J., Miller, P., Kale, L.: Adoption protocols for fanout-optimal fault-tolerant termination detection. In: ACM SIGPLAN Symposium on Principles and Practice of Parallel Programming (PPoPP). ACM (2013)
8. Milthorpe, J., Grove, D., Herta, B., Tardieu, O.: Exploring the APGAS programming model using the LULESH proxy application. Technical report, RC25555, IBM Research (2015)
9. Stewart, R., Maier, P., Trinder, P.: Transparent fault tolerance for scalable functional computation. J. Funct. Program. **26** (2016)
10. The TLA Home Page. http://lamport.azurewebsites.net/tla/tla.html
11. TLA+ specification of the optimistic finish protocol and the replication protocol. https://github.com/shamouda/x10-formal-spec

Global Task Data-Dependencies in PGAS Applications

Joseph Schuchart[(✉)] and José Gracia

High Performance Computing Center Stuttgart (HLRS),
Nobelstraße 19, 70569 Stuttgart, Germany
{schuchart,gracia}@hlrs.de

Abstract. Recent years have seen the emergence of two independent programming models challenging the traditional two-tier combination of message passing and thread-level work-sharing: partitioned global address space (PGAS) and task-based concurrency. In the PGAS programming model, synchronization and communication between processes are decoupled, providing significant potential for reducing communication overhead. At the same time, task-based programming allows to exploit a large degree of shared-memory concurrency. The inherent lack of fine-grained synchronization in PGAS can be addressed through fine-grained task synchronization across process boundaries. In this work, we propose the use of task data dependencies describing the data-flow in the global address space to synchronize the execution of tasks created in parallel on multiple processes. We present a description of the global data dependencies, describe the necessary interactions between the distributed scheduler instances required to handle them, and discuss our implementation in the context of the DASH C++ PGAS framework. We evaluate our approach using the Blocked Cholesky Factorization and the LULESH proxy app, demonstrating the feasibility and scalability of our approach.

Keywords: Parallel programming · PGAS · Task parallelism · RMA

1 Introduction

The decoupling of communication and synchronization in the partitioned global address space (PGAS) programming model allows applications to better exploit hardware capabilities of modern high-performance networks and potentially

We gratefully acknowledge funding by the German Research Foundation (DFG) through the German Priority Programme 1648 Software for Exascale Computing (SPPEXA) in the SmartDASH project and would like to thank all members of the DASH team. We would like to thank the members of the Innovative Computing Lab at the University of Tennessee, Knoxville for their support on PaRSEC.
Joseph Schuchart is a doctoral student at the University of Stuttgart and the main author, claiming exclusive authorship of the design and implementation of the API and distributed scheduler as well as leading authorship of the global task dependency design, the evaluation scenario selection, and interpretation of experimental results.

ⓒ Springer Nature Switzerland AG 2019
M. Weiland et al. (Eds.): ISC High Performance 2019, LNCS 11501, pp. 312–329, 2019.
https://doi.org/10.1007/978-3-030-20656-7_16

increase scalability [2,11,33]. However, consistent states are required to reliably exchange data across process boundaries, which require some form of interprocess synchronization. The simplest forms of synchronization are point-to-point messages and collective operations such as barriers. However, the former break with the concepts of a one-sided programming model while the latter are coarse-granular with a high potential for synchronization slack. Thus, the need for fine-grained synchronization in a one-sided programming model is imminent.

The decomposition of a computational problem into packages of work with well-defined inputs and outputs in the form of *tasks* allows the application to expose a high degree of concurrency to a runtime system and are better suited than traditional work-sharing constructs to exploit ubiquitous multi- and many-core shared-memory systems [7]. Based on the data-flow between tasks, a task graph can be constructed by the runtime system and used to maximize parallelism while ensuring a correct execution order of tasks. The data-flow between tasks can be detected automatically or provided by the user, either in the form of explicit channels between tasks, e.g., C++11 *futures* and *continuations*, or implicitly the through the definition of data dependencies as found in OpenMP [20].

Both approaches have been used to synchronize the execution of tasks in distributed parallel applications, e.g., through the construction of the global task graph in each process or by relying on forms of explicit signals to ensure correct execution order. A detailed discussion of related work is provided in Sect. 3.

In this paper, we propose to employ user-provided descriptions of data-dependencies between tasks in the global address space to ensure correct ordering of global memory accesses within these tasks. Processes only explicitly discover a trimmed task graph, i.e., the tasks they will later execute, while the underlying runtime system automatically discovers and handles edges in the graph that cut across process boundaries. This forms a strictly one-sided task-based programming model that preserves locality awareness. We describe the mechanics of the task graph discovery and necessary scheduler interactions in Sect. 4 before presenting an implementation of our approach in the context of the DASH PGAS abstraction in Sect. 5, which is evaluated using micro benchmarks, the Blocked Cholesky Factorization, and the Lulesh proxy app in Sect. 6, demonstrating both competitive performance and scalability.

2   Background and Motivation

The DASH PGAS abstraction is based entirely on C++14 and thus does not rely on any specific compiler to provide distributed data structures and parallel algorithms working on them. The set of distributed data structures is comprised of both static containers such as one- and multi-dimensional arrays as well as dynamic data structures, e.g., unordered maps and lists. Data access to the elements can be performed similar to containers in the C++ standard template library (STL) such as `std::vector`, including overloaded array subscript operators for random access as well as global and local iterators. A detailed introduction to DASH can be found in [10].

The data distribution in containers is handled by DASH. The user specifies the size of each dimension in a multi-dimensional array together with the desired block distribution pattern and the set of processes across which the container is allocated, called *teams* of *units* in DASH. Units own both private local memory and a portion of the global memory that is accessible by other units. Containers provide locality-aware access methods, allowing units to iterate either over a global range or a range of their local portion, including access through native pointers. The overarching *owner-computes principle* ensures that computation is efficient and global data access is reduced to a minimum.

RMA access primitives such as blocking and non-blocking put and get operations are implemented based on MPI-3 RMA primitives [24,34].

Although previous work has focused on reducing the intra-node communication latency between DASH units by avoiding calls into the MPI library, the data transfer latencies cannot be neglected. For performance critical code regions, performing computation on local data through native pointers is inevitable, requiring (bulk) data exchange between units. Hence, shared-memory parallelism is a promising approach to reducing the amount of data to be communicated across process boundaries by exploiting ubiquitous multi- and many-core architectures to operate on shared data.

An approach to task-based parallelization should be well integrated with the underlying PGAS environment to provide both thread-based parallelization and fine-grained synchronization at a global scale. Following the owner-computes principle and to retain the flexibility of the underlying language, units should only be required to discover the local portion of the global task graph, as depicted in Fig. 1. Since all communication between tasks across process boundaries happens through the distributed DASH containers, the data-flow should be described through dependencies in the global memory space and no additional explicit synchronization and communication channels should be required.

3 Related Work

The Asynchronous PGAS (APGAS) model breaks with the traditional SPMD execution model by reducing the set of initially running processes to a single *place* that spawns tasks using (recursive) `async` statements using remote task invocation [23]. The tasks can be synchronized using `atomic` and `finish` statements. Implementations of APGAS are X10 [8] as well as UPC and Habanero-UPC++ [17].

Several task-based parallel programming models start from a single thread of execution and leave the decision of the place of execution to the scheduler, hiding the locality information from the user. The Chapel language has taken a similar approach using `begin` and `cobegin` to create tasks [6]. In addition, Chapel offers synchronization variables to guard reads and writes to (globally) shared variables for simple producer-consumer patterns. The Charm++ programming system provides a distributed tasking system, which supports the migration of tasks between processes in order to dynamically balance the parallel execution [15].

The Regent project has created a language that is a front-end to the Legion hierarchical data partitioning system and is aiming at extracting distributed task parallelism from a sequential program description [3, 28]. The HPX programming system is the main implementation of a direct global synchronization scheme in which futures are used for both synchronization and communication between tasks in an *active global address space* [14].

Several proposals have been made for unidirectional signaling of data availability. AsyncShmem is built on top of OpenShmem to facilitate distributed task synchronization that allows tasks to wait for state change in the global address space [12]. Notified Access proposed in [4] provides a one-directional notification scheme that can be used to notify the target of an MPI-3 RMA operation about an access but operates on the granularity of a process-wide window and does not help in synchronizing local writes and remote reads. Similarly, CoEvents introduced in Fortran 2015 provide a one-directional signaling scheme, e.g., to signal the availability of data or the completion of read operations [18]. In all cases, unidirectional signaling may require significant efforts by the user to implement complex task synchronization schemes in the global memory space.

The XcalableMP programming model supports tasklets that are synchronized through data dependencies locally and through tags and process information remotely, forming a two-tier two-sided synchronization scheme that is directly mapped onto MPI two-sided communication and OpenMP statements, effectively mimicking MPI message semantics [31].

Several approaches discover the full global task graph on each process to infer the global task graph, including QARK-D [32] and PaRSEC DTD [13], which uses affinity tags provided by the user to determine the place of execution for a task. PaRSEC traditionally uses parameterized task graphs that are generated from a high-level language and does not require dynamic discovery of tasks to detect both local and global dependencies [5]. The StarPU task-system provides support for both global task graph discovery (*sequential task flow*, STF) to automatically infer inter-process dependencies as well as the use of explicit MPI send and receive tasks [1].

Several shared memory tasking libraries exist, including Intel Thread Building Blocks [21] and Cilk-Plus [22], none of which provide a way to express data dependencies. The SuperGlue tasking library [30] offers a C++ interface to define data dependencies between tasks that are automatically versioned to perform the dependency matching.

The OmpSs programming model has been the breeding bed of the tasking approach in OpenMP [9]. Efforts have been made to automatically hide communication by integrating support for two-sided MPI communication in OmpSs [19] but that approach is not applicable to the PGAS programming model since it lacks the inherent synchronization of messages. The ClusterSs approach provides a centralized distributed task-based execution based on the APGAS model [29].

To the best of our knowledge, no previous work has attempted to use user-provided data dependencies to synchronize distributed locality-aware task creation and execution in a PGAS programming environment.

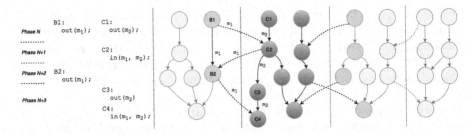

Fig. 1. Distributed task graph with the local portion to be discovered by the process in the center (green) and dependencies across process boundaries to be communicated by the scheduler (dashed lines, blue tasks). The scheduler in the center is unaware of the gray tasks and their dependencies. Phases are used to reliably find dependent tasks across process boundaries, e.g., B1→C2. (Color figure online)

4 Global Task Data Dependencies

In the global tasking model we propose, the main threads of each process execute the application's main routine and dynamically create tasks that will be executed by a set of worker threads and the main thread itself, i.e., there are no explicit parallel regions. A global virtual root task is used as a parent task for the tasks created in the main thread of execution. Tasks themselves may create tasks that are added to the local pool of runnable tasks once their dependencies have been satisfied. However, dependencies may only be used to synchronize sibling tasks, i.e., tasks that have the same parent task. As a consequence, only tasks created by the main threads of execution may be synchronized across process boundaries.

A task consists of an *action* to be executed and a set of *dependency definitions*. A data dependency definition in the global task dependency model includes a *dependency type* $k \in \{in, out\}$, and a reference to a *memory location* in the local or global memory space. Due to the unsynchronized nature of the parallel task creation on multiple processes, we cannot derive a partial order in which the tasks are created. Thus, dependencies reaching across process boundaries could not be reliably matched if tasks from different processes have dependencies on the same global memory location, e.g., B1→C2 and B3→C4 in Fig. 1.

In order to derive this partial ordering and to reliably identify dependent tasks, we extend the task model with the notion of a *phase* $\phi \in \mathbb{N}$, in which tasks and their dependencies are created and which provide a global partial ordering among dependency definitions. The concept of phases has been inspired by the phases that are spawned by global fence or barrier synchronization, which guarantee happens-before relations between global memory accesses and thus the existence of a coherent global state, i.e., all operations *before* the barrier have completed and it is safe to execute new operations that depend on them. Naturally, a blocking barrier across all processes is not desirable in an asynchronous execution model. Instead, task phases model a global state that is guaranteed to be synchronized across processes without any actual communication.

Using phases, the matching of dependencies across process boundaries is done using the following set of rules. Here, *local dependencies* reference a memory location in the local memory space of the process on which they were created while *remote dependencies* reference a memory location in the portion of the global memory space owned by a different process. If a dependency D_1 defined by a task T_1 *matches* another dependency D_2 defined by a task T_2 then the execution of T_2 has to be postponed until after the completion of T_1, noted as T1→T2 below.

$\mathbf{R_1}$: Dependencies only match between sibling tasks.

$\mathbf{R_2}$: Dependencies only match if they reference the same memory location.

$\mathbf{R_3}$: *Input dependencies* match the previous output dependency (RAW dependencies, e.g., C1→C2 in Fig. 1).

$\mathbf{R_4}$: *Output dependencies* match all previous input dependencies up to and including the previous output dependency (WAR and WAW dependencies, e.g., B1→B2 and C2→B2 in Fig. 1).

$\mathbf{R_5}$: *Local dependencies* match local dependencies regardless of the phase (e.g., C3→C4 in Fig. 1).

$\mathbf{R_6}$: *Output dependencies* reside in the phase in which they were specified (e.g., B1 resides in phase N in Fig. 1).

$\mathbf{R_7}$: *Remote input dependencies* match the last output dependency in any previous phase (e.g., C2 in phase $N + 1$ depends on B1 in phase N in Fig. 1).

$\mathbf{R_8}$: *Matching remote dependencies* may not occur in the same phase. For example, the definition of B2 and C2 in the same phase would be erroneous.

These rules allow for the coordination of the execution of tasks created in parallel. Rules R_1–R_4 reflect the dependency model of OpenMP; rules R_4–R_8 are necessary to ensure correct synchronization across process boundaries. As depicted in Fig. 1, phases may contain an arbitrary number of local dependencies and are only required for the matching of remote dependencies. In contrast to using communicating barriers for synchronization, the schedulers can leverage the knowledge about dependencies and phases to detect conflicting global dependencies or missing synchronization thanks to rule R_8. Within a phase, multiple matching dependencies may exist (rule R_5) and the last matching output dependencies is considered the dominant dependency for that particular phase, as implied by rule R_4.

4.1   Creating the Global Task Graph

As described above, the main application threads of each process discover tasks that will eventually be executed locally. The lack of a global view on the task graph requires the detection of edges between tasks reaching across process boundaries (dashed lines in Fig. 1). This is done by the individual scheduler instances exchanging information on remote dependencies and matching them with dependencies of local and other remote tasks. Each process is responsible for handling the dependencies referencing the memory it owns.

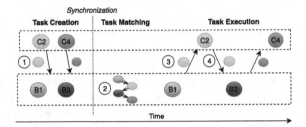

Fig. 2. Interaction of two scheduler instances required during creation, matching, and execution of tasks with dependencies across process boundaries, based on the example in Fig. 1.

While creating the tasks, the scheduler populates the local task graph and communicates any remote dependencies to the scheduler owning the referenced global memory location (① in Fig. 2). Tasks in the first phase can be executed immediately, provided all local dependencies have been satisfied. The execution of tasks in later phases has to be deferred until their dependencies have been handled by the responsible scheduler. The matching is performed in a *task matching step* (② in Fig. 2), which extends the local task graph with the edges that reach across process boundaries based on the global memory owned. Once all edges have been established, all phases leading up to the current phase are released for execution by the worker threads.

Overall, each matching step requires one global collective synchronization operations among the main threads to ensure a consistent global state, i.e., all dependencies up to and including the current phase have been communicated. Matching typically occurs repeatedly during the discovery of the task graph and may be triggered by a phase transition. The matching interval, i.e., the number of phase transitions between matching steps, is variable and a throttling mechanism allows to limit the number of active phases, thus limiting the number of tasks instantiated at any point in time.

4.2   Executing the Global Task Graph

The execution of the task graph happens continuously based on the phases that have been released for execution. Thus, task creation and matching may be overlapped with the execution of tasks by the worker threads. As soon as a task completes its execution, all local dependencies will be released and the tasks are eventually queued for execution as soon as all dependencies have been satisfied. Remote dependencies are released through a signal to the remote scheduler owning the released task (③ in Fig. 2), which subsequently signals the completion of the released task to the scheduler owning the referenced memory location (④ in Fig. 2). Tasks may access local and global memory at any time during their execution.

5   Implementation

We have implemented the global task data dependency model described in Sect. 4 within DASH. At the heart of the implementation are scheduler instances managing the creation and execution of tasks at the individual processes and collaboratively coordinate their execution. Each scheduler manages a thread-pool comprised of a configurable number of POSIX threads.

Schedulers communicate through an active messages queue that is based on MPI and handles the communication completely transparent to the user. A progress thread may be used in the background to handle the communication to (i) ensure timely processing, and (ii) mitigate the overhead of thread-parallel access of the MPI library by funneling messages through it. Alternatively, worker threads may periodically poll the message queue to handle dependency releases. In both cases, DASH requires support for MPI_THREAD_MULTIPLE as tasks may access global memory at any time.

We have implemented support for rescheduling (or cyclic [26]) task-yield and allow tasks to wait for the completion of communication operations without active polling. Tasks may be canceled together with all remaining tasks, e.g., after checking for a termination criterion, either starting from a single process that propagates the cancellation signal or collectively on all processes. Tasks are scheduled in a co-operative manner, i.e., their execution is not interrupted unless they enter a task scheduling point such as yield, a task creation operation, or any other task cancellation point.

In addition to in and out dependencies, DASH also provides a copyin dependency, which constitutes an input dependency that copies the referenced memory range into a user-provided buffer. This transfer can be performed by either one-sided (get) or two-sided communication (send-recv). For the latter, a task together with a remote input dependency is injected at the process owning the referenced memory that triggers a send operation as soon as the dependency has been satisfied. This is especially useful on platforms that do not support remote direct memory access (RDMA) and thus show poor performance when using MPI RMA operations, all while retaining the one-sided programming model. Nevertheless, regular input dependencies are useful in cases where the target memory is non-contiguous or the dependency serves as a sentinel for more complex global memory accesses.

5.1   Example Code

Listing 1.1 shows the implementation of the Blocked Cholesky Factorization, which factorizes a $N \times N$ symmetric positive definite matrix A into its upper triangular matrix U and its transpose, i.e., $A = UU^*$.

We implemented dash::async, which creates a task that executes the provided action (C++ std::function or lambda) once all dependencies specified through dash::out, dash::in, or dash::copyin are satisfied. The specification of phases is done through calls to dash::async_fence (lines 9, 17, and 36).

```
 1  dash::Matrix<2, double> matrix{N, N, dash::TILE(NB),dash::TILE(NB)};
 2
 3  for (int k = 0; k < num_blocks; ++k) {
 4      if (mat.block(k,k).is_local()) {
 5          dash::async([&](){ potrf(matrix.block(k,k)); },
 6              dash::out(mat.block(k,k)));
 7      }
 8
 9      dash::async_fence(); // <- advance to next phase
10      for (int i = k+1; i < num_blocks; ++i)
11          if (mat.block(k,i).is_local())
12              dash::async([&](){
13                  trsm(cache[k], matrix.block(k,i)); },
14                  dash::copyin(mat.block(k,k), cache[k]),
15                  dash::out(mat.block(k,i)));
16
17      dash::async_fence(); // <- advance to next phase
18      for (int i = k+1; i < num_blocks; ++i) {
19          for (int j = k+1; j < i; ++j) {
20              if (mat.block(j,i).is_local()) {
21                  dash::async([&](){
22                      gemm(cache[i], cache[j], mat.block(j,i)); },
23                      dash::copyin(mat.block(k,i), cache[i]),
24                      dash::copyin(mat.block(k,j), cache[j]),
25                      dash::out(mat.block(j,i)));
26              }
27          }
28
29          if (mat.block(i,i).is_local()) {
30              dash::async([&](){
31                  syrk(cache[i], mat.block(i,i)); },
32                  dash::copyin(mat.block(k,i), cache[i]),
33                  dash::out(mat.block(i,i)));
34          }
35      }
36      dash::async_fence();  // <- advance to next phase
37  }
38  dash::complete(); // <- wait for all tasks to execute
```

Listing 1.1. Implementation of Blocked Cholesky Factorization using global task data dependencies in DASH. Some optimizations omitted for clarity.

In the example listing, each process creates only the tasks that output local blocks, e.g., factorization of a block (potrf) is only performed on the unit that owns the block (lines 4–7). The tasks that require the factorized block as input to solve the triangular matrix on the remaining blocks of the current row (trsm, lines 10–15) specify a copyin dependency and will only start executing as soon as the corresponding potrf task completed and the block has been copied into the local user-provided buffer (cache[k]). The scheduler will make sure that blocks are copied only once even if multiple tasks require them as input. The same pattern is used for the tasks executing the gemm and syrk operations.

5.2 Range-Based Task and Dependency Creation

Similarly to the OpenMP taskloop construct, DASH also offers a construct for creating tasks across an input range and allows to define dependencies for the individual tasks. As depicted in Listing 1.2, the dash::taskloop function takes an input range [*begin, end*), optionally a chunk-size (maximum number of elements assigned to each task, line 5) or the number of tasks to be created, and an action to be executed. In addition to the action each task performs on the sub-range assigned (lines 7–9), the user may also provide a function generating the dependencies for each task by assigning them to an insert iterator (lines 11–14). This allows users to synchronize the generated tasks with tasks generated by other task creation constructs.

```
dash::Array<int> arr(N);

if (dash::myid() == 0) {
  dash::taskloop(
    arr.begin(), arr.end(), dash::chunk_size(10),
    // task action
    [&] (auto begin, auto end) {
      // perform action on elements in [begin, end)
    },
    // generate out dependencies on elements in [begin, end)
    [&] (auto begin, auto end, auto deps) {
      for (auto it = begin; it != end; ++it)
        *deps = dash::out(it);
    });
}
```

Listing 1.2. Example of using the `dash::taskloop` in combination with a dependency generator.

6   Experimental Evaluation

We performed our measurements on two different systems: a Cray XC40 (Hazel Hen) installed at HLRS in Stuttgart, Germany, and the Primergy CX1640 M1 system Oakforest-PACS installed at the University of Tsukuba, Japan. The details are listed in Table 1. All codes have been compiled using the Intel compiler 18.0.1 and all threads have been pinned to their respective core using the hwloc library. For OpenMP codes, thread binding was controlled through the environment variable setting KMP_AFFINITY=granularity=fine,balanced.

The numbers presented reflect an average of five repetitions performed on the same set of nodes.

6.1   Micro-benchmarks

Figure 3 displays the results of measuring the overhead of creating and executing DASH tasks with different numbers of dependencies. The measurements were taken using one process on each of the 16 nodes and a single thread per process in order to include both task creation and execution. We measured the creation of 100,000 tasks with different dependency patterns, ranging from zero to 32 dependencies on distinct (but repeating) memory locations.

Table 1. System configurations used. On all systems, the Intel compiler 18.0.1 and MKL 2018.1 were used for compilation.

System	CPU	Network	MPI
Cray XC40 (Hazel Hen)	Intel Xeon E5-2680 v3 (2x12C, 2.5 GHz)	Cray Aries	Open MPI 4.0.0
Oakforest-PACS	Intel Xeon Phi 7250 (68C, 1.4 GHz)	OmniPath	Intel MPI 18.2

Local Output Dependencies. In the case of `local-out`, each task is created with the respective number of output dependencies on different local memory locations, effectively serializing their execution. On the Cray system, the overhead ranges from $0.67\,\mu s$ for a task with no dependency over $1.4\,\mu s$ for a single dependency to $8\,\mu s$ for 32 local dependencies. This puts our implementation in the range of common OpenMP implementations, albeit slightly above both Clang and GCC but below research implementations such as OmpSs [25].

Given the low single-core performance of the KNL system, the overhead for local task dependencies is significantly higher on Oakforest-PACS. Handling a task with a single dependency takes about $5\,\mu s$, of which $2\,\mu s$ are required for task creation and execution, i.e., the handling of the dependency requires about $3\,\mu s$. For 32 local dependencies, the overhead is found at $29\,\mu s$ per task.

Single Target Remote Input Dependencies. In the `remote-in-single` benchmark, a single process creates tasks with input dependencies pointing to unique memory locations on all other remote processes. This benchmark reflects the minimum overhead involved in exchanging information on remote dependencies, their processing on the remote side, and the signaling of their release. We measured the overhead when running either with or without a communication thread processing active messages in the background, as described in Sect. 5. As to be expected, the overhead is higher than for local dependencies, ranging from $2.5\,\mu s$ for a single dependency to up to $34\,\mu s$ for 32 remote input dependencies on the Cray system. With the communication thread enabled, the overhead for a task with 32 remote input dependencies drops to $25\,\mu s$ since the communication is not handled by the thread creating the tasks.

On Oakforest-PACS, the latency rises up to $530\,\mu s$ for 32 remote input dependencies, which is significantly higher than on the Cray system. We attribute this to both the slower serial core performance as well as the OmniPath network, which provides less sophisticated hardware features to support MPI communication than the Aries fabric. However, with the communication thread in the background, the overhead drops to $89\,\mu s$, which constitutes only a factor of three compared to the local dependencies.

Since only a single process is creating tasks with remote dependencies, the target processes of these dependencies can instantly handle the dependencies. Hence, the overhead mainly stems from the inter-scheduler communication.

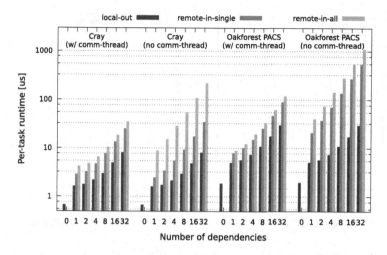

Fig. 3. Average overhead for tasks with different numbers of local and remote dependencies running on 16 nodes of different platforms.

Remote Input Dependencies Between All Processes. For the remote-in-all benchmark, all processes create tasks with remote dependencies pointing to all other processes. This benchmark includes the impact of all processes communicating dependencies, which better reflects real applications in which tasks from multiple processes communicate with each other. We observe latencies between 9 μs for a single remote dependency and up to 215 μs for 32 remote input dependencies on the Cray system. In presence of a communication thread, the overhead is at 35 μs, which is still only slightly more than a microsecond per remote dependency.

On Oakforest-PACS, latencies are significantly higher, ranging from 40 μs to 1092 μs. Similar to the previous benchmarks, the overhead drops significantly in case the communication thread is available: 119 μs for a task with 32 remote dependencies.

While these latencies are higher than for local dependencies for large numbers of dependencies, we expect that only a small fraction of tasks in common applications will exhibit such a high number of remote dependencies as the majority of tasks will have dependencies to local tasks. For small numbers of dependencies, the difference between local and remote dependencies is not prohibitively large and within a reasonable range. For applications with large numbers of remotely dependent tasks, e.g., numerical algorithms such as the Blocked Cholesky Factorization described in Sect. 5.1, the use of a communication thread is highly recommended.

6.2 Blocked Cholesky Factorization

We have measured the performance of the Blocked Cholesky Factorization discussed in Sect. 5.1. Blocks are 2D-cyclically distributed and tasks consume both remote and local blocks to compute local blocks, adhering to the *owner-computes principle*.

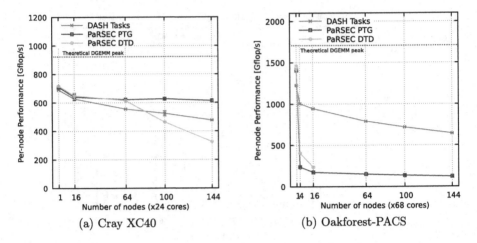

(a) Cray XC40   (b) Oakforest-PACS

Fig. 4. Per-node weak-scaling performance of Blocked Cholesky Factorization of a matrix with leading dimension $N = 25k/node$ and block size $NB = 320$ (higher is better). (DTD runs on Oakforest PACS at scale did not complete within a reasonable time.)

We compare our implementation against both PaRSEC's parameterized task graph (PTG) and dynamic task discovery (DTD) implementations. Other related approaches do not provide comparable scalability: For example, XcalableMP translates tasklets into OpenMP tasks and relies on MPI two-sided communication for inter-process task synchronization, a technique that has been show to not be portable [26]. We were unable to successfully collect measurements for StarPU/Chameleon on both machines.

We performed weak-scaling experiments of the Blocked Cholesky Factorization using matrices with a leading dimension of 25k double precision elements per node, the results of which are depicted in Fig. 4. Both in PaRSEC and DASH, the background communication thread was pinned to a dedicated core, which has proven to yield superior performance. The DASH schedulers perform a matching step every 100 phases, i.e., every 33 iterations of the outermost loop, and the phase throttling was set to 400 simultaneously active phases. s On the Cray system PaRSEC PTG clearly outperforms both DASH ($\approx$20% on 144 nodes) and DTD, which is expected as PTG does not incur the overhead of dynamic task discovery. The dynamic discovery of the global task graph in DTD appears to inhibit the scalability of the benchmark. We tested different block-sizes and found that $NB = 320$ elements yield the best performance for all implementations compared to $NB = 256$ and $NB = 512$.

The `copyin` dependency discussed in Sect. 5 yields better performance using one-sided `get` on the Cray system. However, we found that the Intel MPI implementation does not support the RDMA capabilities of the Omni-Path fabric on Oakforest-PACS, which required the use of two-sided communication in the background. The scalability characteristics of DASH on Oakforest-PACS are similar to the behavior observed on the Cray system. Unfortunately, we were unable to get anywhere near the expected performance for both PTG and DTD at scale. This is part of an ongoing investigation.

6.3 LULESH

To demonstrate the scalability of our approach, we ported the Livermore Unstructured Lagrangian Explicit Shock Hydrodynamics proxy application (LU-LESH [16]) to use DASH in combination with global task dependencies.

We started by replacing the OpenMP work-sharing constructs in the original code of LULESH 2.03 with `dash::taskloop` constructs described in Sect. 5.2. Each task carries a set of dependencies that allows the scheduler to chain chunks of multiple consecutive task-loops to improve cache locality.

An important observation to make is that while traditional work-sharing constructs tend to be well balanced across threads (in the absence of external influence factors such as NUMA effects), the scheduling of tasks created by taskloops is less predictable as some worker threads may be busy executing other tasks. Moreover, in a single iteration LULESH performs computation on the nodes of the unstructured grid, followed by the elements described by the nodes, and regions of elements, each containing multiple parallel loops. While it may be possible to overlap these different computations, we have not attempted to achieve this but instead introduced artificial synchronization between these levels, e.g., to make sure that all tasks operating on the nodes of the grid are completed before starting computation on the elements formed by them. In some cases, the resulting synchronization slack may be hidden by partially overlapping iterations, e.g., force-computation on the nodes may commence before the timestep width for the next iteration has been determined.

In order to achieve proper load-balancing, we control the number of tasks created by the task-loops as described in Sect. 5.2. We found that the number of threads times a factor of five yields the best performance in our experiments. However, this factor may be dependent on the architecture and the problem size.

LULESH employs a 28-point stencil pattern to exchange data with neighboring processes in a 3D grid. We replaced the MPI two-sided communication with global memory arrays into which processes pack the boundary data to be communicated to other processes (similar to the MPI version). The data is then read from global memory on the remote side and unpacked to update the halo regions. Both packing and unpacking have been implemented as tasks—one for each neighbor—with remote dependencies between the packing and unpacking tasks. Thus, the halo updates may be performed as soon as the respective neighbor has completed packing its boundary data relevant for a particular process.

The runtimes of both implementations and the relative speedup are depicted in Fig. 5, which shows the weak-scaling behavior on the Cray XC40 up to 1000 nodes with one process per node and 24 threads per process plus a floating progress thread. A matching step was performed every 20 phases in DASH, which

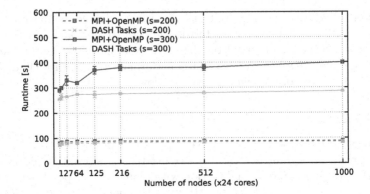

Fig. 5. Weak-scaling runtime and speedup of DASH relative to the reference implementation of the LULESH benchmark with a domain size of 200^3 and 300^3 elements per node at 100 iterations on the Cray XC40 (lower is better).

caused a matching to be performed roughly every four timesteps as each iteration required six phase transitions, one before and one after each data exchange. The phase throttling was set to 60, i.e., tasks for ten consecutive iterations were continuously instantiated simultaneously.

For 300^3 elements per node, the DASH implementation exhibits an increase in runtime of 4% between 64 and 1000 nodes, yielding almost perfect weak scaling in that range. The OpenMP implementation, in contrast, exhibits an increase of 22% in the same range. At this size, we observed a speedup of 25% between the OpenMP and DASH implementation on 1000 nodes, which we attribute to the improved cache utilization as well as partial overlapping of communication and computation of consecutive timesteps in the task-based parallelization.

The results are more stable for $s = 200$. Here, the observed speedup at 1000 nodes of DASH compared to OpenMP is only 3.8% and the overall behavior is more homogeneous. For even lower problem sizes (not displayed), we have observed that the task management overhead prohibits any gains of the task-based parallelization over OpenMP and might eventually lead to a slow-down. It has been shown in the past that a certain minimum task granularity is required for task-based parallelization schemes [27].

Overall, the results demonstrate the feasibility and scalability of our approach. A uniform way of expressing both local and remote dependencies between tasks in a PGAS application while discovering only the local portion of the task graph can lead to significant performance improvements over traditional work-sharing constructs. The required collective synchronization during the task matching does not inhibit scalability as it can be overlapped with the execution of tasks from already matched phases.

7   Conclusion and Future Work

In this paper, we have proposed a new approach for the synchronization of tasks created in a locality-aware PGAS abstraction in which processes only discover the trimmed task graph, i.e., the local portion they will execute. The global execution order of tasks is determined based on a set of dependency definitions of each task that is specified by the user. Loosely coupled scheduler instances at each process communicate dependency information to avoid central coordination and the requirement for global task graph discovery. The synchronization is decoupled from accesses to the global memory space, retaining the potential for random access in distributed data structures.

We are convinced that global task data dependencies are well suited to synchronize one-sided communication as they rely on the global address space for synchronization and communication instead of using unidirectional synchronization mechanisms, explicit two-sided communication, or remote task invocation for inter-process task synchronization, all while providing a simple way to create complex synchronization patterns. Moreover, our approach does not limit the set of language features allowed while discovering the global task graph, e.g., branches based on data locality are perfectly valid.

Using the LULESH proxy app, we have shown that our approach scales to hundreds of nodes while achieving a significant speedup over the reference implementation for larger problem sizes. While the Blocked Cholesky Factorization shows some noticeable overhead compared to PaRSEC PTG due to the dynamic discovery of the local task graph and the exchange of dependency information, our measurements indicate that our approach yields better scalability than a dynamically discovered global task graph.

Overall, the results presented in this paper are encouraging to further pursue this approach. We plan to investigate the integration with other task-based parallelization libraries, such as OpenMP, to ease the transition from regular MPI+OpenMP applications towards DASH. Moreover, we will investigate the potential for automatic tuning of the task creation threshold and task granularity and will elaborate ways to contextualize the virtual root task to provide multiple concurrency contexts with the ability to synchronize tasks across process boundaries.

References

1. Agullo, E., Aumage, O., Faverge, M., Furmento, N., Pruvost, F., Sergent, M., Thibault, S.P.: Achieving high performance on supercomputers with a sequential task-based programming model. IEEE Trans. Parallel Distrib. Syst. (2018). https://doi.org/10.1109/TPDS.2017.2766064
2. Amarasinghe, S., et al.: Exascale software study: software challenges in extreme scale systems. Technical report, DARPA IPTO, Air Force Research Labs (2009)
3. Bauer, M., Treichler, S., Slaughter, E., Aiken, A.: Legion: expressing locality and independence with logical regions. In: 2012 International Conference for High Performance Computing, Networking, Storage and Analysis (SC), pp. 1–11, November 2012. https://doi.org/10.1109/SC.2012.71

4. Belli, R., Hoefler, T.: Notified access: extending remote memory access programming models for producer-consumer synchronization. In: IEEE International Parallel and Distributed Processing Symposium (IPDPS) (2015)
5. Bosilca, G., Bouteiller, A., Danalis, A., Herault, T., Lemariner, P., Dongarra, J.: Dague: a generic distributed DAG engine for high performance computing, pp. 1151–1158. IEEE, Anchorage (2011)
6. Chamberlain, B.L., Callahan, D., Zima, H.P.: Parallel programmability and the Chapel language. Int. J. High Perform. Comput. Appl. **21**, 291–312 (2007)
7. Chapman, B.M., Eachempati, D., Chandrasekaran, S.: OpenMP. In: Balaji, P. (ed.) Programming Models for Parallel Computing, pp. 281–322. MIT Press, Cambridge (2015)
8. Charles, P., et al.: X10: an object-oriented approach to non-uniform cluster computing. In: ACM Sigplan Notices (2005)
9. Duran, A., et al.: OmpSs: a proposal for programming heterogeneous multi-core architectures. Parallel Process. Lett. (2011). https://doi.org/10.1142/S0129626411000151
10. Fürlinger, K., et al.: DASH: data structures and algorithms with support for hierarchical locality. In: Lopes, L., et al. (eds.) Euro-Par 2014. LNCS, vol. 8806, pp. 542–552. Springer, Cham (2014). https://doi.org/10.1007/978-3-319-14313-2_46
11. Gómez-Iglesias, A., Pekurovsky, D., Hamidouche, K., Zhang, J., Vienne, J.: Porting scientific libraries to PGAS in XSEDE resources: practice and experience. In: Proceedings of the 2015 XSEDE Conference: Scientific Advancements Enabled by Enhanced Cyberinfrastructure, XSEDE 2015. ACM (2015)
12. Grossman, M., Kumar, V., Budimlic, Z., Sarkar, V.: Integrating asynchronous task parallelism with OpenSHMEM (2016). https://www.cs.rice.edu/~zoran/Publications_files/asyncshmem2016.pdf
13. Hoque, R., Herault, T., Bosilca, G., Dongarra, J.: Dynamic task discovery in parsec: a data-flow task-based runtime. In: Proceedings of the 8th Workshop on Latest Advances in Scalable Algorithms for Large-Scale Systems, ScalA 2017. ACM (2017). https://doi.org/10.1145/3148226.3148233
14. Kaiser, H., Heller, T., Adelstein-Lelbach, B., Serio, A., Fey, D.: HPX: a task based programming model in a global address space. In: PGAS 2014. ACM (2014). http://doi.acm.org/10.1145/2676870.2676883
15. Kalé, L., Krishnan, S.: CHARM++: a portable concurrent object oriented system based on C++. In: Proceedings of OOPSLA 1993 (1993)
16. Karlin, I., Keasler, J., Neely, R.: Lulesh 2.0 updates and changes. Technical report LLNL-TR-641973 (2013)
17. Kumar, V., Zheng, Y., Cavé, V., Budimlić, Z., Sarkar, V.: HabaneroUPC++: a compiler-free PGAS library. In: Proceedings of the 8th International Conference on Partitioned Global Address Space Programming Models, PGAS 2014. ACM (2014). https://doi.org/10.1145/2676870.2676879
18. Long, B.: Additional parallel features in fortran. SIGPLAN Fortran Forum, 16–23, July 2016. https://doi.org/10.1145/2980025.2980027
19. Marjanović, V., Labarta, J., Ayguadé, E., Valero, M.: Overlapping communication and computation by using a hybrid MPI/SMPSs approach. In: Proceedings of the 24th ACM International Conference on Supercomputing, ICS 2010. ACM (2010). http://doi.acm.org/10.1145/1810085.1810091
20. OpenMP Architecture Review Board: OpenMP Application Programming Interface, Version 4.5 (2015). http://www.openmp.org/mp-documents/openmp-4.5.pdf
21. Reinders, J.: Intel threading Building Blocks: Outfitting C++ for Multicore Processor Parallelism. O'Reilly & Associates, Sebastopol (2007)

22. Robison, A.D.: Composable parallel patterns with Intel Cilk Plus. Comput. Sci. Eng. (2013). https://doi.org/10.1109/MCSE.2013.21
23. Saraswat, V., et al.: The Asynchronous Partitioned Global Address Space Model (2017)
24. Schuchart, J., Kowalewski, R., Fuerlinger, K.: Recent experiences in Using MPI-3 RMA in the DASH PGAS runtime. In: Proceedings of Workshops of HPC Asia, HPC Asia 2018. ACM (2018). https://doi.org/10.1145/3176364.3176367
25. Schuchart, J., Nachtmann, M., Gracia, J.: Patterns for OpenMP task data dependency overhead measurements. In: de Supinski, B.R., Olivier, S.L., Terboven, C., Chapman, B.M., Müller, M.S. (eds.) IWOMP 2017. LNCS, vol. 10468, pp. 156–168. Springer, Cham (2017). https://doi.org/10.1007/978-3-319-65578-9_11
26. Schuchart, J., Tsugane, K., Gracia, J., Sato, M.: The impact of taskyield on the design of tasks communicating through MPI. In: de Supinski, B.R., Valero-Lara, P., Martorell, X., Mateo Bellido, S., Labarta, J. (eds.) IWOMP 2018. LNCS, vol. 11128, pp. 3–17. Springer, Cham (2018). https://doi.org/10.1007/978-3-319-98521-3_1
27. Shudler, S., Calotoiu, A., Hoefler, T., Wolf, F.: Isoefficiency in practice: configuring and understanding the performance of task-based applications. SIGPLAN Not., January 2017. https://doi.org/10.1145/3155284.3018770
28. Slaughter, E., Lee, W., Treichler, S., Bauer, M., Aiken, A.: Regent: a high-productivity programming language for HPC with logical regions. In: SC15: International Conference for High Performance Computing, Networking, Storage and Analysis, pp. 1–12, November 2015. https://doi.org/10.1145/2807591.2807629
29. Tejedor, E., Farreras, M., Grove, D., Badia, R.M., Almasi, G., Labarta, J.: A high-productivity task-based programming model for clusters. Concurr. Comput. Pract. Exp. (2012). https://doi.org/10.1002/cpe.2831
30. Tillenius, M.: SuperGlue: a shared memory framework using data versioning for dependency-aware task-based parallelization. SIAM J. Sci. Comput. (2015). http://epubs.siam.org/doi/10.1137/140989716
31. Tsugane, K., Lee, J., Murai, H., Sato, M.: Multi-tasking execution in PGAS language XcalableMP and communication optimization on many-core clusters. In: Proceedings of the International Conference on High Performance Computing in Asia-Pacific Region. ACM (2018). https://doi.org/10.1145/3149457.3154482
32. YarKhan, A.: Dynamic task execution on shared and distributed memory architectures. Ph.D. thesis (2012)
33. Yelick, K., et al.: Productivity and performance using partitioned global address space languages. In: Proceedings of the 2007 International Workshop on Parallel Symbolic Computation, PASCO 2007. ACM (2007)
34. Zhou, H., Idrees, K., Gracia, J.: Leveraging MPI-3 Shared-memory extensions for efficient PGAS runtime systems. In: Träff, J.L., Hunold, S., Versaci, F. (eds.) Euro-Par 2015. LNCS, vol. 9233, pp. 373–384. Springer, Heidelberg (2015). https://doi.org/10.1007/978-3-662-48096-0_29

Finepoints: Partitioned Multithreaded MPI Communication

Ryan E. Grant[1]([✉]), Matthew G. F. Dosanjh[1], Michael J. Levenhagen[1],
Ron Brightwell[1], and Anthony Skjellum[2]

[1] Sandia National Laboratories, Albuquerque, USA
{regrant,mdosanj,mjleven,rbbrigh}@sandia.gov
[2] University of Tennessee at Chattanooga, Chattanooga, USA
skjellum@utc.edu

Abstract. The MPI multithreading model has been historically difficult to optimize; the interface that it provides for threads was designed as a process-level interface. This model has led to implementations that treat function calls as critical regions and protect them with locks to avoid race conditions. We hypothesize that an interface designed specifically for threads can provide superior performance than current approaches and even outperform single-threaded MPI.

In this paper, we describe a design for partitioned communication in MPI that we call finepoints. First, we assess the existing communication models for MPI two-sided communication and then introduce finepoints as a hybrid of MPI models that has the best features of each existing MPI communication model. In addition, "partitioned communication" created with finepoints leverages new network hardware features that cannot be exploited with current MPI point-to-point semantics, making this new approach both innovative and useful both now and in the future.

To demonstrate the validity of our hypothesis, we implement a finepoints library and show improvements against a state-of-the-art multithreaded optimized Open MPI implementation on a Cray XC40 with an Aries network. Our experiments demonstrate up to a 12× reduction in wait time for completion of send operations. This new model is shown working on a nuclear reactor physics neutron-transport proxy-application, providing up to 26.1% improvement in communication time and up to 4.8% improvement in runtime over the best performing MPI communication mode, single-threaded MPI.

Sandia National Laboratories is a multimission laboratory managed and operated by National Technology and Engineering Solutions of Sandia LLC, a wholly owned subsidiary of Honeywell International Inc. for the U.S. Department of Energy's National Nuclear Security Administration under contract DE-NA0003525. This research was supported by the Exascale Computing Project (17-SC-20-SC), a collaborative effort of the U.S. Department of Energy Office of Science and the National Nuclear Security Administration.

© Springer Nature Switzerland AG 2019
M. Weiland et al. (Eds.): ISC High Performance 2019, LNCS 11501, pp. 330–350, 2019.
https://doi.org/10.1007/978-3-030-20656-7_17

1   Introduction

The Message Passing Interface (MPI) [15] has supported a threaded interface for user applications since 1997. Despite being supported for a long time, MPI multithreading is not widely used today. There are several factors preventing MPI multithreading from widespread use. One factor is that MPI multithreading support remains poorly optimized in some common implementations and their commercial derivatives. Lack of consistency in performance is another major issue preventing widespread use, and this deficiency is understandable: making a highly performant multithreaded MPI library is complex and challenging. Additionally, it can be difficult for thread-based code to interact with MPI in an efficient manner. For these reasons, many hybrid codes today do not allow thread interaction with MPI, opting instead to coordinate to allow a single thread to perform MPI calls. For example, an MPI+OpenMP hybrid code might perform a computation using many threads but still use a single master thread to communicate using MPI.

The MPI threading model treats threads in much the same way as processes. Threads can perform all of the functions available in MPI; however, many codes do not require the full MPI multithreaded support that exists today. Alternative interfaces designed specifically for thread interaction with MPI could be designed to provide easy-to-use semantics and performance benefits over existing MPI interfaces. Performance improvements could be realized by leveraging thread behaviors and isolating the portion of the MPI API that needs to be thread-safe.

Contemporary MPI implementations typically use *pessimistic* serialization to enforce thread safety to MPI calls (*e.g.*, locks), allowing only a single thread to interact within certain MPI critical paths or data (*e.g.*, a given communicator) at a given time. While this restriction may be desirable for a general threading case where the behavior of threads is unknown, it can be problematic for threads that would otherwise not interfere with each other in their participation in a communication. For example, if multiple threads each write to a shared memory buffer using non-overlapping offsets, no interference would occur.

A 2018 survey [2] highlighted application developer concerns with MPI related to the US Department of Energy's Exascale Computing Project. All of the developers not currently using `thread_multiple` cited performance as the reason they were not using it, however, a large majority of those developers (86%) *want* to interact with MPI using multiple threads. Historically, some implementations used a single global lock on the MPI library. However, many implementations have recently moved to locking at a fine granularity. We have used an optimized fine-grain locking MPI for comparison to our proposed MPI threading interface enhancements, *finepoints*, in this work. Finepoints uses lightweight synchronization, requiring only a single atomic for synchronization (which is the minimum synchronization overhead achievable on modern hardware). It also works with emerging hardware to fully offload the threading synchronization overhead. Finepoints is the first solution to offer many of the optimizations that are available to one-sided communication methods in a two-sided model.

In this paper we will detail the design of our proposed solution, finepoints, a partitioned communication interface for MPI. This approach partitions buffers in MPI, allowing threads to contribute individual parts to a single communication operation. We will describe the interface and show the proposed MPI function calls and detail the reasoning behind the design as well as the benefits that the design provides. Next, we will present an implementation of finepoints and evaluate it on a Cray XC40 platform to assess its performance impact. Further, we will detail the changes that we made to two applications to adapt them to use finepoints and show the results of using the interface on a reactor neutron transport proxy application and a finite element code. Finally, we will summarize the results and discuss how these findings relate to the existing work in the area.

This paper makes the following contributions:

- A two-sided, optimizable MPI interface designed specifically for threading/tasking support;
- A design for how finepoints can be fully offloaded to future MPI message matching NIC hardware; and,
- The first finepoints-integrated proxy applications, a reactor neutron transport simulation and a finite element code.

2   Background

The model for multithreading in MPI is simple: threads in a process can access MPI however they wish, using the full interface that is used on a per-process basis in a non-threaded MPI program. There are no modifications to the interface for threads, and all threads share the MPI address (rank) of their parent process. MPI threading modes simply serve to dictate what level of thread-safety is provided by MPI—either MPI_THREAD_MULTIPLE, where all calls are thread safe, or funneled and serialized mode, in which the user is responsible for managing thread-safety with MPI. There is a fourth mode, single, in which threads do not exist. In this paper, we refer to threads as the mechanism by which tasks are run/completed.

MPI provides two main point-to-point interfaces, two-sided send/recv where each message sent matches a receive posted at the target. This results in per-message completion notifications and strong ordering guarantees for messages sent on a given communicator. MPI also provides a one-sided interface called Remote Memory Access (RMA). RMA uses a put/get semantic that can be conceptualized as a remote load/store model. RMA requires that an application explicitly handle synchronization of communication buffers. MPI RMA code typically requires major algorithm changes to use it effectively [14] and its expected use at exascale still remains low (<25% [2]). While work on the RMA model is promising in terms of performance [8,12], the application level code changes required to existing code bases [14] compels exploration of a two-sided model.

The endpoints proposal, which is no longer under consideration by the MPI standardization committee, was an attempt to allow for increased utility for multiple threads (*cf,* [5]). Endpoints addressed threads by assigning a logical

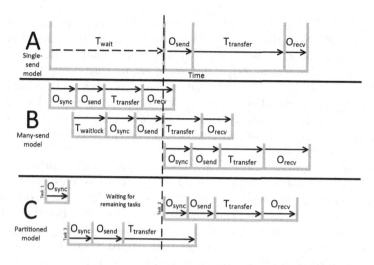

Fig. 1. MPI models for data transmission with multiple tasks/threads. Model A is the traditional single-send approach in an MPI+X applications. Model B is the current multithreaded send-per-thread model. Model C is our proposed partitioned model which leverages the completion model of A and transfer model of B.

address (rank) to each thread or user defined group of threads, enabling per-thread addressability. Endpoints did not fundamentally change the communication model, it only added additional addressability to the existing multithreaded model in MPI. There is no public implementation of MPI endpoints and given its current status with the standards committee, it is unlikely that one will be released in the foreseeable future. Unfortunately, this means that performance comparisons are not possible. However, we can estimate the overheads of Endpoints matching, by emulating it's behavior with a traditional match list implementation that separates traffic by communicator.

2.1 MPI Multithreaded Communication Models

Figure 1 demonstrates the two main threading models used with MPI. Model A shows the single-send (single-threaded) MPI model, where only a single thread calls into MPI, regardless of how many tasks may be used in the non-communication regions of code. There is a time, T_{wait} that is required to wait for all task dependencies on the communication buffer to complete. No communication can happen even if some tasks are ready to send their data. Once all of the data is complete, there is some overhead for issuing the send commands in MPI, O_{send}, after which data is transferred over the network, $T_{transfer}$, and finally some overhead on the receiver-side for matching the message and marking the request as complete, O_{recv}.

Model B demonstrates the many-send model, in which each task sends data as it completes. This results in having no T_{wait} period as data can be sent when it becomes available (all dependencies for the data are complete and it is ready-to-send). Note the use of the time before the dotted vertical line that denotes the beginning of the transfer in model A. However, this also results in synchronization overhead, O_{sync} needed to ensure thread-safety in the MPI library, and $num_{threads}$ times the send and recv overheads. In addition, the message matching overhead for model B will likely be much larger than model A. Because matching is done serially, this message matching overhead will not only significantly increase all of the instances of O_{recv}, it can lead to cascading delays in subsequent instances of O_{recv}.

Therefore, we have two models, A, the single-send model, which cannot take advantage of T_{wait} and B, the many-send model, that has more overhead than model A. In current applications, the single-send model is the more popular approach as it has higher performance in many scenarios. However, there is broad interest in using a model similar to the many-send model as previously discussed [2]. To address this, we propose that a third model, C, that combines the best characteristics of both current models by taking advantage of T_{wait} like model B and offering the minimal receive-side overhead of model A. Model C allows tasks to notify the MPI library that their data is available to send, but allows MPI to make the decision on when to transfer data, ensuring that send overheads and network packet level efficiency can be controlled by MPI. In addition, MPI can manage multiple outstanding operations, allowing model C to take advantage of NIC-level parallelism, unlike model A. The number of receive-side notifications/completions is controllable between 1 and N_{tasks}, allowing for control over receive-side overhead. By setting the number of send-side data partitions to 1, model C can approximate model A; there is no inherent 1:1 relationship between tasks and partitions.

3   Hybrid-Model Design Requirements

There are three requirements for the design of partitioned communication (model C in Fig. 1). First, the design must allow communication to occur when tasks complete, rather than synchronizing on a thread barrier or join before communicating. This addresses the weakness in model A, that there is wasted time due to a monolithic task dependency of all tasks completing before communication. This allows partitioned communication to emulate the strengths of model B, a lack of this monolithic task dependency. We will refer to the productive use of the time that would be spent waiting in model A as early-bird communication.

Second, the design must address the weakness in model B by minimizing or hiding the overheads of thread-safety, send operations, and receive-side overhead. Low receive-side overhead is achieved by reducing number of matching operations and request completions/notifications. There can be an advantage to having multiple completions, namely that task dependencies on a subset of the data can progress when the required remote data becomes available. However, this needs to be balanced with the increased overhead caused by multiple completions. For the purposes of this paper, we choose to minimize receive-side overhead by using a single match/completion operation. This will keep the design in line with the desirable low overhead in model A and avoid matching issues. The last requirement is that the MPI implementation should be free to send data whenever it is most efficient to do so. This allows data to be sent with good wire efficiency (header to payload ratio), a benefit of model A and weakness of model B. By controlling the size of the data sent and allowing for aggregation inside the MPI library we can control the wire efficiency of data transfers for model C. This is something that both models A and B are not able to take advantage of; each send operation is sent as a distinct message in modern MPI libraries.

To allow for easy use/adoption of the partition communication models, there are three main objectives that the design has to meet. The first objective was to align our design with current practice. Existing concurrency models like OpenMP allow for tasks and threads to work cooperatively on a shared buffer—in the most simple sense, like a SIMD model, where multiple data items in a buffer are acted on simultaneously. Threading can be more complicated but the basic concepts behind this approach can be leveraged to better match the thread usage model for MPI. This widely adopted tasking/threading model provides a single buffer that multiple actors (thread, tasks, etc.) can operate on. By matching the semantics of the MPI calls to the semantics of common multithreading models, mismatch can be avoided at the interface level and programmers can easily translate existing threading code to communication.

The second objective was to align our design with legacy practice. Legacy applications have leveraged an MPI+X model with distinct communication and computation phases in a bulk synchronous model. Multi-million-line MPI codes require great effort to modify and revalidate. Therefore, minimal code change at the MPI level is desirable in terms of time and cost for updating and revalidating legacy code bases. This is useful to ensure the widest adoption possible.

Finally, the third objective was to aline our design with anticipated future practices. Proposed models for future applications include task based threading, over decomposition, adaptive workflows, in-situ analytics, etc. These models increase the complexity of requirements for the communication layer of an HPC system. Changing the communication model of legacy and modern codes is a significant undertaking, often performed by non-experts of MPI. To reduce the burden on application developers the interface needs to be adaptable to future hardware and programming models with little to no impact on interface provided by an implementation.

3.1 Finepoints: Partitioned Communication

Finepoints is a MPI interface for partitioned communication designed to match the characteristics of the hybrid communication model C in Fig. 1. Partitioned communication is a new concept in MPI. With partitioned communication we propose breaking the monolithic nature of the single send model by allowing tasks to express data availability to the MPI library by reporting parts of an operation as ready. This allows data to be moved as a portion of a larger operation. The larger operation will have the same receiver-side overhead as the single-send model. We will present the design of finepoints. We target the two-sided communication model in MPI for our design as it is by far the most popular communication method in MPI applications. However, we will discuss the use of MPI's one-sided model where it is a possible option for meeting our requirements.

The first requirement was to use the time that would otherwise be wasted in the case where many threads or tasks need to synchronize before sending any data. Partitioning a send operation accomplishes this goal by notifying MPI as portions of the data buffer become available. This gives MPI the opportunity to send data if doing so is desirable. There are situations in which delaying sending the data is the correct decision, for example, when the available data is too small in size. Another situation in which a system would want to delay data transfer is when the data in the buffer is too fragmented to be sent efficiently. Some networking hardware can efficiently handle strided data or IOvecs, which can describe fragments of data to be collected from memory and sent (gathered) and distributed back to target memory on the receive side (scattered). These features make it desirable to leverage hardware that supports such gather/scatter operations, such as Remote Direct Memory Access (RDMA) as it maps well to these capabilities.

To address the low message processing overhead requirement we must keep the number of messages that MPI must match small, similar to a single-threaded MPI process. One way to get around the matching requirement is the use one-sided communication, which does not provide matching. The drawback to this approach is that the method of completing a given communication with one-sided code is much different than that of two-sided send/recv. Send/recv provides clear message arrival notification as a completed request. One sided communication requires synchronizing a memory window between the sending and receiving nodes. This change in semantics can significantly impact application code, in some cases requiring changing the underlying algorithms to better fit the communication semantics. To avoid these drawbacks a design must leverage two-sided send/recv semantics and must produce as few messages that need to be matched as possible. Along these lines, partitioned communication matches these requirements. It reduces the number of messages that must be processed (matched and notified of completion) but also allows for fine-grained notification of parts of a buffer becoming available to send to MPI. This allows MPI to optimize how the data is sent for any given network architecture, but still allows for the well known send/recv completion semantics. This addresses the issues that can afflict the many-send situation (model B) of each thread/task sending its own messages. This also addresses the third requirement for our design, controllable wire efficiency.

Now that all of the desirable traits and potential designs have been discussed, we can outline a basic design and API for finepoints. Finepoints will use a partitioned send, allowing threads/tasks to notify MPI when portions of a larger shared buffer become available to send. We will only allow a limited number of completions on the receive side to minimize message processing overhead. We can allow some receive side partitioning/notification, but we must be careful not to create too high of an overhead from matching/request completion. Next, we will require some sort of buffer negotiation, as the buffer can arrive in chunks instead of all at once. This can be done using a persistent operation to reduce setup overhead or an on-the-fly one-time-use buffer negotiation. We will provide both interfaces for send operations.

3.2   Partitioned MPI Communication Interface

Partitioned communication in MPI as a concept can be applied to almost all of MPI's existing communication calls, both point-to-point and collectives. For the purposes of our paper, we will only cover point-to-point communication. We present our proposed additions to the MPI-3 or MPI-4 standard in C; for brevity, we omit the Fortran versions of the calls.

The persistent communication approach requires that certain information about the partitioned operation be expressed to MPI prior to writing to any buffers. First, the operation must be initialized; that is, the required information to set up the buffers and synchronization methods must be provided. We propose a MPIX_Partitioned_send_init function call defined below. This function can be used to initialize the partitioned send, which is similar to a persistent operation setup, but introduces the concept of message partitioning.

```
int MPIX_Partitioned_send_init(
    void *buf, int count, MPI_Datatype data_type, int to_rank, int to_tag,
    int num_partitions, MPI_Info info, MPI_Comm comm, MPI_Request *request);
```

Similarly, a recv version of this call must be created to allow for the sender and receiver sides to agree on a buffer for the partial messages (which may be the application buffer on the target side).

```
int MPIX_Partitioned_recv_init(
    void *buf, int count, MPI_Datatype data_type, int from_rank, int from_tag,
    MPI_Info info, MPI_Comm comm, MPI_Request *request);
```

These initialization functions match via tags, sender/receiver rank, and communicator at initialization to form a two-process persistent operation (channel). While wildcard sources/tags may be used for from_rank and from_tag in the MPIX_Partitioned_recv_init call, it is up to the programmer to make sure that there is logical consistency between the sender and receiver that connect during this process. Unlike normal point-to-point persistent send/recv, these operations *may* communicate. To reduce complexity in initialization, these calls should be non-blocking. The output of this function is a request that can be used immediately in a MPIX_Pready call.

When a request is active on the send side, buffer partition elements may be added with the following API:

```
int MPIX_Pready(
    void* buf, int count, MPI_Datatype in_datatype, int offset_index,
    MPI_Request *request);
```

For non-persistent communication, a normal recv operation is used at the target and a partitioned send request can be started with the following API:

```
int MPIX_Ipsend(
    void *buf, int count, MPI_Datatype data_type, int to_rank, int to_tag,
    int num_partitions, MPI_Info info, MPI_Comm comm, MPI_Request *request);
```

When the request is in progress, it waits for num_partitions MPIX_Pready calls. When the number of buffer partitions added equals the num_partitions argument given at initialization, no more partitions may be added prior to a completion operation (MPI_Wait). The total size of the buffer is the count value times the size of the datatype, in bytes, given at initialization.

When using the persistent version of Pready/wait calls (e.g. MPIX_Pready, not MPIX_Ipsend), MPIX_Pready calls for subsequent rounds of communication can only be made after a successful MPI_Wait or MPI_Test call on that request. The buffer should not be altered until it is confirmed that the send operation is complete. This motivates the use of multiple send buffers as it allows tasks to continue to execute and overlap their computation with communication. With even a limited number of buffers, an application can avoid waiting long periods for communication completion. When combined with the non-synchronous nature of MPIX_Pready calls, this will enable applications to spend essentially no time in synchronization barriers for coordinating send operations or waiting on their completion. Tasks will still be required to wait for incoming data if it is not available.

It should be noted that extending the partitioned communication interface to support partial receives is trivial. However, we leave such extensions to future work as the optimization space for receive side partitioning is large and warrants its own full-scale investigation. We instead concentrate on the performance benefits of the send-side partitioning in this paper as an introduction to the general partitioned communication concept.

MPIX_Ipsend calls are expected to return immediately. MPIX_Pready calls are subsequently used to indicate partition readiness. MPIX_Ipsend calls are similar to existing persistent communications interfaces, except that there are no requirements for communication-initiating calls prior to calling MPIX_Ipsend, the setup happens when MPIX_Ipsend is called. It is required that the receiver-side post a non-blocking receive that will match the MPIX_Ipsend call. If no match is found MPIX_Ipsend will return an error code indicating that the operation is not ready and the user should try again. This error reporting is not fatal, following the precedent set by file I/O in MPI.

There are no blocking versions of MPIX_Pready; it is always a non-blocking call. The offset_index is an integer that specifies what internal index the datatypes have in the buffer. For example, for a simple contiguous buffer case, the first element would have index 0. Complex datatypes are supported, and the index associated with those datatypes should be interpreted as their logical placement in the buffer compared to the other expected contributions of datatypes. There is no demand that buffer contributions be non-overlapping in memory; however, we will not define the behavior for overlapping buffer additions here.

MPIX_Pready and MPIX_Ipsend calls can be made thread-safe independently of the other thread concurrency requirements of the MPI library because of the threading isolation that these functions provide. Since partitioned communication does not rely on other parts of the MPI library that have potential thread safety issues, we propose that the finepoints calls use a new threading mode, MPI_THREAD_PARTITIONED, which allows high-performance lock-free MPI calls for the majority of the library by isolating a thread-specific interface for handling concurrency. Partitioned communication need not share significant internal MPI data structures, and the only concurrency required is an atomic fetch and increment to determine if the partitioned operation has reached its num_partitions threshold. Finepoints leverages the knowledge of thread/task interaction at the application and runtime levels to allow for overhead much lower than an MPI implementation with a traditional send/recv type interface could reasonably be expected to provide. An example of finepoints code is provided in Fig. 2 which demonstrates a simple microbenchmark that we will use in Sect. 4.

3.3   Hardware Support for Partitioned Send

We can design full-featured hardware support for partitioned send operations from basic operations of some MPI message matching NICs without the need for new hardware. An example of a networking solution that can support partitioned sends today is Bull's BXI interconnect [3]. Bull's BXI network uses the Portals 4 networking API [1], which supports triggered operations. Triggered operations use a hardware counter on networking devices to accumulate counts of certain events that can be associated with them. Consequently, on the receive side, a Portals-compatible NIC can keep a count of the number of expected contributions to a buffer and deliver immediate notification of completion to the target. The send-side MPI library can leverage triggered operations as well, by staging multiple requested send operations with the different counts on which they are triggered. Using the PtlCTInc function in the Portals 4 API, MPI can perform the bookkeeping required for subsections of the partitioned buffer on the NIC hardware. Once a given sub-partition of the overall buffer has been placed, the hardware automatically triggers the send to occur. This automatic send allows for increased network efficiency while offloading a large portion of the work that would otherwise have to occur in software (counting incoming segments and determining when a request is complete). This concept is the same one behind the mechanism of offloading MPI collectives with Portals-compatible hardware [18]. Therefore, finepoints allows the utilization of network offloading capabilities that are currently being applied for MPI collective offloads to be used for point-to-point communication as well. Networking offload is desirable at exascale [7], and therefore we expect that such offloading capabilities will be widely available in the near future.

```
Data: buf: application buffer, msg_size: message size
Result: transmission of data buffer to remote node using finepoints
if sender then
    MPIX_Partitioned_send_init(&buf, msg_size, MPI_INT,
        receiver_rank, my_tag, num_partitions, info, MPI_COMM_WORLD, &request);
else
    MPIX_Partitioned_recv_init(&buf, msg_size,
        MPI_INT, sender_rank, my_tag, info, MPI_COMM_WORLD, &request);
end
for iteration = 0; iteration++; iteration == 1000 do
    #pragma omp parallel {
    /* We are
       only using one buffer, so need to wait on send completion before re-using it*/
    if !first_loop then
        MPI_Wait(&request);
    end
    compute_loop(compute_time);
    first_loop = false;
    msg_chunk_size = msg_size/omp_get_num_threads();
    if sender && (delay > 0) && my_thread_id == 0 then
        wait(delay);
    end
    if sender then
        MPIX_Pready(&buf,
            msg_chunk_size, MPI_INT, msg_chunk_size*omp_thread_num(), &request);
        /*When all partitions are ready, remote Recv will match and proceed*/
    else
        if my_thread_id == 0 then
            MPI_Recv(&buf, msg_size,
                MPI_INT, sender_rank, my_tag, MPI_COMM_WORLD, &status);
        end
    end
    }
end
comm_time = comm_time / 1000;
```

Fig. 2. Pseudo code for finepoints microbenchmark

4 Experimental Results

In this section, we detail our experimental platform and assess the performance of finepoints via extensive microbenchmark experimentation and the evaluation of two proxy applications, a finite elements code, MiniFE [11], and a nuclear reactor physics code, SimpleMOC [10], both part of the application set for the Exascale Computing Project run by the US Department of Energy (DOE).

To assess finepoints, we have implemented a library on top of MPI that allows partitioned communication (finepoints) to be layered on top of existing MPI calls, particularly the MPI RMA interface. These results demonstrate the performance of a non-hardware implementation of finepoints.

4.1 Experimental Platform

Our experiments were run on a Cray XC40 system. XC40s have two different node types: a dual-socket node with Haswell E5-2698v3 CPUs and 128 GB RAM, and a single-socket node with a Knights Landing (KNL) Xeon Phi 7250 many-core CPU with 96 GB RAM and 16 GB MCDRAM. This model has 68 cores each with support for 4-way SMT. For this reason, microbenchmarks use 64 threads while the application study extends to 256. For purposes of the evaluation, the number of partitions in the subsequent experiments is set to be the number of threads. While there are other configurations available, this is the primary use case we expect to see in finepoints applications. We used the KNL nodes exclusively, as many-core architectures let us explore large amounts of thread concurrency. These results all utilize the same Cray Aries Interconnect with a theoretical maximum bandwidth of 10.2 GiB/s. Open MPI 3.0 is used as the thread-optimized MPI library to interface with our finepoints library. Open MPI's message matching solution combined with different tags for each multi-send message mean that message matching overhead is minimal, approximating the performance of traditional as well as persistent multi-send (`MPI_THREAD_MULTIPLE` overhead is still significant).

4.2   Microbenchmarks

Microbenchmark Setup. In order to evaluate the fine-grain behavior of finepoints, we have created microbenchmarks that assess performance during OpenMP parallel loop execution for data exchanges. Our benchmarks allow for the independent variables of message size, number of threads, compute time per loop, and compute time variation. The compute time variation variable represents typical application performance variation that results from imbalances in the amount of work to be done per process, due to OS noise and process placement on large systems. This variation allows us to explore finepoints ability to leverage the idle thread time caused by this noise, as finepoints decouples individual thread completion from communication dependency. This noise represents the T_{wait} time in the communication models comparison from Fig. 1. To implement this compute time variation, we delay a victim thread by the required noise amount. After this noise is injected, the microbenchmarks communicate using the selected communication model. For single send, the threads synchronize after which a single large message is sent. For multi send and finepoints, each thread sends an equal portion of the message using an MPI_Send or a Pready call. For the single-thread case, this delays the thread synchronization and thus the only send call; for multithread, it is the last send call to occur; and for finepoints, it is the `MPI_Pready` call time for the completing call.

The dependent variable from this microbenchmark is perceived bandwidth. Perceived bandwidth is bandwidth required for an single threaded `MPI_Send` to complete in an equivalent time. This is measured by instrumenting the time of the final thread joining the communication region, where the `MPI_Send` would have been called in the single threaded model, to the completion of all communication for the iteration. From our communication models in Fig. 1, this corresponds to calculating the bandwidth from the all-tasks complete point in time (the dotted vertical line). We do this as it provides a baseline for performance centered on the single-send model, the dominant MPI communication model. For a traditional `MPI_Send`, the perceived bandwidth is the whole transfer time of the message. For finepoints and traditional multi-send, the perceived bandwidth is the bandwidth that the single-send model *would need* in order to complete the communication after the all-tasks complete point to match the wait time of finepoints or multi-send. While these numbers could be presented as time spent waiting after the all-tasks complete point, perceived bandwidth allows a comparison to a well-known metric that can be scaled with trivial effort for future generations of hardware.

Perceived bandwidth can be significantly higher than the actual bandwidth on a system. For example, if 100 workers all need to send one piece of data to a neighbor node and 95 workers complete but 5 workers take significantly longer, 95% of the data transfer can occur with finepoints and multi-send before the last workers reach their communication calls. Thus, the observed communication call could take 95% less time than a call that used the single-thread method, which requires all data to be collected before sending the first byte. Each microbenchmark experiment was run for 50 iterations and the data in this section represents an average over those iterations.

Microbenchmark Results. Our first experiments vary only message size and thread count. Figure 3a shows the performance of finepoints versus send/recv in MPI for both single-thread and traditional multi-send MPI. These results exclude any compute time in the communication loops or any noise.

Figure 3a shows typical trends that are expected by MPI experts. The single-send model's MPI operation is superior to the multi-send model's MPI version and, as lock contention increases with the number of threads, the performance gap between single-send and multi-send models grows, even for our multithreading-optimized MPI implementation. The single-send model clearly outperforms multi-send and finepoints at small message sizes when ignoring the drop in performance that occurs during the eager-rendezvous protocol switch. Breaking up a small message into 16, 32, or 64 parts operates the network in the lower part of a typical bandwidth curve, where packet overheads dominate costs. For small message sizes, performing a single send operation is still preferable, while the benefits of the finepoints approach are clear with larger message sizes. It should be noted that finepoints can accommodate aggregation of smaller messages such that the performance of singlethreaded MPI can be approximated. The results for these benchmarks do not use aggregation.

The performance of small message transfers may appear to be problematic as many MPI applications use small to medium sized messages frequently. However, with the shift towards fewer MPI processes and more threads per process, the overall amount of data needed to be transmitted by a single process will grow. A 64 process MPI-everywhere solution will have to send 64× more data when it is run in a one-process, 64 thread configuration, leading to larger message sizes for multithreaded codes. This will push many application into an area where finepoints performs well. Based on previous work exploring message sizes used by applications of interest [6], we find that message sizes in the 8 KiB–16 KiB range are important and many applications send messages of 1 MiB or more, resulting in the vast majority of network usage for codes. Therefore, when we move to a multithreaded code, we expect messages to be $N_{threads}$ times larger in size, and this is well within the message size range where finepoints is the clear winner. Notably, at a 1 MiB transfer size (total, not per thread), finepoints outperforms the single-send model performance for all thread counts below 64 (results not shown for space). At 64 threads, a 2 MiB transfer is required to outperform the single-send model performance. This performance gap is significant for large transfers when all of the bandwidth curves flatten out. The difference in performance, from 7,200 MiB/s to 9,000 MiB/s on finepoints, represents a significant 25% increase in throughput.

This difference results from several factors. First, finepoints can easily leverage hardware RDMA data transfers, allowing for high-performance messaging. Second, the MPI library *expects* the finepoints transfer to occur; with traditional MPI send/recv, the library must react to the transfer with no advance setup. What is most promising here is that the observed improvement comprises a worst-case outcome for finepoints, since there is no time variance in the compute or noise in the system that allows finepoints to take advantage of available bandwidth in the network while laggard threads finish their compute tasks.

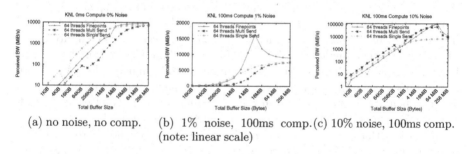

(a) no noise, no comp.   (b) 1% noise, 100ms comp. (c) 10% noise, 100ms comp.
(note: linear scale)

Fig. 3. Partitioned communication with varying noise and compute load

Figure 3b shows finepoints working with a 100 ms compute loop with 1% noise. This reflects real codes on production machines better than no-noise situations do, as 2–4% noise has been common on systems for many years [16]. Both multi-send and finepoints can show bandwidths greater than the available bandwidth from the NIC using this approach because they have the opportunity to send portions of the overall transfer before the final process/thread reaches the communication call. With 64 threads, we see the drawback of MPI's THREAD_MULTIPLE mode. Lock contention is high with large thread counts, impacting the performance of the multi-send approach. While multi-send quickly degrades in performance and even underperforms the single-send model, finepoints gains performance from having many threads. Eventually with large enough message sizes, we see finepoints and multi-send converging back to native wire rates, this happens when there is so much data that the early-bird overlapping cannot preemptively send a large enough portion of the data to see major performance gains. It should be noted that even in these cases, finepoints performance is no worse than the singlethreaded case. Finepoints starts to see a small drop in performance at the 64-thread level illustrated in our Fig. 3b, but still significantly outperforms the best competitor at message sizes of greater than 1 MiB total. To put these bandwidth numbers in context, finepoints with a 8 MiB message will spend only 0.5% of its time waiting for communication with a 100 ms compute loop, compared to 1.9% for the single-send model and 1.3% for multithreaded MPI. This result highlights one of the key performance benefits of finepoints, namely that multiple threads can initiate data movement, exploiting T_{wait} from our communication models without the locking overhead $T_{waitlock}$ and much smaller O_{sync} compared to the multi-send mode.

Shorter compute times can impact the amount of overlap that finepoints can exploit, with compute times of 10 ms demonstrating up to a 3× improvement in performance versus the single-send model as shown in Fig. 4a. Figure 3c shows early-bird communication mostly completing before the final thread arrives at the partitioned communication call. With the chance to send this data in advance, the perceived bandwidth when the final thread reaches the partitioned communication call is 12× greater than a single threaded approach for 64 threads at message sizes of 64 MiB. At a 64 MiB message size finepoints only spends 0.5% of time waiting for communication while the single-send model spends 8.8% and multi-send spends 0.95%. For the 4% noise case, which we expect to be typical of future systems we can observe in Fig. 4b that with reasonable compute times, finepoints can beat single threaded MPI by up to than 9.5× and multi-send by 3.3× in the best case. Thus, early-bird communication can help alleviate a major cost of bulk-synchronous parallelism (BSP). It achieves this result by reducing the time penalty for poor synchronization, reducing the delay after all threads have reached the synchronization point as much as possible.

To ensure that the results observed for finepoints are not a result of the lightweight cores used for the experiments, we have also conducted similar testing on the Haswell partition of our system. These results are omitted for space, but the general trends hold on a Haswell system as well: finepoints outperforms both multi-send and the single-send model for message sizes larger than 1 MB across a spectrum of no-noise to noisy execution. For example, at 32 threads (one thread per core), finepoints beats single by 34% and multi-send by 99% at 64 MiB message sizes with no aggregation, with the latest version of Cray MPICH.

4.3   Message Aggregation Optimizations

The results presented thus far have sent messages as soon as any data was added to the partitioned buffer; however, finepoints can also optimize the transfers out of the partitioned buffer by aggregating traffic to the target node. We have implemented an aggregation scheme that allows the user to specify an aggregation threshold for their network. Our aggregation scheme attempts to combine send operations that occur close together in time that are in contiguous memory,

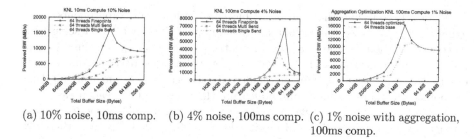

(a) 10% noise, 10ms comp.   (b) 4% noise, 100ms comp.   (c) 1% noise with aggregation,
100ms comp.

Fig. 4. Three experiments exploring the effects of finepoints in situations of short
iteration times, realistic noise, and with aggregation

up to the aggregation threshold size. Timeouts will cause data to move regardless
of aggregation if operations are sufficient spread out in time.

Aggregation is most effective when there is a large number of threads, which
corresponds to more numerous and smaller individual data transfers. Figure 4c
shows the benefit of this aggregation versus a baseline finepoints without aggregation for 64 threads with a 512 KiB aggregation size. We observe that the
aggregation optimization can have large impact on the overall performance of
finepoints at high thread counts. For the 100 ms compute loop results shown, the
maximum gain is 199.5% at 2 MiB, and the optimized version is always better
than the baseline finepoints case.

4.4   Application Proxies

To demonstrate finepoints with an application, we chose two application proxies
to test the impact of finepoints. MiniFE is a proxy application from the Man-
tevo suite [11] that uses conjugate gradient solver on a finite elements problem.
The main communication pattern is a fully packed halo exchange, optimized
for the single-send model. MiniFE is essentially a worst case for finepoints as
it is optimized to send small messages and is highly tuned for the single-send
model. To leverage finepoints in this code, we modified the application in the
most direct manner possible, where each thread sends a subset of the overall
buffer. This results in a significantly larger number of messages being sent by
each peer compared to original serialized code. To provide a comparison to current multithreaded paradigms, we have included a multi-send version as well
that decomposes messages in the same manner of the finepoints version.

Figure 5 shows the results of MiniFE run with 16 nodes (1 process per node)
and a 330^3 problem size per process with no injected variation in the communication phase. Each data point represents the average of three runs. In this graph
we show communication time on the primary y axis and cg-solve time on the
secondary y axis. The general trends in this data show that finepoints performs
better than multi-send but worse than the original serialized code. Because of
a bug we encountered in Open MPI, multi-send runs leveraging more than 32
threads failed to complete. At this scale, the communication in finepoints is a

factor of 2 better than the multi-send baseline. In follow-on experiments leveraging Cray's MPI, we found that multi-send spent 61% of the CG solve time in communication at 256 threads. In contrast, finepoints spends just 11% of its time communicating with 256 threads. As the message decomposition strategy results in a larger number of smaller size messages, it is unsurprising that finepoints spends more time communicating than the single threaded case.

While finepoints does spend a larger percentage of its solve time doing communication than the single-send model (11% vs 2% at 256 threads), there are a two promising things to note. First, this is a worst-case application for finepoints, MiniFE has a highly optimized communication pattern, sending as little data as possible in it's halo exchange. Given this, application developers can use finepoints to leverage multithreaded communication patterns with a small to negligible impact in application performance. Second, the application use of finepoints is unoptimized and cannot take advantage of variations in compute time. In the current implementation, MiniFE exits the parallel region and then starts a new parallel region for communication. This means the time still includes the T_{Wait} portion model A and no early bird communication can occur. This is an example of how an unoptimized finepoints code can perform significantly better than current multithreaded communication models. Leveraging knowledge of the data dependencies and thread behavior, application developers could integrate these communication calls into their compute threads and enable more early-bird communication reducing runtime. This case highlights the fact that, while there are cases where applications will need to be optimized to see benefit from finepoints, the overhead from finepoints is low enough that the impacts to a "worst case" application, with small halo exchanges and little noise are minimal.

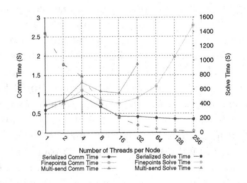

Fig. 5. Finepoints impact on MiniFE performance

SimpleMOC, a reactor physics proxy application from MIT and Argonne National Laboratory, is part of the DOE's ECP application set. We chose this code because it simulates a real problem (albeit not easily adaptable to other problems, which is why it is a proxy application). Also, we can convert its existing communication pattern to partitioned communication without the need to re-factor its data packing routines, making it possible to ensure continued program validity when modified by non–reactor physics experts. This also means that the volume of code changes for such applications are less than 100 lines of code. The changes that need to be made to adopt finepoints should also be easy to implement for application developers who are domain area specialists. We expect that all codes that utilize halo-type message exchanges can benefit from our approach.

SimpleMOC demonstrates the method-of-characteristics technique to solve partial differential equations with a specific application to 3D neutron transport in a light-water nuclear reactor at full scale. SimpleMOC requires multiples of four for MPI process count and communicates only in groups of four; therefore, we have used four KNL nodes for our tests allowing us to use 1024 cores total, with 256 threads per node. Using a larger number of nodes will not provide more insight. Due to the communication pattern used by the code scaling up the number of nodes will simply duplicate the communication pattern. Therefore out results demonstrate the improvement in a given "cell" of the problem breakdown that will be applicable to much larger problem sizes.

For experimental purposes, we have added barriers to the communication portion of the code and included code that allows artificial injection of noise in proportion to the compute loop time. This modification is useful, as we have observed 2%–5% noise impacts in regular runs of the SimpleMOC communication section. By using barriers and artificial injection, we can tightly control the occurrence of this noise in the communication region, making experimentation and understanding easier. We have also run tests without noise controls to demonstrate production performance expectations. In order to let communication begin as soon as possible, we have eliminated the synchronization barrier entirely, allowing the first thread to complete to begin communication (and report the solver completion time). This is the best case for computation as the time reported for our unconstrained finepoints application is the time the first thread gets to the communication point. However, this makes the communication time longer as the communication cannot complete until all compute threads have completed, the performance variation is observed in the communication time and is similar to our large variance case, where overlap occurs, but its benefits are degraded due to the time spent waiting for laggard threads in which there is no communication to perform. The net effect of allowing communication to begin as soon as possible is that the performance variation between threads is observed in the communication phase. Overall this is similar to the time required when 2%–3% variation is injected in the communication phase, but the speedups in overall time shows up in the solve completion due to our eager recording of the solve time and our early start time for communication. All data for SimpleMOC is an average of 10 runs, and we use our aggregation-optimized MPI library with Open MPI 3.0. SimpleMOC was configured according to the recommended small problem size and then scaled in terms of azimuth values (32) and height (1200) to expand the problem size to the MCDRAM capacity on the

KNL. The KNLs were run in quad mode with 100% of MCDRAM operating in cache mode.

The results of this testing are shown in Fig. 6. We can observe that fine-points provides a significant improvement in application performance in both communication time and application total runtime compared to the single-send model optimized version of SimpleMOC. SimpleMOC supports varying numbers of threads in its main compute loop, and we present results using a sweep from 64 threads to 256 threads on each of the 4 KNL nodes.

For the noise controlled runs, communication time improvement sees a low point of 18.5% at 256 compute threads and 10% noise, and it peaks at 26.1% at 64 compute threads and 2% noise. Application runtime improvement ranges from 2.6% for 64 compute threads and 0% noise to 4.8% with 128 compute threads and 2% noise. Overall, both runtime and communication time improvements are relatively similar over the ranges of artificial noise injection because of the nature of the communication that occurs: the communication is small enough in size (approx. 130 MiB total) that even small noise percentages allow good early-bird communication.

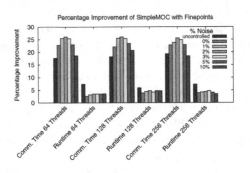

Fig. 6. Finepoints impact on SimpleMOC performance versus the single-send model

5   Related Work

There have been past attempts to integrate threading within MPI, such as FG-MPI [13]. FG-MPI promoted threads to being the equivalent of MPI processes, which while it allowed many concurrent threads, creates a large amount of state for each thread/process. Other efforts have included work on providing benchmarks for testing and profiling MPI RMA multithreaded behavior [8]. The general concept of composing RDMA messages into a large transaction has been explored for application in unreliable datagram networks at the hardware level [9,17]. Similar benchmarks have also been developed for other one-sided communication APIs like OpenSHMEM [19]. Lastly, commercial MPI's such as MPI/Pro, which were designed for internal concurrency and the option of blocking completion notification (to avoid polling), are no longer widely available [4].

Message aggregation is a well known method for networks, having been explored for one-sided communication methods [12], these methods are also common with TCP/Ethernet networking.

The MPI forum had a proposal before it to enhance support for threads through endpoints [5], in which each thread can be assigned a unique rank in an endpoint communicator. However, endpoints never attempted to address the underlying communication model, only add the ability to address messages to specific threads. This work differs from previous efforts by the requirements it places on applications and the corresponding decrease both in resources needed by MPI and in synchronization overhead achieved.

6 Conclusions and Future Work

In this work, we introduced finepoints, a partitioned buffer communication two-sided approach for MPI. Partitioned sends allow data to be transmitted as completed by the application, or else be aggregated by MPI. We discussed the existing concurrency models in MPI and illustrated how desirable features of each model can be combined, resulting in our design of finepoints. Providing threading support with partitioned operations allows for ultra-low overhead thread safety that beats a current highly optimized threading-optimized MPI implementation and fits the existing application code methodologies. A prototype implementation that incorporates early-bird communication provides up to 4.8% improvement in runtime and 26.1% improvement in communications for a reactor physics neutron transport code. Furthermore, this performance improvement did not require major application reformulation, unlike MPI 1-sided communication (RMA).

Partitioned send is only a part of the overall finepoints concept. It is possible to extend finepoints to receive-partitioning. Receive-side partitioning solves a different problem than send-side partitioning; that is, it is an independent concept. The flexibility of receive-side partitioning must be juxtaposed against the increased cost of notification (with reduction of maximum message rate), making it a subject for future study.

References

1. Barrett, B.W., Brightwell, R., et al.: The Portals 4.1 networking programming interface. Technical report SAND2017-3825, Sandia National Laboratories (SNL-NM), Albuquerque, NM, United States (2017)
2. Bernholdt, D.E., Boehm, S., et al.: A survey of MPI usage in the U.S. Exascale Computing Project. Concurr. Comput. Pract. Exp. (2018)
3. Derradji, S. Palfer-Sollier, T., et al.: The BXI interconnect architecture. In: Proceedings of the 23rd Annual Symposium on High Performance Interconnects, HOTI 2015. IEEE (2015)

4. Dimitrov, R., Skjellum, A.: Software architecture and performance comparison of MPI/Pro and MPICH. In: Sloot, P.M.A., Abramson, D., Bogdanov, A.V., Gorbachev, Y.E., Dongarra, J.J., Zomaya, A.Y. (eds.) ICCS 2003, Part III. LNCS, vol. 2659, pp. 307–315. Springer, Heidelberg (2003). https://doi.org/10.1007/3-540-44863-2_31

5. Dinan, J., Grant, R.E., et al.: Enabling communication concurrency through flexible MPI endpoints. Int. J. High Perform. Comput. Appl. **28**(4), 390–405 (2014)

6. Doerfler, D.W., Rajan, M., et al.: A comparison of the performance characteristics of capability and capacity class HPC systems. Technical report, Sandia National Lab. (SNL-NM), Albuquerque, NM, United States (2011)

7. Dosanjh, M.G.F., Grant, R.E., et al.: Re-evaluating network onload vs. offload for the many-core era. In: IEEE International Conference on Cluster Computing (CLUSTER), pp. 342–350. IEEE (2015)

8. Dosanjh, M.G.F., Groves, T., et al.: RMA-MT: a benchmark suite for assessing MPI multi-threaded RMA performance. In: 16th IEEE/ACM International Symposium on Cluster, Cloud and Grid Computing (CCGrid), pp. 550–559. IEEE (2016)

9. Grant, R.E., Rashti, M.J., et al.: RDMA capable iWARP over datagrams. In: IEEE International Parallel & Distributed Processing Symposium (IPDPS), pp. 628–639. IEEE (2011)

10. Gunow, G., Tramm, J.R., et al.: SimpleMOC - a performance abstraction for 3D MOC. In: ANS MC2015. American Nuclear Society, American Nuclear Society (2015)

11. Heroux, M.A., Doerfler, D.W., et al.: Improving performance via mini-applications. Sandia National Laboratories, Technical report SAND2009-5574, vol. 3 (2009)

12. Hjelm, N., Dosanjh, M.G.F., et al.: Improving MPI multi-threaded RMA communication performance. In: Proceedings of the International Conference on Parallel Processing, pp. 1–10 (2018)

13. Kamal, H., Wagner, A.: An integrated fine-grain runtime system for MPI. Computing **96**(4), 293–309 (2014). ISSN: 0010-485X

14. Mendygral, P., Radcliffe, N., et al.: WOMBAT: a scalable and high-performance astrophysical magnetohydrodynamics code. Astrophys. J. Suppl. Ser. **228**(2), 23 (2017)

15. MPI Forum. MPI: A message-passing interface standard version 3.1. Technical report, University of Tennessee, Knoxville (2015)

16. Petrini, F., Kerbyson, D.J., et al.: The case of the missing supercomputer performance: achieving optimal performance on the 8,192 processors of ASCI Q. In: Proceedings of the 2003 ACM/IEEE conference on Supercomputing, p. 55 (2003)

17. Rashti, M.J., Grant, R.E., et al.: iWARP redefined: scalable connectionless communication over high-speed Ethernet. In: International Conference on High Performance Computing (HiPC), pp. 1–10. IEEE (2010)

18. Schneider, T., Hoefler, T., et al.: Protocols for fully offloaded collective operations on accelerated network adapters. In: 42nd International Conference on Parallel Processing (ICPP 2013), Lyon, France, October 2013

19. Weeks, H., Dosanjh, M.G.F., Bridges, P.G., Grant, R.E.: SHMEM-MT: a benchmark suite for assessing multi-threaded SHMEM performance. In: Gorentla Venkata, M., Imam, N., Pophale, S., Mintz, T.M. (eds.) OpenSHMEM 2016. LNCS, vol. 10007, pp. 227–231. Springer, Cham (2016). https://doi.org/10.1007/978-3-319-50995-2_16

Author Index

Printed in the United States
By Bookmasters